SOUNDING OFF!

Music as Subversion/Resistance/Revolution

Maurice Caldwell

RELATED AUTONOMEDIA TITLES IN CULTURE & POLITICS

FILE UNDER POPULAR Theoretical & Critical Writing on Music Chris Cutler

CASSETTE MYTHOS The New Music Underground Robin James, ed.

MAGPIE REVERIES The Iconographic Mandalas James Koehnline

ON ANARCHY & SCHIZOANALYSIS Rolando Perez

GOD & PLASTIC SURGERY Marx, Nietzsche, Freud & the Obvious Jeremy Barris

MARX BEYOND MARX Lessons on the Grundrisse Antonio Negri

THE NARRATIVE BODY Eldon Garnet

MODEL CHILDREN Inside the Republic of Red Scarves Paul Thorez

ABOUT FACE Race in Postmodern America Maliqalim Simone

COLUMBUS & OTHER CANNIBALS The Wétiko Disease & the White Man Jack Forbes

SCANDAL Essays in Islamic Heresy Peter Lamborn Wilson

CLIPPED COINS John Locke's Philosophy of Money Constantine G. Caffentzis

HORSEXE Essay on Transsexuality Catherine Millot

THE TOUCH Michael Brownstein

ARCANE OF REPRODUCTION Housework, Prostitution, Labor & Capital Leopoldina Fortunati

TROTSKYISM & MAOISM A. Belden Fields

FILM & POLITICS IN THE THIRD WORLD John Downing, ed.

ENRAGÉS & SITUATIONISTS IN THE OCCUPATION MOVEMENT René Viénet

ZEROWORK The Anti-Work Anthology Bob Black & Tad Kepley, eds.

MIDNIGHT OIL Work, Energy, War, 1973 – 1992 Midnight Notes Collective

GONE TO CROATAN Origins of North American Dropout Culture Ron Sakolsky & James Koehnline, eds.

THE DAMNED UNIVERSE OF CHARLES FORT Louis Kaplan

¡ZAPATISTAS! Documents of the New Mexican Revolution The Zapatistas

FORMAT & ANXIETY Paul Goodman Critiques the Media Paul Goodman

BY ANY MEANS NECESSARY! Outlaw Manifestoes & Ephemera, 1965 – 70 P. Stansill & D.Z. Mairowitz, eds.

WAR IN THE NEIGHBORHOOD Seth Tobocman

RETHINKING MARXISM Rick Woolf & Steve Resnick, eds.

GULLIVER Michael Ryan

THE DAUGHTER Roberta Allen

ROTTING GODDESS Classical Origins of the Witch Jacob Rabinowitz

SOUNDING OFF!

Music as Subversion/Resistance/Revolution

Edited by

Ron Sakolsky

and

Fred Wei-han Ho

Autonomedia

A companion **Sounding Off** musical CD,
with 77+ minutes of soundtracks by book contributors

HAKIM BEY	SUE ANN HARKEY	NEGATIVLAND	KALAMU YA SALAAM
JEAN BINTA BREEZE	FRED HO	JOHN OSWALD	SCOTT M.X. TURNER
BROTHER RESISTANCE	THOMAS MAPFUMO	PERFORMER'S WORKSHOP	LIZ WAS / MIEKAL AND
CAROL GENETTI	SCOTT MARSHALL	HAL RAMMEL	BATYA WEINBAUM

among others, is available for $10 postpaid from
Autonomedia, POB 568, Brooklyn, New York 11211 USA

Copyright © 1995 Autonomedia and Contributors

Autonomedia
POB 568 Williamsburgh Station
Brooklyn, New York 11211-0568 USA

Phone & Fax: 718-963-2603

Printed in the United States of America

Contents

Part I. *Theorizing Music and Social Change*

"The Sound of Resistance" 13
    Robin Balliger

"Utopian Blues" 29
    Hakim Bey

"Matriarchal Music Making" 41
    Batya Weinbaum

"Beyond Music" 53
    Hal Rammel

"polynoise" 61
    Amendant Hardiker and Miekal And

"knoise pearls" 65
    Liz Was

"Plunderphonics" 67
    Chris Cutler

"Creatigality" 87
    John Oswald

"Fair Use" 91
    Negativland

"Soul Sonic Forces: Technology, Orality, and Black Cultural Practice in Rap Music" 97
    Tricia Rose

"Alternative to What?" 109
    Tom Frank

"World Beat and the Cultural Imperialism Debate" 121
    Andrew Goodwin and Joe Gore

"'Jazz,' Kreolization and Revolutionary Music for the 21st Century" 133
    Fred Wei-han Ho

Part II. *In the Belly of The Beast*

"The Screamers" **147**
    Kalamu ya Salaam

"Music Guerrilla: An Interview with **Fred Wei-han Ho**" **155**
    Miyoshi Smith

"Boyz From the Rez: An Interview with **Robby Bee**" **163**
    Ron Sakolsky

"Who Bombed Judi Bari?" **171**
    Darryl Cherney

"Timber!: An Interview with **Judi Bari**" **173**
    Ron Sakolsky

"Shake, Shake, Whore of Babylon" **179**
    Tuli Kupferberg

"Maximizing Rock and Roll: An Interview with **Tim Yohannon**" **181**
    Scott M.X. Turner

"The Black Wedge Tours:
  'Take Something You Care About and Make It Your Life'" **197**
    Jean Smith

"The Imaginal Rave" **203**
    Cinnamon Twist

"Long Live the Humble Audio Cassette: A Eulogy" **211**
    Scott Marshall

"Plagiarism®: An Interview with the **Tape-beatles**" **217**
    Stephen Perkins

"Recontextualizing the Production of 'New Music'" **227**
    Susan Parenti, Mark Enslin and Herbert Brün

Part III. Shattering The Silence of The New World Order

"Us & Dem" **237**
    Benjamin Zephaniah

"World Music at the Crossroads" **241**
    Ron Sakolsky

"The Rattling of the Drums: Political Expression in World Music" **247**
    Louise Bennett-Coverly, Billy Bragg, Allen DeLeary, and Geoffry Oryema

"Dub Diaspora: Off the Page and Into the Streets" **257**
    Ron Sakolsky

"Nanny" **261**
    Jean Binta Breeze

"Rapso Rebellion: An Interview with **Brother Resistance**" **263**
    Ron Sakolsky

"**Thomas Mapfumo**: The Lion of Zimbabwe" **271**
    Sheila Nopper

"Latin Music in the New World Order: Salsa & Beyond" **277**
    Peter Manuel

"The Singer as Priestess: Interviews with **Celina González** and **Merceditas Valdés**" **287**
    Ivor Miller

"Craft, Raft and Lifesaver: Aboriginal Women Musicians in the Contemporary Music Industry" **307**
    Jilli Streit-Warburton

"Palaam Uncle Sam: An Interview with **Musika** and **Musicians for Peace**, Philippines" **321**
    Tripp Mikich

"Playing Other Peoples' Music: An Interview with **Royal Hartigan**" **331**
    Fred Wei-han Ho

"Singing Other Peoples' Songs" **339**
    Anthony Seeger

Acknowledgements

First, a very special thanks to three people without whose support this project would have been overwhelming: Scott Marshall and Carol Genetti whose layout and design expertise extraordinaire grace the pages in your hands, Scott again for audio wizardry in relation to CD production; and Lisa Hensley for word processing and computer production abilities above and beyond the call of duty.

We would also take this opportunity to acknowledge the generous sharing of time, ideas, skills and nurturance in relation to this project on the part of: Lillian Allen, Jim Allbaugh, Todd Boyd, Rachel Buff, Eugene Chadbourne, David Ciaffardini, John Collins, Bob Diener, Dennis Fox, Michael Franti, Laurie Fuchs, Angela Gilliam, Marvin J. Gladney, Pedro Michel Diaz Gonzalez, "Chako" Habecost, John Hutnyk, Linton Kwesi Johnson, Betty Kano, Charles Keil, Tad Kepley, John Kimsey, Bradley Knopff, Professor Louie, Devorah Major, Music for People, "A-Ron" Nauth, Pablo, Penelope Rosemont, Mtume ya Salaam, Sanjay Sharma, Virinder Singh, C. C. Smith, Karen and Jenny Starr, John Trudell, tentatively a convenience, Gail Tremblay, Tobi Vail, Dennis Warren, and John Zerzan.

For technical support in the publication process, we offer our appreciation to Vicki Lock, Sandy Costa and the former Sangamon State University (now University of Illinois at Springfield).

The following articles originally appeared in whole* or in part** in the publications listed below. We gratefully acknowledge permission to reprint from authors and publishers:

*Robin Balliger "The Sound of Resistance," *Komotion International* #7, 1994.
*Cinnamon Twist "The Imaginal Rave," Tribal Donut pamphlet, 1992. (*Tribal Donut* Productions, 41 Sutter St., San Francisco, CA 94104).
*Chris Cutler "Plunderphonia," *Musicworks* #60, 1994.
*Andrew Goodwin and Joe Gore "World Beat and the Cultural Imperialism Debate," *Socialist Review*, 2013, July/Sept., 1990.
*Tom Frank "Alternative to What?," *The Baffler*, Nov., 1993.
*Peter Manuel "The Soul of the Barrio: Thirty Years of Salsa," *NACLA Report on the Americas*, Vol. 28: 2, pp. 22-29. Copyright 1994 by North American Congress on Latin America, 475 Riverside Dr., #454, New York, N.Y. 10115-01.
**Miller, Ivor "Celina González: Queen of the Punto Cubano," The Beat, Vol. 13, #2, 1994. (Originally commissioned for *Sounding Off!*)
*Stephen Perkins "Plagiarism®: The Collective Vision of the Tape-beatles," *Tractor: A Quarterly Magazine of Iowa Arts and Culture*, Spring 1994. (Tractor, 1103 N. Third St. SE, Cedar Rapids, IA 54021.)
**Hal Rammel "Beyond Music," *Arsenal: Surrealist Subversion*, 4, 1990.
**Tricia Rose "Soul Sonic Forces: Technology, Orality, and Black Cultural Practice in Rap Music." This article orginally appeared in *Popular Music and Society*," (Winter , 1989) under the title "Orality and Technology: Rap Music and Afro-American Cultural Resistance." A reworked version later was published as a chapter in her book, *Black Noise: Rap Music and Black Culture in Contemporary America* (Wesleyan University Press, 1994) under the new title referred to above. Rather than reprint the original we have edited this chapter for inclusion in our text at the author's suggestion so as to have it reflect her current thinking as much as possible.
Ron Sakolsky, **"World Music at the Crossroads," *Sound Choice*, #13, Winter, 1990./**"Brother Resistance," (interview), *Griot: A Journal of Native Consciousness*, Vol. 3, Winter 1993/94./**"Brother Resistance: The Voice of the People," (interview) The Beat, Vol. 12, #2, 1993./*"Dub Poetry Festival International," The Beat, Vol. 12, #5, 1993.
*Anthony Seeger. "Singing Other Peoples' Songs," *Cultural Survival*, Summer, 1991.
*Miyoshi Smith. "Fred Wei-han Ho(un)," (interview) *Cadence*, Vol. 20, #9, Sept., 1994.
**Various Authors. "The Rattling of the Drums," *Cultural Democracy*, #39, Spring, 1990.
**Batya Weinbaum. "Music, Dance and Song: Women's Cultural Resistance in Making Their Own Music," *Heresies*, #22, 1987.
*Benjamin Zephaniah, "Us & Dem," *City Psalms*, Bloodaxe Books, (UK), 1992.

Preface

Come all you guerilla musicians: Native Warriors and Tricksters; Kreoles and Majority-World revolutionaries; womynist sisterhoods and riot girrrlz; chaos magicians and spiritual monkeywrenchers; punks, hiphoppers, and ravers; surrealists, noisicians and plunderphiles; socialists, anarchists, utopians and all the vibrant and complex radical hybrids therein. We are gathered here together in all our subversive beauty and marvelous diversity; our cacophonous disagreements and our glorious contradictions. You the reader can judge our ideas for yourself as you see fit, and construct your own musiopolitical identity accordingly.

We represent collectively the critical voices/sounds of subversion and resistance and the musical visions of revolution; though we are not all here. Some of us are missing in action. Others are available elsewhere, or should be. We are not all-inclusive, but our very existence on the following pages is a start in this direction. We are primarily musicians and cultural activists. Hear our voices. Hear the connection between our music and our struggles. Hear it surge up from inside the belly of the beast or erupt from within the planetary cracks and faultlines of the New World Order. This volume is only the count-off of things to come.

Though we may sound "off" when heard through the tired and insular ears of the dominant culture, in our own terms, we hereby "sound off" in an oppression-detonating explosion of pain, anger, love and joy. Music is our bomb!

Ron Sakolsky   Fred Ho   1995

Dedication

Dedicated to Calvin Massey (1928-1972) and Romulus Franceschini (1929-1994).

Calvin Massey, African American, trumpet player, composer and co-leader of the ROMAS Orchestra, was a mentor to many of the great musicians of twentieth century African American music ("jazz") during the late 1950s and 1960s. While struggling to support himself and his family, Calvin organized benefit concerts for the Black Panther Party and composed the magnificent "The Black Liberation Movement Suite." Sections of the Suite were recorded by Archie Shepp.

Romulus Franceschini, Italian American, composer and brilliant arranger, co-leader of the ROMAS Orchestra with Calvin Massey, whose musical activities were both broadly eclectic and informed by his ardent socialist politics. In 1986, Franceschini and Fred Ho met and collaborated to pay tribute to and perform the music of Calvin Massey and the ROMAS Orchestra. In 1990, Ho and Franceschini co-taught a course, "Music and Social Change," at Stanford University which would later become the idea and catayslt for this book.

James Koehnline

Part I.

Theorizing Music and Social Change

Freddie Baer

Sounds of Resistance

Robin Balliger

Music...site of oral history; sounds of war; social gathering for dancing, pleasure, fun, sex; emotional, spiritual, rapturous like Jimi Hendrix and Mozart's "Requiem"; career, stardom, commodification, cultural imperialism; state censorship; protest songs, punk, nueva cancion, and Fela's "Zombie"; vibration and breath; the reason people go to political rallies!; slave trade and musical codes indomitable as heartbeats; noise, sound, soundtrack; immaterial and uncontrollable; music institutions, discipline and disciplines...

How has music gone from its "old role" as an organizing practice of social groups, to being entertaining fluff or employed for emotional effect in nationalist causes? How can the "political correctness" of music be determined through an "objective" reading of lyrics? Why is it even possible to dissect a song and consider the music itself to be without meaning? These questions point to how music is represented in our society, representations which are not the revelation of some timeless Truth, but constructed by specific societal interests. In the following pages, I develop an understanding of music and noise as social forces, fully involved in the "dialogic process" of social life and as such, an important site of control—and resistance.

Political Music or The Politics of Music

As a practice, music is situated in particular social relationships and locations that are a product of complex intersections of culture, class, gender, etc., in lived experience. Music and representations of music are contextualized activities that have social and political meaning. This view shifts us away from asking: "which music is political?" to "what is the particular politics of a music and how is it political?" What is considered to be music itself is controversial and linked to large-scale ideological formations invested in defining "music" apart from non-music.

This operation is an effect of power, one that functions through discursive strategies that construct "music" as an aspect of civilization, while sound and noise are linked to the uncivilized. In Hieronymus Bosch's famous painting, "Garden of Earthly Delights" (early 16th century), hell is rendered through the din and chaos created by creatures playing fantastic musical instruments which swallow-up and torture the bodies of the dammed. Epitomized by the

Enlightenment and 18th century classical music, societal sound began to be brought under control through dominant representations linking "music" to order/civilization/mind, and "noise" to chaos/the primitive/body. In *Noise: The Political Economy of Music* (1985), Attali argues that a central controlling mechanism of the State is the monopolization of noise emitted in society. "...Music and noises in general, are stakes in games of power. Their forms, sources, and roles have changed along with and by means of the changes in systems of power." Through mechanical reproduction in the 20th century, sound has also been controlled through its incitement. Repressing rhythm and noise has become more selective, while its management has been enabled through the wallpaper-like proliferation and commodification of music.

The dominant constructions of music as non-referential and non-ideological (Western classical music) or as marginalized and primitive (popular and ethnic musics) are implicated in strategies of control that make legitimate music into something transcendental that exists apart from practice. This shields music from being implicated in relations of power and at the same time inhibits understanding about performative practices because it is difficult to conceive of performance or participation as a total experience. The closest we come to conceptualizing a performance that at once mobilizes music/dance/thought/history/play/spirituality etc., is the idea of ritual, but this word is problematic as it still marks off and compartmentalizes human activity. Music is neither transcendental nor trivial, but inhabits a site where hegemonic processes are contested. Placing music back in the world does not reduce music, but gives it social force.

In the following discussion of music and resistance, my purpose, in part, is to explode reified representations of "political music." Discussions of popular music have often suffered from a kind of reductionism by certain Left and reactionary positions, which sense the power of music but are uneasy about its inaccessibility to rational critique and control. I explore how popular music becomes a site of resistance through four lines of investigation: textual analysis focusing on the lyrics of songs; subaltern cultural production; music as performance and its relation to autonomy; and music as a sonic activity or tactic. I argue that oppositional music practices not only act as a form of resistance against domination, but generate social relationships and experience which can form the basis of a new cultural sensibility and, in fact, are involved in the struggle for a new culture.

Textual Analysis or, Bow wow wow yippee yo yippee yay,
bow wow yippee yo yippee yay! (George Clinton "Atomic Dog")

Textual analyses focus on the lyrics in music as the primary or only site of meaning. The words in music have been particularly important as a medium of communication in cultures and historical periods where there are no written texts, texts are only available to a privileged group, or to deliberately subvert the power of the written word. Beyond the notion of "protest songs," lyrics are multivalent, employing discursive strategies which form a poetics of resistance. I will also discuss the limitations of these text-based analyses, particularly with regard to meaning reception, the elision of social context and issues of cultural production, and most obviously, the inability to consider meaning in instrumental music.

Recent literary criticism emphasizes the importance of "voice" in cultural resistance. For oppressed peoples under slavery, in colonial contexts and the underclasses of global capitalism, music has often been a central site for the intervention in dominant discourses and for creating forms of expression that are culturally affirming. Because of the dominance of metropolitan languages, illiteracy or lack of access to print mediums, orality has played a major role in contesting the universalizing discourses of empire. Locating a position of vocality and self-representation is central to creating a counter-narrative, positing a counter-essence and in critically attacking the legitimacy of "objective" knowledge and truth.

Popular forms of music have become an effective site of enunciation and people involved in indigenous struggles have mixed traditional elements of music with rock to reach a mass audience through the circulation of world music. Essays in *Rockin' the Boat: Mass Music and Mass Movements* detail such political music from Hawaii and Australia. In Australia, Aboriginal musicians blend indigenous forms with rock to preserve traditional values, represent their own history and protest oppression. Contemporary Aboriginal music was first influenced by the guitar style and personal song genre of American country-western musicians and in the 1970s became highly influenced by the message of black liberation and reggae music of Bob Marley. Aboriginal Australians are using music as a "political weapon in the long-term struggle of Aboriginal people for dignity, respect, and land rights claims" (Breen). The song lyrics by musician Archie Roach and bands, No Fixed Address and Us Mob, are direct social commentaries, convey the Aboriginal experience in Australia, or are programmatic like a song such as "AIDS, It's a Killer." Breen largely lets the lyrics speak for themselves in his analysis of the music's politics.

In analyzing calypso lyrics of the 1930s and 40s, which are usually thought of as topical social commentary, the lyrics employ various discursive strategies beyond the surface "meaning." Together these devices form a poetics of protest which in some cases utilize techniques of reappropriation usually associated with postmodernism. Three of these discursive strategies are, first, that calypsos were a form of "autoethnography," through which a colonized people could represent themselves and retell history with their image and voice fully included. Second, through irreverence and parody, the calypsonians punctured the screen of colonial superiority by revealing scandals in the British ruling class and challenged the civilizing mission by contrasting it to the actions of the colonizer. Third, calypsos created a counter-narrative to official accounts of events.

As an example, I discuss a song written in the context of colonial rule, global economic depression and socialist organizing of the 1930s. In 1937, a black labor activist named "Buzz" Butler led a wildcat strike of Trinidadian oil workers which resulted in rioting and an extreme use of force by the government. Butler was jailed, but anger over police violence intensified when an official report whitewashing the incident was later released. Below are the last two stanzas of Atilla's calypso, "Commission's Report":

> They said through the evidence they had
> That the riot started at Fyzabad
> By the hooligan element under their leader
> A fanatic Negro called Butler
> Who uttered speeches inflammatory
> And caused disorders in this colony
> The only time they found the police was wrong
> Was when they stayed too long to shoot people down.
> A peculiar thing of this Commission
> In their ninety-two lines of dissertation
> Is there no talk of exploitation
> Of the worker or his tragic condition

Read through the pages there is no mention
Of capitalistic oppression
Which leads one to entertain a thought
And wonder if it's a one-sided report.

Atilla's song thoroughly indicts the official story through mimicking the jargon of the report itself and unmasking media representations. He links the words "commission" and "dissertation" with "exploitation" and "tragic condition," syntactically showing their real connection. Atilla attacks the scapegoating of Butler by reappropriating the language of the media and defusing the "moral panic" induced by such buzz-words as "hooligan," "fanatic," and "inflammatory speeches." In this song, he also brings together the rioting and capitalist oppression, which challenges the controlling mechanism of representing these issues separately; rioting portrayed as unconscious acts of violence, while oppressive economic and social conditions are channeled into 'appropriate' avenues of reform.

However, political communication in music has traditionally been analyzed only in terms of the "self-evident" meaning of song lyrics. Examples of this programmatic approach to political music are common among the organized Left (and in nationalist causes) and are found in Pring-Mill's article, "Revolutionary Song in Nicaragua" (1987). These "didactic songs" include inspirational anthems and historical accounts, as well as songs which are educational, from the learning of multiplication tables to a song that replaces a written manual for the stripping down and reassembly of the "Carabina M-1" (by Luis Enrique Mejía Godoy). Pring-Mill's insights into the emotional meaning and educational uses of these songs are largely gleaned through analyzing a letter by one of the revolutionary leaders, Carlos Nunez Tellez, in which he praises the musical group Pancasán. His article gives little sense of the meaning of these songs in a broader context and, again, the lyrics are considered the only political component. In fact, Pring-Mill states:

> "What may strike one as most surprising about that letter is its total silence regarding the music of such songs, which is simply taken for granted: their didactic and emotive functions, while reinforced by the music, clearly centre on the lyrics. Yet all the most successful songs owe much of their persuasive power to setting and performance—although the contribution of the musical element to the total 'meaning' of a song is something much harder to analyze than that of its text."

This quote speaks to the paradox of constructing political communication only in terms of the text. Whereas the meaning of these songs is only represented as a function of the lyrics, the music is critical to conveying the message. But what is the message of the music? Reading didactic lyrics as literal and complete in the communication of meaning ignores the many subtexts and levels of meaning occurring in the production and performance of music.

Within an analysis of political content based on lyrics, there are problems raised by semiotics such as the unpredictability of sign activity, reception and how meaning is context bound and multiple. In understanding the meaning of songs, musical experience and cultural background are significant factors. In addition, one empirical study suggests only ten to thirty percent of high school and college students "correctly identified the 'intended messages' in songs." In a recent article, Angelica Madeira raises these issues to further ask: "wherein lies popular music's political power?" She doesn't fully address the question, but points in a direction forged by Bakhtin (a Soviet philosopher and literary critic), centering on the "indestructible character and universality of popular culture." She argues that "music is empowering not only because of the explicit political ends it is able to serve, but also because it formulates yearnings and values for an entire generation." While I find the direction of her argument salutary, she neglects to contextualize Bakhtin's writings and how emphasizing nonconformity, irreverence, festivity and pleasure in Stalinist Russia, requires a completely different analysis when applied to the contemporary United States. This highlights the necessity to locate resistance in relation to specific strategies of control and domination.

Understanding the politics of music from a text-based analysis is particularly problematic with forms of music that are heavily coded (possibly to avoid censure), or where the lyrics are of secondary importance or even misleading. And what might "protest lyrics" be in social contexts where the very language of struggle has been co-opted? In an interesting article, Rey Chow analyzes Chinese popular music and how it creates a discourse of resistance in a context where the rhetoric of class struggle has become part of the dominant discourse. In this situation, lightheartedness, emotion and physicality are the central trans-linguistic themes. Chow suggests that meaning is created in the clash of words (often from Chinese history) and rock music, a meaning which becomes audible through "striking notes of difference" from the single voice of official culture. Instead of emphasizing "voice" or "who speaks," Chow suggests we ask "what plays?" and "who listens?" She concludes with the critical distinction between passivity and "silent sabotage," through a literal and metaphorical discussion of the cassette Walkman creating a kind of sonic barrier. These examples show how music is a form of resistance beyond an objectified reading of political lyrics through emphasizing the structure of listening, in which meaning is mutually produced in different contexts.

Cultural Production or, "Classical music, jazz . . .
those are categories of things you buy, that's not music." (Yo Yo Ma, cellist)

In "The Work of Art in the Age of Mechanical Reproduction," Walter Benjamin argues that technologies of artistic reproduction that originated in the early 20th century began to create an undifferentiated visual or musical terrain that separated the artist or author from his /her work. Since this time, critical theory has emphasized the mediation inherent in all mass produced cultural products and two primary positions have developed about mass culture. The first equates economic domination with cultural domination and implicates mass culture in the reproduction of hegemony. The second view argues that mass culture is a site of contestation and that popular music is not a completely controlled and manufactured product of the West. Electric guitars and synthesizers shape the sound of a transnational technoculture which reflects a process of urbanization, not Westernization, as musicians constantly create new sounds for their own purposes. In this section, I detail these arguments, along with ways in which decreasing costs of music technology have facilitated subaltern cultural production and have effectively challenged the hegemony of mass cultural products and ideologies.

Adorno's writings on music represent one extreme in arguments over the role and influence of cultural production in society. For Adorno, the centralized production of popular music is part of a system of control aimed at the creation of mechanized individuals whose habits and desires comply with the needs of capitalism and the State. While his position is understandable, having witnessed the power of music and the "loudspeaker" as employed by the Nazis, Adorno makes the mistake of equating all forms of popular, rhythmic music with sounds that serve dominant interests. His view of popular music and serious music (Western classical) is manichean, and the role of popular music in society is to create escape or distraction, and as a social cement in which the rhythms of popular dance music and jazz produce a standardized individual.

A central problem with Adorno's argument is the positing of a subject as pure receptor. In his work on rock and roll, Grossberg cites communication theories that ascribe a more active role to the audience in the construction of meaning and ideology.

> "...it is the audience that interprets the text, defines its message, 'decodes' it by bringing it into its own already constituted realities, or 'uses' it to satisfy already present needs. In either case, the audience make the text fit into its experiences."

While I agree with Grossberg's contextualizing and creating a dynamic of interaction between mass cultural products and audience, there is a danger of creating a subject in the Americanized sense of individual free will and choice. I am suspicious of theories based on boundaries and difference without thoroughly addressing how the production of difference often conceals a broader conformity that is not only little threat to capitalism but is vital to it.

In addition to the problem of Adorno's subject, his blatant Eurocentrism and dismissal of black cultural forms and their meaning in the context of racial oppression in the United States is, frankly, abhorrent. In a scathing indictment of Horkheimer and Adorno, who were writing in Los Angeles during WWII, Mike Davis states:

> "They described the Culture Industry not merely as political economy, but as a specific spatiality that vitiated the classical proportions of European urbanity, expelling from the stage both the 'masses' (in their heroic, history-changing incarnation) and the critical intelligentsia. Exhibiting no apparent interest in the wartime turmoil in the local aircraft plants nor inclined to appreciate the vigorous nightlife of Los Angeles's Central Avenue ghetto, Horkheimer and Adorno focused instead on the little single-family boxes that seemed to absorb the world-historic mission of the proletariat into family-centered consumerism under the direction of radio jingles and *Life* magazine ads."

Before dismissing the "Culture Industry," it is important to consider the global stratification of the record industry and its economic and cultural influence, in addition to ways in which cultural products are interpreted and appropriated in local contexts. Wallis and Malm provide comprehensive data on the global production and media activity (such as radio airplay) of music and argue that corporate activity in the music industry duplicates large-scale patterns of economic change and distributions of wealth worldwide. Currently, five major record labels "dominate the greater part of the global production and distribution of recorded music. The smaller independents take the risks in the local market, and achieve a high degree of local competence developing artists and repertoire talent which the majors can occasionally exploit internationally." In addition to changes in recording technology, the organization of the music industry, issues of control, authorship, copyright, studio budgets, recording contracts, manufacturing budgets, distribution and payola are major factors in the global flow of mass music products. Through the forces of competition, Simon Frith argues that the industry is intensely conservative, protecting certain styles and their profitability rather than taking risks on new sounds and artists. He concludes that the prevalence of cassette piracy (which is estimated at 66 percent in some markets), and other structural changes in the industry and technology will provide new opportunities for the independents and make cultural production more in tune with the "sounds of the street" and "music as a human activity."

In *Cassette Culture*, Peter Manuel argues that the accessibility of music technology since the mid-1980s has decentered control in the music industry, creating a surge in local music production and the democratization of expression. Manuel sees technology itself as the major determinant of change in musical and political expression away from monopoly and towards pluralism in cultural production, particularly in "developing nations." His study of popular music in India shows an explosion of locally recorded, produced and manufactured cassettes, some of which sell only a few copies, but others become widely popular in ways that could not have occurred with earlier forms of music production and industry control. He argues that this change liberates public expression from the homogenizing and "deculturating" effects of mass media products; preserves folk genres that might otherwise become extinct, as well as fueling "proletarian hybrid genres"; and promotes local and regional identity. While Manuel clearly espouses the revolutionary potential of cassette technology against foreign cultural domination, he admits that the localized quality of cassette "culture" reinforces and may even intensify pre-existing social divisions. Through recorded music and speeches, cassettes have been highly effective in political organizing, a "new media" for grassroots organizing and lower-class empowerment. But cassettes have been utilized by "every major socio-political campaign," including political and religious causes far removed from the "leftist mobilization and subaltern empowerment" envisioned by some.

Developments in music technology and mass communications have created avenues of expression for previously silenced groups, facilitated networks of alternative music like rap and punk, and create the potential for a transnational oppositional culture. By suggesting this potentiality, I do not argue that resistance to either economic or "cultural" imperialism is predicated on new technologies or that a single meaning can be gleaned from these developments. Reformulations of identity through the circulation of popular music products simply raises the possibility of new kinds of organization and community. At the same time, multinational capitalism's "restless search for markets" has meant the increased commodification and consumption of global cultural products, but the social meaning of this marketing and how musicians and cultural producers negotiate this terrain must be addressed in its particularities. Raymond Williams argues that technology is not a predetermined instrument of domination or liberation but "a moment of choice," and instead emphasizes "the intense vitality of some kinds of popular music, always being reached for by the market and often grasped and tamed, but repeatedly renewing its impulses in new and vigorous forms." The next section addresses how popular music production in recorded and live forms interacts with the politics of location.

Performance and The Temporary Autonomous Zone or, "Space is the Place" (SunRa)

The practice of oppressed groups in society trying to achieve "relative autonomy" is historically inseparable from domination itself. Critical studies that go beyond analyzing text and cultural production suggest a linkage between music practices and social formations that seek autonomy from the effects of power in the broadest sense. In developing a complex description of music activity as resistance in such situations, I explore three themes in this section: performance as social organization and cultural empowerment of oppressed groups; music as pleasure, use-value and threat to the necessary commodification of desire under capitalism; music as site of Refusal and the "temporary autonomous zone."

The performance of music is enigmatic from a Western/capitalist perspective because it is often unproductive (materially) and yet it produces (socially). Popular music is a social activity, a site of interaction and ideology, a temporary community that usually includes some type of movement or physical expression that is pleasurable. While music performance is an "extreme occasion" because it is temporal and not repeatable, musicologist John Shepherd states that "all music should be understood within the context of the politics of the everyday." He argues that the activity of music, through its complex system of signification, has the ability to shape awareness, individual subjectivity, and social formations. It is only in the industrialized world that music has become constructed as privileged property, leisure activity or mass distraction. Through its ability to mediate the social—temporally, spatially and bodily—music is a powerful site of struggle in the organization of meaning and lived experience. "Music can at the same time 'territorialize' and 'deterritorialize' the everyday, evoking and transcending its terrains, spaces, and temporalities as these are visually and linguistically mediated."

Beyond music as a site of critique of dominant ideologies, cultural critics have stressed the importance of cultural solidarity that occurs through performance. For the African diaspora and other groups oppressed by colonialism and repressive regimes, cultural expressions of music and dance have been a source of strength and identity formation critical to liberation struggles. Gilroy states that "Black expressive cultures affirm while they protest." This is well demonstrated in the calypso music of Trinidad, which is historically linked to both emancipation and decolonization. The French Catholic tradition of carnival began to be celebrated in Trinidad in the early 19th century and for the next hundred years, carnival, freedom, rioting and music were all linked in various ways. The "yard" was a space of relative autonomy for slaves and through elaborate secret societies and coded forms of communication resistance to slavery was built. By the 1830s, an extensive network of information had evolved as slaves were overheard singing a song in Patois about a successful slave revolt in Haiti. After emancipation, plantation owners replaced slave labor with indentured East Indian immigrants, driving many blacks into urban centers and continued poverty. The tradition of music and expression continued in the urban yard and in the early 20th century carnival music began to be performed in performance "tents." The calypso tents effectively merged a music born in resistance and a broad-based audience into a regularized social gathering through which a counter-narrative to colonial discourse and an emergent cultural identity were shaped. As the songs were performed in front of an audience they were immediately validated or repudiated by the public, and the wit and creativity of the calypsonians were a source of cultural empowerment for all.

Another example of the interlocution of cultural affirmation and political resistance is elaborated by Fairley's discussion of the Chilean group ¡Karaxú!, which was formed shortly after the U.S.-backed coup in 1973. Fairley argues that:

> "…musical meaning is negotiated between elements of performance and between performers and audience. It is inextricably tied to lived experience, political praxis, feelings and beliefs. It is rooted in social and political life…The creation and performance of this music is part of the process of learning to live with, and making sense of, experience—of re-integrating the dis-integrated."

Fairley describes ¡Karaxú!'s performances as important "ritual occasions" to emphasize both the complexity of meaning and inclusion of the audience as integral to the event. Their performances are an active, if symbolically rendered, reminder of historical events and political mobilization in which cultural expression and political commitment survive together in exile.

Second, I address music as pleasure, the politics of forms of pleasure that exist as "use-value" and how this is a threat to the capitalist commodification of desire. With few exceptions, political theory and activity in the West has been constructed as a totally serious and difficult practice. While I would certainly agree with most political activists that the global history of genocidal campaigns, ongoing struggles against oppression and even the smallest acts of social and physical domination evoke both rage and the necessity of political organization and action, I also argue that political ideology and strategies need to be continually reformulated. In this period, which might be thought of as the historic defeat of the Left, questions have been raised about paradigms of political theory and praxis, particularly with regard to the thinking behind slogans like "the road is hard but the future is bright." Constructing politics and pleasure as incommensurable spheres has been a major problem, creating both a denigration of the body (which has been implicated in forms of political tyranny), and it also has difficulty explaining both the attraction and persistence of forms of "entertainment" and "spirituality."

Some theorists are beginning to recognize the need to reintegrate these spheres and develop more complicated notions of resistance distinct from the purely politically instrumental. McClary and Walser critique the traditional Left and musicology for their positivist, Enlightenment-derived approach to meaning in music, and implicate both in systems designed to reinforce norms rather than liberate.

Part of the problem is one that chronically plagues the Left: a desire to find explicit political agendas and intellectual complexity in the art it wants to claim and a distrust of those dimensions of art that appeal to the senses, to physical pleasure. Yet pleasure frequently is the politics of music—pleasure as interference, the pleasure of marginalized people that has evaded channelization. Rock is a discourse that has frequently been at its most effective politically when its producers and consumers are least aware of any political or intellectual dimensions...

In a unique approach, Attali (1985) theorizes historical change in society through a semiotic reading of sound. He maps the global spread of capitalism through the control of societal sound and the "deritualizing" of music's "old code" — locus of social organization, mythology and healing. Attali articulates the difference between music produced by an industry and music as unproductive, an end in itself with the capacity to create its own code. Music is a threat to hegemonic forms of discourse and social relations because it offers the greatest potential to create new forms of communication and create "pleasure in being instead of having." Attali's construction of music as resistance follows from both Marx's theory of commodity fetishism and Foucault's theory of power as the saturation of discourse, social relations and bodies.

> In the seventeenth and eighteenth centuries a form of power comes into being that begins to exercise itself through social production and social service. It becomes a matter of obtaining productive service from individuals in their concrete lives. And in consequence, a real and effective "incorporation" of power was necessary, in the sense that power had to be able to gain access to the bodies of individuals, to their acts, attitudes and modes of everyday behavior (Foucault 1980).

Are there not ways in which music is a constant reminder of the existence of pleasure as use-value and as such poses a threat to a system that necessarily seeks out and exploits all forms of pleasure and energy for productive use?

My third point addresses Attali's notion of music as a site of "reality under construction." This idea is echoed by cultural critics who write on subcultures, black expressive culture and by theorists who articulate resistance in the broadest possible sense—beyond political ideology to a total transformation of values and lived behavior. I suggest thinking about these ideas through a more mobile category that conceives of forms of collective, cultural resistance as the situated practices of specific groups. The "Temporary Autonomous Zone," or TAZ, is useful in articulating this concept and I apply it to music in specific situations. Hakim Bey's theory of TAZ begins with a critique of revolution from two main positions. He argues that the current period is one in which a "vast undertaking would be futile martyrdom" and, coming from an anarchist tradition, he distrusts revolution because of its historical tendency to reinstitute authoritarianism in a different guise. He contrasts revolution with uprising, focusing on this activity as a kind of "free enclave," as festival, and a temporary or limited Refusal in which to "withdraw from the area of simulation." Bey views the TAZ as both a strategy and "condition for life." He states,

> "The TAZ is thus a perfect tactic for an era in which the State is omnipresent and all-powerful and yet simultaneously riddled with cracks and vacancies. And because the TAZ is a microcosm of that 'anarchist dream' of a free culture, I can think of no better tactic by which to work toward that goal while at the same time experiencing some of its benefits here and now."

Ultimately the TAZ is a space beyond the gaze of power and the State. Bey draws inspiration from the spirit of the Paris Commune and the maroon communities of Jamaica and Surinam.

While Bey briefly mentions "music as an organizational principle," Hebdige and Gilroy link African music to a kind of oppositional, utopian space. While both tend to essentialize African music in a way I find problematic, the substance of their discussion of subcultures and black performance traditions speaks to this idea of temporary autonomy. Hebdige stresses the ideological character of everyday activities and how subcultural style in Britain is a symbolic form of struggle against the social order, or "a practice of resistance through style." In describing punk, Hebdige argues that music and dance formed a central site in which to perform revolt that "undermined every relevant discourse" and created an "alternative value system." "Conventional ideas of prettiness were jettisoned...fragments of school uniforms were symbolically defiled...punk dances like the pogo upset traditional courtship patterns...overt displays of heterosexual interest were generally regarded with contempt and suspicion...frontal attacks (on) the bourgeois notion of entertainment or the classical concept of 'high art'..." Hebdige's account resonates with my own involvement with punk in San Francisco in the late 1970s and early 80s. What I found most significant about this scene was that it fostered an ethos of "direct action" through which behavior and ideologies (mostly reactionary positions and some aspects of leftist politics) were overtly challenged and in some cases transformed. This sense of engagement had a significant impact on gender roles as many women were not content to be fans or only singers, but began playing instruments in bands and expressing themselves in numbers that were virtually unprecedented in Western popular music.

Paul Gilroy discusses British punk and its links with reggae through the "two-tone" movement and youth organization, Rock Against Racism, but focuses primarily on black expressive culture as a site of "collective memory, perception and experience in the present...the construction of community by symbolic and ritual means..." Writing on rap, funk and reggae, he argues that the public spaces in which dances occur "are transformed by the power of these musics to disperse and suspend the temporal and spatial order of the dominant culture." In Rastafarianism, "Babylon system" symbolizes the total rejection of "mental slavery," racism and exploitative economic conditions under capitalism; it is "a critique of the economy of time and space which is identified with the world of work and wages from which blacks are excluded and from which they, as a result, announce and celebrate their exclusion." In Gilroy's recent work he also stresses the need to distinguish the "political aesthetics" of different music groups within black popular culture.

My last example centers on an article by Pablo Vila, "*Rock Nacional* and Dictatorship in Argentina" (1992), in which he argues that concerts created a space in which a "we" was constructed that formed a cultural challenge to the ideology of the dictatorship. As the military regime took power in 1976 and sought to disperse all collectivities and suppress traditional political formations, rock concerts became a site of heavily coded oppositional activity. Vila refers to these sites as autonomous spaces of interaction "for broad sections of youth, a refuge, a sphere of resistance, and a channel for participation in the context of a closed and authoritarian society in crisis." The common experience of youth rebellion and its form, the rock concert, became highly politicized in the context of the military dictatorship and the censure of political and cultural expression.

Vila states that the message was in the activity as the music fostered a culture which demanded incorruptibility against *transar* (interactions with the system) and for *zafar* (escape from the system by all possible means). He cites the importance of the *rock nacional* movement for Argentinian youth as "salvaging the meaning of life in a context of lies and terror, consolidating a collective actor as a means of counteracting an individualistic model of life, counterposing a supportive community of actions and interests to the primacy of the market."

In this section I have shown ways in which music as a popular performance medium which engages the body and mind in a collective expression, has the power to transform values, ideology and lived behavior through generating a "temporary autonomous zone." Music is hardly just sound that is passively listened to, but a sonic force that acts on bodies and minds and creates its own life rhythms; rhythms that power recognizes and tries to monopolize through a relentless domination of societal noise. But, because of its unique properties music can be employed as a powerful counter-hegemonic device that goes beyond thought to being. Music as socially organized use-value is a threat to the individuated, consumption-oriented desiring machine of advanced capitalism. As a pleasurable collective expression the practice of music provides important clues to what Foucault describes as the "art of living counter to all forms of fascism" through constantly creating "de-individualization" and how it is "the connection of desire to reality (and not its retreat into the forms of representation) that possesses revolutionary force" (1992).

Sonic Squatting

In this final section I show how subordinate groups have used music as a weapon which is able to penetrate walls and minds. In addition to the fact that drumming can reproduce language, territorialization through sound marks off areas of political or cultural significance and has played a major role in human activities such as religion and war. From kettledrums to bagpipes, sound exhorted troops, relayed commands, and was used to terrify enemies. Sound has remained a potent weapon, a force that disturbs through the fact that it is unhinged from the visual or the knowable and symbolically acts on the imagination, infiltrating and destabilizing power.

In Arguedas' novel, *Yawar Fiesta*, about indigenous struggles in the highlands of Peru, the *wakawak'ras,* or "trumpets of the earth," are a very disturbing sound for the local authorities. The trumpets announce the Yawar Fiesta, an indigenous form of bullfighting that articulates conflict in the novel. While the town of Puquio is geographically divided by class and ethnicity, and controlled by the Civil Patrol, sound is not so easily contained, as the "voices" of the *wakawak'ras* well up "from below" and invade every house, every room, every person. Sound is not only a form of resistance, but an attack on domination materially represented in distinct forms of spatiality.

> "From the four quarters, as the night began, the bullfight music would rise up to the Girón Bolívar. From the Chaupi square, straight up to Girón Bolívar, the *turupukllay* rose on the wind. In the shops, in the pool hall, in the notables' houses, the girls and the townsmen would hear it.
> 'At night that music sounds like it's coming from the graveyard,' they'd say.
> 'Yeah, man. It troubles your mind...'
> 'That *cholo* Maywa is the worst of all. His music goes right down to the depths of my soul.'
> The sound of the *wakawak'ras* interrupted the *mistis'* conversation under the lamps on the corners of the Girón Bolívar; it disturbed the peace of the diners in the houses of the leading citizens. In the Indian neighborhoods, the boys would gather when Don Maywa played...
> Sometimes Don Maywa's trumpet was heard in the town when the Priest was saying the rosary in church with the ladies and girls of the town and with some of the women from the Indian neighborhoods. The bullfight music was dispiriting to those pious souls; the Priest, too, would pause for a moment when the melody came in to him. The girls and ladies would look at one another uneasily, as if the brindled or tawny bulls were bellowing from the church doorway.
> 'Devil's music!' the Vicar would say." (Arguedas)

Beyond associations with the bullfight, the simple moaning of the *wakawak'ras* is complex in its signification, at once recalling the presence of the Indians and the threat posed by their historically incomplete domination by both church and state. The music is particularly powerful in its ability to conjure up unknown aspects of the Other, unleashing fear and anxiety that exists in the minds of the *mistis* (*ladinos*). In this regard it operates as a psychological/spatial tactic that is difficult to contain.

Sound or P.A. systems may create an internal spatiality or "temporary autonomous zone," but through them music can traverse and challenge spatially organized social divisions. In his work on the cultural character of ethnic and class divisions in Cartagena, Colombia, Joel Streicker describes the use of sound as resistance and a "non-spatial way to reclaim space." He historicizes the construction of urban space which has become increasingly divided by class and race to make certain areas "safe" for the "rich" and tourism. The spatial separation of rich and poor is culturally symbolized by the Independence Day Festival which once involved all social groups, but more recently local elites have shaped it into an event which excludes the poor (who are largely of African descent). Many lower class youths have reclaimed the Festival's dance through what Streicker describes as a "budding, racially conscious, popular class cultural movement centered on music and dance called *champeta*." In addition to constructing an alternative identity through African music as opposed to Latin music, the loud sound systems at these dances broadcast the music past the walls of the colonial city. "This music speaks of—and is— a presence that the rich cannot avoid, a nearly dusk-to-dawn siege reminding the wealthy of the popular class' Otherness...and a way for disenfranchised groups to exercise control over space..." Through broadcasting their own music directly into the site of official culture the *champetudos* create a struggle over class privilege and identity through sound.

Conclusion

In this article I have shown how popular music can be a site of counter-hegemonic activity. For explanatory purposes I have deconstructed music activities and forms in an artificial way. Performance and commodification of music products are not clearly bounded and how musicians and audiences negotiate these spheres varies in every situation. There is no correct strategy here. In fact, resistance is necessarily a creative, imaginative process and arguments that purport to have "the one answer" are increasingly suspect. Instead, I argue that music and resistance are shaped in the moment of their coming into being, a musical/political praxis that is negotiated by social actors in particular spatial and temporal locations. As fixity itself is increasingly recognized as a necessary condition for the deployment of power, performative practices like music and dance suggest forms of resistance that produce experience in ever changing forms.

It is important to remember that music is a universal activity that emerged with "culture" as a defining characteristic of human communities. I do not raise this point to suggest some essentialized meaning or origin of music, but to generate further thought about deep cultural assumptions in the West that are prevalent across the political spectrum. In an era when music and the arts are being eliminated from public schools in the United States through specific discourses about the "productive" individual and an emphasis on education that facilitates employment, I argue that these actions have more to do with a particular kind of social reproduction than simply balancing budgets. As music is a common practice of subordinate groups and its practice is a form of social organization, it is an important site of management by dominant forces in society. Finally, I suggest that music draws its power from the fact that it is both ordinary and mystical. Music is something pleasurable that everyone can participate in and create their own bit of magic outside the loop of production and consumption. This is why it is so dangerous.

Acknowledgments

I would like to thank the following people for their encouragement and input on earlier drafts of this paper: Paula Ebron, Sylvia Yanagisako, Mary Louise Pratt, Don Moore, Harumi Befu, Bill Maurer, Joel Streicker, Mat Callahan.

Bibliography

Adorno, Theodor. (1990). On Popular Music. In *On Record: Rock, Pop, and The Written Word.* Simon Frith and Andrew Goodwin, eds. pp.301-314. New York: Pantheon.

Arguedas, José María. (1985). *Yawar Fiesta.* Austin: University of Texas Press.

Attali, Jacques. (1985). *Noise: The Political Economy of Music.* Minneapolis: University of Minnesota Press.

Bey, Hakim. (1991). *T.A.Z.: The Temporary Autonomous Zone, Ontological Anarchy, Poetic Terrorism.* Brooklyn: Autonomedia. (anti-copyright)

Breen, Marcus. (1992). "Desert Dreams, Media, and Interventions in Reality: Australian

Aboriginal Music." In *Rockin' The Boat: Mass Music and Mass Movements*. Reebee Garofalo, ed. pp. 149-170. Boston: South End Press.

Chow, Rey. (1993). "Listening Otherwise, Music Miniaturized: A Different Type of Question about Revolution." In *The Cultural Studies Reader*. Simon During, ed. pp. 382-402. London: Routledge.

Davis, Mike. (1990). *City of Quartz: Excavating the Future in Los Angeles*. New York: Vintage.

Fairley, Jan. (1989). "Analysing Performance: Narrative and Ideology in Concerts by ¡Karaxú!" In *Popular Music*. Vol. 8/1. pp. 1-30.

Foucault, Michel. (1980). *Power/Knowledge: Selected Interviews and Other Writings 1972-1977*. Ed., Colin Gordon. New York: Pantheon.

Foucault, Michel. (1992). Preface. In *Anti-Oedipus: Capitalism and Schizophrenia*. Gilles Deleuze and Felix Guattari. Minneapolis: University of Minnesota Press.

Frith, Simon. (1987). "The Industrialization of Popular Music." In *Popular Music and Communication*. James Lull, ed. pp. 53-77. Newbury Park: Sage.

Frith, Simon. (1989). Introduction. In *World Music, Politics and Social Change*. Simon Frith, ed. pp. 1-6. Manchester: Manchester University Press.

Gilroy, Paul. (1991). *"There Ain't No Black in the Union Jack": The Cultural Politics of Race and Nation*. Chicago: University of Chicago Press.

Gilroy, Paul. (1993). *Small Acts: Thoughts On The Politics of Black Cultures*. London: Serpent's Tail.

Grossberg, Lawrence. (1987). "Rock and Roll in Search of an Audience." In *Popular Music and Communication*. James Lull, ed. pp. 175-197. Newbury Park: Sage.

Hebdige, Dick. (1991), *Subculture: The Meaning of Style*. London: Routledge.

Madeira, Angelica. (1993). "Popular Music: Resistance or Irreverence?" In *Semiotica* 94-1/2. pp. 157-168.

Manuel, Peter. (1993). *Cassette Culture: Popular Music and Technology in North India*. Chicago: The University of Chicago Press.

McClary, Susan and Robert Walser. (1990). "Start Making Sense! Musicology Wrestles with Rock." In *On Record: Rock, Pop, and The Written Word*. Simon Frith and Andrew Goodwin, eds. pp. 227-292. New York: Pantheon.

Pring-Mill, Robert. (1987). "The Roles of Revolutionary Song — A Nicaraguan Assessment." In *Popular Music*. Vol. 6/2. pp. 179-187.

Shepherd, John. (1993). "Popular Music Studies: Challenges to Musicology." In *Stanford Humanities Review*. Vol. 3 No. 2. pp.17-36.

Streicker, Joel. (1994). *"Spatial Reconfigurations, Imagined Geographies, and Social Conflicts in Cartagena, Columbia."* (Unpublished manuscript, Stanford University).

Vila, Pablo. (1992). "Rock Nacional and Dictatorship in Argentina." In *Rockin' The Boat: Mass Music and Mass Movements*. Ed., Reebee Garofalo. pp. 209-230. Boston: South End Press.

Wallis, Roger & Krister Malm. (1984). *Big Sounds from Small Peoples: The Music Industry in Small Countries*. London: Constable.

Wallis, Roger & Krister Malm. (1992). *Media Policy and Music Activity*. London: Routledge.

Williams, Raymond. (1989). *The Politics of Modernism*. London: Verso.

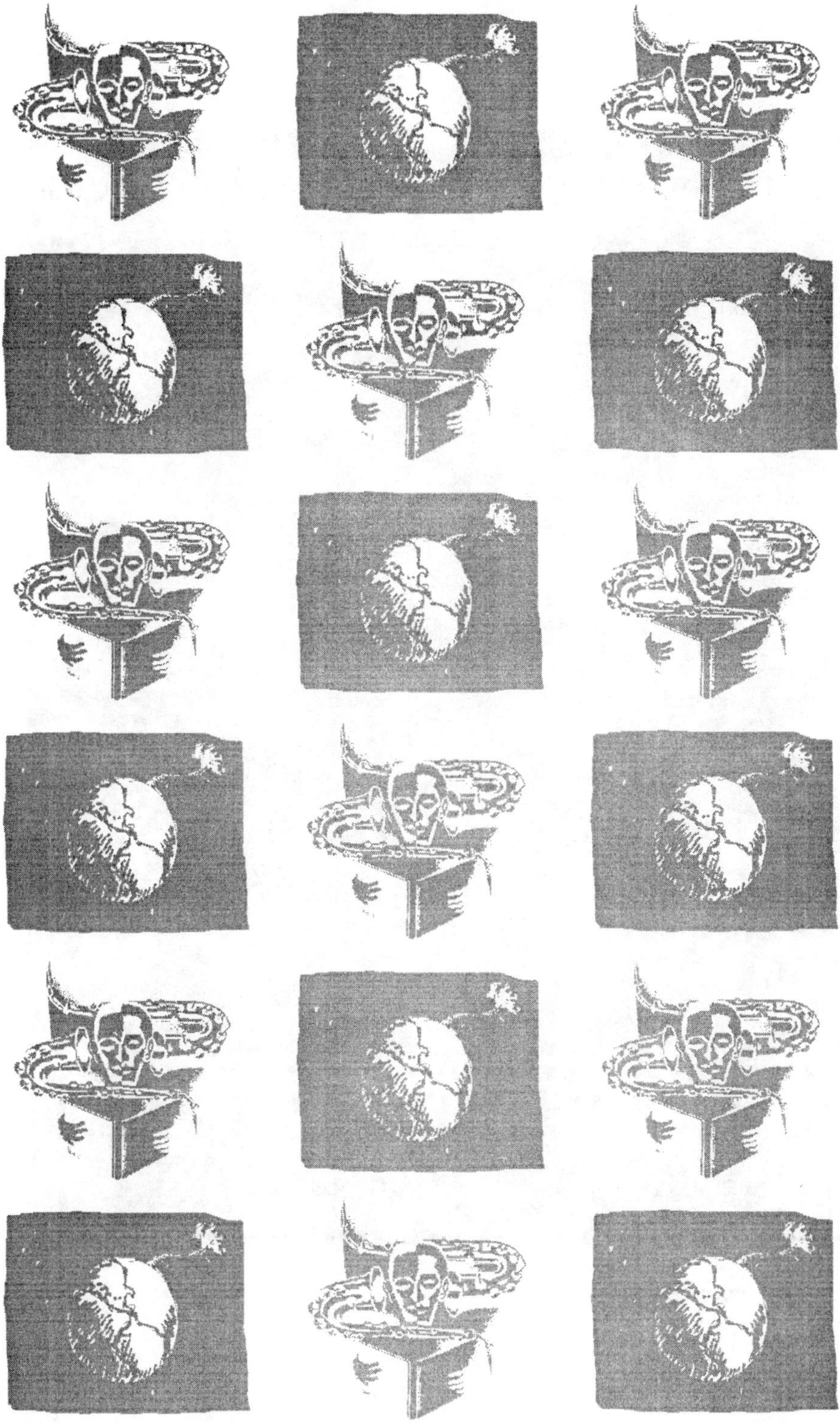

James Koehnline

The Utopian Blues

Hakim Bey

Why is the spirituality of the musician in "High" cultures so often a *low-down* spirituality?

In India, for example, the musician belongs to a caste so low it hovers on the verge of untouchability. This lowness relates, in popular attitudes, to the musician's invariable use of forbidden intoxicants. After the "invasion" of Islam many musicians converted in order to escape the caste system. (The Dagar Brothers of Calcutta, famous for their performance of sacred Hindu music, explained proudly to me that their family had not converted in Mughal times—for worldly advantage—but only much later, and then as Shiites; this proved that their conversion was *sincere*.) In Ireland the musician shared the same Indo-European reputation for lowness. The bards or poets ranked with aristocrats and even royalty, but musicians were merely the servants of the bards. In Dumezil's tripartite structure of Indo-European society, as reflected in Ireland, music seems to occupy an ambiguous fourth zone, symbolized by the fourth province of Munster, the "south." Music is thus associated with "dark" druidism, sexual license, gluttony, nomadry and other *outsider* phenomena.

Islam is popularly believed to "ban" music; yet obviously this is not the case, since so many Indian musicians converted. Islam expresses grave reservations about art in general because all art potentially involves us in multiplicity (extension in time and space) rather than in the unity (*tawhid*) by which Islam defines its entire spiritual project. The Prophet criticized worldly poetry; he criticized realism in art; and he relegated music to social occasions like marriages. (In Islamic societies the minstrels who supply such festal music are often Jews, or otherwise "outside" Islam.) In response to these critiques, Islamic culture developed "rectified" forms of art: —sufi poetry (which sublimates worldly pleasure as mystical ecstasy); non-representative art (falsely dismissed as "decorative" by western art-history); and sufi music, which utilizes multiplicity to *return* the listener to Unity, to induce "mystical states." But this restitution of the arts has never entirely succeeded as an uplifting of the musician. In Tehran in the 1970's, one of the more decadent sufi orders (Safi-Ali-Shahi) had enrolled the majority of professional musicians, and their sessions were devoted to opium smoking. Other musicians were known as hearty drinkers or otherwise *louche* and bohemian types—the few exceptions were pious Sufis in other, more disciplined orders, such as the Nematollahiyya or Ahl-i Haqq. In the Levant, Turkish sufi music leaked out of the *tekkes* and into the taverns, mixed with other

Mediterranean influences, and produced the wonderful genre of Rembetica, with its witty odes to whores, hashish, wine and cocaine.

In the rituals of Afro-American religions, such as Santería, Voudoun, and Candomblé, the all-important drummers and musicians are often non-initiates, professionals hired by the congregation—this is no doubt a reflection of the quasi-nomadic "minstrel" status of musicians in the highly evolved pastoral-agricultural societies of West Africa.

Traditional Christianity places a high value on music but a low value on musicians. Some branches of Protestantism tried to exclude professional musicians altogether, but Lutheranism and Anglicanism made use of them. Church musicians used to be considered an ungodly class of beings, a perception that survives in the reputation for naughtiness of choristers, choir-masters and organists. Thomas Weelkes (1576–1623) represents the archetype: brilliant but erratic (praised justly by Ezra Pound for his wonderful arrhythmic settings of "cadenced prose"), Weelkes was fired from his job at Chichester Cathedral as a "notorious swearer and blasphemer" and drunk, who (according to oral tradition) broke the camel's back by pissing over the organ-screen onto the Dean's head.

Christianity and Afro-American spirituality combined to produce the "Spiritist" churches where music forms the structure of worship and the congregation attains "professional" artistry. The ambiguity of this relation is revealed in the powerful links between sacred "gospel" and worldly "blues," the outcaste music of taverns, and "jazz," the music of the bordello (the very word evokes pure sexuality). The musical forms are very close—the difference lies in the musician, who, as usual, hovers on the very edge of the clearing, the in-between space of the uncanny, and of shamanic intoxication.

In all these cases the music itself represents the highest spirituality of the culture. Music itself being "bodiless" and metalinguistic (or metasemantic) is always (metaphorically or actually) the supreme expression of pure imagination as vehicle for the spirit. The lowness of the musician is connected to the perceived *danger* of music, its ambiguity, its elusive quality, its manifestation as lowness as well as highness—as pleasure.

Music as pleasure is not connected to the mind (or purified elements of spirit) but to the *body*. Music rises from the (inarticulate) body and is received by the body (as vibration, as sexuality).

The logos itself must be given musical expression (in chant, e.g. Koran, plainsong, etc.) for precisely the same somatic reason—the influence of body on spirit (through "soul" or psyche—imagination). Chant is music which *sublimates* the body.

Paradox: —that which is "holy" is "forbidden" (as in the Arabic word *harem* which means either holy or forbidden, depending on context). As Bataille points out, sanctity and transgression both arise from the fracturing of the "order of intimacy", the separation of the "human" from "nature." The "original" expression of this violent break is undoubtedly musical—as with the Mbutu Pygmies, who produce as a collectivity the music of the "Forest" as an expression of their closeness to (yet separatedness from) the wild(er)ness. Subsequent to this "first" expression, a further separation begins to appear: —the musician remains involved in the "violence" of the break with the intimate order in a special way, and so is seen as an uncanny person (like the witch, or the metallurgist). The musician emerges as a *specialist* within a still non-hierarchic society of hunter/gatherers, and the musician begins to take on the sign of the taboo to the extent that the tribe's undivided culture or "collective self" is affronted by this separation or transformation. The undivided culture (like the Mbutu) knows no "musician" in this sense, but only *music*. As division, and then hierarchy, begin to appear in society, the *position* of the musician becomes problematic. Like "primitive" society, these hierarchic "traditional" societies also wish to preserve something *unbroken* at the heart of their culture. If society is "many," culture will preserve a counter-balancing cohesiveness which is the sign of the original sacred order of intimacy, prolonged into the deepest spiritual meanings of the society, and thus preserved. So much for music—but what about the musician?

Hierarchic society permits itself to remain *relatively* undivided by sacralizing the specializations. Music, inasmuch as it is bodiless can be the sign of the upper caste (its "spirituality")—but inasmuch as music *arises from* the body (it is sublimed—it "rises"), the musician (originator/origin of the music) must be symbolized by the body and hence must be "low." Music is spiritual—the musician is corporeal. The spirituality of the musician is low but also ambiguous in its production of highness. (Drugs substitute for the priest's *ritual* highness to make the musician high enough to produce *aesthetic* highness.) The musician is not just low but uncanny—not just low but "outside." The power of the musician in society is like the power of the magician—the excluded shaman—in its relation to wildness. And yet it is precisely these hierarchic societies which create "seamless" cultures—including music. This is true even after the break—in the western tradition—between the "oneness" of melody and the "doubleness" of harmony. And note the reciprocal relation between high and low music—the various Masses on the "Western Wynde," set to a popular tune; the influence of melismatics on the madrigal; the pop influences on Rumi and other Sufis. The ambiguity of music allows it to drift between high and low and yet remain undivided. This is "tradition." It includes the subversive by excluding the musician (and the artist generally) and yet granting them power.

Thus for example the lowly musician Tansen attained the equivalent of aristocratic status in the art-intoxicated Mughal court; and Zeami (the great dramatist of the *Noh* theater of Japan, a form of opera), although he belonged to the untouchable caste of actors and musicians, rose to great heights of refinement because the Shogun fell in love with him when he was 13; to the Court's horror, the Shogun shared food with Zeami and granted courtly status to the *Noh*! For the musician the power of inspiration can be transmuted into the power of *power*. Consider for example the Turkish Janisseries, the Ottoman Imperial Guard, who all belonged to the heterodox (wine-drinking) Bektashi Sufi Order, and who invented military marching bands. Judging by European accounts of Janissery bands, which always speak of the sheer *terror* they induced, these musicians discovered a kind of psychological warfare which certainly bestowed prestige on this very ambiguous group, made up of slaves of the Sultan.

Traditional music always remains *satisfactory* (even when not "inspired") because it remains unbroken—both the high tradition and the low are the same "thing." Indian brass bands—Mozart—the same universe. In Mozart's own character (reflected in his "servant" characters like Leparello) we again discern the figure of the outsider, the gypsy-*wunderkind*, the toy of aristocrats, with a strong link to the low culture of beer-gardens and peasant clog-dances, and a fondness for bohemian excess. The musician is a kind of "grotesque"—disobedient servant, drunk, nomadic, brilliant. For the musician the perfect moment is that of the *festival*, the world turned upside down, the *saturnalia*, when servants and masters change places for a day. The festival is nothing without the musician, who presides over the momentary reversal—and thus the reconciliation—of all separated functions and forces in traditional society. Music is the perfect sign of the festal, and thereby of the "material bodily principle" celebrated by Bakhtin. In the intoxication of conviviality in the *carneval*, music emerges as a kind of utopian structure or shaping force—music *becomes* the very "order of intimacy."

Next morning, however, the broken order resumes its sway. Dialectics alone (if not "History") demonstrates that undivided culture is not an unmixed "good," in that it rests on a divided society. Where hierarchy has not appeared there is no music separate from the rest of experience. Once music becomes a category (along with the categorization of society), it has already begun to be alienated—hence the appearance of the specialist, the musician, and the taboo on the musician. Since it is impossible to tell whether the musician is sacred or profane (this being the perceived nature of the social split) this taboo serves to fill up the crack (and preserve the "unbrokenness" of tradition) by considering the musician as *both* sacred and profane. In effect the hierarchical society metes out punishments to *all* castes/classes for their shared guilt in the violation of the order of intimacy. Priests and kings are surrounded by taboos—chastity, or the sacrifice of the (vegetal) king, etc. The artist's punishment is to be a kind of outcaste paradoxically attached to the highest functions in society. [Note that the poet is not an "artist" in this sense and can retain caste because poetry is *logos*, akin to revelation. Poetry pertains to the "aristocratic" in traditional societies (e.g. Ireland). Interestingly the modern world has reversed this polarity in terms of *money*, so that the "low-caste" painter and musician are now wealthy and thus "higher" than the unrewarded poet.]

The "injustice" of the categorization of music is its *separation* from "the tribe," the whole people, including each and every individual. For inasmuch as the musician is excluded, music is excluded, inaccessible. But this injustice does not become apparent until the separations and alienations within society itself become so exacerbated and exaggerated that a split is perceived in culture. High and low are now out of touch—no reciprocity. The aristos never hear the music of the folk, and vice versa. Reciprocity of high and low traditions ceases—and thus cross-fertilization and cultural renewal within the "unbroken" tradition. In the western world this exacerbation of separation occurs roughly with industrialization and commodity capitalism—but it has "pre-echoes" in the cultural sphere. Bach adapted a "rational" mathematical form of well-temperedness over the older more "organic" systems of tuning. In a subtle sense a break has occurred within the unbroken tradition—others will follow. Powerful "inspiration" is released by this "break with tradition," titanic genius, touched to some extent with morbidity. For the "first time" so to speak the question arises: —whether one says yes or no to life itself. Bach's anguished spirituality (the "paranoia" of the Pietist gambling on Faith alone) was sometimes resolved with a "romantic" effusion of darkness. These impulses are "revolutionary" in respect to a tradition which suffers almost-unbearable contradictions. Their very naysaying opens up the possibility of a whole new "yes." Despite its tremendous inner tension, Bach's music is "healing" because he had to heal himself in order to create it in the first place. Healing—but not un-wounded. Bach as wounded healer.

It's not surprising that people preferred Telemann. Telemann was also a genius—as in his "Water Music"—but his genius remained at home within the unbroken tradition. If Bach is the first modern, he is the last ancient. If Bach is healing, Telemann is *healed*, already whole. His yes is the unspoken yes of sacred custom—naturally, of course, one has never thought otherwise. Telemann is still—supremely—our servant. This kind of "health" is exemplified in only a few composers after Telemann—Mendelssohn, for instance. One might call it "Pindaric," and one might defend it even against "intelligence."

The bohemian life of the modern artist, so "alienated from society," is nothing but the old low-down spirituality of the musician and artisan castes, recontextualized in an economy of commodities. Baudelaire (as Benjamin argued) had no economic function in the 19th century society—his low-down spirituality turned inward and became self-destructive, because it had lost its functionality in the social. Villon was just as much a bohemian, but at least he still had a role in the economy—as a thief! The artist's privilege—to be drunk, to be insouciant—has now become the artist's curse. The artist is no longer a servant—*refuses* to serve—except as unacknowledged legislator. As revolutionary. The artist now claims, like Beethoven, either a vanguard position, or—like Baudelaire—complete exile. The musician no longer accepts low caste, but must be either Brahmin or untouchable.

Wagner—and Nietzsche, when he was propagandizing for Wagner—conceived of a musical revolution against the *broken order* in the cause of a new and higher (conscious) form of the order of intimacy:—integral Dionysan culture viewed as the revolutionary goal of romanticism. The outsider as king. Opera is the utopia of music (as Charles Fourier also realized). In opera music appropriates the *logos* and thus challenges revelation's monopoly on meaning.

If opera failed as revolution—as Nietzsche came to realize—it was because the audience had refused to go away. The opera of Wagner, of Fourier, can only succeed as the social if it becomes the social—by eliminating the *category* of art, of music, as anything separate from life. The audience must become the opera. Instead—the opera became . . . just another commodity. A public ritual celebrating post-sacred social values of consumption and sentiment—the sacralization of the secular. A step along the road to the spectacle.

The commodification of music measures precisely the failure of the romantic revolution of music—its mummification in the repertoire, the Canon—the recuperation of its dissidence as the rhetoric of liberalism, "culture and taste". Wave after wave of the "avant-garde" attempted to *transcend* civilization—a process which is only now coming to an end in the apotheosis of commodification, its "final ecstasy."

As Bloch and Benjamin maintained, all art which escapes the category of mere kitsch contains what may be called the *utopian trace*—and this is certainly true of music (and even "more" true, given music's metasemantic immediacy). Finally it is this *trace* which must serve to counter the otherwise-incisive arguments against music made by J. Zerzan in "The Tonality and the Totality" (see *Future Primitive*, Autonomedia), i.e. that all alienated forms of music serve ultimately as *control*. To argue that music itself, like language, is a form of alienation, however, would seem to demand an "impossible" return to a Paleolithic that is nearly pre–"human." But perhaps the Stone Age is not *somewhere else*, distant and nearly inaccessible, but rather (in some sense) *present*. Perhaps we shall experience not a return to the Stone Age, but a return *of* the Stone Age (symbolized, in fact, by the very *discovery of the Paleolithic*, which occurred only recently). A few decades ago civilized ears literally could not hear "primitive" music except as noise; Europeans could not even hear the non-harmonic traditional classical music of India or China except as meaningless rubbish. The same held true for Paleolithic art, for instance—no one *noticed* the cave paintings till the late 19th century, even though they'd been "discovered" many times already. Civilization was defined by rational consciousness, rationality was defined as civilized consciousness—outside this totality only chaos and sheer unintelligibility could exist. But now things have changed—suddenly, just as the "primitive" and the "traditional" seem on the verge of disappearance, we can *hear* them. How? Why?

If the utopian trace in *all* music can now be heard, it can only be because the "broken order" is now somehow coming to an end. The long Babylonian con is finally wearing thin to the point of translucency, if not transparency. The reign of the commodity is threatened by a mass arousal from the media-trance of inattention. A taste for the authentic appears, suffers a million tricks and co-optations, a million empty promises—but it refuses to evaporate. Instead it condenses—it even coagulates. Neo-shamanic modes of awareness occupy lost or fractal unfoldings of the map of consensus and control. Psychedelics and oriental mysticism sharpen ears, masses of ears, to a taste for the unbroken, the order of intimacy, and its festal embodiment.

Is there actually a *problem* with the commodification of music? Why should we assume an "elitist" position now, even as new technology makes possible a "mass" *participation* in music through the virtual infinity of choice, and the "electric democracy" of musical synthesis? Why complain about the degradation of the aura of the "work of art" in the age of mechanical reproduction, as if *art* could or should still be defended as a category of high value?

But it's not "Western Civilization" we're defending here, and it's not the sanctity of aesthetic production either. We maintain that participation in the commodity can only amount to a commodification of participation, a simulation of aesthetic democracy. A higher synthesis of the Old Con, promising "The Real Thing *now*" but delivering only another betrayal of hope. The *problem* of music remains the same problem—that of alienation, of the separation of consumers from producers. Despite positive possibilities brought into being by the sheer multiplication of resources made accessible through reproduction technology, the overwhelming complex of alienation outweighs all subversive counterforces working for utopian ends. The discovery of "3rd world" music (i.e. primitive and traditional) leads to appropriation and dilution rather than to cross-cultural synergy and mutual enrichment. The proliferation of cheap music-synthesis tech at first opens up new and genuinely folkish/democratic possibilities, like Dub and Rap; but the "Industry" knows very well how to fetishize and alienate these insurrectionary energies:—use them to sell junkfood and shoes!

As we reach out to touch music it recedes from our grasp like a mirage. Everywhere, in every restaurant, shop, public space, we undergo the "noise pollution" of music—its very ubiquity measures our impotence, our lack of participation, of "choice." And what music! A venal and venial counterfeit of all the "revolutionary" music of the past, the throbbing sexualized music that once sounded like the death knell of Western Civilization, now becomes the sonic wallpaper hiding a facade of cracks, rifts, absences, fears; the anodyne for despair and anomie—elevator music, waiting room music, pulsing to the 4/4 beat, the old "square" rhythm of European rationalism, flavored with a homeopathic tinge of African heat or Asian spirituality—the utopian trace—memories of youth betrayed and transformed into the aural equivalent of Prozac and Colt 45. And still each new generation of youth claims this "revolution" as its own, adding or subtracting a note or beat here or there, pushing the "transgressive" envelope a bit further, and calling it "new music"—and each generation in turn becomes simply a statistical mass of consumers busily creating the airport music of its own future, mourning the "sell-outs," wondering what went wrong.

Western classical music has become the sign of bourgeois power—but it is an empty sign inasmuch as its period of primacy production is over. There are no more symphonies to be written in C major. Serialism, 12-tone, and all the 20th century avant-garde carried out a revolution but failed to inflame anyone except a small elite, and certainly failed to deconstruct the Canon. In fact, the very failure of this "Modern" music is somewhat endearing, since it permitted the music to retain some of the innocent fervor of insurrectionary desire, untainted by "success"—Harry Partch for example. But I still remember with horror a scene I once observed in Shiraz (Iran), where the Festival of Arts had invited K. Stockhausen to present his music to "the people" of the city rather than solely to the Tehran aristos and international kulturvultures of the Festival audience. What an embarrassment! And the revolution which swept through town a few years later owed nothing to such "generosity"— except hatred of "decadent" Western music—which it banned. As for "Mozart" (to pick an archetype), how can he be "saved" from the Industry and the Institutions, from CDs and radio, from Lincoln Center and Kennedy Center, from Hollywood and MUZAK? I recall a passage from a Carson McCullers story, in which a poor little girl listens entranced, for the first time, to a 78 of Mozart, through the screen door of a wealthy neighbor—a quintessentially utopian moment. Even the technology of alienation can be "magical"—but only inadvertently, serendipitously, by distortion. A distant radio on a lonely night in a tropical town in Java, say, playing some endless Ramayana-drama till dawn—or for that matter . . . . choose your own favorite (perhaps erotic) moment of memory, marked by some overheard fragment of music. (You'd just better hope that LITE-FM never finds out *which* fragment, because they'll turn it into *nostalgia* and use it to sell your own desire back to you, and taint your sweet memory forever with hucksterish greed.)

. . . . So we admit it—there *is* a problem. All is not necessarily for the best in the world of too-Late Capitalism—Music reminds us of one of those cinematic-vampire-victims, already so drained of life as to be almost one of the Undead—shall we abandon her?

Does any "solution" exist to this problem, any cure which is not a form of reaction, of bombing ourselves back into some ideal past? Is it even valid to base our critique on the assumption that music was or will be "better" at some point in time? Is "degeneration" any better a model than "progress"?

In the first place, is "music itself" in question here, or should we be focused instead on the *production* of music, and on the social structure which informs that production? In other words, perhaps music (short of sheer kitsch) should be considered "innocent," at least by comparison with the constellation of alienation and betrayal and monopolization sometimes called the Industry—the musical arm of the Spectacle, as it were. By comparison, Music is the victim, not the cause of the "problem." And what about *musicians*? Are they part of the Industry, or are they too (like their Muse) mere victims? Part of the problem, or part of the solution? Or is the whole concept of "blame" here no more than the ideology of a subtler Reaction—an incipient Puritanism—another false totality?

If we want to escape any vicious circles of retributive resentment (or musical revanchism) we need a wholly different approach—and if our approach (our strategy) is not to be based on "History"—either of music itself or of production—then perhaps it must be rooted instead in a *utopian poetics*. In this sense, we should not adopt any one utopian system as a model—which would mire us in nostalgia for some lost future—but rather take the idea of utopia itself, or even the emotion of utopia, for a starting point. Music, after all, addresses the *emotions* more immediately than other arts, filtered as they are through *logos* or *image*. (This explains in part why Islam distrusts music.) Music is the most border-permeating of all arts—perhaps not the "universal language," but only because it is in fact not a language at all, unless perhaps a "language of the birds." The "universal" appeal of music lies in its direct link to utopian emotion, or desire, and beyond that to the utopian imagination. By its interpenetration of *time* and *pleasure*, music expresses and evokes a "perfect" time (purged of boredom and fear) and "perfect" pleasure (purged of all regret). Music is bodiless, yet it is *from* the body and it is *for* the body—and this too makes it utopian in nature. For utopia is "no place," and yet utopia concerns the body above all.

As an example (not as a *model*), we might return to Fourier's concept of the opera as it "will be" practiced in utopia, or the societal stage of *Harmony* as he called it. As a "complete art-work" the opera will involve music and words, dance, painting, poetry—in a system based on "analogies" or occult correspondences between the senses and their objects. For instance, the 12 tones in music correspond to the 12 Passions (desires or emotions), the 12 colors, and the 12 basic Series of the Phalanx or utopian community, etc. By orchestrating these correspondences, Harmonian opera will far exceed the paltry music-dramas of Civilization in beauty, luxury, inspiration, not to mention sheer scope. They will utilize the hierographic science of Harmonian art to provide education, propaganda, entertainment, artistic transcendence, and erotic fulfillment—all at once. Sound, sight, intellect, all the senses will respond to the complex multi-dimensional *emblems* of the opera, made up of words and music, reason and emotion, and perhaps even touch and smell. These emblems will create a direct "moral" effect in audience and actors alike (somewhat as Brecht envisioned for "Epic Theater")—and in fact, the tendency in Harmony will be for the audience to disappear, to become part of the Opera (at least potentially) so that the separation between "artist" and "audience"—the proscenium, so to speak—will be broken down, permeated, eventually erased. All Harmonians will be touched with genius in the Opera—this is the purpose of the hieroglyphs, this is their "moral effect." (I'm putting the word in quotes because Fourier hated moralism as much as Nietzsche. Perhaps "spiritual" might be a better term.) This "harmonial association" in the production and experience of the Opera is (for Fourier) a model of the very structure of the utopian community. The phalanx will be spontaneously what the opera is by art. In effect Fourier has rediscovered the primal ritual, the dance/music/story/mask/sacrifice which is the tribe in the form of art, the tribe's co-creation of itself in the aesthetic imagination. Fourier had healed the rift (in his writings, at least—in his imagination)—but not by a *return* to some paradisal perfection of the past. In fact, for Fourier himself, Harmony was not even a state of futurity so much as one of *potential presence*. He believed that if one group (of exactly 1620 people) were to construct a single phalanstery and begin to live by Passional Attraction, the whole world would be converted within two years. Unlike More, Bacon, Campanella and other utopians, Fourier's plans were not meant as ironies nor as critiques nor as science fiction, but as blueprints for non-violent and immediate revolution. In this sense he resembles his (hated) contemporaries Owen and St. Simon—but unlike them he was not interested in the regulation of desire but in its total liberation—and in this he more greatly resembles Blake—or (as Fourier's followers liked to claim) Beethoven, than any of the socialists, whether "utopian" or "scientific."

The disappearance of the audience in Fourier's opera reminds us of nothing so much as the Situationist program for the "Suppression and Realization of Art." Harmonian opera suppresses itself as a separate category of artistic production, with all the consequent commodification and consumption, only to realize itself precisely as "everyday life." But it is an everyday life transformed and systematically informed by the "marvelous" (as the Surrealists put it). It is a communal and individual desiring machine. It is the field of pleasure. It is a luxury—a form of "excess" (as Bataille put it). It is the generosity of the social to itself—like a festival, only more formal, celebration as ritual rather than as orgy. (Of course the orgy is the *other* great organizing principle of phalansterian life!) The opera in this sense *includes us*. From our point of view we can now say that *the music is ours*—not someone else's—not the musician's, not the record company's, not the radio station's, not the shopkeeper's, not the MUZAK company's, not the devil's—but *ours*.

In *Noise: the Political Economy of Music*, (1977), Jacques Atali proposes that this "stage" in music's possible future be called the stage of "Composition"—"a noise of Festival and Freedom," as "essential element in a strategy for the emergence of a truly new society." Composition calls for "the destruction of all simulacra in accumulation"— i.e., it avoids representation and commodification, and mechanical reproduction as "the silence of repetition." "The emergence of the free act, self-transcendence, pleasure in being instead of having" is (violently) opposed to alienation, by which the "musician lost possession of music". In Composition, "to listen to music is to re-write it, 'to put music into operation, to draw it toward an unknown praxis' (Barthes)." Atali warns that "blasphemy is not a plan, any more than noise is a code. Representation and repetition, heralds of lack, are always able to recuperate the energy of the liberatory festival." True composition demands "a truly different system of organization . . . outside of meaning, usage, and exchange," i.e. marked in part by "the Return of the Jongleurs," by "a reappearance of very ancient forms of production," as well as by the invention of new instruments and recycled technologies (as in Dub). Music is separated from Work, and becomes a form of "idleness." "The field of the commodity has been shattered." "Participation in collective play," and "immediate communication," aim to "locate liberation not in a faraway future . . . but in the present, in production and in one's own enjoyment." In this sense, then, "music emerges as a relation to the body and as transcendence": —an erotic relation. In Composition, "production melds with consumption . . .in the development of the imaginary through the planting of personal gardens." "Composition liberates time so that it can be lived, not stockpiled . . . in commodities." Because of the anarchic nature of Composition and the consequent danger of cacophony, *"tolerance and autonomy"* must be presupposed as conditions. Atali also worries about "the impossibility of improvisation," and the lack of musical ability in some persons; nevertheless, these objections are not absolutes—and besides, if we recall the model of Fourier's Opera, we will note that non-musical talents count for as much as musical talents in Harmonial Association. "Composition thus leads to a staggering conception of history, a history that is open, unstable . . . in which music effects a re-appropriation of time and space." "It is also the only utopia that is not a mask for pessimism."

Does the disappearance of the audience already necessitate and predict a sitage "beyond" that of Composition and the Utopian Poetics—a stage of the *disappearance of the musician*? Not according to Fourier. The Passion for music is precisely not the Passion for, say, horticulture—although many Harmonians will be masters of both. But obviously the Opera will still have its "stars," even if these luminaries will also be adept at dozens of other arts and skills. Moreover, thanks to the liberation of all Passions to follow their Attractions, "talent" will increase by stupendous degrees, such that (for instance) "the globe will contain thirty-seven millions of poets equal to Homer" (Fourier in *Theory of the Four Moments*, p. 81)—and untold millions of "stars." In effect however every Harmonian is a star at something; and the opera is only one possible combination or constellation. Thus "the musician" may disappear as a professional, as a separate category or fetish, as a focus of separation—only to re-appear as a kind of shamanic function. Even Fourier, who expected everyone to master at least 12 different *metiers*, understood that utopia must make places for monomaniacs and specialists in ecstasy. Far from disappearing, only now can the "minstrels" (and the "bards") make their re-appearance—as aspects of an integral and creative "personality" of the social. Because *nothing* can be commodified, the musician is at last free to "play," and to be rewarded for play.

Under such conditions, what would become of the *low-down spirituality* of the musician? Utopia is a unity, not a uniformity—and it contains antinomies. Utopian desire never comes to an end, even—or especially!—in utopia. And music will always be the last veil (of 70,000 veils of light and darkness) that separates us from the "order of intimacy." Music will never lose its holy unholiness; it will always contain the trace of the violence of sacrifice. How then could the "blues" ever come to an end—that orgone indigo utopian melancholy caress of sound, that little-bit-too-much, that difference? The *low caste* of the musician will of course be dissolved in utopia—but somehow a certain untouchability will linger, a certain dandyism, a *pride*. The one tragedy that this Harmonian Blues will *never* lament is the loss of the blues of itself, its appropriation, its alienation, its betrayal, its demonic possession. This is the "utopian minimum," the money-back guarantee, the *sine qua non—the music is ours*. At this point a grand dialectical synthesis occurs—the unbroken order and the broken order are *both* "overcome" in the moment of the emergence of a new thing, the low-down utopian blues, the Passional Opera, Composition, the music of utopia dreaming about itself and waking to itself. In heaven itself the harpists will be drunk and disorderly. "And the Angels knock at tavern doors" (Hafez).

The Utopian Blues

Thanks to:

The late George Huddleston, Organist, Christ Church, New Brunswick, NJ
Sasha Zill, soprano saxophone
"Listening with Watson"
Richard Watson (no relation), viola
Jean During, tar, sehtar
Dariush Safvat, Society for Preservation and Propagation of Classical Persian Music
The late Ustad Ilahi of the Ahl-i Haqq
"Barq-i sabz" (Radio Tehran)
The Dagar Brothers, dhrupad
Pandit Pran Nath, vocalist
James Irsay, piano
Tony Piccolo, piano
Martin Schwartz, Rembetica collector
Bill Laswell, basses
Claddagh Records, Dublin
Steven Taylor, guitar

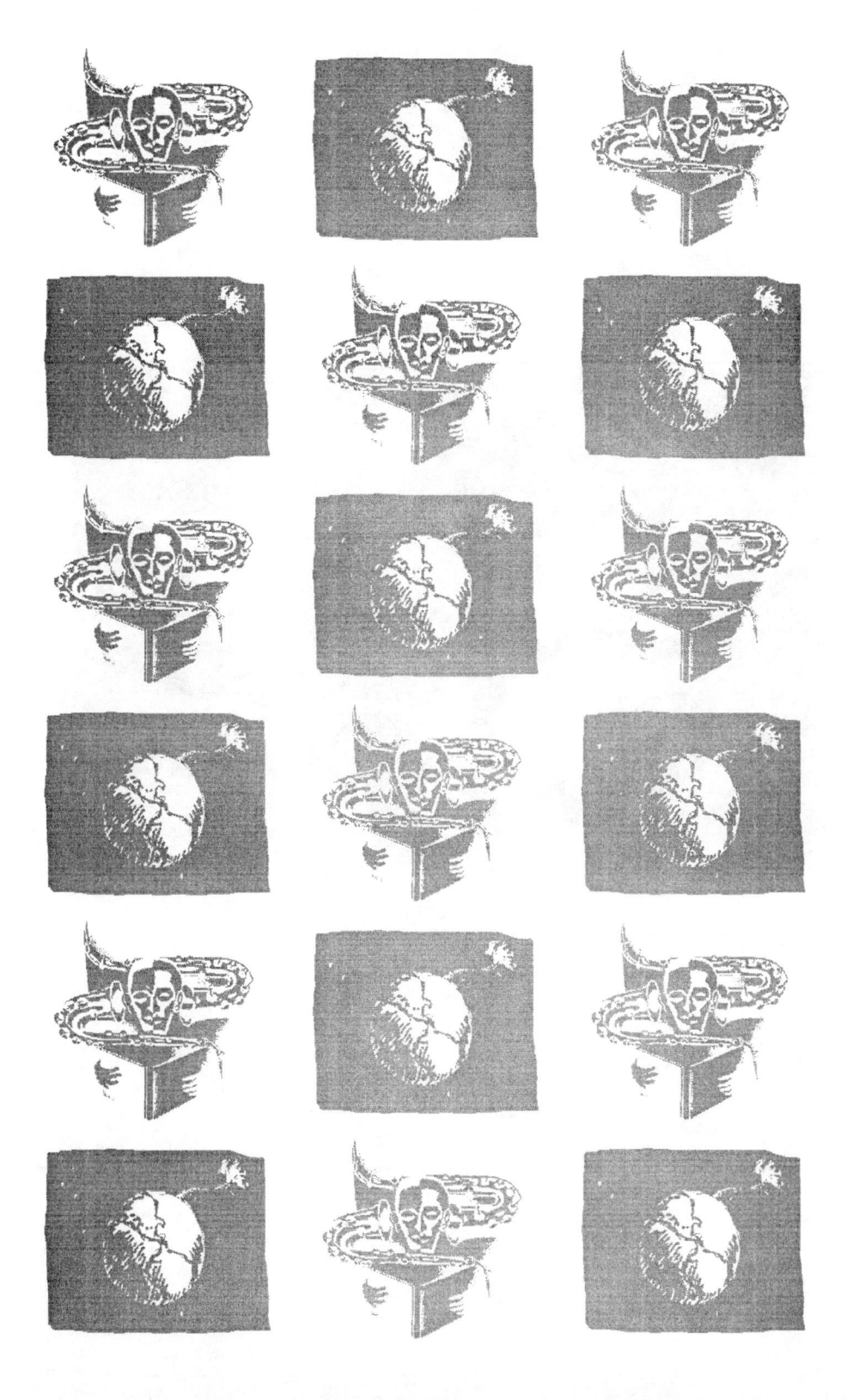

Monica Sjoo

Matriarchal Music Making

Batya Weinbaum

Borealis and Sun lay on their backs now, feet at the tip of the waves, drawing in the sun. As they lay back, each tempted by the surge of the growing warmth between them that they both felt, memories continued of driving around Seneca in Sun's blue VW van together one winter, equipped with woodstove and piano. They took turns. One of them drove. One of them played. They circled the depot 7 times, filling the truck and the air and the sky with their music, then stopped in front of the depot where other women were at the gate. They danced and made music, "waves for peace," trying to make the base fall down. Some of the women at the camp had thought they were insane. Others had come along for the ride. Then two of them had gone traveling, piano and drums in truck. They had played at beaches, oceans, supermarkets. Composing music together at earth spots; taking the sound of the music to gas stations and laundromats, on the way to conferences and festivals. Michigan. EARTHWHEELS, the music had been called. Later they performed with flutes, bells, conch shells and violins. It was a shame, that so much of the creative energy of the women's lands had been withdrawn, reduced to a petty squabbling. They both felt the lapse, as if something had been taken away from them. Together they listened to a wave lap out again.[1]

The creation of women's music festivals by women in the 1980s were positive outgrowths of women's community arts, rather than negative "give women a chance" second rate operations meant to compensate for discrimination.[2] The festivals grew over the last decade, originally being events organized by women producers that brought together women musicians and gathered audiences of women. Gradually, because labor was needed and the producers were operating on short budgets, the audience-community at these festivals began to participate in creating the festivals and building a community. In this article, I'll consider the relation of women's music and women's communities.

For centuries women had been deprived of their own community arts, which had originally taken the form of the communal dancing and singing rites common to "primitive" tribes and natural-world peoples—meaning of course, primitive in the positive sense, not lesser or inferior.[3]

For example, in the islands of Hawaii, the dance known as the *hula* had once been performed as part of the ritual of everyday living, for celebratory and communal purposes.

Women danced in blocks as large as two hundred, as did the men. The European conquerors of the Hawaiian islands drew pictures of large blocks of women dancing together, imitating waves and other natural forms.[4] These dances were misinterpreted as performances for audiences, since the outsiders had no other tradition to interpret what they saw. Colonialists saw the dance as erotic and suppressed it.[5] Only later was the dance commercialized for tourists. Individual women were sketched in erotic poses, broken off from the block of dancing women.[6] This pattern of eroticizing and then suppressing women's dance has been reproduced all over the world. Common comparisons to the hula's history are Indian temple dancing and belly dancing.[7]

The history of women's music making can be traced similarly. In collections of primitive peoples' "mythologies," universal references are made to women's discovery of music.[8] As some of these myths go, women heard the music of the reeds, the singing of the trees, the whispers of ponds. They fashioned natural material instruments, directly derived from natural forms, and started making music. Then men, jealous of the women's natural ability, stole the instruments, made men's houses, and allowed music to be made only within those male walls (unless women's music was purely functional, like singing to genitalia during lovemaking or chanting the birth chant to help the drop of the child from the womb.)

Women were often banned from music making because their music was thought to be destructive to men and male civilization in general, as witnessed in commonly held myths of women's destructive power—the singing of the Sirens that lured men to crash on the rocks of the Siren's island home, the singing of the Ishtar cults in Egypt that purportedly caused men to flagellate themselves, and so on.[9] Once music was bound to an organized patriarchal religion that superceded goddess worship, women lost the collective use of their own bodies simultaneously with the loss of their voices. For instance, consider the male cantors and male-only singing in the synagogues; the all-male Gregorian chanters in the medieval church; and the replacement of women's voices by those of choir boys and *castradi*.

From the perspective of this historical pattern, the rise of women's music festivals where all the arts re-emerge is disruptive to the world at large; or perhaps reformative to the world at large and disruptive to its current civilization. At these festivals, craftwomen, psychics, costume makers, tarot readers, and tattoo artists, acting as traders and sellers, encourage a tribal decorativeness in group symbols and a matriarchal consciousness absent since women controlled sacred space. As Jane Harrison noted in *Ancient Ritual Into Art*, all the arts were derived originally from ritual which created the space for a culture to take form. Indeed, ethnomusicologists have noted that cultures have actually been created by sound—a certain sound rings out and people gather to create their culture, by which is meant the nitty-gritty, the ins and outs, of everyday life.

Thus it is more than coincidental that the women gathering in modern music rituals had begun creating a culture in which, at least temporarily, women were in control and able to rediscover their own bodies, to dance unobserved, and to make loud public music. There arguments were held about where and what to eat, and about the creation and relative importance of rules. The experience of creating culture became more than the passive consumption of culture created by those "others" schooled in the arts. Women were creating the context of symbolic exchange, as a community and in public—or at least in a short-term public made by temporarily excluding onlookers (men).

Thus it is ironic that women culturalists were often not understood as political by those who remained outside of the phenomenon of attempting to restore music makers to their original shamanistic status, recapturing them from "show business." The arts are an integral part of the transformative process and are not just entertainment. The critics of women's culture remained surprisingly unaware of the active process of revitalization that occured at these festivals. The process can be compared to the revitalization based on the re-emergence of songs and dances that accompany or predate nationalistic political movements, such as the famous Ghost Dance campaign of Native American Indian resistance.[10]

Women whose lives have been changed by participating as festival creators have staged spontaneous political happenings such as making waves of sound in front of military bases or in the streets, which cause people to turn around and listen. It is no accident that music and loud street sound were made illegal, and music limited to the restricted area of concert halls. Denial of the right to make sound has much to do with the spread of current imperialistic civilization, which outlawed chants, dances, and indigenous musical instruments as part of its mechanism of conquest. In "Billie Lives,"[11] we have a record of how Billie Holiday's special notes drove stockbrokers to jump out of the window during the Great Crash. Perhaps we can effect politics and help lead to earthly survival if we do the work of finding the right key or note. So we have to rediscover our own sound as women, even if we don't find the chord that makes men lose their minds or that brings the walls of Jericho down. Anything we can do to change the context of sound creation can help loosen the grip of patriarchal civilization. The creation of women's music and festival communities should be seen as part of the retribalization tendency of America's oppressed groups in the '60s and '70s. What kind of communities have women evolved? And do these communities allow for the emergence of a specifically women's music?

Stanley Diamond, in his book *In Search of the Primitive*, discusses certain positive characteristics of the organization of "primitive" communal societies that have been lost in modern civilization. Some of these same characteristics are seen in women's festival "civilization." For example, there is a different relation to the body, that is, public nudity, which appears at these gatherings of women. Second, there is a public ethic that values subjectivity as much as objectivity when formulating policy and rules (seen in the workers' meetings). Third, culture, especially "primitive" culture, functions to create shared meanings, which can be seen as new areas of organization developed in response to the more complex needs of the growing community: at the festivals the healing/medical unity is called "The Womb," not the disembodied and remote name, "clinic"; the safe zone for emotionally overwhelmed women is not called the "psychiatric unit" or "special care" as it is in the modern hospitals, but "Oasis." These healing names actually attract women to the spaces rather than repel them. Thus, they are more often and more easily utilized by women in need. Fourth, schooling and training involve a primary process and not an institutionalized learning situation. Women volunteer to work in areas in which they might have aptitude but not formal training. In fact, this seems to be one of the drawing cards that entices women to work; they can expand to a fuller view of themselves than allowed in the sex-roled external work situation. They can participate in a work culture which the anthropologist Edward Sapir might call "genuine" instead of "spurious." Last, "primitive" economies rest on bartering, trade, and gifts, and this communal economy also emerges at festivals (but only insofar as it does not conflict with the producer's economic needs in terms of external cash flow).

As might be expected, at some point there is a breakdown of the analogy between "primitive" and women's "civilization." After all, the festival communities were and are only temporary pockets of a potential new civilization operating in an advanced capitalist realm. One of the characteristics of "primitive" civilizations which Diamond cites is that there is no body of law which stems from alienation, from us vs. them. Within contemporary women's culture, as within any rising civilization, the creation drama stabilized at some point and alienation did set in. National women's festivals which continue now seem to require a lengthy orientation of first-time participants to the rules previously created. The content of these rules punctures the romantic, mini-revolutionary bubble from which these festivals might be viewed; one hears arguments reminiscent of the debates in Soviet Russia during the '20s and '30s, when it was argued that communism couldn't be pure yet because trade was necessary with the outside, capitalistic world in order for the internal economy to keep going. A "bureaucracy" appeared in the festivals, just as the "State" did in Russia. Arguments over space allocation reduced rule-making to a housekeeping event rather than an exciting immersion in participatory democracy. But the alienation that comes from receiving rather than making rules can be positive. That alienation leads to spin-off festivals, when women frustrated over one issue or another go on to create smaller, more participatory festivals of their own, generally on a regional basis.

Now to consider the women's music and the musicians. It has been pointed out that music makers are ahead of their times, are eccentrics and even deviants.[12] Chris Williamson, for example, is without a doubt a cultural deviant. Appearing as she and others do in a totally institutionalized setting, where participants are dependent on the environment to shelter and feed them, such "star" deviants channel participants in a positive deviant direction (though these festivals surface neither in literature on countercultures nor in feminist sociology or anthropology). But, at first, "women's music" meant only or primarily the stars recorded on the Olivia label, restricting itself to white lesbian soloists performing for white audiences. This ultimately limited audience participation and guarded the performer/audience distinction. At the long-established festivals, performers and audiences became separated by a security force of women who seemed to act out a repressed "cop" mentality, enforcing a hierarchy that has the feel of being of their own devising.

Call the security force "feminist fascism" or what you will, but the makers of women's music continued to operate in a capitalistic-managerial western context and were unaware that women's sounds could actually be shattering. They were often even more unaware of the male nature of their instruments or of the patriarchal stage context in which their new stardom was emerging. But with the struggle for democracy going on within the subculture, including the branching off of "satellites" differentiated from the "mother festivals" on the basis of egalitarianism, space is being created for matriarchal/"primitive" consciousness and reemerging aspects of the tribal lifestyle Diamond cites.

This changing social structure will affect the form the sounds take, since it has been observed by anthropologists that social structure is reflected in the sound of a civilization.[13] Concretely, social change has been brought about at the festivals by protests demanding the music of women of color—protests that have led to such things as Edwina Lee Tylor's drumming on earth brought in trays to the stage or to work shops where women of all races are taught matriarchal African rhythms. Social change is also seen when some local festivals focus so much on the tribal village concept that no specialized musicians ever appear and no stages are erected. For years women creators, writers and artists have looked to pre-patriarchal times for strength; not just in the contemporary feminist period, but by literary greats such as Virginia Woolf and HD concurrent with an earlier wave of feminism.[14]

When we look at pre-patriarchal times, we see women were the originators of music and music-making instruments, although some feminist anthropologists criticize the reclamation of these "myths" saying these stories show women as wild, animalistic and "primitive," as a justification for the need of their taming by men to curb their destructiveness. Or, that these myths glorified women as ephemeral muses. And, there is the large discussion of whether these myths through which we view pre-patriarchal times are real, or projections of consciousness. Nevertheless, it is possible to discern that making music with matriarchal consciousness meant making music and art as the basis for a community-creation ritual. This is the reverse of today's music, which is made largely alone by specialists on machines in studios and played individually on Walkman's to "open up space" in an individual's head while walking down the street or in a confined situation. So what is matriarchal music making? What kind of sound can help us get our feet back on the ground?

First of all, it's making music with what Eric Neuman and other scholars have called matriarchal consciousness.[15] Matriarchal consciousness involved the notion that the universe is abundant and nurturing and plentiful, even though, in this culture, where resources are controlled by men and the patriarchy, individual men may be generous with money when so choosing whereas women (mothers) having less access may be more controlling and stringent. But through early art we see the abundant "giving" imagery of matriarchal consciousness, such as the date palm goddess offering food to the surrounding environ.

Likewise, making music with matriarchal consciousness meant singing to the earth, to return love to her, to encourage her to keep providing with life-sustaining growth. It's making music with inspiration from nature, the moon, and the earth—rather than making music that takes off on the use of tools. Nature consciousness versus tool consciousness, a dichotomy which first many anthropologists and then later many feminists posed as a dichotomy between men and women.

Secondly, making music with matriarchal consciousness is not just jamming. Tribal organizations that lived closer to the earth in which we find more remnants of matriarchal consciousness (as we do with poets, romantics, and impressionists) had very structured music and dance rituals. In Hawaii, where I studied, one was not invited by the *kuma hula* teacher or master to chant or drum—e.g. to make music—until one had studied in the *halau* or dance school for 15 years.

Third, making music with matriarchal consciousness does not mean simply reversing the patriarchy by putting women in the same slots, as those with little or no exposure to feminist culture tend to think. Nor does it mean anti-authoritarian, free form, democratic or "collective." That's making a modern definition of matriarchy to be kind of a knee-jerk reaction to patriarchy. The shamans, or music makers, would go on voyages or visionary quests and return to the group or tribe where they were fed, taken care of, given shelter and listened to for the images of the other world or the messages of spirit they would collect. These were not "processed" or watered down with inputs. These were symbols provided through music and sound to form the consciousness of the community. And traveling musicians, organized to perform at specialized events, only developed when we had dissolution of tribes and the rise of cities, nations and territorialized states which broke up the way it had been when visions through music would cohere and even decide the location of the group.[16]

Fourth, matriarchal music is not cut, pasted and ordered, especially with regard to time. A good metaphor to keep in mind would be that of Susan Griffin, who wrote *Woman and Nature*.[17] She wrote of the way the wildness of the forest was killed by the ordering, classifying drive of patriarchal civilization that veered towards breaking everything up into categories and boxes. This is also reflected in how music became mensurate, or timed and delineated down to the nth degree in notation—sort of a male harnessing of vibrant swirling raw cycling feminine energy, as in a stick | and a grid ≣ to pin ⪅ everything down.

Fifth, the sound of matriarchal music is primitive in the positive sense, or simple.[18] Your classical composition teacher would call it minimalist. But the matriarchal music making perspective would say you don't criticize the "om" for being repetitive; you appreciate it for what it is, and for what it does, which is to clarify the surrounding environmental vibration. Minimal music sounds like a put-down, as if the politics of going back to the simple were not important to reduce an overbureacratized culture which conceals the fact that quite simply taxes support wars. Making a simple, uncomplicated sound can be important to reduce a culture back to harmonious values, as when the Chinese emperor used to send musicians out across the land to collect sounds, to listen to them all, and compose new songs to send out as a way to effect the politics of the state. Although the Confucian state which did that was already patriarchal, we can call this left-over matriarchal use of sound, as the Chinese in matriarchal times used to have rituals where all would sing and dance and go down to the river to make waves of love to keep the peace before the rise of the state.[19]

Another matriarchal element of music making would be to include hearing the sound of the instrument in front of you, rather than imposing a sound by tuning. A tuning, after all, is developed by a certain culture. There are at least 99 tunings I have at home from all over the world, each of them attached to or common in a specific nation-state or culture, all of which are patriarchal or male-dominated at this time. But there is evidence from myth all over the world, here again using myth as evidence without a lengthy discussion of what myth is, of women who used to walk through the woods and by the waters and ponds and hear the sounds of the reeds and the leaves, and let their music flow from there.[20] In other words, you don't conquer or impose; you listen.

Another aspect of matriarchal sound would be to make-do with what you've got. This is making music with what Claude Levi-Strauss and other anthropologists would call *bricoleur* consciousness.[21] This would also be opposed to the civilizing instrumentalist tool-minded consciousness mentioned earlier. (Grids and lines and notation and keys are supposed to be tools, not inhibitors, or punitive weapons and punishers in the work ethic consciousness which dominates music today.[22]) If we adopt the Eastern, non-western perspective, that the performer is there to cleanse the group soul of all who are present, there has got to be some alignment of the music depending on the instrument, the player, the time, the hall and the audience. If we stick to the strictly written form, we do not allow for this form of readjustment and realignment; we make "mistakes."

Black consciousness, which, by some black feminist scholars, has been opposed to white civilizing consciousness, as has "primitive," "women's" and "matriarchal" consciousness, also has this *bricoleur* aspect. If you don't have instruments, or tools, you play your thighs; you "make do"; and if you don't have access to a concert hall, you "make do" with performing your rap on the streets.

Making music with matriarchal consciousness is also visual.[23] Although a violinist I worked with once had classical training, she got into the flow by looking at my hands as I played the keys. I often play by what the patterns of the keys look like together, and I teach that way too. Or I use a synaesthetic sense of mixing colors of light that I can perceive, which might be broken down from an original landscape I had been looking at preparing to do a painting. And, I have had the experience of actually painting in sound. "Primitive" minds used to go from a flow of all these senses, too.[24] What we are discussing here is a synaesthetic versus abstract grid reality, using a different portion of the brain to see a color, or colors, as a focus, and, the receptors thus cleared, letting a sound come through. Most cultural critiques have recognized the damaging, de-personalizing effect of the reduction to black and white in western culture. Some composers, such as Scriabin and Edgar Varese, have revolted against this sterile reality and returned to use of color, and hence matriarchal reality, in composition too.

While there is a similarity between matriarchal-ness in music making and both New Age and eastern music, perhaps it comes down to a question of nature versus nurture. Do women really make music differently than men, out of our nature, or do we merely suffer from lack of nurturance, or active discouragement, in our own culture?

The discrimination against women in both black and white western musical culture has been documented in the forms of active discouragement and burial by being ignored.[25] But it might be more interesting here to note that the resurgence of interest in eastern forms of music making is really a return to matriarchal consciousness. Kay Gardner, a woman composer widely researched in this area, speaks of women making music which is constructed differently than that of male composers all together.[26] It tends to begin with a gesture, she says and to build gradually, adding one note or gesture at a time. Ethnomusicology research shows that eastern musicians do the same. Further, her descriptions of what she calls women's music sound like what Peter Hamel describes as a magical, as opposed to mythical or mental, mode of music.[27] I have concluded that this is because the cultures he writes about utilizing this other kind of mode have more goddesses present in their deitic panopticon and hence more cosmic mother, matriarchal consciousness.

With enough newly sacred space for experimentation with music, dance, and song, the ancient sounds buried since women were suppressed within patriarchal civilization will no doubt resurface. And what would women's own music be like if it did? Composer Kay Gardner, who for several years intentionally did not listen to men's music, suggests that women's compositions are different from men's, that women's are cyclical rather than linear and tend to wind down rather than end within orgasmic crescendo. On the other hand, Pauline Oliveros, another leading *avant garde* woman composer, sometimes described as the female John Cage or the Gertrude Stein of music, holds that women have not composed as much music as men or with the same forcefulness because they are not socialized to tell others what to do. Like similar debates (do women write differently than men, make art differently, etc.) these discussions stem from the "are women different" conundrum.

Perhaps women's minds are just as analytical and linear as men's, and hence their compositions would also be if they had an equal opportunity to compose or perform. These matriarchal compositions might focus on:

1. Modes and scales banned by male authorities such as Plato (sharped 4th, flattened seventh, and a scale combining both researched by Kay Gardner);

2. Earth vibrations such as open fourths and open fifths banned by the patriarchal church as "occult" and "satanic";

3. Matriarchal principles in orchestration such as rotation of instruments to prevent specialization;

4. Musical creation through pictoral sensation and emotive forces rather than through keys and grids;

5. Spirit of place singing in which each gets to illustrate her favorite place in the world by directing the sound patterning of an orchestra.

And what if we did have equal access to musical practice? What does my research in music history and ethnomusicology, as well as my experiences as a musician, reveal would be necessary to reconnect with women's own musical process? First, women would have to have the freedom to take their clothes off and create music uninhibited by imposed social and material forms. In Hawaii, a society once more matriarchal than our own (having female deities, for instance) women and men chanted in the same tonal range, from D above middle C to A below it; husbands and wives chanted only a half step apart. Hawaiian women's voice range would be considered "a man's" in our culture. These women were more centered in their natural bodies, unhindered by the tight clothing subsequently imposed by the missionaries.

Clothes are formally connected with the music of a particular period. By the nineteenth century, when women were once more allowed to make music in public, they performed in the tight corsets and objectified, form-creating clothes, emitting the high "feminine" trills of the European opera singer of Brahm's women's choruses. Stripping ourselves of role-creating female clothing and reembedding our sounds in our bodies would be a precondition to rediscovering a natural women's sound. Even women who have adopted male clothing might discover a female vibratory pattern if allowed to experience creation in a nude state; then they could don whatever costume seemed appropriate for channeling their new musical vibration.[28]

A second suggestion would be to play from emotional impulse and color visualization, rather than by reading abstract written scores as black and white as the costumes donned by orchestra players in western civilization. I suggest this to tap into women's own musical process; when it comes to preserving their work, abstract notation can still be done as a later step in the process. It should be recognized that in the sign system of modern western music, which arose with patriarchal civilization, we have the treble clef (the eternal feminine cycle, albeit with a line through the middle) attached to the staff, the grid of male linear thinking; thus, taking the free-flowing magic of nature once again and fixing it in male dominant form.

But notation was not always black and white. In the beginning of the linear notation of music, color was also used, at least as a coding system. Only gradually did written music become an analytical abstraction, creating a tendency toward composing by mental gymnastics; and some of the most flowing music by men (Eric Satie, Scriabin) was created by color and poetic visualization.

To create from erotic, sensuous and emotional stimulation would be to draw from what has become popularly known as right brain, metaphoric or synaesthetic thinking. Here again we connect with the "primitive" (and in no way inferior) source of sound: tribal singing used to create music tied with visualization and emotion. For example, mourning ritual among the Kahuli entails singing about an ancestor as last seen or remembered in a favorite landscape or habitat: a waterfall, or sacred space in the jungle. The musical visualization is intended to bring about a catharsis judged successful by the lyric's ability to bring out emotion.[29] Or, again to refer to Hawaii, a lover would visualize the loved one and sing a strain deigned to reach him or her; these songs were the vibrator medium through which lovers contacted each other before the telephone. To recontact our own sources of sound we can use what has been dismissed in our civilization as "like a woman," "childlike," or "primitive."

A third route to our own music would be to use forms more common in matriarchal civilization such as rotation of parts and instruments (even if we use western instruments). Certain forms of African drumming, for example, have several parts: each drummer learns all the parts, and those parts are rotated among the players. How might this apply in our search for the matriarchal ear and sound? We might use the instruments of the traditional western orchestra, but in ways that overcome ranking and specialization. The harpist could move to the chair of the first violin; the flautist could move to the seat of the oboist, and so on: a circular game of musical chairs. There is no need to be a purist about the instruments we use. There one can argue that even though men have created rock's electronic technology, it is in women's best interests to claim the form that broadcasts best in this culture.

All my suggestions about how we might recover our own voices have been made to keep women experimenting in a collective search for women's true vibrations. For it is in locating our own clear vibe that we find our strength, and in that strength, our music. Or, perhaps, the other way around?

Endnotes

1 From "The Burdens of a Reader," in Batya Weinbaum, *The Island of Floating Women*. Clothespin Fever Press, San Diego, 1993, pp. 146–47.
2 This is how separate women's spheres in music such as female leagues and orchestras have sometimes been viewed. See *Women in American Music: A Bibliography of Music and Literature*, Westport, Conn., Greenwood, 1979.
3 See Stanley Diamond, *In Search of the Primitive*, Transaction Books, Rutgers, 1974, who conceptualizes the devolution rather than evolution of civilization since "primitive" times.
4 See George Vancouver, *A Voyage of Discovery to the North Pacific Ocean and Around the World in the Years 1790--5*, 1992 (1798), Reprint Service, Irvine, CA., Vol. III, pp. 39–42.
5 See, for example, introduction to Nathaniel Emerson, *Pele and Hiiaka; A Myth from Hawaii*, Charles Tuttle, Rutland, VT, 1978, for missionary condemnation of the hulas as immoral, along with goddess worship.
6 See Daniella Gioseffi, *Earth Dancing: Mother Nature's Oldest Rite*, Mechanicsburg, PA, Stackpole Books, 1980; and Frederique Marglin, *Wives of the God King: The Ritual of the Devadasis of Puri*, Oxford, Oxford University Press, 1985.
7 The sexist western interpretation is depicted in James Michener's novel, *Hawaii*, NY, Faucett, 1994 in which dancers are sent by their fathers to men of other tribes to ward off wars.
8 See K.A. Gourlay, "Sound Producing Instruments in Traditional Society: A Study of Esoteric Instruments and Their Role in Male-Female Relations," *New Guinea Research Bulletin* #60, 1975.
9 For more, see Barbara Walker, *Women's Encyclopedia of Myths and Secrets*, Harper and Row, San Francisco, 1983.
10 For an astute defense of women culturalists, see *Women's Culture Renaissance of the Seventies*, edited by Gayle Kimball, Metuchen, NJ, and London, 1981.
11 Hattie Gossett, *This Bridge Called My Back*. Boston, Persephone Press, 1981, pp.109.
12 See discussion on music, J.M. Yinger, *Countercultures,* Free Press, London, 1982.
13 See for example, Marina Roseman, "The Social Structure of Sound: The Temiar of Peninsular Malaysia," *Ethnomusicology*, September, 1984.
14 Private conversations with Pat Kramer, Ellen Jacobs. See for example Jane Harrison's *Ancient Ritual into Art*, NY, Holt, 1913, which inspired many earlier works such as HD's (Hilda Doolittle's) *Helen in Egypt*, NY, New Directions, 1961. She depicts Helen as a displaced Isis, a goddess enchanting the Greeks because of her possession of secret power chants, symbols and tunes.
15 See Erich Neumann, *The Great Mother: An Analysis of the Archetype.* Princeton, NJ, Princeton University Press, 1964, the best of this genre.
16 Rogan Taylor, *From Shamanism to Show Business to Superstar*, London, A. Blond, 1985.
17 Susan Griffin, *The Roaring Inside Her*. San Francisco, Harper and Row, 1979.
18 Stanley Diamond, *In Search of the Primitive: A Critique of Civilization*, New Brunswick, NJ, Transaction Books, 1987, again takes all the colonialism out of this term.

19 Sukie Colgrave, *Spirit of the Valley: The Masculine and Feminine in the Human Psyche*, JP Torch, Los Angeles, 1981.
20 Listen to women entertaining themselves through full moondancing and self-created music in, for example, *Women's Music from Ghana*, Folkways Records Album #FE 4257, 1981. Obtainable from 43 W. 61st St. N.Y., N.Y. 10023.
21 Claude Levi-Strauss, *Savage Mind*. Chicago, University of Chicago Press, 1968.
22 Here's an example of anti-matriarchal music, Hans von Bulow, cited in Craig Roell, *The Piano in America 1890–1940*, University of North Carolina Press, Chapel Hill, London, Ch.1, p.8: "I crucify, like a good christ, the flesh of my fingers, in order to make them obedient submissive machines to the mind, as a pianist must." This was part of the Victorian work ethic, in which (p. 9) "The piano was to be conquered by the most forceful means..." Scale studies and exercises had to be practiced "with power and energy" several hours a day. This is opposed to the effortless matriarchal music, for example, in which Pele and Hiiaka walked from island to island, in Nathaniel Emerson, *A Myth from Hawaii* (Charles Tuttle, Rutland, VT, 1978), singing to make the ocean give rise to fish and to mend bridges and in general to achieve greater attunement in life.
23 It could also be considered right brain as opposed to left brain. Linda Verlee Williams, *Teaching for the Two-Sided Mind: A Guide to Right Brain—Left Brain Education*, NY, Touchstone, 1986, highlights left and right brain characteristics we might also call patriarchal and matriarchal in music. The left, she says, is analytical and linear like a computer: sequential, working step by step. While the right goes for patterns and wholes, and deals more in visuo-spatial capacities, more like a kaleidoscope, simultaneously combining its parts to create a rich variety of patterns, reshuffling and reassembling pieces in a different relation to each other.
24 See Rudolf Steiner, *Cosmic Memory, Prehistory of Earth and Man*, Blauvelt, NY, Garber, 1981, on the evolution and interchangeability of what we think of as separated sense perceptions.
25 On the burial of women in music, Christine Ammer, in *Unsung: A History of Women in American Music*, Westport, Conn., Greenwood Press, 1980, writes that "indeed women have been writing and performing music for as long as men have. But owing to the social climate of earlier times, their work went unnoticed, unpublished, unperformed, and was quickly forgotten." For discouragement, see several articles in *Women in Music: An Anthology of Source Readings from the Middle Ages to the Present*, edited by Carol Neuls-Bates, Harper and Row, 1982, particularly the section on "The Woman Composer Question" and "Should Women Perform in the Same Orchestra with Men?" She points out the active discouragement, that some instruments were considered unfeminine (introduction). Some have documented how this burial and active discouragement effected black women specifically. See *Black Women in American Bands and Orchestras*, Metuchen, NJ, Scarecrow, 1981, and Sally Placksin, *American Women in Jazz 1900 to the Present*, Seaview, NY, 1982.
26 See interview in Gayle Kimball, *Women's Cultural Renaissance of the 70s*, Metuchen, NJ, Scarecrow Press, 1981.
27 See Peter Hamel's distinction between magical, mythical and mental consciousness in *Through Music to the Self: How To Appreciate and Experience Music Anew*, Rockport, MA, Element Books, 1990 — though he does not correlate with social dominance. For a long time I was troubled by what I read about women's music, eastern music, and "primitive music" sounding the same, as compared with the music of white male western civilization. Then, the more I read about eastern, primitive, and people's of color cultures, the reason

became clear to me: these cultures still had matriarchal aspects predominant in their civilizations. See Christopher Small, *Music of the Common Tongue: Survival and Celebration in Afro-American Music*, NY, Riverrun Press, 1994.

[28] See Elizabeth Taylor, *Strains of Change: The Impact of Tourism on Hawaiian Music*, Honolulu, Bishop Museum 1987 for voice ranging and change with costume; also here *Hula Pa Ho: Hawaiian Drum Dances Vol. 2 Sounds of Power*, Honolulu, Bishop Museum, 1994. *The Naturist* is a good publication explaining the radicalism of nudity.

[29] See Stephen Feld, *Sound and Sentiment: Birds, Weeping, Poetics and Song in Kaluli Expression*. Philadelphia, PA, University of Pennsylvania Press, Conduct and Communication series and the publications of the American Folklore Society, 1990.

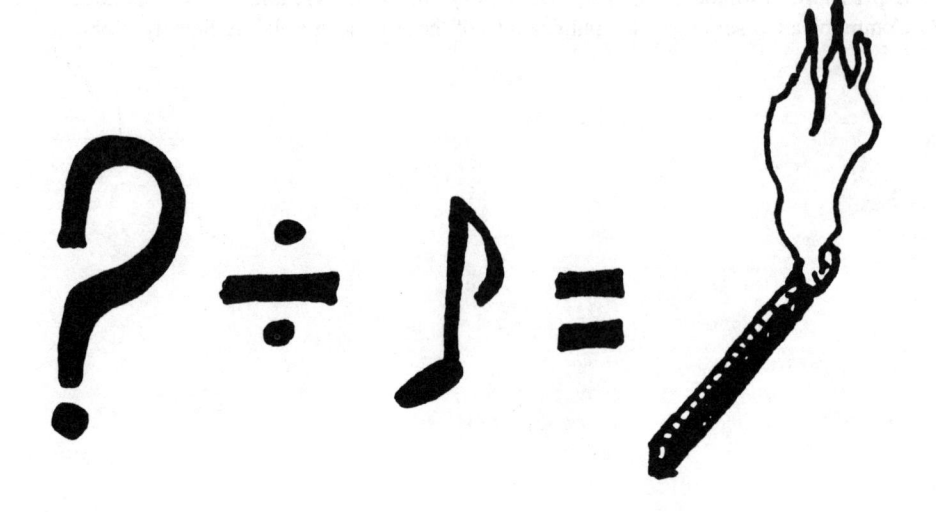

Davey Williams

Beyond Music

Hal Rammel

The following essay originally appeared in ARSENAL: SURREALIST SUBVERSION 4 *in 1990 as a preface for two texts by surrealist musicians Davey Williams ("Beethoven's Thirteenth") and Johannes Bergmark ("Toward a Surrealist Revolution in Music"). A story by LaDonna Smith, Davey Williams' longtime musical collaborator, appeared elsewhere in the same issue.[1] The publication of these texts in Arsenal signaled for me an opportunity to acknowledge the work of a number of significant surrealist voices whose activity represents the first direct and concentrated musical intervention in the movement's history. Written as a preface (not a manifesto), these comments seek to elucidate the connections between contemporary surrealist musical engagement and the work of several of surrealism's earliest practitioners and theorists. Documentation of the intersection of surrealism and music has been fragmentary, too often distorted by, for example, the painter de Chirico's anti-musical bias, André Breton's reported tone-deafness, the turning away from dada stage performance to overt political action, the unrealized collaboration of Antonin Artaud and Edgard Varese. At the same time, surrealists have consistently celebrated the work of composers and performers whose revolutionary paths converage repeatedly with their own. This line of inquiry has been particularly fruitful in the United States with the publication of numerous works on blues, free jazz, comedy music, and improvisation by Franklin Rosemont, Paul and Elizabeth Garon, Joseph Jablonski, Thomas Magee, and others. "Beyond Music" is published here in revised form to reinforce its introductory intent, with apologies to surrealists/musicians whose work is undeservedly omitted.*

Academic and critical commentary on the relations between surrealism and music invariably begin by quoting André Breton's admission in *Surrealism and Painting* (1928) that he found music "the most confusing of all forms," a remark often cited without reference to Breton's later, more carefully considered approach in "Silence is Golden" in 1946.

The entire discussion, however, has heretofore ignored two very significant pieces of evidence. A careful reading of Max Ernst's favored passage that became pivotal to the theoretical background of his *Beyond Painting* (1936) reveals that the exhortation *to hear* as well as *to see* came to surrealists from no less a source than Leonardo da Vinci. Da Vinci wrote in his notebooks (Ernst quoting a nearly identical passage from da Vinci's *Treatise on Painting*):

> When you look at a wall spotted with stains, or with a mixture of different kinds of stones, if you have to invent some scene, you may discover a similarity with different kinds of landscapes... and an endless variety of objects which you could reduce to complete and well-drawn forms. It happens with this confused appearance of walls as it does with the sound of bells in whose jangle you may find any name or word you can imagine.[2]

Perhaps even more remarkably, Breton's reticence found decisive challenge only two years later in a most triumphant and little-heralded *musical* passage in Luis Buñel's *L'Age d'or* (1930). As the young woman protagonist sits before her mirror brushing her hair, we hear the ringing of a bell on the neck of a cow lying across her bed. When the police arrest her lover outside, dogs begin to bark, and as her erotic daydreams intensify, the wind rises to a crescendo before her in the cloudy sky she watches in her mirror. This sequence, considered by Ado Kyrou to be "the most magnificently poetic" in the history of film, can also be heard as a composition of sounds of desire in magnificently powerful juxtaposition.[3] Almost seventy years have passed since the publication of *Surrealism and Painting*, and to the early surrealists' theoretical doubts regarding music, music has not listened. In the intervening decades barely a sound on the planet has not felt ignition in the transformative surge of the African diaspora and its progeny in Afro-Caribbean and African American musicking. While the forces of repression seem ever more pervasive and pernicious each passing year, music has increasingly expressed people's hunger for freedom and a better world. For decades, too, surrealists have recognized important comrades on these fronts, where improvisation and psychic automatism share their intense celebration of the Moment, untamed and irreducible, pivot-point of urgently desired revolution.

Echoing da Vinci's observations, Ornette Coleman, speaking of his early years in Fort Worth, Texas in the 1940s, tells us that "musicians...would always talk about 'playing the bells.' They could hear free voices coming from the skies."[4] The notion that the course of a musical encounter might be based on free voices as opposed to rigid prescription (e.g. conventional tonality, fixed meter) as exemplified in the early recordings of Ornette Coleman, Cecil Taylor, Sun Ra, and Albert Ayler was indeed in the air in the middle decades of this century, reaching quite isolated poetic outposts. Painter, poet, musician Tristan Meinecke, active with the "automatist" painters in Chicago in the 1950s, and later a participant in exhibitions with the Chicago surrealist group, reports:

> In the late 40s and early 50s I played a lot of automatistic music. Several of us would get together and start playing without having any idea what the others were doing. Each of us would play a different tune, simultaneously—or we'd play instruments we didn't really know how to play.[5]

In this context it is quite valuable to recall guitarist Derek Bailey's advisory note in his *Improvisation: Its Nature and Practice in Music* regarding the increasingly frequent re-writing of the history of the beginnings of free improvisation: "...free improvisation wasn't 'started' by anybody."[6]

While our interests here veer sharply away from the historical (criticism that surrealism failed to produce its own body of music reveal only the critic's misapprehension of the surrealist project), it is, however, essential to introduce the revelatory musics of Davey Williams and LaDonna Smith. The release of the first recordings of the duo *trans* (LaDonna Smith's violin, viola, and voice: Davey Williams' acoustic and electric guitar, and banjo) in the mid-70s in Birmingham, Alabama heralded the wedding of free jazz and free improvisation with the surrealist techniques of pure psychic automatism, the paranoiac-critical method, and objective chance.[7] In a series of unique recordings on their own label *trans museq* (e.g. *Jewels, Direct Waves, Locales for Ecstasy*), in performances worldwide with their many musical collaborators, and in their editorship of *the improvisor*, the only international journal of free improvisation, this duo continues to explore this marriage of diverse musical cultures, consistently pursuing the liberatory image, freely improvising on all fronts.[8] "Free improvisation is not an action resulting from freedom; it is an action directed toward freedom."[9] All that follows seems hardly possible without deep acknowledgement of their articulate (verbal and non-verbal) contributions to these discussions.

To situate a discussion of surrealist musical practice we must first and foremost avoid the distraction of music. We must look or, rather, listen, beyond music. At the same time, however, the sense of looking illuminates the intangibility of this investigation by reference to visual experience, inquiry into "the regions of visible sonics."[10] To propose metaphors of terrain admits a visual analog to sound and permits the identification of sound image as a unit of expression. Indeed this analogy may itself serve musical discovery, as in Davey Williams' *Listening Post*:

> In this system, attention while playing is focused on whatever intuitive imagery the sound of the music might suggest. These visual stimuli are then fed back into musical use, becoming the center of attention, and it is this distraction to which the musical playing becomes a kind of soundtrack, hopefully always at the service of the moment's evolving scenarios.[11]

Retrospectively, suggesting that there is a point at which looking and listening are not perceived as separate sensations, the simplest substitution of auditory association for retinal casts the following statements in new light:

> The vice called *Surrealism* is the unregulated and passionate use of the narcotic *image*, or rather of the uncontrolled provocation of the image for itself and for what it involves in the realm of the representation of unforeseeable disturbances and of metamorphoses: for each image at every blow forces you to revise the whole Universe.[12]

> The task of the right eye is to peer into the telescope, while the left eye peers into the microscope.[13]

Surrealism desires that sounds offer, in the words of Antonin Artaud, "an insidious extension of the invisible, the unconscious at hand."[14] Thus, sounds proceed at the bidding of an inner model, just as surrealist painting, beckoning in an automatic voice which may enter with varying, but always certain, degrees of premeditation. As further delineated by Breton in *Artistic Genesis and Perspective of Surrealism* in 1941:

...a work can be considered surrealist only in proportion to the efforts the artist has made to encompass the whole psychophysiological field (in which consciousness constitutes only a very small segment). Freud has demonstrated that at these unfathomable depths there reigns the absence of contradiction, the relaxation of emotional tensions due to repression, a lack of the sense of time, and the replacement of external reality by a psychic reality obeying the pleasure principle alone. Automatism leads us in a straight line to this region.[15]

Adherence to this inner model calls into question the value of external prescription, offers release from art-about-art aestheticism, from the numbing sentimentality of mass-mediated "adult sounds," from the noise of civilization's authoritarian machinery, glorified in war by futurist declaration. This search sets its course not for "new sounds" (though it may call for the abolition of civilized sounds),[16] but for the liberating sounds of social transformation where such dead ends and diversions wither away. "To reveal the marvelous in its most undeniable mediums and intensities, music may have no higher aspiration than to make visible that kite lamp delicately tethered, aloft in the constant invisible storm that we perceive all our lives as signal-precipitating weather."[17] So a journey proceeds in all directions: "True spirit must show itself everywhere at once."[18]

Living in this world so unrelentingly bludgeoned by man-made miseries, human's seemingly limitless capacity for subjugation and acquisition, does such interior exploration reflect retreat from social and political realities? It is an old argument. Breton confronted these issues in his address to the "Left Front" in Prague in 1935 published as *Political Position of Today's Arts,* a response I will quote at length as it struck me so decisively facing accusations of "post-revolutionary concerns" in the mid '60s. In this passage, Breton contrasts the painting of Gustave Courbet, who participated in the destruction of the Vendome column in 1871, but who in no manner portrayed such themes in his painting, with the painter Jacques-Louis David, who graphically depicted scenes from the first French Revolution in his work:

> As far as Courbet is concerned, we must recognize that everything happens as if he had decided that there must be some way to reflect his profound faith in the betterment of the world in everything that he tried to evoke, some way to make it appear somehow in the light that he caused to fall on the horizon or on a roebuck's belly... Here, then, was a man of mature sensibilities and, most importantly, one at grips with certain of the most intoxicating circumstances in all of history. These circumstances lead him, as a man, to risk his life without hesitation; they do not lead him to give directly polemical meaning to his art.[19]

The essence of such choices for Courbet and for surrealism lies in the sense that within innermost reaches (along roads that lead out as well as in) the apparent dichotomies of life and death, real and imagined, past and future, above and below cease their contradictory status, that, indeed, pathways between this world and our waking life exist and point in grander directions resolving our most visceral and violent conflicts. On this point in the late 1920s George Bataille and André Breton parted ways, Bataille denouncing notions regarding "the 'elevation of any man's spirit' as 'imbecilic.'"[20] Breton coined the term *miserabilism* ("the depreciation of reality in place of its exaltation") befitting Bataille's flights of excremental fancy. Antoin Artaud in 1927 voiced this crucial difference more personally: "What divides me from the Surrealists is that they love life as much as I despise it."[21]

Much of contemporary culture remains mired in *miserabilism*: the eroticism of American films in which orgasm is immediately followed, if not interrupted, by a bullet in the head; music concerts testifying to the power of media and microphone assemble masses of people in "counter-cultural" spectacles that are little more than celebrations of social manipulation; arts so constrained by rigid intention and concept that their only reflection mirrors deterioration, decay, and death, physically and emotionally; public education so impoverished and fractured as to obliterate history beyond the lives of celebrities, politicians, and their hideous scandals; a planet where hardly a nook or cranny exists that has not been polluted by advertising, selling products whose ingredients, assuming that these products may one day breakdown into their ingredients, will poison all living things for centuries into the future.

In defiance of the miserable, surrealism defends the Marvelous in a vision of liberatory social possibilities that embody both the fragility and resilience of its innermost revelations, defined in the immediacy of a moment's grandeur inexplicably persisting in the face of chillingly scant evidence supporting any hope for a better future. In this world in the death-grip of greed and self-aggrandizing power, we remain, in the words of poet Mary Low, co-author with Juan Brea of the 1937 *Red Spanish Notebook*, "Alive in Spite Of."[22]

Returning to musical dimensions, summoned "in the service of a subversive group of sounds, which is always evolving,"[23] what lies at stake is the poetic spirit, eloquently defined by Franklin Rosemont, in reference to jazz improvisation, as "that climate of readiness for the actualization of the Marvelous."[24] In this climate, where the absolute necessity is watchfulness, marvels appear at every turn, thriving on the unexpected. Consider this experience related by surrealist/percussionist Thomas Magee, describing an evening of playing music with Harry "the Hipster" Gibson:

> While working at Donte's one night, I watched as Harry got carried away on an especially fast-tempo boogie, and began pounding the high keys with the heavy-heeled hustler's-style wingtip of his right foot. Completely into the excitement of the moment, he booted that thing so bad he kicked a key out of Donte's piano! I still remember seeing it fly into the air, describing a steady curlicue as it went into the audience. My spirits were exceptionally high on this evening, and when I saw that key escape from its piano, it seemed to me that it had deliberately chosen to do so of its own will, as if to escape punishment! Instantly my mood became one of uncontrollable delight, throwing me into a laughing fit so intense that it threatened to throw me off my stool as well, and it took every bit of concentration that I could gather to keep myself from losing the very up-tempo shuffle.[25]

The wide, joyous leap of Harry the Hipster's frantic key proscribes its liberating arc, so archly musical across our future. The tempo accelerates. Flocks of gulls congress with swarms of bees to instigate the overthrow of civilization's oppressively melodic intentions. Strings break, drum kits lost in senseless dimuendos lie tattered in their wake. "Six bows for every violin! Timbales to each raccoon!" Ostriches reveal themselves to be the most creative in devising musical hybrids of old watch parts with bits of gravel and feathers. Trios, quartets, septets, and aimless soloists, human and marsupial, clatter in wondrous disorder as every possible omniverous song is sung at once. "Where are the winds?" An oboe is carried in by stag beetles and handed to a child. Day and night reverse order. Pages fly away from open books. The tempo is hot. The time is now.

Endnotes

1 *Arsenal: Surrealist Subversion* 4, ed. Franklin Rosemont (Chicago: Black Swan Press, 1990). "Beyond Music," "Toward a Surrealist Revolution in Music," and "Beethoven's Thirteenth" are printed together on pages 56—58. LaDonna Smith's "Operating Table" appears on page 144. Articles on Bob Marley, Memphis Minnie, Cecil Taylor, and Charles Mingus appear elsewhere in this issue along with reviews of recordings by Cecil Taylor, Douglas Ewart, Fred Anderson, and Russell Thorne.
2 *Leonardo da Vinci as a Musician*, ed. Emanuel Winternitz (New Haven and London: Yale University Press, 1982), p. 134.
3 Luis Buñuel's interests in sound and music, evident in his first two films, *Un Chien andalou* (1929) and *L'Age d'or* (1930), appear in his first published literary work "Instrumentation" (1922) which includes definitions such as "Piccolo: ants' nest of sound" and "Cymbals: shattered light." See Francisco Aranda's *Luis Buñuel: A Critical Biography* (New York: Da Capo Press, 1976), pp. 251–252.
4 Ornette Coleman is quoted by Nat Hentoff in his liner notes to *Something Else! The Music of Ornette Coleman* (Contemporary S 7551).
5 Tristan Meinecke, "Symposium on Surrealism," *Cultural Correspondence* No. 12–14 (Summer 1981), p. 77.
6 Derek Bailey, *Improvisation: Its Nature and Practice in Music* (London: The British Library National Sound Library, 1992.), p. 85.
7 Free improvisation, a musical locus occupying a position perhaps even further at the margins of contemporary musical activity than free jazz, has nonetheless remained an undiminished wellspring of inspired musicking for the past 35 years. Embracing a consistent bias toward collective expression without any prearrangement of structure or tonality (and without the lead voice/supporting voices form typically associated with jazz), free improvisation shares much with African American musical expression, of particular note its celebration of the unique instrumental voice of each individual contributor at the service of shared discovery.

Valuable introduction to the theoretical background of pure psychic automatism, the paranoiac-critical method, and objective chance can be found in *What is Surrealism?*, an anthology of André Breton's selected writings edited and introduced by Franklin Rosemont (New York: Pathfinder Press, 1978). This and many other surrealist publications are readily available from Black Swan Press, P.O. Box 6424, Evanston, IL 60204.
8 Recordings by LaDonna Smith and Davey Williams are available from *trans museq*, 1705 12th Street South, Birmingham, Alabama, 35205. *The improvisor: the international journal of free improvisation* is available from the same address.
9 Davey Williams, "Towards a Philosophy of Improvisation," *the improvisor* No. 4 (Summer 1984), p. 33.
10 Davey Williams, liner notes to *Criminal Pursuits: Electric Guitar Solos* (*trans museq* 8).
11 Ibid.
12 Louis Aragon, *Le paysan de Paris*, quoted in Jacqueline Chénieux-Gendron, *Surrealism* (New York: Columbia University Press, 1990), p.61.
13 Leonora Carrington, *Down Below* (Chicago: Black Swan Press, 1983), p. 18.
14 Antonin Artaud, quoted in J. H. Matthews, *The Imagery of Surrealism* (Syracuse: Syracuse University Press, 1977), P. 48.

[15] André Breton, "Artistic Genesis and Perspective of Surrealism," *Surrealism and Painting* (New York: Harper and Row, 1965), p. 70.
[16] See Johannes Bergmark, "For a Wild Music," *the improvisor* Vol. 10 (1993), pp. 22–23, and "Call for the Hidden Sounds," *Experimental Musical Instruments*, forthcoming.
[17] Davey Williams, "Concerning the Music That Will Be," *the improvisor* Vol. II, No. 2 (Winter 1982), p. 29.
[18] André Breton, "Political Position of Surrealism," *Manifestoes of Surrealism* (Ann Arbor: University of Michigan Press, 1969), p. 221.
[19] Ibid., p. 219.
[20] Georges Bataille, "The 'Ole Mole' and the Prefix Sur in the words Surhomme (Superman) and Surrealist," *Visions of Excess: Selected Writings*, 1927-1939 (Minneapolis: University of Minnesota Press, 1985), p. 43.
[21] Antonin Artaud, "In Total Darkness, or The Surrealist Bluff," *Antonin Artaud: Selected Writings* (New York: Farrar, Strauss and Giroux, 1976), p. 141.
[22] Mary Low, *El Triunfo de La Vida* (Alive in Spite Of) (Miami: Ediciones del Tauro, 1981).
[23] LaDonna Smith and Davey Williams, liner notes to *Locales for Ecstasy* (*trans museq* 9).
[24] Franklin Rosemont, "The New Argonautica," *City Lights Anthology* (San Francisco: City Lights Books, 1974), p. 220. See also Franklin Rosemont's "Black Music and the Surrealist Revolution," *Arsenal: Surrealist Subversion* 3 (Chicago: Black Swan Press, 1976) pp. 17–27.
[25] Thomas Magee, letter to the author, 1984.

NOISE IS THE CHAOS ENTITY SPEAKING

Dreamtime Collective

polynoise

information abstracts for
the electromagnetic spectacle
— radical codes for
brainwave interference

*Amendant Hardiker
& Miekal And*

I believe that the use of noise to make music will continue and increase until we reach a music produced through the aid of electrical instruments which will make available for musical purposes any and all sounds that can be heard. Photoelectric, film, and mechanical mediums for the synthetic production of music will be explored. Whereas, in the past, the point of disagreement has been between dissonance and consonance, it will be, in the immediate future, between noise and so-called musical sounds. The present methods of writing music, principally those which employ harmony and its reference to particular steps in the field of sound, will be inadequate for the composer who will be faced with the entire field of sound. New methods will be discovered, bearing a definite relation to Schöenberg's twelve-tone system and present methods of writing percussive music and any other methods which are free from the concept of a fundamental tone.

The principle of form will be our only constant connection with the past. Although the great form of the future will not be as it was in the past, at one time the fugue and at another the sonata, it will be related to these as they are to each other through the principle of organization or man's common ability to think.

—John Cage (from *The Future of Music: Credo*, 1937)

Great tools take much time to be manufactured.... The Great Tone is the tone that goes beyond all usual imagination.

—Lao-tzu

Noise has entered our waking conscience, forcefully & can not be relinquished to the un/sub conscience. There lies within noise a manner of empowerization that is both organic & suggestive. By an external manipulation of erotic desirability, by a concentrated rehearsal of memory, of the most complete & instantaneous global recollection. Noise constitutes all that remains undigested, confused & in opposition. At the end of the 2nd millennium the properties of noise include as its subset consonance & rhythm since they are no longer obtainable in their original purity.

No virgin harmony remains unspoilt by the ravages of industrial continuity. Noise is the diamond of the future, mined & recycled for its luster, for its clues to the nature & construction of infinity. Noise reproduces in all directions with nucleic passion, with spidery unpredictability.

To describe globularity without noise as an essential resource is no longer possible. Civilization has now exhausted most of its non-renewable energy & has invested nothing toward technology appropriate to the conversion of noise into an international energy & initiative. Simply for the global exchange of information, noise is conspicuously apropos. Beyond dialect yet suggestively communicable, it is a direct transmission, acculturated to specific ambiguity. It speaks to or thru a possible understanding, catalyzing disparate info & imagery. Categorical noise is a program of thoughts, conceptual noise is an imaginative omnibus of investigations. An impoverished listener would likely become numb to the invariability & the repetitive, would sleepwalk endlessly & think in predictable motor rhythms. A concerted attention to noise phenomena would defeat that spell, offer a propulsion within the interior of hyper action. The affectation of noise inseminates a non-emotional life force.

Inventing Noise

We can also see, in resonance, that all objects have a sound component, a second shadow existence as a configuration of frequencies. Nikola Tesla, one of the great geniuses of the electrical age, strapped a small oscillating motor to the central beam in his Manhattan laboratory and built up a powerful physical resonance that conducted through the building and into the earth to cause an earthquake in which buildings shook, panes of glass broke and steam pipes ruptured over a twelve block area. He was forced to stop it with a blow from a sledge hammer. Tesla stated that he could calculate the resonant frequency of the earth and send it into strong vibration with a properly tuned driver of adequate size and specific placement.
—Bill Viola, *The Sound of One Line Scanning*

...the curtain rose upon an orchestra of weird funnel-shaped instruments directed by Signor Luigi Russolo. It is impossible to say that the first of the "noise-spirals" performed "The Awakening of a Great City," was as exhilarating as Futurist art usually is; on the contrary, it rather resembled the sounds heard in the rigging of a Channel-steamer during a bad crossing, and it was, perhaps, unwise of the players—or should we call them the "noisicians?"—to proceed with their second piece, "A Meeting of Motor-cars and Aeroplanes," after the pathetic cries of "No more!" which greeted them from all the excited quarters of the auditorium.
—London *Times*, June 15, 1914

The builder of noise machines can now return to positively constructing the composite possibilities of the historic noise. Immediate recall will access thousands of noisebits for spontaneous aural hallucinations & these noisebits, or tiny audio memories comprise a founding influence on behavior, digression, dream, imagination, & action... They are to be considered profound form & source of neuro-psychical energy, without which a being in the late 20th century would no longer be able to function as an accessory to their own environment. This observation can be substantiated quite readily experienced in the context of metropolitan living or in the most remote hideaway. That sensory stimulation, via sound/noise is central to our location on this planet & would be all too continuous of an impression for any ear capable of listening intently & openly. Noise is the international language, easily understood or processed beyond any boundary of dialect or orientation. The sound of walking, radio static, a ratchet, a bellowing tube, share an index of understandings in the universal & collective experience. The sound of dumbbells caroming down a stair & a wild night of noise coming to past 300 years ago or 3000 before that. Every noise partnering or coupling with every simultaneous inertia. A fortune of itching mad audio. An orchard of incrustaceous cacaphonemes. No noise adheres to previous understanding more than the edge of noise, where all sound constructs further sonifications.

Tonal blasphemy in radio kingdom, tonal hierarchy may well perish beneath the weight of noisiness.

Inner Noisversation

There is no such thing as experimental music, which is a fond utopia; but there is a very real distinction between sterility and invention. The ostriches demonstrate to us the existence of danger—with their heads tucked under their folded wings
—Pierre Boulez

Every manifestation of life is accompanied by noise. Noise is therefore familiar to our ears and has the power to remind us immediately of life itself. Musical sound, a thing extraneous to life and independent of it,... has become to our ears what a too familiar face is to our eyes. Noise, on the other hand, which comes to us confused and irregular as life itself, never reveals itself wholly but reserves for us innumerable surprises. We are convinced, therefore, that by selecting, coordinating and controlling noises we shall enrich mankind with a new and unsuspected source of pleasure.

—Luigi Russolo

Russolo: Accumulating a philosophy of noise that doesn't idolize monotony & boredom approaches a radical response to the imitation of industrial culture. One could only await the construction of noise neologue, perhaps akin to the contrivance of Webern's 12 tone endless permutations....

Antheil: A bomb of discrete sounds evasively amplified & implanted out of sight in parks, bus stops, hallways, highway rest areas & any non-implemented public arena would access the global soundscape to masses of the unsuspecting.

Russolo: The subliminal after effects would be perfectly alarming!

Antheil: Repoliticizing noise as a tool of subterfuge & indictment is consistently ignored. Compare a demonstration with people banging pots & pans to a demonstration with noise conspirators recreating the chaos of warfare & political turmoil, of ubiquitous riot & radio interference.

Russolo: Without hedging toward any manner of resolution, there is the tendency to want to make noise identifiable, digestible in the way that a song is consumed & I think that this urge strips the potential moving force of noise from its context. The sound of a dog barking or a car screeching to a halt are harmlessly absorbed by cognition. Nothing about the listening mechanism of the brain is altered. Now 100 layers of independent noise material implanted at the base of a being's skull would initiate a complete rearrangement of molecular structure.

anartisticality

Discard & confuse the six tones, smash & unstring the pipes & lutes, stop up the ears of the blind musician K'uang, & for the first time the people of the world will be able to hold on to their hearing. —Chu'ang Tzu

Actually the word that we have been using for a couple years is anartistic, to refer specifically to a notion of cultural anarchy which is improvised ritual & intuitive responses to acquired cultural taste. I think the most radical thought/material contemporary to our planet is noise. & by noise I mean all kinds of noise; architectural noise, paint noise, sculptural noise, behavioral noise, idea noise, graffiti noise, language noise, xerox noise, psychic noise, computer noise... Our experiment is to invent tactics & strategies which are operable in a world of all possible noises. The year 2000 is only minutes away & our modes of thinking are entrenched in western industrial rationalism. Our form of anarchy is reconstructive. It takes all the possible noises & words & mixes them into the widest imaginable vocabulary from which we chose our actions & ideas.

Wholly unleashed on the unsuspecting, noise is not a candy, a suppressant, but given its viable ability to cauterize the unknown & the overly emoted sense of being, noise can be the missing pill of proximity. Taken readily with frequency there is eventual clarity amid the chaos. To spread thru the manner of listening in all directions sensory, the assimilation of noise is a combatant against feebleness, or is the constitution of bearing a specific weight. The noise of the future is the combination of all noise past. Conceived memory wise, noise has the unlimited potential of subscribing to every contradiction, such as one might expect from a juxtaposition of dreams. Noise leads to no conclusions yet is an equation of solutions.

Liz Was

knoise pearl #1

INTENTIONAL KNOISE

Even if intentional audio noise continues to be resisted, even outlawed, the reality of (unintentional) noise will remain. When the population explodes to the point where no radio can blare alone, noise is inevitable. On a street corner in your average city, juxtaposition & rich layering of sounds can be heard. Regardless of whether it is pleased or annoyed, the fact is THE MODERN EAR HAS ALREADY GROWN ACCUSTOMED TO THIS AUDIO TAPESTRY, and must learn to deal with more & more sound in the future. Our species will not only adapt to but eventually feed off of the AURAL GLUT. "Knoise is the most neglected resource in our society today," says Amendant Hardiker.

It is only a matter of time when the intentional creation of extreme audio juxtapositions & excessive layering of sounds will be accepted too. But before that can happen the iron triad rule of harmony, 4/4 rhythm, & the tempered scale must be rusted away—& along with it, audio morality. (Note the radical changes in visual morality accomplished by the fashion world's adoption of modern art. Just about anything goes now, especially for women, especially in the cities, & even some moderately conservative clothes are made in fabrics which 30 years ago would've caused stares & frowns. But with sound, we are still in the middle ages, even kids, natural knoisicians, are still "meant to be seen & not heard.")

James Koehnline

knoise pearl #2

AN EARFUL OF KNOISE

An unprejudiced ear can behave like glue in the perceiving of knoise. Like the zen mind, undistracted by distaste or confusion, it can hear a variegated, dense or chaotic mass as one coherent whole. Thus the perceptive but unperturbed listener of knoise experiences the same frenzied calm as that of the knoisician playing. In fact, besides the obvious physical difference between playing & listening, I consider the knoise-listener (the knoisee?) to be a knoisician as well. (By knoisee I refer to those who make it a point to listen to knoise & who in some manner or other enjoy or need it.)

We must be crazy, or sick, most people think of those of us who love knoise. No, but we further our own evolution by seeking out that which intitially disturbs us. And what this adaptation consists of is THE OPENING OF OUR EARS. A marvelous thing, but you can't open your ears if your mind is closed.

Scott Marshall

Plunderphonics

Chris Cutler

"New art and music do not communicate an individual's conception in ordered structures, but they implement processes which are, as our daily lives, opportunities for perception"
—John Cage, on the influence of Marshall McLuhan on his music

INTRODUCTION
"Sounds like a dive downwards as a sped up tape slows rapidly to settle into a recogniseable, slightly high-pitched Dolly Parton. It continues to slow down, but more gradually now. The instruments thicken and their timbres stretch and richen. Details unheard at the right speed suddenly cut across the sound. Dolly is changing sex; she's a man already; the backing has become hallucinatory and strange. The grain of the song is opened up and the ear, seduced by detail lets a throng of surprising associations and ideas fall in behind it. The same thing is suddenly very different. Who would have expected this extraordinary composition to have been buried in a generic country song, 1000 times heard already and 1000 times copied and forgotten?"

So I hear John Oswald's version of Dolly Parton's version of "The Great Pretender," effectively a recording of Oswald playing Parton's single once through, transformed via varispeed media (first a high speed cassette duplicator, then an infinitely variable speed turntable, finally a hand-controlled reel-to-reel tape—all edited seamlessly together). Apart from the *economy* of this single proceedure of controlled deceleration, which is, as it were, *played* by Oswald, no modifications have been made to the original recording. However, although the source is plainly fixed and given, the choice, treatment and reading of this source are all highly conscious products of Oswald's own intention and skill. So much so indeed that it is easy to argue that the piece, although "only" Parton's record, undoubtedly forms, in Oswald's version, a self-standing composition with its own structure and logic—both of which are profoundly different from those of the original. Oswald's "Pretender" would still work for a listener who had never heard the Parton version, and in a way the Parton version never could. Though the Parton version is, of course, *given*—along with and against the plundered version. What Oswald has created—created because the result of his work is something startlingly new—is a powerful, aesthetic, significant, poly-semic but highly focussed—and enjoyable—sound artifact; both a source of direct listening pleasure and (for our purposes) a persuasive case for the validity and eloquence of its means.

John Oswald's "Pretender" and other pieces, all originated from existing copyright recordings but employing radically different techniques, were included on an EP and later a CD. Both were given away free to radio stations and the press. None was sold. The liner notes read: "This disc may be reproduced but neither it, nor any reproductions of it are to be bought or sold. Copies are available only to public access and broadcast organisations, including libraries, radio or periodicals.."

The 12" EP, *Plunderphonics*, consisting of four pieces "Pretender" (Parton), "Don't" (Presley), "Spring" (Stravinsky), "Pocket" (Basie) was made between 1979–1988 and released May 1988, with some support from the Arts Council of Canada. The CD, containing these and twenty other pieces, was realised between 1979–89 and released October 31, 1989 and was financed entirely by Oswald himself.

Between Xmas eve 1989 and the end of January 1990 all distribution ceased and all extant copies were destroyed. Of all the plundered artists, it was Michael Jackson who pursued the CD to destruction. Curiously, Jackson's own plundering—for instance the one minute and six seconds of The Cleveland Symphony Orchestra's recording of Beethoven's Ninth which opens Jackson's "Will you be there?" on the CD *Dangerous*, for which Jackson claims no less than six credits, including the composer copyright (adding plagiarism to sound piracy)—seems to have escaped his notice.

Necessity and Choice Continued

In 1980, I wrote that "from the first moment of the first recording, the actual performances of musicians on the one hand, and all possible sound on the other, had become the proper matter of music."[1] I failed, however, to underline the consequence that 'all sound" has to include other people's already recorded work; and that when all sound is just raw material, then recorded sound is *always* raw—even when it is cooked.

This omission I wish now in part to redress.

Although recording offered all audible sound as material for musical organisation, art music composers were slow to exploit it, and remain so today. One reason is that the inherited paradigms though which art music continues to identify itself have not escaped their roots in notation, a system of mediation which determines both what musical material is avalable and what possible forms of organisation can be applied to it. The determination of material and organisation follows from the character of notation as a discontinous system of instructions developed to model visually what we know as Melody, Harmony and Rhythm—represented by, and limited to, arrangements of *fixed tones* (quantised, mostly twelve to an octave) and *fixed durations* (of notes and silences). Notation does not merely quantise the material, reducing it to simple units but, constrained by writability, readability and playability, is able to encompass only a very limited degree of complexity within those units. In fact the whole edifice of Western Art Music can be said, after a fashion, to be constructed upon and through notation[2] which, amongst other things, *creates* "the composer," who is thus constitutionally bound to it.

No wonder then that recording technology continues to cause such consternation. On the one hand it offers control of musical parameters beyond even the wildest dreams of the most radical mid-twentieth century composer, on the other it terminally threatens the deepest roots of the inherited art music paradigm, replacing notation with the direct transcription of performances, and rendering the clear distinction between performance and composition null.

Perhaps this accounts for the curious relationship between the art music world and the new technology, which has, from the start, been equivocal, or at least highly qualified, (Edgard Varese notably excepted). And it is why the story I shall have to tell is so full of tentative High Art experiments that seem to die without issue, and why, although many creative innovations in the new medium were indeed made on the fringes of High Art, their adoption and subsequent extension has come typically through other, less ideologically intimidated (or less paradigmatically confused ?) musical genres. Why was this? I am suggesting that it is because the old art music paradigms and the new technology are simply *not able* to fit together.[3]

For art music then, recording is inherently problematic—and surely Plunderphonics is recording's most troublesome child, breaking taboos art music hadn't even imagined. For instance, while Plagiarism was already strictly off limits (flaunting unnegotiable rules concerning originality, individuality and property rights). Plunderphonics was proposing routinely to appropriate as its raw material not merely other people's tunes or styles but finished recordings of them! It offered a medium in which, far from art music's essential creation *ex nihilo*, the origination, guidance and confirmation of a sound object may be carried through *by listening alone*.

The new medium proposes, the old paradigms recoil. Yet I want to argue that *it is precisely in this forbidden zone that much of what is genuinely new in the creative potential of the new technology resides*. In other words, the moral and legal boundaries which currently constitute important determinants in claims for musical legitimacy, impede and restrain some of the most exiting possibilities in the changed circumstances of the age of recording. History to date is clear on such conflicts: the old paradigms will give way. The question is—what to?

One of the conditions of a new art form is that it produce a metalanguage, a theory through which it can adequately be described. A new musical form will need such a theory. My sense is that Oswald's "Plunderphonics" has brought at last into sharp relief many of the critical questions around which such a theory can be raised. For by coining the name, Oswald has identified and consolidated a musical practice which until now has been without focus. And like all such namings it seems naturally to apply retrospectively, creating its own archaeology, precursors and origins.

Originality

Of all the processes and productions which have emerged from the new medium of recording, PLUNDERPHONICS is the most consciously self-reflexive; it begins and ends only with recordings, with the *already played*. Thus, as I have already remarked, it cannot help but challenge our current understanding of originality, individuality and property rights. To the extent that sound recording as a medium negates that of notation and echoes in a transformed form that of biological memory, this should not be so surprising.[4] In ritual and folk musics, for instance, originality as we understand it would be a misunderstanding—or a transgression—since proper performance is repetition. Where personal contributions are made or expected, these must remain within clearly prescribed limits and iterate sanctioned and traditional forms. Such musics have no place for genius, individuality or originality—as we know them—or for the institution of intellectual property. Yet these were precisely the concepts and values central to the formation of the discourse that identified the musical, intellectual and political revolution that lay the basis for what we now know as the classical tradition. Indeed they were held as marks of its superiority over earlier forms. Thus, far from describing *hubris* or transgression, originality and the individual voice became central criteria of value for a music whose future was to be marked by the restless and challenging pursuit of progress and innovation. Writing became essential, and not only for transmission. A score was an individual's signature on a work. It also made unequivocal the author's claim to the legal ownership of a sound blueprint. "Blueprint" because a score is mute and others have to give it body, sound, and meaning. Moreover, notation established the difference and immortality of a work in the abstract, irrespective of its performance.

Copyright

The arrival of recording, however, made each performance of a score as permanent and fixed as the score itself. Copyright was no longer so simple.[5] When John Coltrane recorded "My Favourite Things," a great percentage of which contained no sequence of notes contained in the written score, assigning the composing rights to Rogers and Hammerstein hardly recognised the compositional work of Coltrane, Garrison, Tyner and Jones. A percentage can now be granted for an "Arrangement," but this doesn't satisfy the creative input of such performers either. Likewise, when a collective improvisation is registered under the name, as often still occurs, of a bandleader, nothing is expressed by this except the power relations pertaining in the group. Only if it is registered in the names of all the participants, are collective creative energies honoured (and historically, it took decades to get copyright bodies to recognise such "unscored" works, and their status is still anomalous and poorly rated[6]). Still, this is an improvement—until the mid-seventies, in order to claim a composer's copyright for an improvised or studio originated work, one had to produce some kind of score constructed from the record: a topsy-turvy practice in which the music created the composer. And to earn a royalty on a piece which started and ended with a copyright tune but had fifteen minutes of free improvising in the middle, a title or titles had to be given for the improvised parts, or all the money would go to the author of the bookending melody. In other words, the response of copyright authorities to the new realities of recording was to cobble piecemeal compromises together in the hope that, between the copyrights held in the composition and the patent rights granted over a specific recording, most questions of assignment could be adjudicated—and violations identified and punished. No one wanted to address the fact that recording technology had called not merely the mechanics but the adequacy of the prevailing *concept* of copyright into question.

It was Oswald, with the release of his Not-For-Sale EP and then CD who, by naming, theorising and defending the use of "macrosamples" and "electroquotes," finally forced the issue.

It was not so much that the principles and processes involved were without precedent, but rather that through Oswald they were at last brought together in a focused and fully conscious form. The immediate result was disproportionate industry pressure, threats and the forcible withdrawal from circulation and destruction of all extant copies. This, despite the fact that the CD in question was arguably an original work (in the old paradigmatic sense), was not for sale (thereby not exploiting other people's copyrights for gain) and was released precisely to raise the very questions which its supression underlined but immediately stifled. Nevertheless, the genie was out of the bottle.

The fact is that, considered as raw material, a recorded sound is technically indiscriminate of source. All recorded sound, as recorded sound, is information of the same quality. A recording of a recording is just a recording. No more, no less. We have to start here. Only then can we begin to examine, as with photomontage (which takes as its strength of meaning the fact that a photograph of a photograph is—a photograph) how the message of the medium is qualified by a communicative intent that distorts its limits. Judgements about what is plagiarism and what is quotation, what is legitimate use and what is, in fact if not law, public domain material can not be answered by recourse to legislation derived from technologies that are unable even to comprehend such questions. When "the same thing" is so different that it constitutes a new thing, it isn't "the same thing" anymore—even if, like Oswald's hearing of the Dolly Parton record, it manifestly is the 'same thing' and no other. The key to this apparent paradox lies in the protean self-reflexivity of recording technology, allied with its elision of the acts of production and reproduction—both of which characteristics are incompatible with the old models, derived from notation, from which our current thinking derives and which commercial copyright laws continue to reflect.

Thus plunderphonics as a practice radically undermines three of the central pillars of the art music paradigm: *originality*—it deals only with copies, *individuality*—it speaks only with the voice of others, and *copy rights*—the breaching of which is a condition of its very existence.

Recording History: the Gramophone.

As an attribute unique to recording, the history of plunderphonics is in part the history of the self-realisation of the recording process; its coming, so to speak, to consciouness.[7]

Sound recording began with experiments in acoustics and the discovery that different pitches and timbres of sound could be rendered visible by attaching a needle to a membrane, causing the membrane to vibrate with a sound and allowing the needle to engrave its track in a plate or cylinder moving at a fixed speed. Such experiments were conducted only to convert otherwise invisible, transient sound into a "writing" (phono-graph means "voice-writer")—a fixed visible form that would allow it to be seen and studied. It was some 50 years before it occurred to anyone that by simply reversing the process, the sound thus written could be recovered. And it wasn't until the late 1870's that the first, purely mechanical, phonograph was constructed, still not sure what it was for, appearing variously as a novelty item, talking doll mechanism and "dictaphone." The music gramophone really started to take hold after the electrification of the whole process in 1926, but the breakthrough for the record as a producing (as opposed to reproducing) medium, came only in 1948 in the studios of French Radio with the birth of *Musique Concrete. There were no technological advances to explain this breakthrough*, only a thinking advance; the chance interpenetrations of time, place and problematic. The first *concrete* pieces, performed at the *"Concert de Bruits"* in Paris by engineer Pierre Schaeffer, were made by manipulating gramaphone records in real time, employing techniques embedded in their physical form: varying the speed, reversing the direction of spin, making "closed grooves" to create repeated ostinati, etc. Within two years the Radio station, in the face of resistance from Schaeffer, had re-equipped the studio with tape recorders and Schaeffer, now head of the *group de musique concrete*, continued to develop the same aesthetic of sound organisation and to extend the transformational procedures learned through turntable manipulations with the vastly more flexible resources of magnetic tape. Other composers began to experiment with disc manipulation around the same time, including Tristam Cary in London and Mauricio Kagel in Buenos Aires. Tape had completely displaced direct to disc recording by 1950, and the studio that was to become an instrument was the tape studio. Disc experiments seemed merely to have become a primitive forerunner to tapework. It is curious that, in spite of the intimacy of record and recording, the first commercially available *Musique Concrete* on disc was not released until 1956.

Tape

Where the gramophone was an acoustic instrument, the magnetic recorder, also invented at the end of the nineteenth century, was always electrical. The gramophone, however, had numerous initial advantages; it was easier to amplify (the recoverable signal was louder to start with), and as soon as Emile Berliner replaced the cylinder with the disc and developed a process to press copies from a single master (1895), records were easy to mass produce. Wire—and then tape—were both much more difficult. For these and other reasons, tape was not regularly employed in music until after WW2, when German improvements in recording and playback quality and in stable magnetic tape technology were generally adopted throughout the world. Within five years, tape had become standard in all professional recording applications.

The vinyl disc meanwhile held its place as the principle commercial playback medium, and thus the ubiquitous public source of recorded sound. This divison between the professionally productive and socially reproductive media was to have important consequences, since it was on the gramophone record that music appeared in its public, most evocative form; and when resonant cultural fragments began to be taken into living sound art, it was naturally from records, from the "real" artifacts that bricolagists would draw. But before we get to this part of the story, I want to take a quick look at some plundering precedents in some other fields.

History: Plunder

From early in this century conditions existed that one would expect to have encouraged sound plundering experiments as a matter of course. Firstly, the fact of sound recording itself, it's existence, its provision of a medium which offers the sonic simulacrum of an actual sound event in a permanent and alienable form. Moreover, in principle, a sound recording, like a photograph, is merely surface. It has no depth, reveals no process and is no palimpsest. It's just there; always the first, always a copy. It has no aura, nor any connection to a present source. And with its special claims toward objectivity and transparency, the tongue of a recording is always eloquently forked, and thus already placed firmly in the realm of art.[8]

Secondly, montage, collage, borrowing, bricolage have been endemic in the visual arts since at least the turn of the century. The importation of readymade fragments into original works was a staple of cubism (newspaper, label samples, advertising etc.), futurism and early Soviet art. Dadaists took this much further (Schwitters above all, and the photomontagists) and, as early as 1914, Marcel Duchamp had exhibited his bottle rack, a work in which, for the first time, a complete unmodified object was simply imported whole into an "art space." Yet, strangely, it waited 25 years for John Cage in his "Imaginary Landscape No. 1" (1939) to bring a gramaphone record into a public performance as an instrument—and he still only used test tones and the effect of speed changes. Having said this, I recently learned that at a DADA event in 1920 Stephan Wolpe used 8 gramophones to play records at widely different speeds simultaneously—a true precedent but without consequences; and of course Ottorino Resphigi did call for a gramophone recording of a nightingale in his 1924 *"Pina di Roma"*—a technicality this, but imaginative nonetheless (though a bird call would have sufficed). Moreover, Darius Milhaud (from 1922), Moholy-Nagy at the Bauhaus (1923) and Edgard Varese (1936) had all experimented with disc manipulations, but none eventually employed them in a final work. Paul Hindemith and Ernst Toch did produce three recorded "studies" ("Grammophonmusik," 1929/30), but these have been lost, so it is difficult to say much about them, except that judging from the absence of offspring, their influence was clearly small.[9] More prescient, because the medium was more flexible, were sound constructions made by filmmakers in the late '20s and '30s, using techniques developed for film, such as splicing and montaging, and working directly onto optical film soundtrack—for instance, in Germany, Walter Ruttman's "Weekend," and Fritz Walter Bischoff's lost "Sound Symphony:" "Hallo! Hier Welle Erdball" and, in Russia, constructivist experiments including G.V. Alexandrov's "A Sentimental Romance" and Dziga Vertov's "Enthusiasm." There had also been some pieces of film music which featured "various treatments of sounds...probably created with discs before being transferred to celluliod, by such composers as Yves Baudrier, Arthur Honneger and Maurice Jaubert."[10] The ideas were around, but isolated in special project applications. And strangely, optical recording techniques developed for film in the '20s, although endowed with many of the attributes of magnetic tape, simply never crossed over into the purely musical domain—despite Edgard Varese's visionary proposal in 1940 for an optical sound studio in Hollywood, a proposal which, needless to say, was ignored.

With so many precedents in the world of the visual arts and the long availability of the means of direct importation and plunder, it does seem surprising that it took so long for there to be similar developments in the world of music. And when, at last, the first clear intimations of the two principle elements crucial to plunderphonic practice did arrive, they arrived in two very different spheres, each surrounded by its own quite separate publicity and theory. The key works were Pierre Schaeffer's early experiments with radio sound archive discs (e.g., "Study of a Turntable," 1948) and John Cage's unequivocal importation of readymade material into his "Imaginary Landscape No. 4" (1951) for twelve radios—where all the sounds, voices and music were plundered whole, and at random from the ionosphere. (In 1955, "Imaginary Landscape No. 5" specified as sound material 42 gramophone records). Thus although Schaeffer used pre-recorded materials, these were "concrete" sounds, not already recorded compositions, while Cage, with a different intention, certainly made his construction out of "copyright" works, *but this fact was purely incidental to the intention of the piece.*

It wasn't until 1961 that an unequivocal exposition of plunderphonic techniques arrived in James Tenney's celebrated "Collage No.1 (Blue Suede)," a manipulation of Elvis Presley's hit record "Blue Suede Shoes." The gauntlet was down; Tenney had picked up a "non-art," lowbrow work and turned it into "art"; not as with scored music by writing variations on a popular air, but simply by subjecting a gramophone record to various physical and electrical proceedures.

Still no copyright difficulties.

To Refer or Not To Refer

Now, it can easily be argued that performances with—and recordings comprising—readymade sounds, including other people's completed works, reflect a concern endemic in 20th century art with art media in and of themselves, apart from all representational attributes. This can take the form, for instance, of an insistence that all that is imitation can be stripped away, leaving only sensual and essential forms with no external referents; or a belief that all semiotic systems consist of *nothing but* referentiality—signalled by the addition, as it were, of imaginary inverted commas to everything. But it is only a loss of faith, or illusion, or nerve that stands between this century's younger belief in "pure" languages and today's acceptance of the "endless play of signification."

Moreover, *Plunderphonics* can be linked, historically and theoretically, to both perceptions. Thus a recording may be considered as no more than the anonymous carrier of a "pure"—which is to say a non-referential—sound, or it may be an instance of a text that *cannot exist without reference*. In the first way, as Michel Chion's "Ten Commandments for an Art of Fixed Sounds" makes clear, "the composer makes a complete distinction between sounds and their source... (having) got rid of the presence of the cause..."[11] Here the goal is to "purify" the sound, to strip it of its origin and memories (though it may well be that that same erased origin remains still to haunt it).

In the second way the recording—for instance, a sample—may be no more than a fragment, a knowing self-reference, a version, and may be used to point at this very quality in itself.

As a found (or stolen) object, a sound is no more than available—for articulation, fragmentation, re-origination; it may be given the form of pure "acousmatics" or made an instance of the availability and interchangability (the *flatness*) of a recording, it's origin not so much erased as rendered infinitely relative. These applications, of course, do not exhaust it: as a pirated cultural artifact, a found object, as debris from the sonic environment, a plundered sound also holds out an invitation to be used *because* of its cause, and because of all the associations and cultural apparatus that surround it. And surely, what has been done with "captured" visual images (Warhol, Rauschenberg, Lichtenstein..) or directly imported objects (Duchamp, the mutilated poster works of Harris, Rotella, De la Villegle et al.)—all of which *depend upon* their actuality and provenance—can equally be done with captured "images" of sound.

Plundered sound carries, above all, the unique ability not just to *refer* but to *be*; it offers not just a new means but a new meaning. It is this dual character that confuses the debates about originality which so vex it.

High and Low

Popular musics got off to a slow start with sound piracy, nevertheless, they soon proved far more able to explore its inherent possibilities than art musics, which even after fifty years of sporadic experiment remained unable rigorously to do so. It is interesting perhaps that Tenney, who made the most radical essay into unashamed plunder, chose popular music as his primary source. In a later piece, "Viet Flakes" from 1967, he mixed pop, classical and Asian traditional musics together, and in so doing drew attention to another significant facet of the life of music on gramophone records, namely that, in the same way that they conceal and level their sources, records as objects make no distinction between "high" and "low" culture, "Art" and "pop."[12] A record makes all musics equally accessible—in every sense. No special clothes are needed, no expensive tickets need be bought, no travel is necessary, one need belong to no special interest or social group, nor be in a special place at a special time. Indeed, from the moment recordings existed, a new kind of "past" and "present" were born—both immediately available on demand. Time and space are homogenised in the home loudspeaker or the headphone, and the pop CD costs the same as the classical CD and probably comes from the same shop. All commodities are equal.

For young musicians growing up in the electric recording age, immersed in this shoreless sea of available sound, electronics, Maltese folk music, bebop, rhythm and blues, show tunes, film soundtracks and the latest top ten hit were all equally on tap. Tastes, interests, studies could be nourished at the pace, and following the desire, of the listener. Sounds, techniques and styles could flit across genres as fast as you could change a record, tune a dial or analyse and imitate what you heard. A kind of sound intoxication arose. Certainly it was the ideas and applications encountered in recorded music of all types which led a significant fringe of the teenage generation of the late '60s into experiments with sound, stylistic bricolages, importations, the use of noise, electronics, "inappropriate" instruments and—crucially—recording techniques.[13] The influence of art music and especially the work of Varese, Schaeffer, Stockhausen and others can not be overestimated in this context, and more than anything, it would be the crossplay between high and low art that would feature increasingly as a vital factor in the development of much innovative music. In plunderphonics too, the leakages, or maybe simply synchronicities between productions in what were once easily demarcated as belonging in high or low art discourses, are blatant. Indeed, in more and more applications, the distinction is meaningless and impossible to draw.

But there are simpler reasons for the special affinity between low art and plundering. For instance, although the first plunder pieces (viz., the early *concrete* and the Cage works mentioned) belonged firmly in the Art camp, blatant plundering nevertheless remained fairly off limits there, precluded essentially by the non-negotiable concern with originality and peer status—and also with the craft aspect of creating from scratch: originating out of a "creative centre" rather than "just messing about with other people's work." The world of low art had few such scruples, indeed, in a profound sense, plundering was endemic to it—in the "folk" practices of copying and covering for instance (few people played original compositions), or in the use of public domain forms and genres as vessels for expressive variation (the blues form, sets of standard chord progressions, and so on). The twentieth century "art" kind of originality and novelty simply was not an issue here. Moreover, in the "hands on," low expectation, *terra nova* world of rock, musicians were happy to make fools of themselves rediscovering America the hard way. What I find especially instructive was how, in a sound world principally mediated by recording, high and low art worlds increasingly appropriated from one another. And how problems that were glossed over when Art was Art and there was no genre confusion (like Tenney and Trythall's appropriation of copyright, but lowbrow, recordings) suddenly threatened to become dangerously problematic when genres blurred and both plunder and original began to operate in the same disputed (art/commercial) space.

Low Art Takes a Hand

Rock precedents for pure studio tapework were Frank Zappa, with his decidedly Varese-esque concrete pieces on the LPs *Absolutely Free, Lumpy Gravy* and *We're Only In It For The Money*, all made in 1967 (*Money* also contains an unequivocally plundered surf music extract), and The Beatles' pure tapework on "Tomorrow Never Knows" from the 1966 LP *Revolver*. "Revolution No. 9," on the *White Album*, is also full of plundered radio material. In the early '60s, radios were ubiquitous in the high art world and in some intermediary groups, such as AMM and FAUST (in the latter, on their second UK tour, guest member Uli Trepte played "Space Box"—a shortwave radio and effects as his main instrument).

Such examples, taken with (i) the increasing independence, confidence and self-consciousness of some rock musicians; (ii) a generation of musicians coming out of art schools; (iii) the mass availability of ever cheaper home recording equipment; and, (iv) a climate of experiment and plenitude, made straightforward plunder inevitable.[14] This promise was first substantially filled by The Residents. Their second released album, *Third Reich and Roll*

76 Plunderphonics

(1975), a highly self-reflexive commentary on rock culture and hit records, curiously employed a technique analogous to that used by Stockhausen in 1969 for his Beethoven Anniversary recording, *Opus 1970*, which had nothing to do with influence and everything to do with the medium. What Stockhausen had done was to prepare tapes of fragments of Beethoven's music which ran continuously through the performance of the piece. Each player could open and shut his own loudspeaker at will, and was instantaneously to "develop" what he heard instrumentally (condense, extend, transpose, modulate, synchronise, imitate, distort). To different ends The Residents followed a similar proceedure: instead of Beethoven, they copied well known pop songs to one track of a 4-track tape, to which they then played along (transposed, modulated, distorted, commented on, intensified), thus building up tracks. Though they subsequently erased most of the source material, you can often, as with *Opus 1970*, still hear the plundered originals breaking through.

In 1977, it was The Residents again who produced the first unequivocal 100% plunder to come out of pop, following in the high art footsteps of Tenney's Presley based "Collage No.1" and the later, more successful 1975 work "Omaggio a Jerry Lee Lewis" by American composer Richard Trythall (plundered from various recordings of Lewis' "Whole Lotta Shakin' Goin' On"). Trythall comments: "...like the table or newspaper in a cubist painting, the familiar musical object served the listener as an orientation point within a maze of new material... the studio manipulations... carried the source material into new, unexpected areas, while maintaining it's past associations." (Programme note on ReR CMCD). The Residents' work was a 7" single titled "Beyond the Valley of a Day in the Life" with subtitle: "The Residents Play The Beatles / The Beatles Play The Residents." It came packed as an art object in a numbered, limited edition and hand silkscreened cover, but was sold to—and known by—a rock public. One side of this single was a cover version of the Beatles' song "Flying." The other was pure plunderphonics. This whole side was assembled from extracts dubbed off Beatles records, looped, multitracked, composed with razor blades and tape. It is an ingenious construction, and remains a kind of classic.

Sampling and Scratching

Although there were some notable experiments and a few successful productions, tape and disc technologies made plundering difficult and time consuming, and thus suitable only for specific applications. What brought plundering to the centre of mass consumption, low-art music was a new technology that made sound piracy so easy that it didn't make sense *not* to do it. This development was Digital Sampling, launched commercially by Ensonic in the mid-1980s. Digital sampling is a purely electronic digital recording system, which takes (samples) "vertical slices" of sound and converts them into on/off information, into data, which tells a sound producing system how *to reconstruct*, rather than *reproduce* it. Instantly.

At a fast enough sampling rate, the detailed contours of a sound can be so minutely traced that playback quality is compatible in quality with any analogue recording system. The revolutionary power associated with the digital system was that the sound, when stored, consisted of information in a form that could be transformed, edited or rewritten electronically, without "doing" anything to any actual analogue recording, but only to a code. This really is a kind of a writing. When it is stored, modified or reproduced, no grooves, magnetized traces or any other contiguous *imprint* link the sound to its means of storage (by imprint I mean as when an object is pressed into soft wax and leaves its analogue trace). It is stored rather as discrete data, which act as *instructions* for the eventual reconstruction of a sound (as an object when electronically scanned is translated only into a binary code). Digital sampling allows any recorded sound to be linked to a keyboard or to a MIDI trigger and, using electronic tools (computer software) to be stretched, visualised on screen as waveforms and rewritten or edited with keys or a light pencil. All and any parameters can be modified and any existing electronic processing effects applied. Only at the end of all these processes will an audible sound be recreated. This may then be listened to, and if it is not what is wanted, reworked until it is and only then saved. It means that a work like Cage's four-minute "Williams Mix" (the first tape collage made in America), which took a year to cut together, could now be programmed and executed quite quickly using only a domestic computer. The mass application is even more basic. It simply puts any sound it records, or which has been recorded and stored as software, on a normal keyboard, pitched according to the key touched. The user can record, model and assign to the keys any sounds at all. At last here is a musical instrument which is a recording device and a performing instrument—*whose voice is simply the control and modulation of recordings*. How could this technology not give the green light to plundering ? It was so simple. No expertise was needed, just a user friendly keyboard, some stuff to sample (records and CDs are easy, and right there at home) and plenty of time to try things out. Producing could be no more than critical consuming; an empirical activity of Pick 'n' Mix. Nor is that all. Sampling was introduced in a musical climate where low art plundering had already deeply established itself in the form of "scratching," which, in its turn echoed in a radically sophisticated form the disc manipulation techniques innovated in high culture by Hindemith and Koch, Milhaud, Varese, Honnegger, Kagel, Cary, Schaeffer et.al., but now guided by a wholly different aesthetic.

From Scratch

The term "scratching" was coined to describe the practice of the realtime manipulation of 12" discs on highly adapted turntables and it grew up in U.S. discos, where DJs began to programme the records they played, running them together, cutting one into another on beat and in key, superimposing, crossfading and so on. Soon this developed to the point where a good DJ could play records as an accompanying or soloing instrument, along with a rhythm box, other tracks, singing. New and extended techniques emerged—for instance, the rhythmic slipping of a disc to and fro rapidly by hand on a low friction mat to create rhythms and cross rhythms—alongside old Concrete techniques: controlled speed alterations and *sillons fermées* riffs. ("Two manual decks and a rhythm box is all you need. Get a bunch of good rhythm records, choose your favorite parts and groove along with the rhythm machine. Using your hands, scratch the record by repeating the grooves you dig so much. Fade one record into the other and keep that rhythm box going. Now start talking and singing over the record with your own microphone. Now you're making your own music out of other people's records. That's what scratching is" —Sleeve note on Malcolm McLaren's *B-BU-BUFFALO GALS*, 1982.) It was only after scratching had become fashionable in the mid -'70s in radical Black disco music that it moved back toward Art applications, adopted quite brilliantly, by Christian Marclay (who used all the above techniques and more, incorporating also an idea of Milan Knizac's, who had, since 1963, been experimenting with deliberately mutilated discs, particularly composite discs comprising segments of different records glued together. Of course, everything Marclay does (like Knizac) is 100% plundered, but on some recordings, he, too—like Oswald on his seminal "Plunderphonics" recordings—creates works which, echoing Tenney and Trythall, concentrate on a single artist, producing a work which is about an artist and made only from that artist's sonic simulacrum. Listen, for instance, to the Maria Callas and Jimi

Hendrix tracks on the 10" EP "More Encores" (subtitled "Christian Marclay plays with the records of Louis Armstrong, Jane Birkin & Serge Gainsbourg, John Cage, Maria Callas, Frederic Chopin, Martin Denney, Arthur Ferrante & Louis Teicher, Fred Frith, Jimi Hendrix, Christian Marclay, Johann Strauss, John Zorn").

Marclay emerged to prominence as a member of the early eighties "New York Scene," on the experimental fringe of what was still thought of unequivocally as low art. He emerged into prominence out of the context of disco and scratching, not *concrete* or other artworld experiments with discs (though they were part of his personal history). His cultural status (like the status of certain other alumni of the the New York school, such as John Zorn) slowly shifted, from low to high, via gallery installations and visual works, and through the release of records such as "Record Without a Cover" (1985), which has only one playable side (the other has titles and text pressed into it) and comes unwrapped with the instruction: "Do not store in a protective package," or the 1987 grooveless LP, packaged in a black suede pouch and released in a limited and signed edition of 50 by Ecart Editions. Marclay's work appears as a late flowering of an attenuated and, even at its height, marginal high art form, reinvented and reinvigorated by low art creativity. It traces the radical interpenetrations of low and high art in the levelling age of sound recording; the swing between high art experiment, low art creativity and high art re-appropriation, as the two approach one another until, at their fringes, they become indistinguishable. *This aesthetic levelling is a property of the medium* and this indistinguishability signals not a collapse, but the coming into being of a new aesthetic form.

Oswald Plays Records

Curiously, the apotheosis of the record as an instrument—as the raw material of a new creation—occurred just as the gramophone record itself was becoming obsolete and when a new technology that would surpass the wildest ambitions of any scratcher, acousmaticist, tape composer or sound organizer was sweeping all earlier record/playback production systems before it. Sampling, far from destroying disc manipulation, seems to have breathed new life into it. Turntable techniques live on in live House and Techno. Marclay goes from strength to strength, more credits appear on diverse CDs listing "turntables," and younger players, like Otomo Yoshihide, are emerging with an even more organic and intimate relation to the record/player as an expressive instrument. It is almost as if sampling had recreated the gramophone record as a craft instrument, an analogue, expressive voice, made authentic by nostalgia. Obsolescence empowers a new mythology for the old phonograph, completing the circle from passive repeater to creative producer, from dead mechanism to expressive voice, from the death of performance to its guarantee. It is precisely the authenticity of the 12" disc that keeps it in manufacture; it has become anachronistically indispensible.

Disc–Tape–Disc

Applications of a new technology to art are often first inspired by existing art paradigms, frequently simplifying or developing existing procedures. Then new ideas emerge that more directly engage the technology for itself. These arise as a product of use, accident, experiment or cross-fertilization, but always through hands-on interaction. New applications then feed back again into new uses of the old technologies and so on round. For a long time such dynamic interpenetrations can drive aspects of both. Painting and film, for instance, have just such a productive history. A similar process could be traced in the tension between recording and performance. A particularly obvious example of this is the way that hard cuts and edits made with tape for musical effect inspire *played* "edits"—brilliantly exemplified in the work of John Zorn.[15] This process can be traced more broadly, and more profoundly, in the growth and refinement of the new sound aesthetic itself, which, from its origins in the crisis in art music at the turn of the century to contemporary practices in many fields, is characterised by the dynamic interactions between fluid and fixed media. New instrumental techniques inform, and are informed by, new recording techniques. Each refines a shared sonic language, sets problems, makes propositions. Each takes a certain measure of itself from the other; both living and dead: "Records are... dead" as Christian Marclay carefully points out.

More Dead than Quick

What is essential, and new, is that by far the largest part of the music that we hear is recorded music; live music making up only a small percentage of our total listening. Moreover, recording is now the primary medium through which musical ideas and inspiration spread (this says nothing about quality, it is merely a quantitative fact). For example, one of the gravitational centres of improvisation— which is in every respect the antithesis of fixed sound or notated music—is its relation to recorded sound, including recordings of itself or of other improvisations. This performance-recording loop winds through the rise of jazz as a mass-culture music, through rock experiments, and on to the most abstract noise productions of today. Whatever living music does, chances are that the results will be recorded. And this will be their immortality. In the new situation, *it is only what is **not** recorded that belongs to its participants, while what is recorded is placed inevitably in the public domain*. Moreover, as noted earlier, recorded music leaves its genre community and enters the universe of recordings. As such the mutual interactions between composers, performers and recordings refer back to sound and structure and not to particular music communities. Leakage, seepage, adoption, osmosis, abstraction, contagion: these describe the life of sound work today. They account for the general aesthetic convergence at the fringes of genres once mutually exclusive—and across the gulf of high and low art. There is a whole range of sound work now about which it simply makes no sense to speak in terms of high or low, art or popular, indeed where the two interpenetrate so deeply that to attempt to discriminate between them is to fail to understand the sound revolution which has been effected through the medium of sound recording. Plunderphonics addresses precisely this realm of the recorded. It treats of the point where both public domain and contemporary soundworld meet the transformational and organisational aspects of recording technology; where listening and production, criticism and creation elide. It is also where copyright law from another age can't follow—where, as Oswald himself remarked: "If creativity is a field, copyright is the fence."

Pop Eats Itself

I want now to look at some of the many applications of *Plundering* beyond those of directly referential or self-reflexive intent like those of Tenney, Trythall, The Residents, Oswald and Marclay.

First, and most obvious, is the widespread plundering of records for samples that are recycled on Hip Hop, House and Techno records in particular, but increasingly on pop records in general. This means that drum parts, bass parts (often loops of a particular bar), horn parts, all manner of details (James Brown whoops etc.) will be dubbed off records and built up layer by layer into a new piece. This is essentially the same proceedure as that adopted by the Residents in their Beatles piece, except that nowadays the range and power of electronic treatments is far greater than before, and the results achieved of far greater technical complexity. Rhythms and tempi can be adjusted and sychronised, pitches altered, dynamic shape rewritten, and so on. Selections sampled may be traceable or untraceable, it need not matter. Reference is not the aim so much as a kind of creative consumerism, a bricolage assembly from parts. Rather than start with instrument(s), or a score, you start with a large record and CD collection and then copy, manipulate and laminate.

Moral and copyright arguments rage around this. Following several copyright infringement cases, bigger studios employ someone to note all samples and register and credit all composers, artists and original recording owners. "Sampling licences" are negotiated and paid for. This is hugely time consuming and slightly ridiculous and really not an option for amateurs and small fish. Oswald's recent work "Plexure," for instance, *has so many* tiny cuts and samples on it that, not only are their identities impossible to register by listening, but compiling credit data would be like assembling a telephone directory for a medium sized town. Finding, applying, accounting and paying the 4000+ copyright and patent holders would likewise be a full-time occupation, effectively impossible. Therefore such works simply could not exist. We have to address the question whether this is what we really want.

For now I am more interested in the way pop really starts to eat itself. Here together are cannibalism, laziness and the feeling that everything has already been originated so that it is enough now endlessly to reinterpret and rearrange it all. The old idea of originality in *production*, gives way to another (if to one at all) of originality in *consumption*, in hearing.

Cassiber

Other applications use plundered parts principally as sound elements which relate in a constitutive or alienated way to the syntax of a piece. They may or may not bear referential weight, this being only one optional attribute which the user may choose to employ. The Anglo-German group Cassiber uses just such techniques, where samples act both as structure and as fragments of cultural debris. Cassiber creates complexities; no piece is reducable to a score, a set of instructions, a formula. Simultaneity and superimposed viewpoints are characteristic of much of the work, as is the tension between invention and passion on the one hand and 'dead' materials on the other. When the group was formed, singer Christoph Anders worked with a table stacked with prepared cassettes, each containing loops or raw extracts taken from from all manner of musics (on one Cassiber piece, there might be fragments of Schubert, Schoenberg, The Shangri-La's, Maria Callas and Them). The invention of the sampler put in his hands a similar facility, except with more material, and infinitely greater transformational power, all accessible immediately on a normal keyboard. It means that, options impossible—though desired—before, can now be simply played. They can be as unstable as any performed musical part. And as discontinuous. Cassiber's use of familiar fragments, though these are often recogniseable—and thus clearly referential—doesn't depend on this quality, which is accepted merely as a possible aspect—but rather on their musical role within the piece. Where House, Rap etc., use samples to reinforce what is familiar, Goebbels and Anders use them to make the familiar strange, dislocated, more like debris. But (and this is the key) as structural rather than decorative debris. It is an affect only plundered materials can deliver.

The Issue

What is the issue ? Is it whether *sound* can be copyrighted, or snatches of a performance? If so, where do we draw the line—at length, recognizability? Or does mass produced, mass disseminated music have a kind of folk status; is it so ubiquitous and so involuntary (you *have* to be immersed in it much of your waking time) that it falls legitimately into the category of 'public domain'? Since violent action (destruction of works, legal prohibition, litigation and restraint) have been applied by one side of the argument, these are questions we can not avoid.

Review of Applications

A.> *There it is:* Cases such as that of Cage, in "Imaginary Landscapes 2 and 4," where materials are all derived directly from records or radio and subjected to various manipulations. Though there are copyright implications, the practice implies that music picked randomly "out of the air" is simply *there*. Most of Cage's work is more a kind of *listening* than of producing anyway.

B.> *Partial importations:* For example "My Life In The Bush Of Ghosts" and the work of Italians Roberto Musci and Giovanni Venosta spring to mind. In both, recordings of ethnic music are used as important voices, the rest of the material being constructed around them. The same might be done with whale songs, sound effects records and so on; I detect political implications of the absence of copyright problems on such recordings. At least, it is far from obvious to me why an appeal to public domain status should be any more or less valid for "ethnic" music than it is for most pop—or any other recorded music.

C.> *Total importation:* This might be rather thought of as interpretation or re-hearing of existing recordings. Here we are in the territory of Tenney, Trythall, The Residents, Marclay and quintessentially, of Plunderphonic pioneer John Oswald. Existing recordings are not randomly or instrumentally incorporated so much as they become the simultaneous *subject* and *object* of a creative work. Current copyright law is unable to distinguish between a plagiarised and a new work in such cases, since it's concerns are still drawn from old pen and paper paradigms. In the visual arts, Duchamp, with readymades, Warhol with soup cans and Brillo boxes, Lichtenstein with cartoons and Sherry Levine with rephotographed "famous" photographs are only some of the many who have, one way or another, broached the primary artistic question of "originality" which Oswald too can't help but raise.

D.> *Sources irrelevant:* Where recognition of parts plundered is not necessary or important. There is no self-reflexivity involved; sound may be drawn as if "out of nothing," or bent to new purposes, or simply used as raw material. Also within this category falls the whole mundane universe of sampling or stealing "sounds": drum sounds (not parts), guitar chords, riffs, vocal interjections, etc., sometimes creatively used, but more often simply a way of saving time and money. Why spend hours creating or copying a sound when you can snatch it straight off a CD and get it into your own sampler-sequencer?

E.> *Sources untraceable:* Manipulations which take the sounds plundered and stretch and treat them so radically that it is impossible to divine their source at all. Techniques like this are used in electronic, concrete, acousmatic, radiophonic, film and other abstract sound productions. Within this use lies a whole universe of viewpoints. For instance, the positive exploration of new worlds of sound and new possibilities of aestheticisation, or—the idea that there is no need to originate any more, since what is already there offers such endless possibilities, or—

the expression of an implied helplessness in the face of contemporary conditions, namely, everything that *can* be done *has* been done and we can only rearrange the pieces...

This is a field where what may seem to be quite similar procedures may express such wildly different understandings as a hopeless tinkering amidst the ruins, or a celebration of the infinitude of the infinitesimal.

Comments

Several currents run together here. There is the technological aspect: plundering is impossible in the absence of sound recording. There is the cultural aspect: since the turn of the century, the importation of readymade materials into artworks has been a common practice, and one which has accumulated eloquence and significance. The re-seeing, or re-hearing, of familiar material is a well-established practice, and in high art at least, accusations of plagiarism are seldom raised. More to the point, the two-way traffic between high and low art (each borrowing and quoting from the other) has proceeded apace. Today it is often impossible to draw a clear line between them (witness certain advertisements, Philip Glass, Jeff Koons, New York subway graffiti...). It seems inevitable that in such a climate, the applications of a recording technology that gives instant playback, transposition and processing facilities, will not be intimidated by the old proscriptions of plagiarism or the ideal of originality. What is lacking now is a discourse under which the new practices can be discussed and adjudicated. The old values and paradigms of property and copyright, skill, originality, harmonic logic, design and so forth are simply not adequate to the task. Until we are able to give a good *account* of what is being done, *how* to think and speak about it, it will remain impossible to adjudicate between legitimate and illegitimate works and applications. Meanwhile, outrages such as that perpetrated on John Oswald will continue unchecked.

1. On Proportion

Current copyright law differs from country to country, but in general follows international accords. It certainly allows "fair use," which would include parody, quotation and reference, though these may need to be argued and defended. This is a minefield in which only lawyers profit. So where the Beatles had to pay up for quoting "In The Mood" at the end of "All You Need Is Love" and Oswald had his work destroyed, Two Live Crew's parody of Roy Orbison's "Pretty Woman" got off free as "fair use." Or take Negativland's parody on U2's "I Still Haven't Found What I'm Looking For" (1991). This was also recalled and destroyed after Island Records sued the group and its record company, identifying illegally stolen samples as one of the main causes. But Negativland are famous precisely for their tapework and cut-up techniques, as well as their sharp fragmentalising and commenting on the media debris by which we are all, like it or not, daily assaulted. This piece was (i) funny, (ii) telling, (iii) not commercial—in all these respects, unlike the record by Two Live Crew. It and the group and the record company all got hammered (all copies recalled and destroyed, $25,000 fine and other financial penalties, assignation of Negativland's rights to Island Records). Now compare the case of disco mixers DNA who made a techno manipulation of Susanne Vega's song "Tom's Diner," released it on an independent label, sold a few thousand copies and then, when Vega's record company heard it, were offered not a crippling lawsuit but a deal for an "official" release.

Questions of works unstarted, or only circulating privately, or of a climate where ideas and opportunities are simply abandoned—all for fear of copyright difficulties—are not even broached here.

There is no proportion because there is no clarity. The rethinking of copyright law is long overdue. Recording has been with us now for more than 100 years.

2. *Everyday Sample and Plunder*

"A typical group's producer has a machine like a Linn/Akai MPC60, which has twelve pads like a drum machine, lots of memory for sequencing, and most important, it's a sampler, too. This person spends time at home with their huge record collection, finding suitable bits to build a new song with. Usually they'll start with a drum loop, perhaps from a James Brown record—1, 2, maybe 4 bars. Then a loop with a bass line (maybe with drums on too), say from the Zapp band—1 or 2 bars. Horn section from an Earth, Wind and Fire album, electric piano from some incredibly obscure funk album, add a few more drum loops to fatten it up and give it a rolling, driving feel. Some percussion, tambourine, hi-hat samples (a lot of producers have their own "signature" hi-hat and tambourines which they use on all their stuff and won't tell anyone where they sampled them from; if you recognise it you're a true fanatic scholar of all the old records. The 808 Kick drum is a major part of the sound, the "boom." It comes from the Roland TR 808 drum machine if you turn the decay on the bass drum all the way up. Very few people actually own an 808, but there are plenty of samples around. You can also make a good boom by sampling an oscillator, somewhere between 60–100 Herz and adding a regular kick drum sample to it. The sound is so deep it can be way up in the mix like it's supposed to be and not get in the way of anything else.

So all these loops and sounds are put on different pads on the MPC60 and sequenced into a song form. Before it's actually a song, with breaks, choruses and so on, the whole big rolling pile of samples and loops is called a "beat". But to arrive at this, getting all the loops and samples—most of which were originally in different tempi—to play in perfect synch with one another, is a whole job in itself. They all have to be synched up with the metronome in the sequencer. Drummers speeding up and slowing down within the four bars of a sample, horn sections slightly behind or ahead of the beat—all the natural human "imperfections" sometimes make it necessary to break a loop into two or four separate segments, shortening or lengthening each to get it "in time." All these loops have little idiosyncracies, people talking, band/audience members shouting, stuff going on in the background, scratches and pops from the old vinyl, all of which add up and contribute to the overall end sound.

When it's been shaped into a song, it's all printed on the multitrack, each sample and loop on its own track and the "live" parts are added; maybe a bass guitar, wah wah guitar, sax. Then the vocals and scratches. The scratches are added by the DJ, the guy with the turntable and crates full of old records. The DJ is almost like a soloist, and spaces are left in the song structure for scratching, the same way a rock band leaves a space for a guitar solo and for fills and flavoring throughout the song. They're really good at knowing just where to get the right little phrases and sounds which somehow relate to the lyrics of the song, often rearranging the words of an old song, or piecing lines from several songs together to make them say what they want for the new song. A really great DJ is unbelievable, and fun to watch and listen to: real performers."

—From my Interview with BOB DRAKE, *ReR Quarterly,* Vol 4. No.1.

84   Plunderphonics

Endnotes

[1] In "Necessity and Choice in Musical Forms," part III (i) from *File Under Popular,* November Books/Autonomedia, revised edition 1992.

[2] As I have argued in "Necessity and Choice," II (i), ibid.

[3] There were sporadic experiments, as we shall see, and notably Varese grasped the nettle early. Pierre Shaeffer made the radical proposal, but precisely from his work as an engineer, and not emerging out of the Art music tradition. A few followed, Stockhausen, Berio, Nono and others, and new schools formed which in part or whole abandoned mediating notation (concrete, electronic, acousmatic, electroacoustic musics, for example), but these too tried to retain, so far as was possible, the old status and values for their creators, merely replacing the score with direct personal manipulation, and continuing to make the same claims to originality, personal ownership, creation *ex nihilo,* etc. John Cage was an interesting exception; his originality and individuality were claimed precisely in their negation.

[4] For the full argument of this claim see, once again, "Necessity and Choice in Musical Forms" part III (ii), in my *op cit.*

[5] The first Copyright Act in England was passed in 1709. The current Act dates from 1956 and includes rights of the author to remuneration for all public performances (including broadcasts, jukeboxes, muzak, fairground rides, concerts, discotheques, film, TV and so on) as well as for recordings of all kinds. The recording is copyrighted seperately from the composition, so that every individual recording of a composition also has an owner.

[6] Most copyright bodies discriminate between works which earn a lot by the minute ("serious" composed works) and those which earn a little (pop music, for instance and improvised-compositions). Criteria for making such decisions vary, reflecting the prejudices of the day.

[7] Which is to say, where it raises questions that reflect upon its own identity.

[8] And through its documentary authenticity also in the realm of the political, as the purity of the retouched photograph and doctored tape attest.

[9] Hugh Davies recently brought to my attention a report from a 1993 conference in Berlin where it was reported that in the mid-eighties Hindemith's discs had been offered to the director of a German musicological institute. He refused them, after which they were almost certainly destroyed.

[10] Hugh Davies, "A History of Sampling," *ReR Quarterly,* Vol. 4, No. 1.

[11] Michel Chion, "L'Art des sons fixes," *Editions Metamkine*, Fontaine 1991.

[12] I shall treat the quotation marks as read from here on.

[13] See *File Under Popular* chapters on "The Residents," "Necessity and Choice," "Progressive Music in the U.K." passim.

[14] I remember coming home from school and putting on records at 16 or 78 rpm, two secondhand radios tuned between stations or at random, and similar mixtures already recorded on tape, filling the room with "noise." I was more or less unaware of experimental music at the time and discovered this pleasure just by messing about. I'm sure this was just "in the air" at this time and nothing so unusual. Or as John Oswald notes: "As a listener my own preference is the option to experiment. My listening system has a mixer instead of a receiver, an infinitely variable speed turntable, filters, reverse capability, and a pair of ears." John Oswald. *Plunderphonics, or,* audio piracy as a compositional prerogative, *Musicworks*, 34.

[15] Zorn's work is of course strongly influenced by early cartoon soundtracks, recorded in real time with constant changes, following the cuts and twists in the film. One way Zorn achieves this effect

is to use relays of players, one grouping jumping in as another concludes. Sections can be very short and cuts extreme. Zorn cuts genres together as well as quotes and bursts of noise. Listening can be like spinning a radio dial, but has always that special energetic and virtuosic quality that comes from its having been played in real time.

Discography

Cassiber. *A Face We All Know*. 1990. ReR, CCD.
Marclay, Christian. *More Encores*. EP. 19 No Man's Land, NML 8816.
Musci/Venosta. *Messages and Portraits.*. CD 1990, ReR, MVCD1.
Negativland. *U2*. 1991. Released by SST as SST CD 272 (destroyed).
Oswald, John. *Plunderphonics*. EP, 1988, released by John Oswald.
    Plunderphonics. CD, as above 1989 (destroyed).
    Discosphere. CD. ReR 1991.
    Plexure. CD. Avant DIW, Japan.
Residents, The. 7" single "The Beatles play the Residents/The Residents play the Beatles," Ralph records 1974, reissued on the CD *Third Reich'n Roll* as a bonus track, ESD 80032.
Schaeffer, Pierre. CD reissues INA.GRM C1006, 1007, 1008, 1009.
Stockhausen, Karlheinz. *Opus 1971*. Deutsche Gramophone.
Tenney, James. "Collage No. 1 (Blue Suede)" (1961) released on *Selected Works* . CD, Artifact recordings as FP001, 1992. "Viet Flakes" issued by *Musicworks on* MW56, 1993.
Trythall, Richard. *Hommagio a Jerry Lee Lewis*. 1971. Released by CRI as CRI SD 302, reissued on CD by ReR on the collection *CMCD* 1980.

John Oswald

Creatigality

John Oswald

If creativity is a field, copyright is the fence. We each own property of our creative efforts and the extent to which trespassing is tolerable is entirely up to us. When we hear of a song snatcher being apprehended it's a case of artist's arrest in the form of a civil law suit. There are no actual copyright police listening for burglars of sound.

Many of you would like to know exactly the extent to which a song or sound can legally be copied or sampled without permission. Speculators venture that a few bars, or seconds, or perhaps a snare shot is allowable appropriation. Actually, there is no minimum duration below which the copyright of sound lapses. If the procurement is recognized and objected to, you could be sued. Even so, you may feel compelled to lift a sample from a record or CD—an imitatable string sound perhaps. Not many of us could afford to hire the Chicago Symphony for a sampling session.

Or you may worry that the catchy tune in your mind's ear is inadvertently not really yours, and epithets of plagiarism and derivativeness await. It is conceivable that one might accidentally write an unoriginal tune. For the majority of composers, working within the structure of diatonic sequences from the twelve equal tempered divisions of the octave, there is always the worry that the new melody is actually from some forgotten source, or has a coincidental similarity to an existing composition. In a future time depicted in Spider Robinson's speculative story "Melancholy Elephants," the copyright office, with its formidable archives of existing melodic combinations, constantly rejects the earnest efforts of composers as being unoriginal. While more tunes are being written, fewer possible tunes remain to be written.

Interestingly enough, while imitation of melody can invoke litigation, anyone's style is up for grabs. The components of creativity lie on both sides of the copyright fence. Thus the Elvis Clone Syndrome. One can copy his look, dress, sound and moves exclusively for one's own profit. Nevertheless, each ersatz Elvis is a gyrating billboard for the original—imitation is financial flattery.

Look at it this way. Music is information and, as such, is a renewable resource. Intellectual real estate is infinitely divisible. The big difference between the taking of physical property and the taking of intellectual property is that in the latter case the original owner doesn't lose the property. They still have it. Theft only occurs when the owner is deprived of credit. Unfortunately, the fear that copyrightholders will forbid access causes some borrowers to plunder covertly. Sneakiness pervades the industry, pilfered riffs and snitched sounds proliferate, hidden in everything from patches to platinum product.

The blatant reuse of recorded sound is harder to find. Some composers, contemporary Robin Hoods, are making music which, in the tradition of Charles Ives (who wrote at a time when public domain had some currency) and Carl Stallings (the seminal cartoon composer who freely quoted from the extensive song library of his employer, Warner Brothers), directly refers to and transforms the familiar. Ives was an unnoticed pioneer in what was, at the turn of the century, the open frontier of music. Stallings worked on a large ranch where he creatively roamed, rarely encountering the fences of copyright. We now live in the condos of our own compositions and wouldn't dare ask neighouring composers for the loan of something to sweeten a track.

Thomas Edison's professed aim was to make his phonograph "the greatest musical instrument in the world." This curious notion seems to imply that the record player could transcend the role of being merely a reproducer of music. It's doubtful that Edison envisioned the scratch techniques of the descendants of Grandmaster Flash, who strum a groove with a stylus prick.

Take the case of Master Mix producer Steve Stein. Master Mix DJs., working dance clubs and radio, use records as macro-samples, constantly changing and combining the copyrighted sounds of songs. Stein's collages are conglomerates of actual recordings of Otis Redding, Walter Cronkite, Led Zeppelin and a host of others combined in novel juxtapositions. He composes with familiar recordings the way most musicians compose with familiar chords. Unwilling to use evocations or impersonations, he insists, "You want the thing. You don't want the almost thing." Indeed, few of us are satisfied with "sounds-like" imitations, from FM Bosendorfers to bargain bin facsimiles of "almost" the Boss. Stein's audacious *verité* collages hit a satisfying chord in many listeners. They're authentically familiar and at the same time they're brand new, stimulating interest in the electronically "quoted" artists.

And so, the vinyl borrowings burrowed in the mix have recently surfaced in hip hop hits like the M.A.R.S. "Pump Up the Volume." No credit is given for the appropriations but aural identification is a snap. Record companies didn't appreciate the quotes by extraterrestrials in Dickie Goodman's retrofit hit "The Flying Saucer" back in the fifties. Where does tolerance end now? Since no one knows no credit is given to the sources of these procurements.

Some copyright holders see such appropriation as potentially harmful to the integrity of the original material. I disagree. Imitation does glut a market, but transformation revitalizes it. Creative listening is, in effect, discouraged by copyright law which seeks to protect artists from the trivialization of their work. Dolly Parton transposed down a fourth (i.e. from 45rpm to 33 1/3rpm) becomes a handsome tenor, slightly more elegiac. Does this aural sex change trivialize Ms. Parton's work or rather, does it provide some of us with an opportunity for appreciation and a new reason to buy her records?

Others argue that the original sounds (of an orchestra for example) are acquired at great expense, and widespread electronic appropriation devalues the source. Similar arguments were to be heard at the dawn of the recording era when musicians feared that live music would be replaced by the mechanical reproduction of piano rolls and Edison cylinders. With the advent of synthesizers whole groups of conventional instruments seemed to face extinction. Perhaps we will soon see "do not sample" labels embossed on traditional instruments.

It is unfortunate that music has no "...," the two fingers of each hand which indicate credit given. Yet the danger in rigid enforcement of copyright is the restriction of potential access, legitimate reference, and the healthy trading of ideas and sounds. The creative act must be to some extent a derivative process. Total originality is incomprehensible. Even so, the most derivative artists are those usually the least willing to acknowledge their inspirational debts.

Originality takes a different tact. Stravinsky said, "A good composer does not imitate, he steals," echoing Milton's definition of plagiarism as occurring when the work "is not bettered by the borrower." One wrests ownership from existing work only by improving upon it. *Plunderphonics* is a term I've coined to cover the counter-covert world of converted sound and retrofitted music, where collective melodic memories of the familiar are minced and rehabilitated to a new life. A "plunderphone" is an unofficial but recognizable musical quote. The blatant borrowings of the privateers of sound are a class distinct from common samplepocketing, parroting and tune thievery.

Thus art progresses by innovation and chameleonization. It is difficult to assess how new technology will eventually affect the musical environment. Home taping for instance, rather that destroying the record industry, seems to have vitalized it. Given access to the verb "record" as well as the noun, consumers are now able to edit unwanted material from commercial releases and to assemble more varied collections than any one record company could possibly provide. Records, tapes and CDs sell partly because the consumer now has more ways to listen to them.

Am I glorifying as musical creativity the habits of hyperactive listeners? Is there a line between Stein and Stravinsky? I think they walk a similar purpose. A composer listens with instruments. Anything from a wire to a wireless can be used creatively as a musical instrument. Making a sample is the same as tuning a string—you are specifying a configuration to be used in the making of music. There is meaning and value even in very short durations (we're talking milliseconds here) of well-known records. Think of the bits-of-hits contests on the radio in which hit parade listeners identify songs from a barrage of brief fragments. Listening to plodding renditions on *Name That Tune* while trying to remember the words is an anachronistic activity; sounds are usually recognized instantly or not at all. These fragments of timbre are inextricably associated with the whole. They have become the new language of music, using a syntax of rhythm and melody.

Sampling, like creativity itself, is a derivative activity. Making a sample is the same, in effect as tuning a string—you are specifying a configuration to be used in the making of music. Samples won't replace all pianos; but they will continue to evoke pianos. Likewise a sample or a quote from existing music refers to the original in a positive sense, more than it steals from it. It's not necessary to tear down the fences of copyright when you can enter by the gate. If you sample, give the credit due. And if you have been sampled, consider the credit you've been given.

U2

NEGATIVLAND

Fair Use

Negativland

As Duchamp pointed out many decades ago, the act of selection can be a form of inspiration as original and significant as any other. Throughout our various mass mediums, we now find many artists who work by "selecting" existing cultural material to collage with, to create with, and to comment with. In general, this continues to be a direction that both "serious" and "popular" arts like. But is it theft? Do artists, for profit or not, have the right to freely "sample" from an already "created" electronic environment that surrounds them for use in their own work?

The psychology of art has always favored fragmentary "theft" in a way which does not engender a loss to the owner. In fact, most artists speak freely about the amount of stuff they have stolen at one time or another. In the realm of ideas, techniques, styles, etc., most artists know that stealing (or call it "being influenced" if you want to sound legitimate) is not only OK, but desirable and even crucial to creative evolution. This proven route to progress has prevailed among artists since art began and will not be denied. To creators, it is simply obvious in their own experience.

Now some will say there is a big difference between stealing ideas, techniques, and styles which are not easily copyrighted, and stealing actual material, which is easily copyrighted. However, aside from the copyright deterrence factor which now prevails throughout our lawbound art industries, we can find nothing intrinsically wrong with an artist deciding to incorporate existing art "samples" into their own work. The fact that we have economically motivated laws against it does not necessarily make it an undesirable artistic move. In fact, this kind of theft has a well-respected tradition in the arts extending back to the Industrial Revolution.

In the early years of this century, Cubists began to attach found materials such as product packaging and photographs to their paintings. This now seems an obvious and perfectly natural desire to embody or transform existing things into their own work as a form of dialogue with their material environment. And that "material" environment began to grow in strange new ways. Appropriation in the arts has now spanned the entire Century, crossing mediumistic boundaries, and constantly expanding in emotional relevance from beginning to end regardless of the rise and fall of "style fronts." It flowered through collage, Dada's found objects and concept of "detournement," and peaked in the visual arts at mid-century with Pop Art's appropriation of mass culture icons and mass media imagery. Now, at the end of this century, it is in music where we find appropriation raging anew as a major creative method and legal controversy.

We think it's about time that the obvious aesthetic validity of appropriation begins to be raised in opposition to the assumed preeminence of copyright laws prohibiting the free reuse of cultural material. Has it occurred to anyone that the private ownership of mass culture is a bit of a contradiction in terms?

Artists have always perceived the environment around them as both inspiration to act and as raw material to mold and remold. However, this particular century has presented us with a new kind of influence in the human environment. We are now all immersed in an ever-growing media environment—an environment just as real and just as affecting as the natural one from which it somehow sprang. Today we are surrounded by canned ideas, images, music, and text. My television set recently told me that 70 to 80 percent of our population now gets most of their information about the world from their television sets. Most of our opinions are no longer born out of our own experience. They are received opinions. Large increments of our daily sensory input are not focused on the physical reality around us, but on the media that saturates it. As artists, we find this new electrified environment irresistibly worthy of comment, criticism, and manipulation.

The act of appropriating from this media assault represents a kind of liberation from our status as helpless sponges which is so desired by the advertisers who pay for it all. It is a much needed form of self defense against the one-way, corporate-consolidated media barrage. Appropriation sees media, itself, as a telling source and subject, to be captured, rearranged, even mutilated, and injected back into the barrage by those who are subjected to it. Appropriators claim the right to create with mirrors.

Our corporate culture, on the other hand, is determined to reach the end of this century while maintaining its economically dependent view that there is something wrong with all this. However, both perceptually and philosophically, it remains an uncomfortable wrenching of common sense to deny that when something hits the airwaves it is literally in the public domain. The fact that the owners of culture and its material distribution can claim this isn't true is a tribute to their ability to restructure common sense for maximum profit.

Our cultural evolution is no longer allowed to unfold in the way that pre-copyright culture always did. True folk music, for example, is no longer possible. The original folk process of incorporating previous melodies and lyrics into constantly evolving songs is impossible when melodies and lyrics are privately owned. We now exist in a society so choked and inhibited by cultural property and copyright protections that the very idea of mass culture is now primarily propelled by economic gain and the rewards of ownership. To be sure, when these laws came about there were bootlegging abuses to be dealt with, but the self-serving laws that resulted have criminalized the whole idea of making one thing out of another.

Our dense, international web of copyright restrictions was initiated and lobbied through the Congresses of the world, not by anyone who makes art, but by the parasitic middle men of culture—the corporate publishing and management entities who saw an opportunity to enhance their own and their clients' income by exploiting a wonderfully human activity that was proceeding naturally around them as it always had: the reuse of culture. These cultural representers—the lawyers behind the administrators, behind the agents, behind the artists—have succeeded in mining every possible peripheral vein of monetary potential in their art properties. All this is lobbied into law under the guise of upholding the interests of artists in the marketplace, and Congress, with no exposure to an alternative point of view, always accomodates them.

That being the case, there are two types of appropriation taking place today: legal and illegal. So, you may ask, if this type of work must be done, why can't everyone just follow the rules and do it the legal way? Negativland remains on the shady side of existing law because to follow it would put us out of business. Here is a personal example of how copyright law actually serves to prevent a wholly appropriate creative process which inevitably emerged out of our reproducing technologies.

In order to appropriate or sample even a few seconds of almost anything out there, you are supposed to do two things: get permission and pay clearance fees. The permission aspect becomes an unavoidable roadblock to anyone who may intend to use the material in a context unflattering to the performer or work involved. This happens to be exactly what we want to do. Dead end. Imagine how much critical satire would get made if you were required to get prior permission from the subject of your satire? The payment aspect is an even greater obstacle to us. Negativland is a small group of people dedicated to maintaining our critical stance by staying out of the corporate mainstream. We create and manufacture our own work, on our own label, on our own meager incomes and borrowed money. Our work is typically packed with found elements, brief fragments recorded from all media. This goes way beyond one or two, or ten or twenty elements. We can use a hundred different elements on a single record. Each of these audio fragments has a different owner and each of these owners must be located. This is usually impossible because the fragmentary nature of our long-ago random capture from radio or TV does not include the owner's name and address. If findable, each one of these owners, assuming they each agree with our usage, must be paid a fee which can range from hundreds to thousands of dollars each. Clearance fees are set, of course, for the lucrative inter-corporate trade. Even if we were somehow able to afford that, there are the endless frustrations involved in just trying to get lethargic and unmotivated bureaucracies to get back to you. Thus, both our budget and our release schedule would be completely out of our own hands. Releases can be delayed literally for years. As tiny independents, depending on only one release at a time, we can't proceed under those conditions. In effect, any attempt to be legal would shut us down.

So OK, we're just small potato heads, working in a way that wasn't foreseen by the law, and it's just too problematical, so why not just work some other way? We are working this way because it's just plain interesting, and emulating the various well-worn status quos isn't. How many artistic prerogatives should we be willing to give up in order to maintain our owner-regulated culture? The directions art wants to take may sometimes be dangerous, the risk of democracy, but they certainly should not be dictated by what business wants to allow. Look it up in the dictionary—art is not defined as a business! Is it a healthy state of affairs when business attorneys get to lock in the boundaries of experimentation for artists, or is this a recipe for cultural stagnation?

Negativland proposes some possible revisions in our copyright laws which would, very briefly, clear all restrictions from any practice of fragmentary appropriation. In general, we support the broad intent of copyright law. But we would have the protections and payments to artists and their administrators restricted to the straight-across usage of entire works by others, or for any form of usage at all by commercial advertisers. Beyond that, creators would be free to incorporate fragments from the creations of others into their own work. As for matters of degree, a "fragment" might be defined as "less than the whole," to give the broadest benefit of the doubt to unpredictability. However, a simple compilation of nearly whole works, if contested by the owner, would not pass a crucial test for valid, free appropriation. Namely: whether or not the material used is superceded by the new nature of the usage, itself—is the whole more than the sum of its parts? When faced with actual examples, this is usually not difficult to evaluate.

Today, this kind of encouragement for our natural urge to remix culture appears only vaguely within the copyright act under the "Fair Use" doctrine. The Fair Use statutes are intended to allow for free appropriation in certain cases of parody or commentary. Currently these provisions are conservatively interpreted and withheld from many "infringers." A huge improvement would occur if the Fair Use section of existing law was expanded or liberalized to allow any partial usage for any reason. (Again, "the whole is greater than the sum of its parts" test.) If this occurred, the rest of copyright law might stay pretty much as it is (if that's what we want) and continue to apply in all cases of "whole" theft for commercial gain (bootlegging entire works). The beauty of the Fair Use Doctrine is that it is the only nod to the possible need for artistic freedom and free speech in the entire copyright law, and it is already capable of overriding the other restrictions. Court cases of appropriation which focus on Fair Use and its need to be updated could begin to open up this cultural quagmire through legal precedent.

Until some such adjustments occur, modern societies will continue to find the corporate stranglehold on cultural "properties" in a stubborn battle with the common sense and natural inclinations of their user populations.

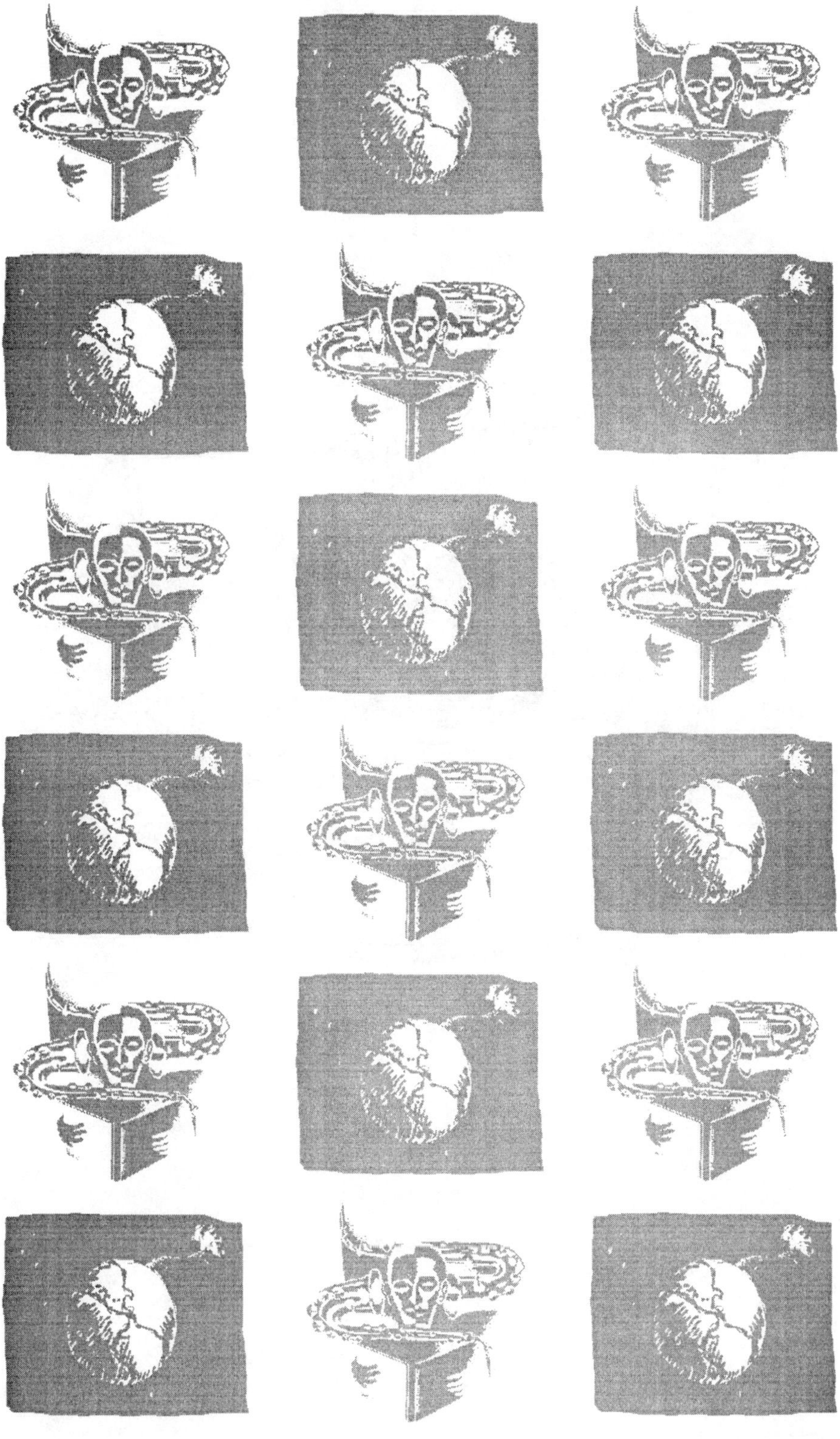

Esau Underhill

Soul Sonic Forces: Technology, Orality, and Black Cultural Practice In Rap Music

Tricia Rose

Rap music has inspired me because I know that when Chuck D tells you to 'bring the noise,' he's telling you that it's hard. And when you hear the tribal beat and the drums, they are the same drums of the African past that draws the community to war. The drum beats are just faster, because the condition is accelerating so they've got to beat faster. And when your feet are jumping, dancing...it's the spirit attempting to escape the entrapment. When you feel that the children have gone mad, if you don't feel it, and when you look at the dances you don't see it and when you listen to the music and you don't hear a call, then you missed the jam.

—Sister Souljah[1]

'The sound,' I tell them, that's the final answer to any question in music—the sound.

—Max Roach [2]

In the spring of 1989, I was speaking animatedly with an ethnomusicology professor about rap music and the aims of this project. He found some of my ideas engaging and decided to introduce me, and describe my project to, the chairman of his music department. At the end of his summary, the department head rose from his seat and announced casually, "Well, you must be writing on rap's social impact and political lyrics, because there is nothing to the music." My surprised expression and verbal hesitation gave him time to explain his position. He explained to me that, although the music was quite simple and repetitive, the stories told in the lyrics had social value. He pointed out rap's role as a social steam valve, a means for expression of social anger. "But," he concluded, referring to the music, "they ride down the street at 2:00 A.M. with it blasting from car speakers, and (they) wake up my wife and kids. What's the point in that?" I immediately flashed on a history lesson in which I learned that slaves were prohibited from playing African drums, because, as a vehicle for coded communication, they inspired fear in slaveholders. I suggested that perhaps the music was more complicated than it seemed to him, that a number of approaches to sound and rhythm were being explored in rap music. He listened but seemed closed to such possibilities. Having had some experience with these sorts of "what I don't know can't penetrate me" exchanges, I knew it would be prudent to disengage from this brewing disagreement before it became a long and unpleasant exchange. The ethnomusicology professor who had introduced me ushered us out of the chairman's office.

For the music chairman, automobiles with massive speakers blaring bass and drum heavy beats looped continuously served as an explanation for the insignificance of the music and diminished rap's lyrical and political salience as well. The music was "nothing" to him on the grounds of its apparent "simplicity" and "repetitiveness." Rap music was also "noise" to him, unintelligible yet aggressive sound that disrupted his familial domain ("they wake up my wife and kids") and his sonic territory. His legitimate and important question, "What is the point of that?" was offered rhetorically to justify his outright dismissal of the music, rather than presented seriously to initiate at least a hypothetical inquiry into a musical form that for him seemed at once to be everywhere and yet going nowhere. Let us take his question seriously: What is the point of rap's volume, looped drum beats, and bass frequencies? What meanings can be derived from the sound rap musicians have created? How is the context for its consumption connected to both its black cultural priorities and its sociological effects? His dismissive question is a productive point of entry into understanding rap's sonic power and presence. Rap's distinctive bass-heavy, enveloping sound does not rest outside of its musical and social power. Emotional power and presence in rap are profoundly linked to sonic force and one's receptivity to it. As Sister Souljah reminds her audience at Abyssinian Baptist Church: "When you feel the children gone mad, if you don't feel it... when you listen to the music and you don't hear a call, then you missed the jam."

Rap's black sonic forces are very much an outgrowth of black cultural traditions, the postindustrial transformation of urban life, and the contemporary technological terrain. Many of its musical practitioners were trained to repair and maintain new technologies for the privileged but have instead used these technologies as primary tools for alternative cultural expression. This advanced technology has not been straight forwardly adopted; it has been significantly revised in ways that are in keeping with long-standing black cultural priorities, particularly regarding approaches to sound organization. These revisions, especially the use of digital samplers, have not gone unnoticed by the music industry, the legal system and other institutions responsible for defining, validating, and policing musical production and distribution. Sampling technology and rap producers' commercially profitable use of sampled sounds have seriously challenged the current scope of copyright laws (which are based on notated compositions) and raised larger, more complex questions regarding fair use of musical property and the boundaries of ownership of musical phrases.

Rap's use of sampling technology, looped rhythmic lines, coupled with its significant commercial presence also raises questions about the relationship between industrial imperatives and their impact on cultural production (for example, formulas that streamline the sale of music as commercial radio's four-minute song cap or rap's reuse of previously recorded music). Or, are there cultural explanations for the musical structures in rap's use of electronic equipment?

At the same time as rap music has dramatically changed the intended use of sampling technology, it has also remained critically linked to black poetic traditions and the oral forms that underwrite them. These oral traditions and practices clearly inform the prolific use of collage, intertextuality, boasting, toasting, and signifying in rap's lyrical style and organization. Rap's oral articulations are heavily informed by technological processes, not only in the way such oral traditions are formulated, composed, and disseminated, but also in the way orally based approaches to narrative are embedded in the use of the technology itself. In this contentious environment, these black techno-interventions are often dismissed as nonmusical effects or rendered invisible. These hybrids between black music, black oral forms, and technology that are at the core of rap's sonic and oral power are an architectural blueprint for the redirection of seemingly intractable social ideas, technologies, and ways of organizing sounds along a course that affirms the histories and communal narratives of Afro-diasporic people.

* * *

> The organizing principle which makes the black style is rhythm. It is the most perceptible and the least material thing.
> —Léopold Sédar Senghor[3]

> Rhythm. Rap music is so powerful because of rhythm.   —Harmony[4]

Rap's rhythms—"the most perceptible, yet least material elements"—are its most powerful effect. Rap's primary force is sonic, and the distinctive, systematic use of rhythm and sound, especially the use of repetition and musical breaks, are a part of a rich history of New World black traditions and practices. Rap music centers on the quality and nature of rhythm and sound, the lowest, "fattest beats" being the most significant and emotionally charged. As rapper Guru has said, "If the beat was a princess, I'd marry it."[5] Many of the popular "Jeep beats" feature dark, strong, prominent, and riveting bass lines.[6] These musical lines dominate production—even at the expense of the rapper's vocal presence. The arrangement and selection of sounds rap musicians have invented via samples, turntables, tape machines, and sound systems are at once deconstructive (in that they actually take apart recorded musical compositions) and recuperative (because they recontexualize these elements creating new meanings for cultural sounds that have been relegated to commercial wastebins). Rap music revises black cultural priorities via new and sophisticated technological means. "Noise" on the one hand and communal countermemory on the other, rap music conjures and razes in one stroke.

These revisions do not take place in a cultural and political vacuum, they are played out on a cultural and commercial terrain that embraces black cultural products and simultaneously denies their complexity and coherence. This denial is partly fueled by a mainstream cultural adherence to the traditional paradigms of Western classical music as the highest legitimate standard for musical creation, a standard that at this point should seem, at best, only; marginally relevant in the contemporary popular music realm (a space all but overrun by Afrodiasporic sounds and multicultural hybrids of them). Instead, and perhaps because of, the blackening of the popular taste, Western classical music continues to serve as the primary intellectual and legal standard and point of reference for "real" musical complexity and composition. For these reasons, a comparative look at these two musical and cultural forces is of the utmost importance if we are to make sense of rap's music and the responses to it.

Rhythmic Repetition, Industrial Forces, and Black Practice

Unlike the complexity of Western classical music, which is primarily represented in its melodic and harmonic structures, the complexity of rap music, like many Afro-diasporic musics, is in the rhythmic and percussive density and organization.[7] "Harmony" versus "rhythm" is an oft-sited reduction of the primary distinctions between Western classical and African-derived musics. Still, these terms represent significant differences in sound organization and perhaps even disparate approaches to ways of perception, as it were. The outstanding technical feature of the Western classical music tradition is tonal functional harmony. Tonal functional harmony is based on clear, definite pitches and logical relations between them; on the forward drive toward resolution of a musical sequence that leads to a final resolution: the final perfect cadence. The development of tonal harmony critically confined the range of possible tones to twelve tones within each octave arranged in only one of two possible ways, major or minor. It also restricted the rhythmic complexity of European music. In place of freedom with respect to accent and measure, European music focused rhythmic activity onto strong and weak beats in order to prepare and resolve harmonic dissonance. Furthermore, as Christopher Small has argued, Western classical tonal harmony is structurally less tolerant of "acoustically illogical and unclear sounds, sound not susceptible to total control." Other critical features of classical music, such as the notation system and the written score—the medium through which the act of composition takes place—separate the composer from both the audience and the performer and sets limits on composition and performance.[8] This classical music tradition, like all major musical and cultural developments, emerged as part of a larger historical shift in European consciousness:

> [We see] changes in European consciousness that we call the Renaissance having its effect in music, with the personal, humanistic viewpoint substituted for the theocratic, universalistic viewpoint of the Middle Ages, expressed in technical terms by a great interest in chords and their effects in juxtaposition, and specifically in the perfect cadence and the suspended dissonance, rather that in polyphony and the independent life of the individual voice.[9]

Rhythm and polyrhythmic layering is to African and African-derived musics what harmony and the harmonic triad is to Western classical music. Dense configurations of independent, but closely related rhythms, harmonic and nonharmonic percussive sounds, especially drum sounds, are critical priorities in many African and Afro-diasporic musical practices. The voice is also an important expressive instrument. A wide range of vocal sounds intimately connected to tonal speech patterns, "strong differences between the various registers of the voice, even emphasizing the breaks between them," are deliberately cultivated in African and African-influenced musics.[10] Treatment, or "versioning," is highly valued. Consequently, the instrument is not simply an object or vehicle for displaying one's talents, it is a "colleague in the creation." And, most important for this discussion, African melodic phrases "tend to be short and repetition is common; in fact, repetition is one of the characteristics of African music." Christopher Small elaborates:

> A call-and-response sequence may go on for several hours, with apparently monotonous repetition of the same short phrase sung by a leader and answered by the chorus, but in fact subtle variations are going on all the time, not only in the melodic lines themselves but also in their relation to the complex cross-rhythms in the accompanying drumming or hand clapping...The repetitions of African music have a function in time which is the reverse of (Western classical) music—to dissolve the past and the future into one eternal present, in which the passing of time is no longer noticed.[11]

Rhythmic complexity, repetition with subtle variations, the significance of the drum, melodic interest in the bass frequencies, and breaks in pitch and time (e.g., suspensions of the beat for a bar or two) are also consistently recognized features of African-American musical practices. In describing black New World approaches to rhythm, Ben Sidran refers to Rudi Blesh's notion of "suspended rhythm" and Andre Hodier's description of "swing" as rhythmic tension over stated or implied meter.[12] Time suspension via rhythmic breaks—points at which the bass lines are isolated and suspended—are important clues in explaining sources of pleasure in black musics.

Approaches to sound, rhythm, and repetition in rap music exhibit virtually all of these traits. Rap music techniques, particularly the use of sampling technology, involve the repetition and reconfiguration of rhombic elements in ways that illustrate a heightened attention to rhythmic patterns and movement between such patterns via breaks and points of musical rupture. Multiple rhythmic forces are set in motion and then suspended, selectively. Rap producers construct loops of sound and then build in critical moments, where the established rhythm is manipulated and suspended. Then, rhythmic lines reemerge at key relief points. One of the clearest examples of this practice is demonstrated in "Rock Dis Funky Joint" by the Poor Righteous Teachers. The music and the vocal rapping style of Culture Freedom has multiple and complicated time suspensions and rhythmic ruptures of the musical and lyrical passages.[13] Busta Rhymes from Leaders of the New School, reggae rapper Shabba Ranks, British rapper Monie Love, Trech from Naughty by Nature, B-Real from Cypress Hill, and Das Efx are known especially for using their voices as percussive instruments, bending words, racing through phrases, pausing and stuttering through complicated verbal rhythms.

These features are not merely stylistic effects, they are aural manifestations of philosophical approaches to social environments. James A. Snead, working along the same lines as Small, offers a philosophical explanation for the meaning and significance of repetition and rupture in black culture. As we shall see, musical elements that reflect world views, these "rhythmic instinctions," are critical in understanding the meaning of time, motion, and repetition in black culture and are of critical importance to understanding the manipulation of technology in rap.

* * *

The rhythmic instinction to yield to travel beyond existing forces of life. Basically, that's tribal and if you wanna get the rhythm, then you have to join a tribe.
—A Tribe Called Quest[14]

The outstanding fact of late-twentieth-century European culture is its ongoing reconciliation with black culture. The mystery may be that it took so long to discern the elements of black culture already there in latent form, and to realize that the separation between the cultures was perhaps all along not one of nature, but of force.
—James A. Snead[15]

Snead suggests that the vast body of literature devoted to mapping the cultural differences between European—and African—derived cultures, which has characterized differences between European and black cultures as a part of "nature," are in fact differences in force; differences in cultural responses to the inevitability of repetition. Snead argues that repetition is an important and telling element in culture, a means by which a sense of continuity, security, and identification are maintained. This sense of security can be understood as, in fact, a kind of "coverage," both as insurance against sudden ruptures and as a way of hiding or masking undesired or unpleasant facts or conditions. Snead argues quite convincingly that all cultures provide coverage against loss of identity, repression, assimilation, or attack. Where they "differ among one another primarily [is] in the tenacity with which the 'cover-up' is maintained...grafting leeway to those ruptures in the illusion of growth which most often occur in the déjà vus of exact repetition." He suggests that when we view repetition in cultural forms we are not viewing the same thing repeated, but its transformation, "repetition is not just a formal ploy, but often the willed grafting onto culture of an essentially philosophical insight about the shape of time and history.... One may readily classify cultural forms based on whether they tend to admit or cover up these repeating constituencies within them."[16]

Snead claims that European culture "secrets" repetition, categorizing it as progression or regression, assigning accumulation and growth or stagnation to motion, whereas black cultures highlight the observance of repetition, perceiving it as circulation, equilibrium. In a fashion resembling Small, Snead argues that Western classical music uses rhythm mainly as "an aid in the construction of a sense of progression to harmonic cadence (and) repetition has been suppressed in favor of the fulfillment of the goal of harmonic resolution." Similarly, musicologist Susan McClary points out that "tonal music" (referring to the Western classical tradition) is "narratively conceived at least to the extent that the original key area—the tonic—also serves as the final goal. Tonal structures are organized teleologically, with the illusion of unitary identity promised at the end of each piece."[17]

To the contrary, Snead claims that black cultures highlight the observance of repetition, perceiving it as circulation and equilibrium, rather that as a regulated force that facilitates the achievement of a final harmonic goal. Drawing on examples in literature, religion, philosophy, and music, Snead elaborates on the uses and manifestations of repetition in black culture. For our purposes, his analysis of the meaning of repetition in black music is most relevant, specifically his description of rhythmic repetition and its relationship to the "cut":[18]

> In black culture, repetition means that the thing circulates, there in an equilibrium.... In European culture, repetition must be seen to be not just circulation and flow, but accumulation and growth. In black culture, the thing (the ritual, the dance, the beat) is there for you to pick up when you come back to get it. If there is a goal... it is always deferred; it continually 'cuts' back to the start, in the musical meaning of a 'cut' as an abrupt, seemingly unmotivated break (an accidental da capo)) with a series already in progress and a willed return to a prior series.... Black culture, in the 'cut,' 'builds' accidents into its coverage, almost as if to control their unpredictability.[19]

Deliberately "repetitive" in force, black musics (especially those genres associated with dance) use the 'cut' to emphasize the repetitive nature of the music by "skipping back to another beginning which we have already heard," making room for accidents and ruptures inside the music itself. In this formulation., repetition and rupture work within and against each other, building multiple circular musical lines that are broken and then absorbed or managed in the reestablishment of rhythmic lines.

Rap music uses repetition and rupture in new and complex ways, building on long-standing black cultural forces. Advances in technology have facilitated an increase in the scope of break beat deconstruction and reconstruction and have made complex uses of repetition more accessible. Now, the desired bass line or drum kick can be copied into a sampler, along with other desired sounds, and programmed to loop in any desired tempo or order. Rap music relies on the loop, on the circularity of rhythm and on the "cut" or the "break beat" that systematically ruptures equilibrium. Yet, in rap, the "break beat" itself is looped—repositioned as repetition, as equilibrium inside the rupture. Rap music highlights points of rupture as it equalizes them.

Snead calls James Brown "an example of a brilliant American practitioner of the 'cut'" and describes the relationship between established rhythmic patterns and the hiatus of the cut in Brown's work as a rupture that affirms the rhythmic pattern while it interrupts it. "The ensuing rupture," Snead claims, "does not cause dissolution of the rhythmic; quite to the contrary, it strengthens it." Snead's reading of James Brown as a brilliant practitioner of the "cut" is a prophetic one. Published in 1981, a number of years before hip-hop producers had communally declared James Brown's discography the foundation of the break beat, Snead could not have known that Brown's exclamations ("hit me!"/"take it to the bridge!"), rapid horn and drum accents, and bass lines would soon become the most widely used breaks in rap music.

Snead's approach presumes that music is fundamentally related to the social world, that music, like other cultural creations, fulfills and denies social needs, that music embodies assumptions regarding social power, hierarchy, pleasure, and worldview. This link between music and larger social forces, although not widely held in the field of musicology, is also critical to the work of Susan McClary, Christopher Small, and French political economist Jacques Attali. McClary, Small, and Attali demystify the naturalized, normalized status of nineteenth-century classical musical structures and conventions, positing an understanding of music's role as a way of perceiving the world and suggesting that every musical code is rooted in the social formations and technologies of its age.[20] These historically and culturally grounded interpretations of technological "advances" shed light on naturalized aesthetic parameters as they are embodied in equipment, illustrating the significance of culture in the development of technology.

Grounding music as a cultural discourse dismantles the causal link between rap's sonic force and the technological means for its expression. Rap producers' strategic use of electronic reproduction technology particularly sampling equipment, affirms stylistic priorities in the organization and selection of sounds found in many black diasporic musical expressions. Although rap music is shaped by and articulated through advanced reproduction equipment, its stylistic priorities are not merely by-products of such equipment.

On the question of repetition as a cultural force, Attali and Snead part company. For Attali and other cultural theorists, repetition is primarily considered a manifestation of mass culture, a characteristic of culture in the age of reproduction. The advent of recording technology signaled the emergence of a society of mass production and repetition. Repetition is, therefore, equated with industrial standardization, Attali claims, music becomes an industry and "its consumption ceases to be collective."[21] Similarly, Adorno describes the "break" in pre-swing jazz as "nothing other than a disguised cadence" and explains that, "the cult of the machine which is represented by unabated jazz beats involves a self-renunciation that cannot but take root in the form of a fluctuating uneasiness somewhere in the personality of the obedient."[22] "In mass culture," Fredric Jameson claims, "repetition effectively volatizes the original object—so that the student of mass culture has no primary object of study."[23]

Repetition does, in fact function as part of a system of mass production that structures and confines creative articulation; along these lines Adorno, Jameson, and Attali offer vital criticisms of the logic of massified culture in late capitalistic societies. Yet, repetition cannot be reduced to a repressive, industrial force. Nor is it sufficient to understand repetition solely as a by-product of the needs of industrialization. I do not mean to suggest that any of the cultural theorists would claim that repetition was nonexistent in preindustrial society. However, their focus on repetition as an industrial condition encourages mischaracterizations of the black popular cultural phenomenon, particularly those forms that privilege repetition and are prominently positioned in the commodity system.

If we assume that industrial production sets the terms for repetition inside mass-produced music, then how can alternative uses and manifestations of repetition that are articulated inside the commodity market be rendered perceptible? Rap music's use of rhythmic lines constructed with sampled loops of sound are particularly vulnerable to misreadings or erasures along these lines. Working inside the commodity market and with industrial technology, rap music uses rhythmic forces that are informed by mass reproduction technology, but it uses it in ways that affirm black cultural priorities that sometimes work against market forces. Yet, none of this is visible if all mass-produced repetition is understood primarily as a manifestation of mass culture. If rap can be so overwhelmingly mischaracterized, then what other musical and cultural practices have collapsed into the logic of industrial repetition, labeled examples of "cult-like" obedience? Adorno's massive misreading of the jazz break, beside betraying a severe case of black cultural illiteracy, is another obvious example of the pitfalls of reading musical structures in the popular realm as by-products of industrial forces.

Adorno, Jameson, and Attali, by constructing repetition as if it were a singular force, strongly suggest that mass production sets the terms for repetition and that any other cultural forms of repetition, once practiced inside systems of mass production, are subsumed by the larger logic of industrialization. Consequently, no other mass-produced or mass-consumed forms that privilege forms of repetition are accessible or relevant once inside this larger logic of industrial repetition.

Positioning repetition in the late capitalist markets as a consequence of that market, marginalizes or erases alternative uses of and relationships to repetition that might suggest collective resistance to that system. Repetition, then, is all too easily vilified, collapsed into the logic of the commodity system and is employed as a means by which to effectively erase the multiplicity of cultures and traditions present in contemporary Western societies. I am not suggesting that black culture supersedes the effects of commodification. Nor am I suggesting that black cultural priorities lie outside of (or completely in opposition to) mass cultural industries. Quite to the contrary, this is a call for readings of commodification that can accommodate multiple histories and approaches to sound organization. I am mostly concerned, here, with facile and all-too-frequent readings of repetition that apply and naturalize dominant cultural principles and consequently colonize and silence black approaches, which, in the case of American popular music especially, have significant and problematic, dare I say, racist, implications....[24]

Rap music is a technologically sophisticated and complex urban sound. No doubt, its forebears stretch far into the orally influenced traditions of African American culture. But the oral aspects of rap are not to be understood as primary to the logic of rap nor separate from its technological aspects. Rap is fundamentally literate and deeply technological. To interpret rap as a direct or natural outgrowth of oral African-American forms is to romanticize and decontextualize rap as a cultural form. It requires erasing rap's significant sonic presence and its role in shaping technological, cultural, and legal issues as they relate to defining and creating music. Retaining black cultural priorities is an active and often resistive process that has involved manipulating established recording policies, mixing techniques, lyrical construction, and the definition of music itself.

The lyrical and musical texts in rap are a dynamic hybrid of oral traditions, postliterate orality, and advanced technology. Rap lyrics are a critical part of a rapper's identity, strongly suggesting the importance of authorship and individuality in rap music. Yet, sampling as it is used by rap artists indicates the importance of collective identities and group histories. There are hundreds of shared phrases and slang words in rap lyrics, yet a given rap text is the personal and emotive voice of the rapper.[25] The music is a complex cultural reformulation of a community's knowledge and memory of itself. Rap lyrics and the sampled sounds that accompany them are highly literate and technological, yet they articulate a distinct oral past.

Like many groundbreaking musical genres, rap has expanded popular aural territory. Bringing together sound elements from a wide range of sources and styles and relying heavily on rich Afrodiasporic music, rap musicians' technological in(ter)ventions are not ends in and of themselves, they are means to cultural ends, new contexts in which priorities are shaped and expressed. Rap producers are not so much deliberately working against the cultural logic of Western classical musics as they are working with and among distinctly black practices, articulating stylistic and compositional priorities found in black cultures in the diaspora. As has been made clear, these practices do not take place in a cultural and political vacuum. Raps sonic forces are often contested on the grounds that they are not creative, constitute theft, and are nonmusical. In other cases, these black approaches to the use and manipulation of new technologies are rendered invisible as they are joyfully appreciated. Sampling, as employed by rap producers, is a musical time machine, a machine that keeps time for the body in motion and a machine that recalls other times, a technological process whereby old sounds and resonances can be embedded and recontextualized in the present. Rap technicians employ digital technology as instruments, revising black musical styles and priorities through the manipulation of technology. In this process of techno-black cultural syncretism, technological instruments and black cultural priorities are revised and expanded. In a simultaneous exchange rap music has made its mark on advanced technology, and technology has profoundly changed the sound of black music.

Endnotes

[1] Sister Souljah speaking at "We Remember Malcolm Day" held at Abyssinian Baptist Church in Harlem, New York, 21 February 1991.

[2] Cited in Mitch Berman and Susanne Wah Lee, "Sticking Power," *Los Angeles Times Magazine*, 15, September 1991, pp. 23–50.

[3] Léopold Sédar Senghor, "Standards critiques de l'art Africain," *African Arts/Arts d'Afrique*, Vol. 1, No. 1, (Autumn 1967), excerpted in John Miller Chernoff, *African Rhythm and African Sensibility: Aesthetics and Social Action in African Musical Idioms* (Chicago: University of Chicago Press, 1979), p. 22.

[4] Rose interview with female rapper Harmony, 14 June 1991.

[5] GangStarr, "Step in the Arena," *Step in the Arena* (Chryalis, 1990).

[6] Jeep beats are rap songs with especially heavy bass and drum sounds that are intended for play in automobiles, preferably with customized stereo systems. Album titles such as *Terminator X & The Valley of the Jeep Beats* (Columbia Records, 1991) and Marley Marl, *In Control*: Volume I, advertised as an album designed for "your steering pleasure," illustrate the centrality of heavy prominent beats in rap production. The August 1991 issue of *The Source*, a popular magazine that covers hip hop music culture and politics, also featured a Jeep slammers section that reviewed recent releases based in part on their value as jeep beats. Favored albums received comments such as, "fatter beats, thunderous beats, and street feel."

[7] Chernoff, *African Rhythm*; Dick Hebdige, *Cut n Mix: Culture, Identity and Caribbean Music* (London: Methuen, 1987); Levine, *Black Culture, Black Consciousness*; Maultsby, *Africanisms*; Eileen Southern, *The Music of Black Americans* (New York: Norton, 1971).

8 Christopher Small, *Music, Society, Education: An Examination of the Function of Music in Western, Eastern and African Cultures with its Impact on Society and its Use in Education* (New York: Schirmer, 1977), pp. 20–21. See also Christopher Small, *Music of the Common Tongue* (New York: Riverrun Press, 1987).

9 Small, *Music, Society, and Education*, pp. 9–10. See also John Storm Roberts, *Black Music of Two Worlds* (New York: William Morrow, 1974).

10 Rap's "human beat box" shares many vocal sounds found in African vocal traditions. Mark Dery describes this link: "The hums, grunts and glottal atacks of Central Africa's pygmies, the tongue clicks, throat gurgles and suction stops of the Bushmen of the Kalahari Desert, and the yodeling, whistling vocal effects of Zimbabwe's *m'bira* players all survive in in the mouth of percussion of such 'human beat box' rappers as Doug E. Fresh and Darren Robinson of the Fat Boys." Marc Dery, "Rap!" *Keyboard*, November 1988, p. 34.

11 Small, *Music, Society, Education*, pp. 54–55.

12 See also Ben Sidran, *Black Talk New York*: Holt, Reinhart & Winston, 1971), and Olly Wilson, "Black Music as Art," *Black Music Research Journal*, no. 3, 1–22, 1983.

13 Poor Righteous Teachers, "Rock Dis Funky Joint," *Holy Intellect* (Profile, 1990). See also Ice Cube, "The Bomb," *AmeriKKKa's Most Wanted* (Profile, 1990), and the Fu-schnickens, *Take It Personal* (Jive, 1992). Bear in mind that not all rap music deploys these characteristics equally. In particular, some of the earliest rap recordings used the instrumental side of a disco single verbatim as the sole musical accompaniment. This may, in part, be due to limited musical resources, as disc jockey performances that predate these recordings demonstrate substantial skill and complexity in rhythmic manipulation.

14 A Tribe Called Quest, "Youthful Expression," *People's Instinctive Travels and the Paths of Rhythm* (Jive Records, 1989/1990).

15 James A. Snead, "On Repetition in Black Culture," *Black America Literature Forum*, Vol. 15, No. 4, p. 153, 1981. Special thanks to AJ for this reference.

16 Snead, "Repetition," pp. 146–47. Culture is one of the most complex words in the English language. Culture, as I use it and as Snead uses it, is both a "whole way of life," which is manifest over the whole range of social activiities but is most evident in 'specifically cultural' activities—a language, styles of art, kinds of intellectual work; and an emphasis on a 'whole social order' within which a specifable culture in style of art and kinds of intellectual work, is seen as the direct or indirect product of an order primarily constituted by other social activities." From Raymond Williams, *The Sociology of Culture* (New York: Schocken, 1981), pp. 11–12. See also Raymond Williams, *Keywords* (Glasgow: Fontana, 1976).

17 Snead, "Repetition," p. 152, my italics; Susan McClary, *Feminine Endings* (Minneapolis: University of Minnesota Press, 1991), p. 155.

18 Snead also demonstrates that the recovery of repetition in twentieth-century European literature (e.g., Joyce, Faulkner, Woolf, Yeats, and Eliot) suggests that the dominance of nineteenth-century repression of European traditions that favored privileged uses of repetition and verbal rhythm in the telling "in favor of the illusion of narrative verisimilitude" may have "begun to ebb somewhat." Ibid., p. 152. For a range of discussions on form and meaning in black music and culture, see Graham Lock, *Forces in Nature: The Music and Thoughts of Anthony Braxton* (New York: Da Capo Press, 1988); Wole Soyinka, *Myth, Literature and the African World* (New York: Cambridge University Press, 1990); and Gates, *The Signifying Monkey*. Gates affirms Snead's argument regarding the centrality of repetition in black culture: "repetition and revision are fundamental to black artistic forms from painting and sculpture to music to language use," p. xxiv.

[19] Snead, "Repetition," p. 150.
[20] Susan McClary and Richard Leppert, eds., *Music and Society: The Politics of Composition, Performance and Reception* (New York: Cambridge University Press, 1989), and McClary, *Feminine Endings; Small, Common Tongue, and Music, Society, Education*; Jacques Attali, *Noise: The Political Economy of Music* (Minneapolis: University of Minnesota Press, 1985).
[21] Attali, *Noise*, p. 88.
[22] Theodore W. Adorno (with the assistance of George Simpson), "On Popular Music," in Simon Frith and Andrew Goodwin, eds., *On Record: Rock, Pop and the Written Word* (New York: Pantheon, 1990), p. 313. Also see T. W. Adorno, "On the Fetish-Character in Music and the Regression of Listening," in Andrew Arato and Eike Gebhardt, eds., *The Essential Frankfurt School Reader* (New York: Continuum, 1982), pp. 288–89.
[23] Fredric Jameson, "Reification and Utopia in Mass Culture," *Social Text*, Winter, 137, 1979.
[24] Richard Middleton's *Studying Popular Music* (Philadelphia: Open University Press, 1990) attempts to grapple with the question of repetition in popular music in his chapter on pleasure, value, and ideology in popular music (see esp. pp. 267–93). He finds that "popular common sense tends to see repetition as an aspect of mass production and market expoitation but often also associates it with the phenomenon of being 'sent,' particularly in relation to 'hypnotic' rhythmic repetition and 'primitive' audience trance.... How can we square a psychology of repetition and the historically specific Adornian notion of repetition as a function of social control?" (pp. 286–87). Middleton suggests that multiple determinations are operative at once. To illustrate his point, he compares Freud, Barthes, Deleuze, Guattari, Jameson, Rosolato, and Lacan on the question of repetition. The multiple determinations he offers cannot accomodate the kind of black approach to repetition as articulated by Snead and Small. In fact, none of the approaches he offers ground black practices in African traditions. Although he is quite aware of black cultural influences in popular music, in his mind these influences do not reflect an alternative approach to cultrural production; they are discrete black practices that are not constructed as a part of a larger approach. So, although he agrees that black musics privilege repetition (although not rhytmically complex uses of repetition, but "riffs, call-and-reponse, short unchanging rhythmic patterns"), it is a technique, not a manifestation of an alternative approach.
[25] See *Spin* (October 1988) for a hip hop slang dictionary.

Over the course of 1995, XRT will present several live
showcase opportunities for our listeners to enjoy
restaurants. This special sponsorship provi
opportunity to spotlight your busines
listeners.

Tom Frank

Alternative To What?

Tom Frank

It's Not Your Father's Youth Movement

There are few spectacles corporate America enjoys more than a good counterculture, complete with hairdos of defiance, dark complaints about the stifling "mainstream," and expensive accessories of all kinds. So now that the culture industry has nailed down the twenty-somethings, it comes as little surprise to learn that it has also uncovered a new youth movement abroad in the land, sporting all-new looks, a new crop of rock 'n' roll bands, and an angry new 'tude harsher than any we've seen before. Best of all, along with the media's Columbus-like discovery of this new "underground" skulking around exotic places like Seattle, consumers have been treated to what has undoubtedly been the swiftest and most profound shift of imagery to come across their screens since the 1960s. New soundtracks, new product design, new stars, new ads. "Alternative," they call it. Out with the old, in with the new.

Before this revelation, punk rock and its descendents had long been considered commercially unviable in responsible business circles because of their incorrigible angriness, their implacable hostility to the cultural climate that the major record labels had labored so long to build, as well as because of their difficult sound. Everyone knows pop music is supposed to be simple and mass-producible, an easy matter of conforming to simple genres, of acting out the standard and instantly recognizable cultural tropes of mass society: I love love, I'm sad sometimes, I like America, I like cars, I'm my own person, I'm something of a rebel, I'm a cowboy, on a steel horse I ride. And all through the '80s the culture industry knew instinctively that the music that inhabited the margins couldn't fit, didn't even merit consideration. So at the dawn of punk the American media, whose primary role has long been the uncritical promotion of whatever it is that Hollywood, the record labels, or the networks are offering at the time, lashed out at this strange, almost unfathomable movement. "Rock Is Sick," declared the cover of *Rolling Stone*. The national news magazines pronounced the uprising to be degeneracy of the worst variety, then proceeded to ignore it all through the following decade. Its listeners were invisible people, unmentionable on TV, film, and radio except as quasi-criminals. And in the official channels of music-industry discourse—radio, MTV, music magazines—this music and the tiny independent labels that supported it simply didn't exist.

But now, it seems, the turning of generations and the inexorable logic of the market have forced the industry to reconsider, and it has descended in a ravenous frenzy on what it believes to be the natural habitats of those it once shunned. Now we watch with interest as high-powered executives offer contracts to bands they have seen only once, college radio playlists become the objects of intense corporate scrutiny, and longstanding independent labels are swallowed whole in a colossal belch of dollars and receptions. Now *Rolling Stone* magazine makes pious reference to the pioneering influence of defunct bands like Big Black and Mission of Burma whose records they ignored when new. Now we enjoy a revitalized MTV that has hastily abandoned its pop origins to push "alternative" bands round the clock, a 50-million-watt radio station in every city that calls out to us from what is cleverly called "the cutting edge of rock." And now, after lengthy consultation with its "twenty-something" experts, the mass media rises as one and proclaims itself in solidarity with the rebels, anxious to head out to Lollapalooza on the weekend and 'mosh' with the kids, don flannel, wave their fists in the air, and chant lyrics that challenge parental authority.

Time magazine has finally smelled green in the music of what it longingly calls "the hippest venues going," and, in its issue of October 25, 1993, flings itself headlong into the kind of reckless celebrationism usually reserved only for the biggest-budget movies and the most successful TV shows. Salivating over the "anxious rebels" of "a young, vibrant alternative scene," it is all *Time* can do to avoid falling over itself in a delirious pirouette of steadily escalating praise. The magazine breathlessly details every aspect of the youngsters' deliciously ingenuous insurrection: they're "defiant," they're concerned with "purity and anticommercialism," they sing about "homes breaking," and—tastiest of all—they're upset about "being copied or co-opted by the mainstream." But for all this, *Time's* story on "alternative" rock never once mentions a band that is not a "co-optation," that still produces records on an actual independent label. As per the usual dictates of American culture, only money counts, and indie labels don't advertise in *Time*. So Pearl Jam, a major-label band that has made a career out of imitating the indie sounds of the late eighties, wins the magazine's accolades as the "demigod" of the new "underground," leading the struggle for "authenticity" and against "selling out."

Of course this is poor reporting, but journals like *Time* have always been more concerned with industry boosterism and the hard, profitable facts of making credible the latest packaging of youth culture than with a vague undefinable like "news." Thus while we read almost nothing about the still unmentionable world of independent rock, we are bombarded with insistences that Pearl Jam is the real rebel thing, the maximum leaders of America's new youth counterculture—assertions that are driven home by endless descriptions of the band going through all the varieties of insurgent posturing. They have a "keen sense of angst," and singer Eddie Vedder feels bad about the family problems of his youth. He rose to success from nowhere, too: he was a regular guy with a taste for living on the edge (much like the people in ads for sneakers and cars and jeans), a "gas station attendant and high school dropout," who thought up the band's lyrics while surfing. But Eddie's real sensitive also, a true Dionysian like Mick Jagger, with a "mesmerizing stage presence" that "reminded fans of an animal trying to escape from a leash." In fact, he's so sensitive that certain of the band's lyrics aren't included with the others on the album sleeve because "the subject matter is too painful for Vedder to see in print."

The gushing of official voices like *Time* make necessary a clarification that would ordinarily go without saying: among the indie-rock circles which they mimic and from which they pretend to draw their credibility, bands like Pearl Jam are universally recognized to suck.

Almost without exception, the groups and music that are celebrated as "alternative" are watery, derivative, and strictly second-rate; so uniformly bad, in fact, that one begins to believe that stupid shallowness is a precondition of their marketability. Most of them, like Pearl Jam, play pre-digested and predictable versions of formulaic heavy guitar rock, complete with moronic solos and hoarse masculine poutings. There is certainly nothing even remotely "alternative" about this sound, since music like this has long been the favorite of teenage boys everywhere; it's just the usual synthetic product, repackaged in a wardrobe of brand new imagery made up of thousands of fawning articles and videos depicting them as "rebels" this or "twenty-something" that. A band called the Stone Temple Pilots, who grace the cover of other national magazines, have distinguished themselves as the movement's bargain boys, offering renditions of all the various "alternative" poses currently fashionable: all in one package the consumer gets sullen angst, sexual menace, and angry pseudo-protest with imitation punk thrown in for no extra charge. Another group called Paw is exalted by their handlers and a compliant media as the premier product of the ever-so-authentic Kansas "scene," complete with album-cover photographs of farms and animals; their lukewarm mimicry of Nirvana hailed as a sort of midwestern "grunge." Never mind that the band's founders come from a privileged Chicago background and that they have long since alienated most of Lawrence's really good bands by publicly crowing that one of their number killed himself out of jealousy over Paw's major-label success. The sole remarkable feature of these otherwise stunningly mediocre bands is their singers' astonishing ability to warble the shallowest of platitudes with such earnestness, as though they have actually internalized their maudlin, Hallmark-worthy sentimentality. But we aren't supposed to be concerned with all this: the only thing that matters is that the latest product be praised to the skies; that new rebels triumph happily ever after over old.

As ever, the most interesting aspect of the industry's noisy clamoring and its self-proclaimed naughtiness is not the relative merits of the "alternative" culture products themselves, but the shift of imagery they connote. Forget the music; what we are seeing is just another overhaul of the rebel ideology that has fueled business culture ever since the 1960s, a new entrant in the long, silly parade of "countercultural" entrepreneurship. Look back at the ads and the records and the artists of the pre-Nirvana period: all the same militant protestations of non-conformity are there, just as they are in the ads and records and artists of the 70s and the 60s. Color Me Badd and Wham! once claimed to be as existentially individualist, as persecuted a group of "anxious rebels" as Rage Against the Machine now does. But by the years immediately preceding 1992, these figures' claims to rebel leadership had evaporated, and American business faced a serious imagery crisis. People had at long last tired of such obvious fakery, grown unconvinced and bored. No one except the most guileless teeny-boppers and the most insecure boomers fell for the defiant posturing of Duran Duran or Vanilla Ice or M.C. Hammer or Bon Jovi; especially when the ghettos began to burn, especially when the genuinely disturbing sounds of music that was produced without benefit of corporate auspices were finding ever wider audiences.

By the beginning of the new decade, the patina of daring had begun to wear thin on the eighties' chosen crop of celebrity-rebels. Entire new lines of insolent shoes would have to be designed and marketed; entire new looks and emblems of protest would have to be found somewhere. Consumerism's traditional claim to be the spokesman for our inchoate disgust with consumerism was hemorrhaging credibility, and independent rock, with its Jacobin "authenticity" obsession, had just the things capital required.

Out went the call for an "alternative" from a thousand executive suites, and overnight everyone even remotely associated with independent rock in Seattle—and Minneapolis,

Chapel Hill, Champaign, Lawrence, and finally Chicago—found themselves the recipients of unsolicited corporate attention. Only small adjustments were required to bring the whole universe of corporate-sponsored rebellion up to date, to give us Blind Melon instead of Frankie Goes to Hollywood; 10,000 Maniacs instead of Sigue Sigue Sputnik. And suddenly we were propelled into an entirely new hip paradigm, a new universe of cool, with all new stars and all new relationships between the consumer, his celebrities, and his hair.

And now Pepsi is no longer content to cast itself as the beverage of Michael Jackson or Ray Charles or even Madonna: these figures' hip has been obsoleted suddenly, convincingly, and irreparably. Instead we watch a new and improved, an even more anti-establishment Pepsi Generation, cavorting about to what sounds like "grunge" rock; engaged in what appears to be a sort of oceanside slam dance. *Vanity Fair*, a magazine devoted strictly to the great American pastime of celebrating celebrity, hires the editors of a noted "alternative" zine to overhaul its hipness; *Interview*, the great, stupid voice of art as fashion, runs a lengthy feature on college radio, the site of the juiciest, most ingenuously "alternative" lifestyle innovations in the land. Ad agencies and record labels compete with each other in a frenzied scramble to hire leading specimens of the "alternative" scene they have ignored for fifteen years. Even commercial radio stations have seen the demographic writing on the wall and now every city has one that purports to offer an "alternative" format, featuring musical hymns to the various rebellious poses available to consumers at malls everywhere.

In the same spirit the Gap has enlisted members of Sonic Youth and the cloying pop band Belly to demonstrate their products' continuing street-cred; Virginia Slims has updated its vision of rebel femininity with images of a woman in flannel sitting astride a motorcycle and having vaguely '60s designs painted on her arm. Ralph Lauren promotes its astoundingly expensive new line of pre-weathered blue jeans and flannel shirts with models done up in "dreadlocks" and staring insolently at the camera. The United Colors of Benetton hone their subversive image by providing the costume for indie-rock figure "Lois." Another firm offers "Disorder Alternative Clothing" for the rebellious grungy "few who are tired of the mainstream." Quite sensibly, the makers of Guess clothing prefer imagery of an idealized "alternative" band, played by models, to the real thing, since actual rock 'n' rollers rarely sate the company's larger obsession with human beauty. So there they stand, in a pose that just screams "authentic": four carefully unshaven guys in sunglasses, grimaces, and flannel shirts, each with a bandana or necklace suspended carefully from their neck, holding guitar cases and trying to look as hardened, menacing, and hip as possible, with a lone blonde babe clinging off to one side. In another ad the Guess Clothing fantasy band are pictured "in concert," a flannel-clad guitarist spotlit with eyes closed, stretching one hand out to the heavens in an anthemic consumer epiphany.

But the most revealing manifestation of the new dispensation is something you aren't supposed to see: an ad for MTV that ran in the business sections of a number of newspapers. "Buy this 24-year-old and get all his friends absolutely free," its headline reads. Just above these words is a picture of the 24-year-old referred to, a quintessential "alternative" boy decked out in the rebel garb that the executives who read this ad will instantly recognize from their market reports to be the costume of the "twenty-somethings": beads and bracelets, a vest and T-shirt, torn jeans, Doc Martens and a sideways haircut like the Jesus and Mary Chain wore in 1985. His pose: insolent, sprawled insouciantly in an armchair, watching TV of course. His occupation: consumer. "He watches MTV," continues the ad, "Which means he knows a lot. More than just what CDs to buy and what movies to see. He knows what car to drive and what credit cards to use. And he's no loner. What he eats, his friends eat. What he wears, they wear. What he likes, they like."

Thus with the "alternative" face-lift, "rebellion" continues to perform its traditional function of justifying the economy's ever-accelerating cycles of obsolescence with admirable efficiency. Since our willingness to load up our closets with purchases depends upon an eternal shifting of the products paraded before us, upon our being endlessly convinced that the new stuff is better than the old, we must be persuaded over and over again that the "alternatives" are more valuable than the existing or the previous. Ever since the 1960s hip has been the native tongue of advertising, "anti-establishment" the vocabulary by which we are taught to cast off our old possessions and buy whatever they have decided to offer this year. And over the years the rebel has naturally become the central image of this culture of consumption, symbolizing endless, directionless change, an eternal restlessness with "the establishment"—or, more correctly, with the stuff "the establishment" convinced him to buy last year.

Not only did the invention of "alternative" provide capital with a new and more convincing generation of rebels, but in one stroke it has obsoleted all the rebellions of the past ten years, rendered our acid-washed jeans, our Nikes, our DKNYs meaningless. Are you vaguely pissed off at the world? Well, now you get to start proving it all over again, with flannel shirts, a different brand of jeans, and big clunky boots. And in a year or two there will be an "alternative" to that as well, and you'll get to do it yet again.

It's not only the lure of another big Nirvana-like lucre-glut that brings label execs out in droves to places like Seattle, or hopes of uncovering the new slang that prompts admen to buy journals like *The Baffler*. The culture industry is drawn to "alternative" by the more general promise of finding the eternal new, of tapping the very source of the fuel that powers the great machine. As *Interview* affirms, "What still makes the genre so cool is not its cash potential or hype factor but the attendant drive and freedom to create and discover fresh, new music." Fresh new music, fresh new cars, fresh new haircuts, fresh new imagery.

Thus do capital's new dancing flunkeys appear not in boater hat and ingratiating smile, but in cartoonish postures of sullen angst or teen frustration: dyed hair, pierced appendages, flannel shirt around the waist. Everyone in advertising remembers how frightening and enigmatic such displays were ten years ago when they encountered them in TV stories about punk rock, and now their time has come to be deployed as the latest signifiers of lifestyle savvy. Now it's executives themselves on their days off, appearing in their weekend roles as kings of the consumer hill, who flaunt such garb, donning motorcycle jackets and lounging around the coffeehouses they imagine to be frequented by the latest generation of angry young men. Of course every other persecuted-looking customer is also an advertising account exec or a junior vice president of something-or-other; of course nobody would ever show up to see a band like, say, the New Bomb Turks or Prisonshake in a costume like this. As ever, *Interview* magazine, the proudest exponent of the commercialization of dissent, explains the thinking of the corporate mandarin who has now decided to dude himself up in a Sid Vicious leather jacket and noticeable tattoo. Punk, as the magazine triumphantly announces in a recent issue, has been successfully revived as a look only, happily stripped of any problematic ideological baggage: maybe '90s punk is just a great high style. Some will slash their own clothes, and others will clamor after the fashions of rule-slashing designers. (Are there ever any designers who don't claim to "slash rules?") If your mother doesn't like it, who cares? If your kid is embarrassed, stand proud. If your bosses fire you for it, screw 'em. And if people stare at you in the street, isn't that the point?

So on we plod through the mallways of our lives, lured into an endless progression of shops by an ever-changing chorus of manic shaman-rebels, promising existential freedom—sex! ecstasy! liberation!—from the endless trudge. All we ever get, of course, are some more or less baggy trousers or a hat that we can wear sideways. Nothing works, we are still entwined in vast coils of tawdriness and idiocy, and we resolve not to be tricked again. But lo! Down the way is a new rebel-leader, doing handstands this time, screaming about his untrammelled impertinence in an accent that we know could never be co-opted, and beckoning us into a shoe store. Marx's quip that the capitalist will sell the rope with which he is hanged begins to seem ironically incomplete. In fact, with its endless ranks of beautifully coiffed, fist-waving rebel boys to act as barker, business is amassing great sums by charging admission to the ritual simulation of its own lynching.

Interlude: Come Around to My Way of Thinking

Perhaps the only good thing about the commodification of "alternative" is that it will render obsolete, suddenly, cleanly, and inexorably, that whole flatulent corpus of "cultural studies" that seeks to appreciate Madonna as some sort of political subversive. Even though the first few anthologies of writings on the subject only appeared in 1993, the rise of a far more threatening generation of rock stars has ensured that this singularly annoying pedagogy will never become a full-fledged "discipline," with its own lengthy quarterly issued by some university press, with annual conferences where the "subaltern articulations" of "Truth or Dare" are endlessly dissected and debated.

Looking back from the sudden vantage point that only this kind of image-revolution affords, the scholarship of academia's Madonna fans now appears as predictable in its conclusions as it was entertaining in its theoretical pyrotechnics. After careful study of the singer's lyrics and choreography, the professors breathlessly insisted, they had come upon a crucial discovery: Madonna was a gender-questioning revolutionary of explosive potential, a rule-breaking avatar of female empowerment, a person who disliked racism! One group of gaping academics hailed her "ability to tap into and disturb established hierarchies of gender and sexuality." Another celebrated her video "Vogue" as an "attempt to enlist us in a performance that, in its kinetics, deconstructs gender and race," an amusing interpretation, to be sure, but also one which could easily have been translated into academese directly from a Madonna press kit.

The problem is not that academics have abandoned their sacred high-culture responsibilities for a channel changer and a night at the disco, but that in so doing they have uncritically reaffirmed the mass media's favorite myths about itself. Discovering, after much intellectual twisting and turning, that Madonna is exactly the rebel that she and her handlers imagine her to be, is more an act of blithe intellectual complicity than of the "radicalism" to which the Madonna analysts believe they are contributing. After all, it was Madonna's chosen image as liberator from established mores that made her so valuable to the culture industry in the first place. It doesn't take a genius to realize that singing the glories of pseudo-rebellion remains to this day the monotone anthem of advertising, film, and TV sitcom, or that the pseudo-rebel himself—the defier of repressive tradition, ever overturning established ways to make way for the new; the self-righteous pleasure-monad, changing identity, gender, hair color, costume, and shoes on a whim—is more a symbol of the machine's authority than an agent of resistance. But academics seem to have missed the point. For years the culture industry has held up for our admiration an unending parade of such self-proclaimed subverters of middle-class tastes, and certain scholars have been only too glad to play their part in the strange charade, studying the minutiae of the various artists' rock videos and deciding, after long and careful deliberation, that yes, each one is, in fact, a bona fide subversive. How thoroughly had they come around to the Industry's way of thinking; how desperately did they want to, want to get along!

But thanks to the rise of "alternative," with its new and vastly improved street "cred," sneers, and menacing hairdos, the various postmodern courses by which each scribbler arrived at his or her conclusion that Madonna is "subverting" from within, and the particular costly academic volume in which they presented their "findings" are now, thankfully, finally, and irresistibly made irrelevant. Just as Madonna's claims to rebel authenticity have been made suddenly laughable by an entirely new package of much more rebellious rebel imagery, so their works are consigned to the same fate. Academia's Madonna fans have built their careers by performing virtually the same task, with a nice intellectual finish, as the toothy hosts of "Entertainment Tonight," and now they are condemned to the same rubbish bin of instant forgetting. Their embrace of corporate culture has brought them face to face with its unarguable conclusions, the steel logic of its unprotestable workings: obsolescence.

In at least one sense, then, the triumph of Urge Overkill is a liberation. At least we will never, ever have to hear this favorite Paglian (or, should we say, all-American) platitude chanted for the thousand-and-first time: "I admire Madonna because she's a woman who's totally in control of her career." And since it will take at least three years for the first close readings of the "Sister Havana" video to appear in assigned texts, let us enjoy the respite and ponder the strange twists of history that brought academia so closely into line with the imperatives of mass culture.

In this spirit, I offer the following observation.

Perhaps the saddest aspect of all this is not scholars' gullible swallowing of some industry publicist's line, or even their naïve inability to discern Madonna's obvious labor-fakery. The real disappointment lies in their abject inability to recognize "popular culture" anywhere but in the officially-sanctioned showplaces of corporate America; their utter dependence on television to provide them with an imagery of rebellion. Even as they delved deeper and deeper into the esoterica of poststructuralist theory, investing countless hours scrutinizing bad rock videos frame by frame, they remained hopelessly ignorant of the actual insurgent culture that has gone on all around them for fifteen years, for the simple reason that it's never made MTV. And academics, the wide-eyed, well-scrubbed sons and daughters of the suburbs, cannot imagine a "counterculture" that exists outside of their full-color, 36-inch screens. So in TV-land as well as the academy, Madonna was as "radical" as it got. Thus did the role of criticism become identical to that of the glossy puff magazines, with their well-practiced slavering over the latest products of the Culture Industry: to celebrate celebrity, to find an epiphany in shopping, a happy heteroglossia in planned obsolescence. As for their interpretations, the professorial class might just as well have been proclaiming the counter-hegemonic undercurrents of "Match Game" or the patriarchy-resisting profundity of Virginia Slims advertising.

Imagine what they could do if they only knew about Borbetomagus or Merzbow!

Fuck You and Your Underground

At the center of the academics' intricate webs of Madonna-theories lay the rarely articulated but crucial faith that the workings of the culture industry, the stuff that comes over our TV screens and through our stereos, are profoundly normal. The culture-products that so unavoidably define our daily lives, it is believed, are a given—a natural expression of the tastes of "the people." This has long been a favorite sophistry of the industry's paid publicity flacks as well: mass culture is fundamentally democratic. The workings of the market ensure that the people get what the people want; that sitcoms and Schwarzenegger and each of the various sneering pop stars are the embodiment of the general will. Thus, as the academic celebrators of Madonna were always careful to assert, those who insist on criticizing Madonna are deeply suspicious, affected adherents of an elitist and old-fashioned aesthetic that unfairly dismisses "low" culture in favor of such insufferably stuffy pastimes as ballet and opera.

This anti-elitist theme is, quite naturally, also a favorite in sitcoms and movies, which establish their hegemony over the public mind by routinely bashing various stock snobs and hapless highbrow figures. Advertising repeatedly strikes the same note: a drink called "Somers" is to gin, one ad asserts, as a bright green electric guitar, implement of transgressive cool, is to an old brown violin, squeaky symbol of the slow-moving. A Pizza Hut commercial similarly juxtaposes a moralizing, old-fashioned stuffed-shirt man who is filmed in black and white, with a full-color, rock 'n' roll rendition of the restaurant of revolt. And when the straw man of "cultural elitism" is conjured up by the academics for its ritual stomping, the feeling is exactly the same. There is only the dry, spare, highbrow of the privileged and the lusty, liberated lowbrow of the masses, and between these two the choice is clear.

This, then, is the culture of "the people." Never mind all the openly conducted machinations of the culture industry—the mergers and acquisitions, the "synergy," the admen's calculations of "penetration" and "usage pull," the dismantling of venerable publishing operations for reasons of fiscal whimsy. What the corporations have decided we will watch and read and listen to is somehow passed off as the grass-roots expressions of the nation. And this is a crucial financial distinction, since the primary business of business is no longer, say, making things or exploiting labor, but manufacturing culture, finding the means to make you buy and consume as much as you possibly can, convincing you of the endless superiority of the new over the old, that the solution to whatever your unhappiness may be lies in a few new purchases. It is a truism of the business world that Coke and Pepsi don't make soda pop; they make advertising. Nike may pay Asian laborers starvation wages, but their most important concern is convincing us that it is meaningful, daring, and fulfilling to spend over one hundred dollars for a pair of sneakers. If you feel a burning need to understand "culture," get out of the coffee house and buy yourself a subscription to *Advertising Age*.

The media-flurry over the definition of the "twenty-somethings" provides an interesting example of the ways in which "popular culture" is made, not born. Between the multitude of small presses and independent record labels that were founded, produced, and distributed by young people over the last decade, we have been a remarkably articulate, expressive group. But this is not what was meant when the various lifestyle journalists and ad agency hacks went looking for "Generation X." The only youth culture that concerned them was the kind that's pre-fabricated for us in suites on the Sunset Strip and Madison Avenue, and the only question that mattered was how to refine this stuff so that we, too, could be lured into the great American consumer maelstrom. Take a look at the book *13th Gen* by Neil Howe and Bill Strauss, the most baldfaced attempt to exploit the culture industry's confusion about how to pigeonhole us. As with the *Time* article on Pearl Jam, the book's lengthy cataloguing of "twenty-something" culture never once even mentions an actual indie-label band or a magazine produced by young people; all that matters are the movies, the TV sitcoms, the major-label records that are targeted our way. The book's press kit (which, again, you aren't supposed to see) explicitly cast *13th Gen* as a useful guide for executives in the advertising, public-relations, and election-winning industries. We are to be sold, not heard.

Under no condition is "popular culture" something that we make ourselves, in the garage with electric guitars and second-hand amplifiers, on the office photocopier when nobody's looking. It is, strictly and exclusively, the stuff produced for us in a thousand corporate boardrooms and demographic studies. "Popular culture" doesn't enlighten, doesn't seek to express meaning or shared aspects of our existence; on the contrary, it aims to make people stupid and complacent. "Popular culture" sells us stuff, convinces us to buy more soap or a different kind of shirt, assures us of the correctness of business paternalism, offers us a rebel fantasy world in which to drown our never-to-be-realized frustration with lives that have become little more than endless shopping trips, marathon filing sessions.

"Popular culture" is the Enemy; Rock 'n' Roll is the Health of the State

In such a climate, the old highbrow/lowbrow categorization becomes utterly irrelevant: who cares about the intricacies of Brahms when the world is being made and unmade anew every day by the power-tie and mobile-phone wielding commissars of public awareness? The great American cultural conflict has nothing to do with the clever *pas de deux* of affected outrage acted out by sputtering right-wingers and their blustering counterparts in Soho and Hollywood. It is not concerned with twaddle like "family values" or "cultural elitism," but with a much more basic issue: the power of each person to make his own life without the droning, quotidian dictation of business interests. If we must have grand, sweeping cultural judgments, only one category matters anymore: the adversarial. The business of business is our minds, and the only great divide that counts in music, art, or literature, is whether or not they give us the tools to comprehend, to resist, to evade the all-invasive embrace.

But between the virtual monopoly of business interests over the stuff you spend all day staring at and the decision of the academics to join the burgeoning and noisy legion of culture industry cheerleaders, very little that is adversarial is allowed to filter through. Our culture has been hijacked without a single cry of outrage. However we may fantasize about Madonna's challenging of "oppressive tonal hierarchies," however we may drool over Pearl Jam's rebel anger, there is, quite simply, almost no dissent from the great cultural project of corporate America, no voice to challenge television's overpowering din. You may get a different variety of shoes this year, but there is no "alternative," ever.

And yet it is not for nothing that the rebel is the paramount marketing symbol of the age. Beneath all the tawdry consumer goods through which we are supposed to declare our individuality—the earrings, the sunglasses, the cigarettes, the jackets, the shoes; beneath the obvious cultural necessities of an obsolescence-driven business regime, we find something deeply meaningful in the image of the free-spirit. We need the rebel because we know that there is something fundamentally wrong.

"Something fundamentally wrong." So ubiquitous is this feeling, so deeply entrenched is this unspoken but omnipresent malaise, that it almost seems trite as soon as the words are set on the page. And yet only the simplest, least aware, and most blithely comfortable among us retain any sort of faith in the basic promises of our civilization. Violence, fear, deterioration, and disorder are the omnipresent daily experiences of one class; meaninglessness, mandatory servility, and fundamental dishonesty inform every minute in the lives of another. Conrad's horror and Eliot's futility have become the common language of everyday life. We want out, and the rebel, whether of the "artistic," beatnik variety, the inner-city gangster type, or the liberated star-figures of "alternative" rock, has become the embodiment of our longings.

It is due only to the genius of the market that these desires have been so effectively prevented from achieving any sort of articulation, so cleverly and so imperceptibly channeled into dumb politics and simple acts of consuming, into just more and more and more of the same.

We may never be able to dismantle the culture of consumption and we will almost surely never achieve any sort of political solution to the problems of this botched civilization. Quite simply, no platform exists from which the monomessage of the media might be countered. The traditional organs of resistance, enfeebled by decades of legislative attack and a cultural onslaught they do not comprehend, have either made their peace with consumerism or cling to outdated political goals.

But through the deafening mechanical yammering of a culture long since departed from the rails of meaning or democracy, through the excited hum of the congregation gathered for mandatory celebrity-worship, there is one sound that insists on making sense, that speaks piercingly through the fog of fakery, the airy, detached formulas of official America. Punk rock, hardcore, indie rock, the particular name that's applied is not important: but through its noise comes the scream of torment that is this country's only mark of health; the sweet shriek of outrage that is the only sign that sanity survives amid the stripmalls and hazy clouds of Hollywood desire. That just beyond the silence of suburban stupidity, the confusion of the parking lots, the aggression, display, and desperate supplication of the city streets, the possibility of a worthy, well-screamed no survives. Just behind the stupefying smokescreens of authorized "popular culture" seethes something real, thriving on the margins, condemned to happy obscurity both by the marketplace, to whose masters (and consumers) its violent negation will be forever incomprehensible, and by the academic arbiters of "radicalism," by whom the "culture of the people" is strictly understood to be whatever the corporate donors say it is. Unauthorized and unauthorizable, it clamors in tones forbidden amid the pseudo-rebel propriety of the cultural avenues of the empire: complete, overriding disgust; routine degradation under the tutelage of the machine; a thousand mundane unmentionables like the sheer exhausting idiocy of shopping, the dark and not at all amusing vacancy of celebrity (because no matter what skillful postmodern maneuvers of ironic rationalization they make, the institution of celebrity requires, at its base, the unironic, and very real, mental surrender of millions of people in such places as Toledo and Detroit and Kansas City), the grinding inescapable ruination of the everyday, the mind-numbing boredom, the You're All Twisted, violence, distrust, anger. It is the frenzied transgression of the TV mandatory, the sudden giggling realization that something has finally come close, confronted the electronic fist with such forceful extremist honesty, with an openness so utterly foreign to the "realistic" violence of the Hollywood blockbuster, the scopophilia of the sex drama. For them it's fantasies of the comfortable *cul-de-sac* with state-of-the-art security equipment, the fine car, the airborne curfew enforcement unit, the Lake Forest estate, the Westchester commute; for us it's the secession, the internal exile, the purging clean pure no; the unnuanced thrashing release, the glorious never never never, the Won't Fit the Big Picture, the self-losing refusal to ever submit, the I'm not not not not not not not your academy.

For this expression of dissent there has been no Armory show, no haughty embrace by aesthetes or editors. The only recognition it has garnered is the siege equipment of the consumer age, a corporate-sponsored shadow movement that seeks to mine it for marketable looks, imitable sounds, menacing poses. A travelling youth circus patterned, of course, after the familiar boomer originals of Woodstock and Dead shows, is invented to showcase the new industry dispensations. But so strange, so foreign to the executive are our "punk rock" rantings that they are forced to hire "youth consultants" to explain us to them, to pay marketing specialists vast sums to do nothing but decode our puzzling signifiers. For while we were discovering paths of resistance, the people who are now manufacturing, marketing, and consuming "alternative" product were busily transforming themselves into mandarins at business school, were honing themselves dumber and dumber at the college paper, were practicing their professional skills in the bathrooms of the frat houses. Only lately have they discovered that we're "hip," that our look has "potential," that our music "rocks."

So now, with their bottomless appetite for new territory to colonize, they've finally come around to us. For years they were too busy working their way up the corporate ladder to be bothered, but now what we have been building has begun to look usable, even marketable. But they won't find it easy. Ours is a difficult country, with all sorts of arcane pitfalls that will require an ever-mounting payroll of expensive consultant-guides, many of whom will lead them astray just for the sheer joy of seeing the machine seize up, of watching suburbanites wander about clad in ridiculous slang and hairdos. (Who was it that foisted Paw on A&M?)

We will not be devoured easily. Few among us are foolish enough to believe that "the music industry" is just a bigger version of the nextdoor indie label, just a collection of simple record companies gifted mysteriously with gargantuan budgets and strange powers to silence criticism. Few consider the glorified publicity apparatus that we call media as anything other than an ongoing attack by the nation's owners on the addled minds of the great automaton audience. We inhabit an entirely different world, intend entirely different outcomes. Their culture-products aim explicitly for enervated complacency; we call for resistance. They seek fresh cultural fuel so that the machinery of stupidity may run incessantly; we cry out from under that machine's wheels. They manufacture lifestyle; we live lives.

So as they venture into the dark new world of hip, they should beware: the natives in these parts are hostile, and we're armed with flame-throwers. We will refuse to do their market research for them, to provide them amiably with helpful lifestyle hints and insider trend know-how. We are not a convenient resource available for exploitation whenever they require a new transfusion of rebel street cred; a test-market for "acts" they can someday unleash on the general public. And as they canvass the college radio stations for tips on how many earrings and in which nostril, or for the names of the "coolest" up-and-coming acts, they will find themselves being increasingly misled, embarrassed by bogus slang, deceived by phantom blips on the youth-culture futures index, anticipating releases from nonexistent groups. It has taken years to win the tiny degree of autonomy we now enjoy. No matter which way they cut their hair or how weepily Eddie Vedder reminisces about his childhood, we aren't about to throw it open to a process that in just a few years would leave us, too, jaded and spent, discarded for yet a newer breed of rebels, an even more insolent crop of imagery, looks, and ads. Sanity isn't that cheap.

ASSAULT REPORT

Vibes of the Time

SABOTAGE

Superpower Contention

Ron Sakolsky

World Beat and the Cultural Imperialism Debate

Andrew Goodwin & Joe Gore

Contemporary debates about global culture can be characterized by a tension between two competing (although not necessarily conflicting) approaches: on the one hand there is a long tradition of Marxist and neo-Marxist analyses of imperialism, in which culture and the arts are seen to reflect the international organization of social relations. In a variety of ways which we will elaborate later in this essay, this position sees inequalities in the economic and political spheres refracted in the arts and media. More recently, however, media and cultural studies scholars have developed models that de-emphasize the importance of ownership and that examine the potentially subversive and/or "progressive" nature of the Western culture industries.

That debate forms one axis for discussion in our exploration of World Beat music. The other related site of debate concerns the specifics of World Beat, or World Music, itself. Here we refer both to those forms of music which fuse traditional and third world musics with sounds and structures derived from Anglo-American pop, and to Western appropriations of non-Western folk musics. In response to recent interest in World Musics, two opposing camps can be distinguished. In the first place, critics of the burgeoning market for non-Western pop identify old forms of exploitation, as Anglo-American musicians re-appropriate and perhaps even corrupt traditional third world cultures—often with inadequate financial recompense or (in the case of Paul Simon's *Graceland* project)[1] in the teeth of politically progressive opposition. On the other hand, a more optimistic scenario is sketched out by those critics who see World Beat as a progressive intervention within Western culture. As we will suggest in this essay, the inadequacies of the two positions on World Beat (the first is too cynical, the second is too naive) mirror, and surely partially derive from the inadequacies of the cultural imperialism positions outlined earlier.

The emergence of World Beat as a new category of popular music over the last ten years suggests an element of feedback in the "one-way flow" which has often characterized global communications. Where many on the left have seen rock and pop music as classic examples of cultural imperialism (not only for third world nations, but also for Europeans—and Canadians—hostile to the commercial culture of the United States), World Beat turns the tables, opening up a line of communication *from* music producers in Africa, Latin America, Asia and Eastern Europe, to listeners in the United States and Western Europe (especially in

Britain and France, where World Beat is circulated more widely than in the United States). Furthermore, World Beat's use of the forms of commercial Anglo-American culture defies simple notions of "media imperialism," in which the products of the West are defined as purely hegemonic and/or instrumental for transnational capitalism.

In this essay we want to consider the political implications of World Beat music, through an analysis of the very complex ways in which popular music intersects issues of cultural and media imperialism. Although we do have some general suggestions to make regarding the wider debate about cultural imperialism, we believe that it is more important to note the need for political analyses of popular culture which pay far greater heed to the specificities of media forms. In the case of World Beat, even elementary musical analysis reveals the dangers of conflating the particularities of diverse media (film, print, television, music, etc.) into a catch-all category of "media imperialism."

The Construction of World Beat

The term World Beat was coined by Dan Del Santo, an Austin, Texas-based bandleader and DJ. (Jack Kerouac wrote about tuning into a cosmic "world beat" in the final pages of *On the Road*, and if there isn't a conscious connection between this and later uses of the term, the link between the Beat aesthetic and rock and roll is obvious enough.) Del Santo's 1982 album *World Beat* followed in the wake of earlier country music and R&B efforts—this music blended R&B, afrobeat and calypso forms. In 1983 the term was adopted by a loose aggregation of San Francisco musicians (Joe Gore among them), who wanted a convenient label for their fusion of rock, funk, African and Afro-Caribbean musics. This movement attained considerable regional popularity and some national media attention before fizzling out in the mid-1980s.

Since then the term World Beat has become a fashionable label for any music that originates in, or borrows substantially from, the musical traditions of regions other than North America and Western Europe. Even some American and European "minority" musics have been accommodated under the World Beat umbrella; zydeco, Celtic sounds and Bulgarian folk music have each found themselves newly categorized in this way. Indeed, many of the smaller, "independent," World Beat record companies began as folk labels—Rounder, Shanachie and Hannibal, for instance.

It is clear then that the construction of World Beat as a genre is not simply a musicological phenomenon. Folk musics which do not employ the fusions characterized by North American and European musicians, or by African and Caribbean musicians influenced by rock and funk, have nonetheless been marketed as World Beat. A case in point is the Bulgarian State Radio and Television Female Vocal Choir *(Le Mystere des Voix Bulgares)*, whose largely traditional music is released on Nonesuch (a label which pioneered the remarkable "Explorer" series in the 1960s). This music, which would once have been categorized under the older label of "International Music," was considered, in 1988, to be on the cutting edge of "new" music in North America.[2]

This repackaging of older, folk forms is at work also in the promotion of the South African vocal group Ladysmith Black Mambazo, who rose to international fame after its appearance with Paul Simon, in recording and performing the *Graceland* music. Neither Ladysmith Black Mambazo nor the Bulgarian State Radio and Television Female Vocal Choir have much in common with, for instance, Ofra Haza—a Yemenite disco singer who sounds like a Middle Eastern version of Madonna. Yet the widespread circulation of both kinds of World Beat (folk musics and various Western/Third World fusions) has created an environment in which, to paraphrase Lyotard, it is commonplace to consume Celtic harp music in the morning, Bruce Springsteen in the afternoon, and Middle Eastern disco grooves in the evening.

The eclecticism inherent in most World Beat music does not, however allow us to make an easy case for its coherence or novelty as a musical genre or category. As long as mass-media pop music has existed, it has colored the content of local musics. Pop has at various times appropriated sounds from around the world—as with the calypso craze of the 1950s, or the Latin dance fads that have periodically swept the globe. Non-Western songs have been hits, whether performed by "genuine" non-Western performers (e.g., Miriam Makeba's "Pata Pata," Cameroon bandleader Manu Dibango's proto-disco hit "Soul Makossa"), or, more often than not, by American or Anglo pop artists (e.g., the Andrews Sisters' "Rum and Coca-Cola," Buster Poindexter's "Hot Hot Hot," originally recorded by the Montserrat musician Arrow). Recordings of music from around the world have been available for as long as there have been recordings, and mainstream pop artists have never been reluctant to add "exotic" touches to their music in order to cash in on a musical trend.

So what is truly new about World Beat? In the first place, World Beat has been constructed by musicians, critics, and entrepreneurs as a genre in itself, so that it is now a promotional label (like "heavy metal" or "soul") with its own sections in record stores, its own magazines, specialty shops, and labels (Shanachie/Ethnopop/World Beat, GlobeStyle, WOMAD, Original, Earthworks, etc.), festivals (Britain's WOMAD event), radio ad television programs (National Public Radio's *Afropop*, the *Beats of the Heart* documentary series), and so on. World Beat is now institutionalized within the music and media industries. The form of that institutionalization is deeply shaped by Anglo-American hegemony in the music media. For world music to reach Western ears, it must be presented in a way that will enable it to compete in the musical marketplace. World music has been pitched as yuppie-directed exotica *(Le Mystere des Voix Bulgares)*, "quality" art-rock (Salif Keita, Youssou N'Dour), dance craze (Manu Dibango, Mory Kante, Ofra Haza, Cheb Khaled), mystical mind-expansion (The Beatles/Brian Jones/Led Zeppelin usage—still invoked on the 1989 Rolling Stones LP, *Steel Wheels*, on the track "Continental Drift"), and as scholarly folklore studies (the Nonesuch Explorer series, the Ocora series).

Secondly, however, there *is* a musicological component to the newness of World Beat. The way non-Western music is being used is less mediated than previously—the perceived purity of the music is an important factor in its appeal to Westerners. This is not to say that non-Western musics are not already mediated (we criticize the notion of an essential folk "purity" below), but rather that World Beat music often subordinates rock and pop forms to an indigenous third world rhythm, melody or arrangement. Also, the use of non-Western musics is a key element in recent debates within the community of pop musicians and rock critics. Certainly, much of the current popularity of world music stems from the many Anglo-American pop artists who have incorporated global sounds and styles into their music; such as the Talking Heads *(Remain in Light)*, Peter Gabriel *(So)*, Malcolm McLaren *(Duck Rock)*, Paul Simon *(Graceland)*, and Sting *(Nothing Like the Sun)*.[3]

Many Western listeners initially encounter non-Anglo-American musics through artists such as these. Often the musicians are quite upfront about their use of world music, and Peter Gabriel in particular has been at pains to promote it; for instance through his support for Britain's WOMAD organization, and more recently in his participation with the Real World record label and recording studio.

But while current stylistic appropriations seem to proceed with a great deal more respect for the lender culture than was the case in the past, there has nonetheless been much debate about the morality of sounds in mainstream Western pop. In these controversies, which are frequently aired in the music press, we see a displaced account of the debate about cultural imperialism, in which the real issue of Western domination of channels of cultural production and (more importantly) distribution is taken up as a narrowly *moral* question concerning the practices of individual musicians. This accusation of music "theft" thus constitutes the simplest and most commonly aired link between the World Beat phenomenon and the debate about cultural imperialism.

Police and Thieves

Does World Beat music constitute a form of cultural exploitation, in which Western musicians use their economic power to steal music from their less fortunate Third World counterparts? This is the simplest issue raised in this complex debate. It seems easy enough to dismiss the argument by pointing out that music, unlike diamonds or minerals, is not depleted; this was the response of The Police drummer Stewart Copeland, when asked if his World Beat album *The Rhythmist* was exploitative. But his rebuttal misses the point that third world musicians might constitute the equivalent of cheap labor. It is important to register that the question of exploitation is based on the fact that Western musicians "cash in" on indigenous cultural traditions without offering adequate recompense. However, the nature of popular music renders the issue a good deal more complex than is the case in other forms of the mass media.

One problem with the argument that World Beat is exploitative is its sometimes simplistic notion of the relation between Third World and Anglo American musical forms, which takes us to the heart of a major complication in understanding contemporary rock and pop music in terms of the debate about cultural imperialism. In a useful survey of the issues, Oliver Boyd-Barrett has listed four components in the media imperialism thesis: the media contents themselves; a set of industrial arrangements; a body of values; and the shape of the communication vehicle.[4]

Media contents are the most obvious and commonly discussed aspect of the debate, where it is often noticed that cultural exports from Anglo-American media organizations to Third World nations occur in disproportion to cultural imports. By *a set of industrial arrangements*, Boyd-Barrett refers to the manner of organizing cultural production—for instance, the Hollywood studio system has been copied in India; and some African nations attempted to emulate the British Broadcasting Corporation when they established their "own" radio and television systems. *A body of values* comprises ideas of media professionalism: what constitutes "entertainment"? Who decides what is "news"? How should narratives be organized? *The shape of the communication vehicle* refers to the nature of the format—the daily newspaper, the soap-opera, the pop song, etc.

Boyd-Barrett's scheme is useful because it enables us to distinguish between aspects of the process whereby third world nations may be subject to Western cultural power. This delineation of the debate takes us beyond questions of ownership, so that inequalities in cultural power can be traced even to those forms which are owned and controlled by non-Western institutions. The argument is that local media forms may be implicated in cultural imperialism through their roots in the Western cultural industries.

It is easy to see how these points might relate to music. The *media contents* component of the argument references the question of the imbalance of Western rock and pop sold in the third world when compared to the availability of non-Western music in North America and Europe. The question about *a body of values* would ask whether or not non-Western musicians adopt Anglo-American definitions of what "good" music is, and whether the impact of Western media changes the social functions of music. A key question here would be whether Western musical technology changes the nature of global music, perhaps through its tendency to rationalize rhythms (via the drum machine) and tonal possibilities (via electronic keyboards).[5] *The set of industrial arrangements* would be relevant here in terms of looking at how non-Western nations organize their music industries.[6]

However, while the argument about *the shape of the communication vehicle* applies very well to mass media such as film and television (where third world nations have often found themselves copying notions of what a movie or a newspaper should be), in the case of postwar popular music the situation is more involved. As Simon Frith has written, "It is worth remembering that migration—the compulsory diaspora of Africans—has had a much greater impact on popular music history than even the cultural imperialism of the Anglo-American entertainment industry."[7] In other words, the complicating factor here is that the communication vehicle has already been globally-shaped, before it is "exported" from the West.

There are at least three stages in this process. The most recent concerns the impact of musical imperialism itself—the fact that so many third world musicians have grown up listening to Anglo-American rock and soul. So while the material on the Talking Heads' album *Remain in Light* was, according to the band, inspired by Nigerian afrobeat, that music was in turn heavily influenced by American soul—in particular the recordings of James Brown (as afrobeat's founder Fela Kuti has clearly acknowledged), The "purity" of Third World music must always be questioned, not only for dangerous (we would say racist) ideological assumptions about the "authenticity" of non-Western cultures, but also for empirical flaws in the argument.[8] Critics of the media imperialism thesis have always argued that Western culture might be used in new and perhaps creative ways when it is received in non-Western nations. They view the simple Marxist theories of the 1970s as inadequate, because they were too reductive in assuming superstructural consequences of patterns of ownership, and because the global audience for Anglo-American culture is misrepresented as a passive constituency.[9] In afrobeat music there is living evidence of this fact: musicians like Fela Kuti, far from being helpless dupes of a Coca-Cola culture, went on to use what they heard to produce a new kind of music.

Secondly, there is, an earlier stage of cultural interaction, which is obvious when we consider the African roots of James Brown's music and indeed of the whole aesthetic of rock, which derives in considerable measure from African musical practices. To make this case, however requires a rejection of simplistic notions of African music as merely "repetitive" and tuneless, and European music as stiff and "unfunky." These are surely myths of grand proportions, but it is true that if modern pop were stripped of its Europeanisms it would *sound* a lot more like Western pop than if it were stripped of its Africanisms. It is difficult to argue, therefore, that rock music is "Western" in quite the same way that Hollywood cinema or British television news are.

A third layer of complexity about the origins of the "communication vehicle" is suggested by musicologist Philip Tagg, who has recently addressed the issue of race in popular music by noting some of the inconsistencies and historical inaccuracies in common-sense notions of "black" and "white" musics.[10] Tagg argues that most of the elements considered quintessentially "black" in Anglo-American pop are to be found in European and/or other non-African musics (blue notes, call-and-response patterns and improvisation), while the one major component which is truly alien to the European tradition (polyrhythm) is so peculiar to specific areas of the African continent that to label it generically "African" is a misnomer. (This myth of a unitary "Africa" is one to which we will return later.) Furthermore, Tagg argues that the degree of intermingling of musical traditions in the formation of US popular music is such that even the term

"Afro-American" is questionable, since it denies the black American contribution, by implying a "pure" non-black American music that probably never existed. Tagg's position is important for the World Beat debate since it so carefully deconstructs the separate categories that are supposedly being fused in the "new" form, while also pointing to the implicitly racist discourses that often operate in discussions of so-called "black" and "white" musics.

To return to the question of whether World Beat is exploitative, even if one could identify "pure" musical elements of national and regional cultures, the problems of calculating appropriate compensation are mind-boggling. As detailed by Roger Wallis and Krister Malm, the 1976 "Tunis Model Law for Folklore" proposed that users of folklore heritage must obtain licensing from the appropriate culture.[11] If such a model were adopted (and this is merely the embodiment of a concept that lies behind many leftist assumptions about global culture), the Talking Heads' record company would need to calculate how much compensation was due to the band themselves, how much to Fela Kuti, how much to James Brown before him, and how much to the generation of African musicians who preceded him! Clearly the almost incomprehensible complexity of musical influence, counter-influence and dissemination undermines any simple notion of "one-way flow" in the world of global music.

Acknowledgment (and non-acknowledgment) can take as many forms as appropriation itself. Western performers can borrow non-Western sounds or procedures in a generalized sense (as with the Talking Heads' afrobeat-derived material), surround themselves with non-Western performers (as have Peter Gabriel and Paul Simon), or use actual musical material drawn form non-Western sources. It is interesting to compare how two black American artists have dealt with this last scenario; the opening cut of Michael Jackson's 1982 album *Thriller*, "Wanna Be Startin' Somethin'," features a vocal breakdown lifted from Manu Dibango's "Soul Makossa." Jackson, however, claimed sole authorship. When George Clinton used the vocal refrain from Fela Kuti's "Mr. Follow Follow" as the hook for his 1983 recording "Nubian Nut," Kuti was given a composer's credit.

Malcolm McLaren's 1983 album *Duck Rock* presents an even kinkier situation. On one hand, the record is a virtual World Beat manifesto; the record's packaging and liner notes make quite clear where the music is drawn from, and McLaren is explicit about his own role as master of ceremonies, rather than "musician" (he doesn't play any instrument and appears only occasionally on the record in a rather limited vocal capacity). McLaren's global bricolage dates back to the early 1980s, when he introduced Burundi drumming techniques into the music of British pop star Adam Ant, and then repeated the exercise with Bow Wow Wow on "C-30, C-60, C-90, Go." *Duck Rock*'s cut-and-paste stylistic juxtapositions say a great deal about cultural relativism, and the marginalization of the musician-as-*auteur* constitutes a statement that many critics will see as typical of the new global postmodernism. McLaren raids township jive, rap, disco music, and progressive rock and reconstructs them into a collection that he calls his own. Yet McLaren and producer Trevor Horn commit one of the most infamous examples of plagiarism in pop history, claiming authorship of "Jive My Baby Jive" and "Double Dutch," when the songs were note-for-note copies of two songs by the South African group The Mahotella Queens ("Thina Siyakhanyisa" and "Jive Mabone"). McLaren and Horn also claim composer credits for two sections of traditional (indeed, *sacred*) Afro-Cuban music, "Obatala" and "Legba."[12]

These examples (along with similar controversies surrounding Paul Simon's *Graceland* LP)[13] indicate that it is insufficient to respond to the claims of exploitation by noting that there is no "pure" music, or by asserting the complex Afro-American shape of the communication vehicle of rock music. Certainly those facts do need to be aired and taken account of in any discussion of global music, and they certainly make the debate a good deal more complicated than it is in relation to broadcasting or cinema. But it is also true that World Beat has generated instances of exploitation, rooted in the privileged position of Western musicians vis-a-vis the recording and publishing industries. This point suggests a link with the wider debate about cultural imperialism in the global music business.

We Are The World

Far from constituting an aberration within cultural imperialism, World Beat can be seen as an *effect* of those processes. Writing in 1977, Boyd-Barrett defined media imperialism as:

> the process whereby the ownership, structure, distribution or content of the media in any one country are singly or together subject to substantial external pressures from the media industries of any other country or countries without proportionate reciprocation of influence by the country so affected.[14]

More recently, critics such as Armand Mattelart have noted the importance of transnational corporations in the control of global information and entertainment.[15] Fred Fejes takes account of this role when he identifies media imperialism according to its results, as "the process by which modern communication media have operated to create, maintain and expand systems of domination and dependence on a world scale."[16]

World Beat music might be identified as Western pop stars appropriating non-Western sounds, as third world musicians using Western rock and pop, or as the Western consumption of non-Western folk music; in each case it is evidently an effect of the kinds of processes outlined above. World Beat fusions exist because of the development of Western technologies such as the digital sampling computer, which has assisted in the appropriation of Third World musics by Anglo-American rock stars.[17]

World Beat exists because of the impact of rock and soul on Third World musicians. And World-Beat-as-folk is an effect of a new, and possibly postmodern, interest in exotica which is made possible by the global reach of the western-based music industry. One question that follows from this notion of World Beat as an effect of cultural imperialism is the question of capital: who profits from these processes? The question is easily answered. Most of the capital flows, of course, to multinational record companies based in the United States, Britain, and France. The more difficult question is this: what do these processes mean?

In recent years there has been a trend within academic discussion towards re-evaluating the terms of the media imperialism debate. Writing about the international television industry, scholars such as Jeremy Tunstall, Thomas McPhail and Chin-Chuan Lee have questioned the very basis for seeing significant inequalities in media ownership noting the emergence of developed or developing media powers within the Third World, or refusing to reductively conflate economic and cultural power.[18] Tunstall and other critics of the media imperialism thesis have also suggested the degree to which this work illegitimately moves from describing ownership patterns to imputing cultural effects.

In the field of popular music, the study of media imperialism is highly underdeveloped, but a few recent studies suggest parallels with the critique of media imperialism. Dave Laing has explicitly questioned the extent of media dominance through an account of the importance of record piracy.[19] He argues that the unauthorized sale of cassettes in the Third World is so pervasive as to significantly skew the relationship between ownership and control in the international marketplace, and that paradoxically this indigenous enterprise is more harmful to the development of local music than the operation of the multinationals themselves. Roger Wallis and Krister Malm consider the global music scene to be at least partially autonomous from the economic sphere of production,[20] highlighting the importance of language in maintaining space for the development of non-Anglo-American forms, or most significantly music which struggles with dominant practices through fusion.[21] They show how language differences can act as a brake on homogenizing trends in the global market for culture.

John Lennon is credited with once saying of the Beatles: "The Russians put it out that we were capitalist robots. Which we were, I suppose." And yet while that remains a marvelous insight, studies abound which show that the *audience* for Western rock, including the Beatles, is anything but robotic. A recent book about world music contains numerous accounts of the various ways in which musicians resist and reappropriate Western forms in ways that defy simple ideas of imperialist domination: young people in Yugoslavia forming their own music groups after hearing the Beatles, musicians in Israel mixing traditional "Oriental" musics and Western dance-floor rhythms, and West African musicians fusing big band jazz styles with indigenous forms.[22] One manifestation of World Beat that clearly illustrates this kind of resistance is where third world musicians appropriate and incorporate Western pop into new kinds of music.

But these arguments do not necessarily undermine a sophisticated theory of cultural dependence (including a Marxist one), since they are mostly based on a recognition of the unequal struggle between third world musicians and multinational mass-mediated pop. However, an adequate account of World Beat needs to take account of relative autonomy in the sphere of culture (including music), and must come up to date with the new media research emphasizing the active, creative role of popular culture consumers. It is also essential to avoid conflating meaning and national identity: the fact that a piece of music is written or recorded in a particular country tells us nothing about its meaning. The pop music of Abba is not resistant to Anglo-American trends merely because it emanates from Sweden. And much of the World Beat sounds that are consumed as "authentic" Third World music in the United States are in fact produced in London and Paris.

In relation to World Beat, this complexity suggests three tasks. First, the question of Western dominance needs to be examined *musically*. Instead of focusing narrowly on questions of ownership (although these issues clearly do significantly determine which artists will succeed in North America and Europe), we need a theory of global *discourse*: which is to ask, to what extent are developments in World Beat dependent on their compatibility with Western definitions of music? As we have already suggested, this question is made all the more difficult to answer due to the transcultural nature of Western pop. It is notable, however, that those World Beat artists who have had the most success in the West are those whose music fits dominant Anglo-American ideas of dance-pop—Ofra Haza's *Shaday* album and Mory Kante's European hit single "Ye Ke Ye Ke," for instance.

Secondly, however, we must consider the importance of audience perceptions that defy the musicological account sketched out here. If rock music is perceived as "Western," then its meaning may imply (for some audiences) the various associations of the West, regardless of the actual origins of the communication vehicle itself. Only empirical research can answer this question, and it is obviously one that will be answered differently amongst different social groups in different parts of the world.

Thirdly, it is necessary to ask some hard questions about the consumption of World Beat itself. In the first place, we have very little idea about what Western pop (World Beat or not) actually means in its various global contexts. Charles Hamm has pointed out that even music as insipid and trite as the Live Aid records ("Do They Know It's Christmas?" and "We Are The World") may take on meanings in Botswana or Zimbabwe that Western criticism can miss.[23] Conversely, we have no idea what third world sounds mean in the West. Here again we need to disavow economic, ethnic, or geographical reductionism. World Beat is not necessarily "progressive" solely by virtue of its country of origin, the color of the musicians or the name on the record label. The question of use was painfully spelled out in the 1970s, when British skinhead groups saw no contradiction between their violent racism and their devotion to reggae music.[24]

Stuart Cosgrove has pointed out that for many World Beat fans in the West, what is offered is exoticism—world music sounds as aural tourism.[25] Here we confront the problem of the construction of an undifferentiated, usually African, "Other." Any view of "Africa" for instance, as either unitary or "pure" is quite clearly empirically unfounded and potentially racist, and the creation of an "African Other" in the western subcultures of World Beat (and in rap music's newfound Afrocentricity) needs to be examined critically. It is here in particular that one needs to consider the pervasive presence of discourses of imperialism which have long outlived the actual practices of colonialism. In merely inverting the interpretation of an Africa or the Orient that remains undifferentiated, do contemporary World Beat and rap culture notions of globalism actually help to reproduce ethnocentric ways of seeing (and hearing) the world?

Reading musical texts thus involves not only criticizing simple theories of media imperialism; it also means researching the presence of hegemonic reading formations which occur beyond the arena of media production. Too often the argument for an active, creative audience is conflated with a political analysis. Our point is that the move from production to consumption is not, as it is simplistically assumed in some recent critiques of media imperialism, a straightforward matter of recovering progressive, counter-hegemonic, modes of consumption. The alternative to economically reductive approaches using theories of audience passivity is too often a simple inversion, in which an autonomous sphere of culture is the site of creative freeplay of meaning and progressive politics. In fact, it is quite possible (indeed likely) that audiences will sometimes construct *reactionary* meanings from the products of the global culture industries.

Go With the Flow?

To return to our initial question: To what extent does World Beat represent two-way flow of communication? In their conclusion to *Big Sounds from Small Peoples*, Wallis and Malm outline four models of cultural interaction: cultural exchange, where music is exchanged equally between two cultures; cultural dominance, where one culture is forced onto another with no reciprocation; cultural imperialism, where money, resources and notions of culture are transferred from one group to another; and transculturation, where the features of a number of cultures are combined within the framework of the transnational media. Although World Beat is itself largely an effect of the third process (cultural imperialism), the complexity of the *results* of such practices are demonstrated in the fact that this new form usually falls into the last category—transculturation.

The availability of "world music" both in its original form and as filtered through Western pop artists represents a genuine, if limited, penetration of the Anglo-American musical soundscape. The "enlightened" form of appropriation practiced by some Anglo-American pop stars is clearly an improvement on past forms of cultural exchange. However, media imperialism is not perpetuated by pop musicians, but by the Western cultural hegemony inherent in the structure of the global mass media. As we noted earlier, the musicians themselves confuse this issue (as do most rock critics and journalists) by reducing the broad problem concerning the organization of the cultural industries to issues of personal ethics.

Referring back to Boyd-Barret's definition of media imperialism, it is clear that to a limited degree World Beat does represent a "reciprocation" and is therefore an encouraging trend. World Beat certainly shows us that reductive theories which conflate economics and meaning, ownership and ideology, are outdated and invalid. Nonetheless, the World Beat phenomenon hardly constitutes "*proportionate* reciprocation." It does not, therefore, undermine the fundamental point of the cultural imperialism theorists.

This is not to deny the weaknesses in seeing the cultural imperialism issue only in terms of "flow" (or Boyd-Barret's category of "contents"), for it is undeniable that this question does not exhaust what is at stake. In relation to World Beat music, the point of unequal flow does not encompass either the reception of that music amongst music makers, nor its meaning in the ears of consumers. We have tried to demonstrate, however, that both those questions can be tackled within a sophisticated non-reductive understanding of transnational power; these questions do not, in other words, negate the importance of understanding World Beat as a phenomenon of inequitable global resources and discourses.

What must be abandoned, however, are the twin errors displayed in many left assumptions about World Beat and its relation to global music in general. We have shown how these mistakes connect with the opposing "progressive" lines held by fans, critics, and musicians. In the first place, reductive Marxist accounts, like cynical insider dismissals of rock star "exploitation" of Africans, are not only too simple, they are actually empirically wrong. They describe neither the process of producing World Beat music nor the practice of consuming it. Secondly, however, we must scrutinize the knee-jerk optimism that has developed in its place. Just as many "cultural studies" academics (some of whom describe themselves as Marxists) rarely demonstrate the "progressive" merits of popular culture that they claim to be there in the text (while ignoring the numerous ways in which it is potentially available for active, *reactionary* consumption), so fans of World Beat tend to celebrate its politics too unconditionally.

We have tried in this article to suggest some ways in which the merits of World Beat can be understood in relation to a non-reductive, musically specific, version of the cultural imperialism thesis. But doing this must also involve an acknowledgment that when we provide a mode in which the (global) audience is active, we have yet to identify what that means *politically*. Pop audiences will not be made counter-hegemonic by scholarly or devotional fiat.

> Our thanks to Leslie Kauffman and members of the Bay Area *Socialist Review* for their helpful suggestions in writing this paper.

Endnotes

[1] See Charles Hamm, "Graceland Revisited," *Popular Music*, Vol. 8, No. 3 (October 1989); and the critical response by Dave Laing, *Popular Music*, Vol. 9, No. 1, (January 1990).

[2] An even more bizzare instance of music industry labeling concerns the 1990 Grammy award given to Peter Gabriel's *Passion* LP—an instrumental album inspired by pan-Islamic musics, which won in the "New Age" category.

[3] The debate even spilled over into the controversies about sampling in rap, when Eric B. and Rakim used a snatch of an Ofra Haza vocal on their dance floor re-mix "Paid in Full (Seven Minutes of Madness)," which was in its turn used on the M/A/R/R/S dance record "Pump Up The Volume."

[4] Oliver Boyd-Barrett, "Media Imperialism: Towards an International Framework for the Analysis of Media Systems," in James Curran et al., eds., *Mass Communication and Society* (London: Edward Arnold, 1977).

5 Many drum machines do not allow for the "elastic" placement of the beat, just as most electronic keyboards make micro-tonal composition impossible. While it might by objected that advances in electronic technology are gradually invalidating these points, it is typically the case that the "advances" are more available and affordable in North America and Europe.
6 For an empirical discussion of some of these questions see Roger Wallis & Krister Malm, *Big Sounds From Small Peoples* (London:Constable, 1984).
7 "Editor's Note," in Simon Frith, ed., *World Music, Politics and Social Change* (Manchester & New York: Manchester University Press, 1989), p. 72.
8 John Collins & Paul Richards have shown, for instance, how West African highlife and ju-ju musics are influenced respectively by Western dance orchestras and Brazilian music. See "Popular Music in West Africa" in Frith, *World Music*.
9 A typical example of this work is the research on the television show Dallas, which has been shown to generate an extraordinary variety of responses outside the United States. See, for instance, Ien Ang, *Watching Dallas* (New York & London: Methuen, 1985) and Elihu Katz & Tamar Liebes, "Decoding Dallas: Notes From a Cross-Cultural Study," in Horace Newcomb, ed., *Television: A Critical View* (New York & Oxford: Oxford University Press, Fourth edition, 1987).
10 Phillip Tagg, "Open Letter: Black Music, Afro-American Music and European Music," *Popular Music*, Vol. 8, No. 3 (October 1989). An interesting, if musicologically unsound, view of the myth of "pure" African-ness in rock culture is also suggested by Robert Pattison's *The Triumph of Vulgarity: Rock Music in the Mirror of Romanticism* (Oxford:Oxford University Press, 1988).
11 Roger Walls & Krister Malm, *Big Sounds from Small Peoples*.
12 This well-known scandal is carefully traced in Craig Bromberg's *The Wicked Ways of Malcolm McLaren* (New York: Harper&Row, 1989), pp. 253-275.
13 Steven Feld discusses similar issues in relation to Paul Simon's *Graceland* LP, in "Notes On World Beat," *Public Culture*, Vol. 1, No. 1 (Fall 1988); see also Charles Hamm, "Graceland Revisited."
14 Boyd-Barrett, "Media Imperialism."
15 Armand Mattelart, *Multinational Corporations and the Control of Culture: The Ideological Apparatuses of Imperialism* (Brighton: Harvester Press, 1979).
16 Fred Fejes, "Media Imperialism: An Assessment," *Media, Culture, & Society*, Vol. 3, No. 3 (July 1981).
17 The centrality of the sophisticated and at that time hugely expensive digital sampling computer in the production of *Duck Rock* is made clear in Bromberg, *The Wicked Ways of Malcolm McLaren*. Similarly, Peter Gabriel's blending of African musics and rock was prompted in part by his access to a Fairlight music computer—an instrument that was, at that time, available to a very few musicians and producers in the West.
18 Jeremy Tunstall, *The Media Are American: Anglo-American Media in the World* (London:Constable, 1977); Thomas McPhail, *Electronic Colonialism: The Future of International Broadcasting and Communication* (London/Beverly Hills: Sage, 1981); Chin-Chuan Lee, *Media Imperialism Reconsidered: The Homogenizing of Television Culture* (London/Beverly Hills: Sage, 1980).
19 Dave Laing, "The Music Industry and the 'Cultural Imperialism' Thesis," *Media, Culture & Society*, Vol. 8, No. 3 (July 1986).
20 Wallis & Malm, *Big Sounds from Small Peoples*.
21 A fascinating study along these lines is Motti Regev's account of "oriental" pop music in Israel, "The Music Soundscape as a Contest Area: 'Oriental music' and Israeli Popular Music," *Media, Culture &Society*, Vol. 8, No. 3 (July 1986)
22 Frith, *World Music, Politics, and Social Change*.
23 Charles Hamm, "Afterword," in Frith, *World Music, Politics, and Social Change*.
24 An excellent study of the complexities of such questions is provided in Simon Jones, *Black Culture, White Youth: The Reggae Tradition from JA to UK* (Basingstoke: Macmillan, 1988).
25 Stuart Cosgrove, "Global Style?" *New Statesman & Society*, September 9, 1988.

Darrell Johnson

"Jazz," Kreolization and Revolutionary Music For The 21st Century

Fred Wei-han Ho

I do not use the term "jazz"[1] just as I do not use such terms as "Negro," "Oriental," or "Hispanic." Oppressed peoples suffer from their history, identity, and culture being defined, (mis)represented and explicated by our oppressors. The struggle to redefine and reimage our existence involves the struggle to reject the stereotyping, distortions, and devaluing embodied in the classifications of conquerors and racists. In essence, the struggle over how to describe past and present reality is to change reality.

Well, then, so what term should be used instead of "jazz"? Implicit in the asking of this question is that calling it 20th-century American (or African American) music is either inadequate or inaccurate. Yet, while the continual usage of the term "jazz" marginalizes, obfuscates and denies the fact that this music is quintessentially American music, it is the music of an American oppressed nationality and not the music of the dominant European American. It is white supremacist racism that will not properly and justly accept both the music and its creators in a position of equality.

However, a satisfactory replacement for "jazz" has yet to emerge and continues to be part of the ongoing struggle to dismantle white supremacy and Eurocentrism in American culture and society. At times, certain terms have gained some currency, such as Rahsaan Roland Kirk's "Great Black Music," or Archie Shepp's "African American Instrumental Music," or Max Roach preferring to say, "The music of Louis Armstrong, the music of Charles Parker, etc.," or I recall Billy Taylor simply saying "20th-century American music." Some might argue that "jazz" should be reclaimed and that its meaning should be transformed from a pejorative term and usage to a celebratory and "in-your-face" defiance, as militant gays and lesbians have reappropriated the once-derogatory and insulting "queer" and "fag." It is noted that "black" was once a term loaded with negativity which the Black Liberation Movement transformed to symbolize pride and self-respect.

But the fact is that it took a movement of oppressed peoples for self-determination to project new terms and meanings and to replace reactionary and oppressive ones. Clearly, the movement for Black Power and Black Liberation must be led and controlled by black or African American people. While according to 19th-century racist blood quantum legislation in the U.S., anyone with "one drop" of African blood was to be considered "black," another reality holds true for the genetics and culture of African Americans: both are a hybrid. Neither is mainly "African" or mainly "American" (in its dominant, mainstream understanding and context), but a "kreolized"[2] identity—a revolutionary new cultural and social identity, forged in struggle against an oppressive society that still largely excludes, denies, and denigrates (i.e., "niggerizes" or "chinkifies" or "spicifies") entire peoples.

Kreolization among the oppressed is intrinsically related to resistance to oppression in the socio-political context. We need only to look at American national music, which is quintessentially African American. The slave songs or spirituals employed the double entendre of coded, two-level meaning in their lyrics. Singing in English, the language of the slave master, and using Christian biblical references (the slave master's religion), the songs were a form of underground communication and a celebration of the spirit and act of rebellion. Musically, African American music has been characterized as a synthesis of Western European tonal harmony and West and Central African modal melodicism. African American music has been the revolutionary music of the 20th century not just for the U.S., but for the planet as well. It has revolutionized the world of music by introducing new instrumentalization (e.g., the drum kit) or refiguring other instruments (e.g.s., the saxophone, the piano more as a rhythm and less as a harmonic instrument, the stringbass played primarily pizzicato and in a role as time keeper and less played acro as a melodic line). It has aesthetically transformed the very components of melody (e.g., the primacy of improvisation), rhythm (e.g., the concept of swing), and harmony (e.g.s., parallel voicings, "blue notes," and altered chord changes).

Art-for-art's sake ideologues may argue with me: Were the singers and musicians politically conscious or were they simply making music from their cultural milieu. Since much of the music, art and culture of an oppressed people are not deemed worthy of scholarly attention by the dominant society, we lack the honest and indepth interviews and historiography to clearly assert a conscious political design. But even if the performers were simply "creating" from their experiences, clearly those experiences are contextualized by their social, political and economic conditions. As Marx stated, conditions shape humans; that's why we must struggle to make those conditions more humane. Part of that struggle for humanity is music-making—its particular forms and expressive character are shaped by the material, social and cultural conditions. If we understand the concept of nationality and discard the falsity of "race," then obviously so-called white people can play "jazz" and have made important contributions. However, while the music continues to incorporate influences from many cultures and experiences, it remains African American. So-called "whites," can embrace and identify with African American culture, but as long as the system of white supremacy exists they will always be "whites" whether or not they consciously desire to be so. Though well intentioned or skillful "whites" might make interesting music within the idiom, they can never be innovators or cultural/artistic leaders in relation to the cultural forms of oppressed nationalities because those forms are inevitably and intrinsically bound up with the oppression and struggle of our peoples—i.e., our survival and development is a refusal to identify with, submit and capitulate, to the oppressor. While kreolization is a fact, we seek to avoid the "false" and objectionable kreolization that is about assimilation and acculturation with the dominant oppressor culture and society and seek instead "true" kreolization, the free and voluntary intermingling, cultural synthesis and crossfertilization which occurs at the bottom of society, among the varying oppressed peoples. We can see this today among Chicano, Dominican, Puerto Rican, Asian and Pacific Islander youth, who, while often lacking much identity with their own nationality, will tend to identify with African American culture and radical politics. To choose "black" over "white" reflects and strengthens a potential anti-imperialist bond. However, "real" kreolization is a synthesis and not imitation or simple identification with another.

On the other hand, cultural imperialism, while masking as cultural blending/borrowing/mixing, enforces dominant privilege, power and profit. "Jazz," Rock, and most popular music in the U.S. are basically African American. However, through white cultural imperialism these forms have been assimilated, and therefore become "acceptably" American. Since the exportation of American pop music around the world happens within the context of American cultural imperialism, it typically is not the culture of the oppressed African American people that is exported but rather the "Americanization" of African American culture. Yet by linking our common struggles and mutually-shared identity as oppressed nationalities, rather than subscribing to nationalism or ethnicity, we can begin to form a basis for genuine cultural synthesis (i.e., in an African context, Fela Kuti identifying and drawing from the music of the "I'm Black-and-Proud" James Brown rather than say, a white cover artist like Elvis Presley or, more recently, Paul Simon, Malcolm McLaren, David Byrne or Buster Poindexter). Artistic crossfertilization proceeds from a deep respect and consciousness of the richness and complexity of the varying oppressed nationality heritages. A revolutionary kreolization is the interdependent, interconnected struggle to forge a common identification as oppressed peoples. New cultural forms will inevitably flow from this unity.

The struggle of oppressed nationalities in the U.S. is to transform the very conception of "American" to its multicultural, multinational and multilingual reality. That struggle is inherently revolutionary: more than a proclamation of multiculturalism or integration into the dominant mainstream, but an attempt to dismantle the entire institutional power structure of white supremacy and Eurocentrism. As a young Chinese (Asian) American growing up in the 1970s, I was profoundly drawn to and inspired by African American music as the expression of an oppressed nationality, for both its social role as protest and resistance to national oppression, and for its musical energy and revolutionary aesthetics. I identified with its pro-oppressed, anti-oppressor character: with whatever militancy the musicians displayed, with its social history of rebellion and revolt, and with its musical defiance to not kow-tow to, but challenge and contest, Western European "classical" music as well as commercialized American Pop music.

"Jazz" is the music that embodies and expresses the contradictions of the century, fundamentally rooted to the world's division between oppressor, imperialist nations, and the liberation struggles of the oppressed nations and nationalities. "Jazz" emerged as formerly-rural African American laborers traveled north to the urban industrial and commerce centers of Chicago, Kansas City, Detroit, St. Louis, New York and Philadelphia. A new music arose with a new class of urban workers, grafting a rich and unique African American music of formerly enslaved plantation laborers, rural tenant farmers and migratory workers upon the sophisticated, cosmopolitan, industrial, and multiethnic urban culture of growing capitalist America.

No longer field songs, blues, or southern; the music brings along these cultural precedents, yet they are transformed. All of the characteristics of African American music that are distinctive are transformative: the Western European concert tradition of metronomic sense of time and general singularity of rhythm vis-à-vis the grafting of West and Central African multiple and layered rhythms produces the polyrhythmicality of African American 20th century music; the fixed pitch and fixed diatonic temperment of Western European concert music vis-à-vis West and Central African modalism and non-fixated pitch produces the blue notes of African American music; the primacy of written notation in Western European concert music vis-à-vis West and Central African oral tradition produces a revolutionary unity of composition and improvisation for 20th century African American music, and the primacy of the conductor and composer for Western European concert music vis-à-vis call and response/soloist-leader and group that progresses to player-as-leader-as-soloist-as-virtuoso improviser/performer/composer. The music has, in these transformations, developed a high degree of sophistication and complexity, utilizing and combining both compositional/notational and improvisational/oral tradition features.

Yet, due to national oppression, "jazz" was, ironically, spared the canonization and institutionalization that the concert music of Western Europe underwent as part of the establishment of white supremacist settler-colonialism in U.S. society. Thus the music became both a folk/popular music and an art/classical music that could be performed and enjoyed in not only the "lowest" of venues but the "highest" concert halls. Accordingly, until recently, the music, by its very positionality as the creative expression of an oppressed nationality excluded from most of American mainstream society (except when acceptably "covered" by white artists), resisted the calcification and ossification that "classical" music had undergone. For the most part, "jazz" has never looked back to the past as "classical" music has—fixated upon finer and finer degrees of perfection in the interpretation of past "classic" treasures. Rather, "jazz" has been about the present ("Now is the Time") and the future ("Space is the Place"). Its entire history has been about the freeing of time, pitch and harmony from fixed, regulated, predictable standards. Every major innovation in the history of the music has been from the struggle of musicians to attain greater and greater levels of expressive freedom through liberating the two basic fundamentals of music: time (meter) and sound (pitch/temperament/harmony).[3]

New and Refigured Instrumentation

A new instrument was introduced to the world of music during the 1890s and early 1900s in the U.S.A.: the drum kit. The multiple, layered rhythms of both West and Central African and New Orleans drum ensembles merged into a kit played by one person instead of several players. For the first time, one individual using all four limbs played several percussion parts simultaneously. European instruments such as the piano and bassviolin (string bass) were transformed both in their role and in their manner of playing. In the Western European orchestra, their roles were primarily melodic. But, in the African American music ensemble, both instruments became part of the "rhythm section." The piano's role is both rhythmic and harmonic. The string bass, now rarely played in its traditionally Western European arco or bowed manner, is played primarily pizzicato or plucked, supplying rhythm, keeping time and providing a harmonic foundation. Piano playing (especially in "comping"—from the word "accompaniment") now involves a rhythmic approach to harmony—supplying chordal/harmonic percussion-like rhythms. Eventually, by the 1960s, as musicians sought to more boldly escape from fixed, Western temperament, the piano was either left out entirely or played without regard to conventional harmony. Pulse and some establishment of tonality was left to the bass. Even the drum kit no longer was confined to keeping time or to meter. Certainly Max Roach since the 1940s has demonstrated the melodic artistry of the drum kit.

Probably, the most characteristically "jazz" instrument is still the saxophone. Created by a Belgian, Adolphe Saxe, in the 1840s in France, the saxophone would have become an obsolete, novelty instrument, with the exception of some works by French and Belgian composers, if it were not for its role in 20th century African American music. Replacing the clarinet, the saxophone became the "voice" of the "jazz band." Heretofore, popular music had been predominantly a vocal music performed by singers. With the saxophone, an instrumental popular music emerged. Much has been made of the saxophone's vocal-like qualities. In one of the clearest examples of the dialectical nature of African American 20th century music, horns perform like voices (from cries, shouts, screams, hollers and talkin' to its yakety-yak burlesque-y humor and caricature) and voices perform like horns (from the inflection and phrasing of the human voice to "scat" soloing).

Indeed, every feature of the music is an expressing of revolutionary dialectics. Demarcations are dissolved between soloist and ensemble, between the elements of melody, time and harmony, between composition and improvisation, between "tradition" and "avant garde," between "artist" and "audience," between "art" and "politics," between "western" and "eastern." If there is any "tradition," it is the continual exploding of time and pitch in a quest of greater human expressiveness and a deeper spiritualizing of the music that is fundamentally rooted, in my view, in the struggle to end all forms of exploitation and oppression and to seek a basic "oneness" with life and nature. The various ideological/spiritual pronouncements of musicians are necessarily reflections of this quest and struggle.

Much ballyhoo has been made about essentializing "jazz" as basically blues, swing, and improvisation—that if these are lacking, then the music ain't "jazz." Interestingly, the proponents of this dogma can range the ideological and political spectrum from black cultural nationalists to black and white neo-conservatives.

Blues

In my view, blues is not simply a "style," nor a 12-bar, AAB form, nor a certain chordal progression. Musically, blues is first and foremost a unique system of temperament: African American temperament! It is not, as Eurocentric musicology may attempt to codify, flatted or lowered thirds, sevenths, and fifths (notated in Western musical theory as sharp or raised seconds, dominant sevenths, or sharp or raised 11ths). Blue notes can be played on Western instruments without fingering minor thirds, dominant (flatted) sevenths and flatted fifths if the player has the African American temperament. The African American system of blues temperament is the product of synthesizing the Western European fixed, diatonic temperament system with an amalgam of West and Central African pitch and modal systems. With this new temperament system, the distinction between major and minor is irrelevant. Dr. Royal Hartigan has described it as African Americans trying to get the Western seven note scale back to the five notes common to many West and Central African pentatonic systems (though he also recognizes that there are seven note African scales).

Many "authentic" blues performers will actually retune their instruments to be more "in tune" with being bluesy. Similarly, there are "inauthentic" players who might perform the mechanics of the blue notes by fingering a minor third, etc., but sound unblue. The key aspect is not a fixed style (Baraka's "noun") but a process or approach to music making (Baraka's "verb")[4] that is highly African whereby the blurring of pitch is done to reach an emotive and spiritual catharsis—in West and Central Africa, literally to "allow the gods to descend"—and thereby affirm both personal and communal humanity in the face of inhumanity.

Secondarily, blues is a "form." The 12-bar AAB form has become, in the analogy made by LeRoi Jones/Amiri Baraka, another case of the verb-to-noun syndrome. It has been so thoroughly appropriated by (white, mainstream) "American" music in rock, country and western, disco, etc., that the "standard" blues form has practically ceased to be the blues! Historically, blues "form" has been expressed in 12 bars, 10 bars, 8 bars, 11-1/2 bars, 12-1/2 bars, 13 bars, 16 bars, etc. There have been blues based on three and more chords, blues based on one chord, and blues based on no chords.

Without getting into a discussion of the "blues sensibility," which Kalamu ya Salaam (1993) terms a "post-reconstruction expression of peoplehood culturally codified into an aesthetic,"[5] that is very significant and meaningful to an understanding of the blues both socially and culturally; in my view, the blues musical form is best understood as a musical representation of African American poetry. Blues pre-dates "jazz" as a sung, vocal genre—a griot tradition that has become secularized and existentialized (individual self-expressionism). In "jazz," blues is metamorphasized, once sung now instrumental, once performed by an individual now by an ensemble, once literal now nonliteral. The blues form cannot be reduced to simply a number of bars, a type of chord progression, or a phrase structure. To do so is to be guilty of Eurocentric codification and mechanical empiricism, suffocating the music's essence and creative, dynamic being as an expression of an African American oppressed nationality. The music, thus, has no wrong notes, no wrong progression or fixed number of bars, so long as, if I can interpret LeRoi Jones/Amiri Baraka's *Blues People*, it has the feel, the expressiveness of African American life and culture. Once it has been thoroughly codified and appropriated by the mainstream, dominant oppressor culture; then it ceases to be.

Swing

African American "swing" is not, as some Eurocentric musicologists would try to characterize it in Western musical paradigms, syncopation.[6] Nor is it a "tripleted feel." Rather, speaking in musical terms, it is a hybrid concept of time/pulse and rhythm that has resulted from the miscegenation of West and Central African triple meter, multiple rhythmic layering, with Western European duple meter and singular rhythm. This "3 inside of 2," is fundamentally a West and Central African-descended phenomenon, evidenced in all African diasporic musics, in which more than one time and more than one rhythm coexist.

Enslaved Africans in the Diaspora developed their own types of "swing" in Cuba, Haiti, Puerto Rico, Brazil, etc. In African America, due to the particular banning of drums by the oppressors; a unique type of "swing" developed in which a sense of time and rhythm no longer could be conveyed by drums, but was adapted and reinterpreted in singing, instrument playing and a collective, internal "feel," and expressed in body movement, dance, "pattin' juba," language and vocal inflections. Since drums and drumming were illegal and banned, the West and Central African drumming, percussion and rhythmic traditions came through in everything else—musical and extramusical. Some have characterized African American swing as a rhythmic energy and life force—a far greater phenomenon than simply the role of meter and rhythm in Western European music. Indeed, it is a form of African-based kinetics, a multiple rhythmic perspective; a shared communal bond of time, motion and energy. It is simultaneously both exciting and relaxing (what Archie Shepp has characterized as the tension and beauty of being both on the front and back-edge of the beat—its forward and laid back quality). The beat can swing whether it be in units of three or two; in patterns of 2, 3; the common 4; or 7, 7, 11, 15, 9, 13, etc. Swing can be in time, different time and in no time! It is found in the music of Baby Dodds and Sid Catlett swinging in 4/4, to odd meters done by Max Roach, to the polyrhythms of Elvin Jones, to the free, "no time" of Sunny Murray.

Improvisation

Finally, let me address the issue of composition/notation and improvisation. Some have argued that once the music has too much notated composition (implying that improvisation is necessarily diminished), then it becomes more "European" and less "African American." Initially, Western European music had quite a lot of improvisation, the result of player/composers under economic pressure to quickly come up with new works to entertain and satisfy their aristocratic employers. Though they were "literate" and trained, improvisation facilitated both economic expediency and met their own creative urge to avoid the repetitive boredom of performing the same "hits" the same way all the time. As solo and small group works expanded to large ensembles and extended compositions, and paying audiences required their favorites to be replicated as faithfully as the "first"; notation assumed greater and greater dominance.

African American music has never, until recently, had to face the prospects of institutionalization, canonization, and the standardization and codification of a ruling class (presently, bourgeois) classical music. Paradoxically, as the art and music of an oppressed nationality, it was free to be free. Duke Ellington's orchestra could play every night for years the same show music and still retain spontaneity and freshness, no matter how much notation, choreography and staging was set. As "jazz" took on more of an "art" music (i.e. primarily listened to and not danced to) aspect, and the "jazz" composer (who still could be a player/leader) began to pen extended works such as suites, ballet, music-theater and film scores, the best and strongest writing always allowed for and enhanced spontaneity and improvised contributions by the players. Indeed, to truly play the music was to achieve a state of complete memorization and internalization in which the written page was no longer looked at, but the players played from understanding and interaction. This is the essence of the African American music ensemble and composition: in which the whole becomes greater than the sum of its parts. The identity of the parts and whole, of player and composer, of notation and performance, of composition and improvisation; are inseparable, mutually dependent and interpenetrate.

Notation *qua* notation is not the enslaver, the oppressor of spontaneity and improvisation. Calcification, Europeanization, de-African Americanization, cooptation—whatever word one chooses to accuse and decry—is not so much caused by musical deviations and practices, but by, in my view, ethical[7] violations. Clearly, in Ellington's large-scale works, the essence of African American musical spontaneity is reflected in highly composed music. There are players who play "correct" "jazz" but it is sterile and reactionary. There are "jazz" artistic directors who have pronounced certain black musicians not playing "Black Music." The revolutionary musical aspects of 20th century African American music are part of an extramusical ethical/spiritual/socio-political context—the commitment, attitude, resistance, perseverance, celebration, love and joy in the face of oppression, brutality, poverty, persecution and exclusion. Archie Shepp expressed it in poetic language: "Jazz is the lily in spite of the swamp." It is the triumph of the human spirit, of spirituality and ethicality in the midst of cannibalistic and corrupting capitalism.

The carrier of the music (the musician) must not violate the ethical bond between the music and the people (i.e., a bond of merit, of excellence, of meaning, of purpose, of significance in the people's aspirations and efforts to be free). It is a responsibility that transcends careers, critical praise, conservatory training and cash. It is the music's fundamental affirmation and celebration of humanity, a commitment to liberation rooted in formerly enslaved peoples from Western and Central Africa becoming an oppressed nationality—African Americans—in the age of internationalized commodity production and exchange where cash is God.

"Jazz" was born in the contradictions of our epoch. The music changes just as the people, the society, the world, change. African Americans in the 20th century have been the largest and leading oppressed nationality in U.S. society. Their political, social, and cultural impact has been revolutionary. Into the 21st century, Spanish-speaking oppressed nationalities will become numerically the largest group of oppressed nationalities, while

Asian/Pacific Islanders are proportionally the fastest growing oppressed nationality. Facing the most extreme and desperate conditions, revolts by indigenous peoples are increasing, including armed struggle (c.f., Chiapas, Mexico) to defend their land and way of life. In the years to come, in a process that has already begun, a new music will arise, rooted in all that has come before, yet moving with greater volatility in the transformation, alteration, and explosion of time and sound; thereby changing music itself.

The petty machinations of trying to "institutionalize" "jazz," the reactionary "back to the tradition" (tradition is not something one can or should go back to, but to move from), the business-suited corporate and government legitimation and acceptability of "jazz," all violate the spirit, the sacred bond between culture and people, the ethics of the aesthetics. A new "jazz," (maybe something that won't use this term because it has become so coopted and reactionary) will draw on the heritage of the past, but will be a hybrid that is reflective of the music of all oppressed peoples fighting imperialism.

My own case might be instructive here. Up until 1986 I characterized my music as "jazz" with Asian American thematic and musical references (i.e., "Asian American jazz"). During many years of committed cultural work within the "Movement," I was struggling with the question: what makes Chinese American music Chinese American? What would make for an Asian American musical content and form that would be transformative of American music as well, and not simply be subsumed in one or another American musical genre such as "jazz." I began to embark upon a course which I now articulate as creating "an Afro-Asian new American multicultural music." Taking Mark Izu's significant leadership in the incorporation of traditional Asian instrumentation (in his case, mostly in improvised or incidental approaches), I began to explore such an incorporation in a composed, orchestrated manner. With no desire to be a Sinophile or Asian traditional music academic, yet recognizing the importance of studying and drawing from traditional formic structures, I wanted to capture and evoke the spirit of folk music in both (solo and ensemble) performance and in composition.

Earlier in 1985, in New York City, at the request of Jodi Long, then a member of my Asian American Art Ensemble, I had composed music for her multimedia work "Bound Feet," which incorporated the Chinese double reed *sona* and the Chinese two-stringed fiddle, the *erhu*, orchestrated with Western woodwinds, contrabass, and multiple percussion. I wrote the *sona* and *erhu* parts in Chinese notation, an ability I had acquired from my days leading a Chinese folksinging group. Though "Bound Feet" was only performed twice, I was personally excited by the musical results of this embryonic integration of Eastern, nontempered, and Western, tempered, instruments. While employing my own "jazz" voicing in the harmonization of the parts, I had struck upon some new, fresh and unusual timbral qualities from this combination. This synthesis of Chinese and African American components seemed to be a musical analogy for the Chinese American identity, or even further, something Afro-Asian in sensibility.

In 1986–7, I then embarked upon composing what was to become the first modern Chinese American opera, "A Chinaman's Chance." I wanted this new opera to be an extension of the traditional Chinese opera in America that was once so active in the Chinatown communities before World War Two. My concept was to utilize the woodfishhead and syllabic verse chants as episodic narration. I collaborated with the Chinese musicologist Guang Ming Lee, whom I had met at a "Jazz and World Music" symposium at Wesleyan University in the summer of 1986. We utilized both Cantonese and Beijing opera melodic styles, integrated with African American rhythmic, harmonic and orchestrational influences. I wrote the bilingual libretto (with sections drawn from historical narratives and the epilogue based on a Genny Lim poem), which was more of a history lesson than a conventional plot/story, though it is a story of the transformation of the Chinese immigrant god, Kwan Gung, as metaphor for the transformation of the Chinese to becoming Chinese American. It was a major struggle to fund a stage production. In April 1989, a one-time full stage performance finally happened. The Celestial Orchestra did not perform in the pit as per Western opera tradition, but was situated right on stage in accordance with Chinese opera practice—part of the drama itself. Along with *erhu* and *sona*, the orchestra consisted of "jazz" players on saxophones, bassoon, western strings and "jazz" rhythm section with Chinese opera percussion. (Since Chinese music lacks brass, I only employed strings, woodwinds and percussion.)

In the process of realizing this opera, I struggled with two major vexing issues that confront the creation of a truly multicultural synthesis. First, the integration of two vastly different musical traditions requires bi- or multi-cultural musicians and artists, willing to stretch beyond their traditional roles and approaches. As such experimental works sorely lack financial resources, it is hard to sustain the years of rehearsal and interfacing needed to forge such an interactive musical dialogue and exchange. Such projects, aimed at forging a multicultural music, have taken many years of effort, working with a stable core of musicians who are themselves in the process of understanding the concept for which I am striving. The Chinese artists with whom I work are not only master musicians within their own traditions and context, but are also open to playing my music, which they call *"jen chi gwai"* (literally, "very strange"). Their initial skepticism toward combining Chinese and jazz music has since given way to genuine excitement and commitment. Also, among the "western" players, I have found a musical and socio-political comradeship with Iranian American tenor saxophonist, Hafez Modirzadeh, whose own "chromodal discourse" conception toward both saxophone performance and composition is a shared theoretical and practical approach to synthesizing tempered and non- and variable tempered music. In his case, between Persian and African American. I also share comradeship with the world music and "jazz" percussionist Dr. Royal Hartigan. His astounding comprehensive fluency in percussion traditions from all around the world has achieved such a multicultural synthesis in the world of rhythm.

Secondly, the very compositional process must struggle to be a real synthesis, and not a pastiche or juxtaposition of contrasting cultural styles. Most world music/world beat intercultural collaborative efforts are limited in the extent to which a real synthesis has manifested. When practiced by people of color in a shallow, superficial manner, it's "chop sueyism." When practiced by culturally imperialistic whites, I have regarded these efforts as "exoticism." In opposition to the Christopher Columbus Syndrome of cultural imperialism, a genuine multicultural synthesis is the embodiment of revolutionary internationalism in music. Rather than coopting different cultures, it seeks revolutionary transformation, predicated upon anti-imperialism in both the musical respect and integrity accorded as well as social equality between peoples. Depending on one's position, I am either leaving or expanding "jazz." Whichever the case may be, I do not compose from "tunes" or "chord changes" or even "grooves." Though I am still primarily a "Western" artist, my music has been a search for approaches that are beyond East and West (hence the initial name of my most recent bi-coastal chamber group, The Journey Beyond the West Orchestra, now re-named The Monkey Orchestra).

During the late 1980s, I collaborated with Kulintang Arts, a Filipino American music and dance group in the Bay Area, on my musical theatre epic, "A Song for Manong." I found kulintang to be highly significant to my own vision as it is a cultural tradition that has continuously resisted western colonialism in the Philippines. It pre-dates the contact with Spain, therefore it is not hispanicized. This encounter directed me to draw upon exploring and developing a music that seeks to violate the sensibilities of the white imperialist bourgeoisie. Music, in which the very sound, by its aesthetics of what is considered pleasing or beautiful to the ear, is in diametrical opposition to the sensibilities and values of the oppressor; can, at the same time, be liberating and catalytic to the oppressed by its envisioning through sound a precursor for a new role. Prior to its present neo-conservative state, "jazz" had been such a revolutionary American 20th century music.

The fall season of 1989 marked a significant advance in my forging of an Afro-Asian New American Multicultural Music. Jack Chen, the octogenarian president of the Pear Garden in the West, commissioned me to write the music for an episode extracted from the Chinese classic serial adventure novel, "Journey to the West." Chen and The Pear Garden must be highly credited for preserving the Chinese opera tradition, and it has been Chen who has given me such tremendous support in presenting all my new Chinese American works on the west coast. Chen, I believe, regards my work as an important advance to the tradition of Chinese American performing arts. Composing "Monkey Meets the Spider Spirits," a twenty five minute Afro-Asian score for ballet, resulted in the formation of The Journey Beyond the West (JBTW)—now The Monkey Orchestra. This short episode premiered during Chinese New Year of 1990 and the response was ecstatic. Not only had we created the first Chinese American ballet, with a libretto sung totally in (Mandarin) Chinese, but more significantly, created a music score that defied categorization as either Chinese or "jazz" music, but was a unique and unusual hybrid.

For there to be new music, there has to be a new type of ensemble, i.e., players directed into new musical and social relationships. The JBTW (Monkey) Orchestra consists of three Chinese instrumentalists playing *pipa*, *sona*, and *erhu*, along with players versed in "jazz" playing trombone, multiple percussion that combined Chinese opera percussion and drum set (Royal Hartigan), three saxophonists, string bass, and a very special, variable temperament (chromodal) tenor saxophone part specifically written and conceived for Hafez Modirzadeh. I deliberately chose not to include the piano so as not to be bound by western temperament and harmony.

For Chinese New Year in 1991, I composed a new episode, "Uproar in Heaven," which in terms of the story line, is the beginning of what now has become a four-part musical suite-cum-serial adventure and revolutionary allegory. I have taken great artistic license in revising the classic Chinese stories of Journey to the West, and have renamed the work, "Journey Beyond the West: The New Adventures of Monkey." I have explicitly heightened revolutionary allegorical themes in my reinterpretation of the Monkey adventures: for example, Monkey's defiance of ruling class authority, Monkey's disregard for the sanctity of private ownership of the means of production, the struggle for redistribution of wealth, violence as a means of ruling class control, class struggle, the journey as the forging of a united front among the oppressed; and, in "Monkey Meets the Spider Spirits," the political and class nature of love and the fallacy of transcendental love, etc. A much longer score (45 minutes), "Uproar in Heaven" represents the fruition of a new, Chinese American multicultural music.

Interestingly, I have been one of the few Asian American male artists to deal with the oppression of Asian and Asian American women: e.g., "Home is Where the Violence Is" (1992), an anti-domestic violence performance art work; "Song of the Slave Girl" (1989), the extended aria of a Chinese prostitute circa west coast/19th century; "Picture Bride" (1992), collaboration with Korean American dancer/choreographer Peggy Choy about Japanese and Korean arranged marriage in Hawaii's sugar plantation experience; "Bound Feet" (1985), Jodi Long's text/dance work, about the oppressive feudal Chinese feminine beauty practice; "Lan Hua Hua" (1990), a reworking of a traditional Chinese folk song that was a protest of arranged marriages; "What's A Girl to Do?" and "Rockin' in Revolution/Drowning in the Yellow River"

(1984), based on Janice Mirikitani's poetry. And of course, love songs about and for Asian Americans: "Shao Heh Bao" (Chinese language); "We'll Make Tomorrow!"; a self-criticism for womanizing, "I'm Sorry (for Kayo and Sayo)." A new work is "Yes Means Yes, No Means No, Whatever She Wears, Wherever She Goes!", a suite dedicated to WHAM! (Women's Health Action and Mobilization) and BWARE (Brooklyn Women's Anti-Rape Exchange). Such works are simultaneously about women's oppression, creating revolutionary aesthetics and changing the relations of cultural production.

My goal is a radical unity of form and content.

Endnotes

1 Several etymologies have been asserted for the word "jazz." I find the less credible ones to assert an African derivation, as certain of these words are from languages not spoken south of the Sahara and therefore not likely to be in common usage among the West African, sub-Saharan peoples enslaved and brought to the Americas. More likely, "jazz" comes from either the word "jass" or "jizz" which referred to semen, as originally piano music was common to houses of prostitution, although perhaps this is only the place people not of African American origins first heard it rather than in black clubs, at house parties, in parks, and in the street. Another explanation is that "jazz" comes from the French verb, *jasser* (New Orleans, the "birthplace" of the music, was a French colonial territory) which means to "chatter nonsensically" (i.e. gibberish). In either case, the word "jazz," as used by the oppressors, has a pejorative context, as do many terms from the legacy of colonialism and oppression.

2 Spelled with a "k," "kreolization" is a concept advanced by Ms. Dorothy Désir-Davis, to be distinguished from "creolization" of M. Herskovitz, et al., pertaining to the intermixing in the Caribbean. Kreolization is from the perspective of cultural and social cross-fertilization, a process that leads to the formation of entirely new identities and cultures, and, often in the case of oppressed-oppressor relations, it is selectively appropriated by dominant social groups into the dominant identity and culture, but politicized and deracinated.

3 A perspective put forward by Dr. Royal Hartigan, which, I, too, share.

4 LeRoi Jones (Amiri Baraka), *Blues People*. William Morrow: NY, 1963.

5 Kalamu ya Salaam, *What Is Life?* Third World Press, 1993.

6 Extensive syncopation (the emphasis on "off" or "weak" beats) is very prevalent in the musical cultures of the Pacific Islands and Southeast Asia and other parts of the world. But none of these musics "swing" in the African American sense, though it can be asserted that they have their own forms of "swing."

7 An ethical mandate between the music, the musician, and the people:

    1. *Speak to the People* (the music has and will embody messages, either explicitly in the form of lyrics and/or song titles or implicitly—in sound and spirit);

    2. *Go to the People* (perform music where the people can enjoy it);

    3. *Involve the People* (dissolve the separation between artist and audience, between professional and amateur);

    4. *Change the People* (revolutionize the consciousness, values, aesthetics, and actions of the people).

Carol Genetti

Part II.

In the Belly of the Beast

photo: Andrew Rawson

The Screamers
What The Revolutionary Poets, Volunteers All, Are Supposed To Do
(for Amiri Baraka, 7 Oct. 1994)
Kalamu ya Salaam

poet/musician
who else to elevate the souls of blk folk into the future,
who bold enough to chronicle the death daring of maroon guerrillas
& the daily milk spill & hammer break resistance tactics
of all the rufuses & earthas of our race,
who better to capture the cooing to lull fat cheeked brown babies
to sleep & the incantations to propagate the oral histories
of how we became who we be?

poet/musician
articulating the African speech sensibilities of tonal languages,
the syntax, structures & ironic uses of vocabularies
orated as dialectical song, like how one word, e.g. "shit,"
depending on context & inflection, can mean so much more
than excrement as in "that shit was happening!" or could mean
very precisely doo-doo & nothing more as in "that ain't shit,"
such wonderous word wizardry a philosophically dynamic world view

revolutionary poet/musician
speaking the people's tongue
let the congregation say "ashe" (Ah-Shay)

poetry, the emotional essentialism of symbolic language,
is so important to us that all our best musicians in their
terribleness be sounding like they talking, giving
state of the race addresses with every solo, taking horns
& strings and making them sing but modeled on the yodel
of the black voice shouted at full throttle or hummed
with subtle sensitivity, the murmured moan of a west african choir
chanting felicitous greetings to the dawn or carthartic mourning
decoring an elder's last go round, the ecstatic stutter of lovers

The Screamers

chortling in the throes of orgasm, the war whoop going over the side
of the slave ship or hitting the overseer upside the head
with his own damn whip, that bad black voice, the cookers
smoking the tops of their horns screeching into the sacred
falsetto of upful feelings and the shibboleths of speaking in tongues,
as bad as our music be the truth is the musicians all want to be poets
really, really that is why the holy ones with beards
& wild hair have ancient horns which bellow like millions of negroes
 screaming for freedom in the midnight, and why our blessed
sisters throw their heads back, close their dark lidded eyes, open
their black, brown & beige throats and transport
us to another place & time where joy & pain are one & the same
making music so potent it possesses us & commands us
dance in a circle, thrash on the floor, scream
like funkateers jamming to james brown like
church stalwarts getting happy and shouting like
rappers reading the riot act to the masses:
say yo, say ho, disrupt the status quo

revolutionary poet/musician
breaking the silence of submission
with the shout of resistance
let the congregation say "ashe"

the real deal is not simply mastering the techniques of poeting, but
indeed advocating the empowerment of the exploited, the oppressed,
every poem an unfurled flag indicating which side the battle our work
falls on in this mad time crisis emergency red full of black folk killing
each other, killing each other dead, on the stoop reach up & pull out
your heart, your guts, put a bullet in your head because of something
somebody else claim you said, drive by and leave lead
& brass castings all in the streets turning our communities
 into morgues and cemeteries, children going to school carry
books & guns, knives, this is a mad & murderous time of black
on black crime, brutus bloodhounds stabbing our backs
everytime we try to unify all us selves into a togethered oneness
& our enemies employ willing negro cultural assassin gate keepers,
send these suckers gleefully skipping after us while validating
the national agendas of the otherman via the ny times
& sunday paragons of pseudo liberal, so-called moral integrity,
can you dig the gaul of killers brazenly instructing the victims
on the correct way to act humanly, or else they unleash grouchy
intellectual goons who illtelligently attempt to bludgeon us
into a stoop standing submission on the basis that our people,
the creators of america's sole significant contribution to world culture,
that we, the producers of armstrong, duke, bird, diz, monk and trane,
not to mention mahalia jackson, marion anderson, paul robeson, blind tom,

robert johnson, jimi hendrix and thousands of others, that we who produced
the most profound artists of the twentieth century & if you want writers
try to find a peer of william edward burghardt dubois' collected works,
from suppression to reconstruction to crisis to souls dubois enunciates
& elucidates the sweeping arc of our humanity, so to say that we
— about whom dubois wrote, from whom dubois was created — to say
that we must be alienated, made a thing apart in order to create
great art, nigger please, how can stand stoop so low, such pathetic
self alienation would be a laughable self negation were the rich not
giving up genius awards to dark skinned disciples of whiteness
honoring rear garde machinatious performance art pieces which de-evolve
racial amnesia to heretofore unfathomed depths, what say you
fellow scribes & purveyors of the word do you think that this is a time
for poets to only be chilling & illing incessantly talking about what
we do or don't in bed with what or whom, & how our color shouldn't
matter or is this a time to scream against the system, don't you think
we need books that tell us how our enemies look, make clear
who our allies are, give us instructions for healing our hurts
& delineate devotional acts of faith which will reinforce our struggle
& make us feel like fighting for freedom as well as feel
like falling in love with our own life affirming selves?

poet/musician
be grander than the western canon
be the sniper shooting out the eyes of enemy colored artillerers
let the congregation say "ashe"

& while we all want to eat & enjoy modern creature comforts still
comprador corruption via accommodationist versifying is a vileness
that not even phyliss wheatley would condone as she used her
18th century poems to help keep the abolitionist movement going
didn't we know as sun ra always sang, it's after the end
of the world, the end of their old world & time now to construct
our new world, revolutionary poets should wake us from the dead,
this dying we do daily in this artificial time manufactured by capitalism's
mutation into obsolescence obsession & consumer cannabalism, this time
that fund prez george clinton accurately predicted, remember
funkadelic standing on the verge and shouting from the stage
"america eats its young," an accurate description of our nationstate
in every city where our numbers soar to ten thousand or more

revolutionary poets/musicians
are supposed to be dangerous and feared
cover yankers and coat pullers,
let the congregation say "ashe"

The Screamers

but who's afraid of clown poets, def jam poets,
sound and fury poets without one iota of substance poets,
poets who can't write but who give killer interviews?
poets who are jazz poets but are never where the music is?
poets who win awards but have never demonstrated in their life?
poets who can scan & deconstruct text but who can't dance?
poets who write praise poems for their enemies?
poets who are more comfortable in germany than africa?
poets who never talk bad about the government until their grants run out?
poets who are for being down with the people but who only fly first class?
poets who write about the black experience but never in black publications?
who's afraid of them kind of poets, no one and nothing
them kind of poets are like sellout griot jester judases who, for a few pieces
of silver, will shout any silly song presidents & kings pay these poetic
prostitutes
to sing wrap their lips around for awards & prizes or sometimes just simply
a user friendly pat on the behind, ain't they got no shame, naw, none,
they got careers & publishing contracts, academic chairs and fellowships, but
they ain't got no shame and now comes the performance poet
arriving on the set mtv-ing verse that sounds like
advertisements for "i'm crazy, you're crazy, america is crazy,
and it's ok to be crazy" and that's really crazy, what do we be saying,
where do we stand, are we supporting our people in time of anger & need
or are we looking for movie rights and a hip career?

poet /musician
our people need to be moved by your insights & inspiration, not
encouraged to buy the overpriced products of your patrons
let the congregation say "ashe"

hey, we revolutionary poets are supposed to be social screamers,
spirit summoners, secular shouters and sacred sermonizers,
& not just publicists & cheerleaders mindlessly rah-rahing capital
by chanting at large mo money, mo money, mo money,
hey, we revolutionary poets are supposed to be dangerous
supposed to be enemies of whomever & whatever harms our people
but hey, big time buppie poet blowing up & going pop
who can't be revolutionary while giving head to capitalism, sucking
on the dicks of dead presidents, i know we all got contradictions
but damn sam when you be selling sneakers to kids while adidas banks
big bucks what you become is not a poet but a shoe salesman, a counter-
revolutionary shoe salesman, word to be heard my fawley if revolution is
really your goal than drop kick your 12's verbally & literally up the asses
of those who profit on our poverty & impoverish our pockets through
the legalized thievery of conspicuous consumption, who use the co-signing
of celebrities to create a false consciousness that values brands on our behinds
& nothing on our minds so the mega merchants can steal us blind

poets/musicians
saying yo, saying ho, revolution
disrupting the status quo
let the congregation say "ashe"

revolution is what we need even when we don't know it, even
when we are too afraid, too underdeveloped to face our hard realities,
revolution is what we need even after neocolonialism & the malignant
cancer of negro politicians have diarrhea run amok on our body politic,
revolution is what we need even beneath a fall in the face of friendly fire
& especially when put down by the ire of paddy roller critics in white face
come to push us back in place into the line of enemy fire by decrying
the wit & wordplay of our work as unartistic political propaganda
as if there is something wrong with talking bad about our enemy
& they mammy —raise your glass, sip a brew, here's a toast
to the slave master crew: fuck you and the ship you floated in on, fuck
the pledge allegiance & that spangled banner song & fuck your flunkies
& their tired doo-doo, in fact fuck your mammy and your whole cave crew —
revolution & conscious change is the eternal & deep seated inner ethos
of our people, revolution, some of us was always, always, & always for overturning
the system, & change, like we as a people never, never fully
accepted the neat european way our tormentors said stuff had to be done
which is why we eats fried fish and chicken today only fried instead
of in palm oil, fried in vegetable oil & lard, lawdy lard, the lard really
the thing so physically & mentally unhealthy, if jesus ever does make it back
it will have to be as a liberation theologist macking the rhetoric of change,
a revolutionary poet ciphering about healing the sick, housing the homeless,
feeding the hungry, & reciting poems called scriptures, imagine god is here
writing poetry, do you think her words would be in iambic pentameter
or even in english for that matter, it is a euro-centric conceit to think
that god is male, white and english speaking when no great religions
have ever come from the minds & caves of europe

poets/musicians
we are part of the whole, the cosmos & universe
life is our god, creation our destiny, & being beautiful
& nurturing is the only nation totally worthy of our citizenship
let the congregation say "ashe"

revolutionary poets/musicians
tomorrow belongs to those who create it, who
struggle for future & seize opportunities, who
love people & respect earth, who write poems loud & so hard
we shutter & smile the first time we hear the words uttered, conceive
verse so soft & encouraging we recite whole stanzas over and over
to loved ones, to friends, family & kin, odes so humane, healthy &

mentally rejuvenating the rimes become new birth anthems,
powerful kick images smashing mainstream negativity,
healthy heart embracing forward motion exhortations,
therapeutic cauterizing critiques which staunch backward flow,
uprising vivid invocations of engaged imaginations visioning alternated irations,
superhonest limitation revelations tempered by judicious retification,
bold self investigations of breath & inhalations,
precision audit takings of social health & waste elimination,
environmental surveying of gender & generational liberation,
cartographing & documentation of social transformation,
wordsmiths, moral messengers & ethical explorers, we've work to do
& must be audacious in our doing & unapologetic in bringing the noise,
the blusey sounding of our deepest creed, today tonight yesterday & tomorrow,
wherever we find our people in sorrow, revolution is what we really need

poet/musician
how you sound is how you are &
for now, for the escalating upliftment of the downpressed
for the ancients & ancestors, the ways they resisted & the legacies they leave
for today's first upside the head of our own backwardness
for moving up on ever pushing to the next level & the next
for revolutionary poetry hugged & welcomed by conscious
& progressive forces no matter how small (six in somebody's
basement plotting subversion or thousands in the street singing at a rally
chanting the party line: say yo, say ho, disrupt the status quo)
forever, for always, for the love of life & each other

let the congregation say "ashe"

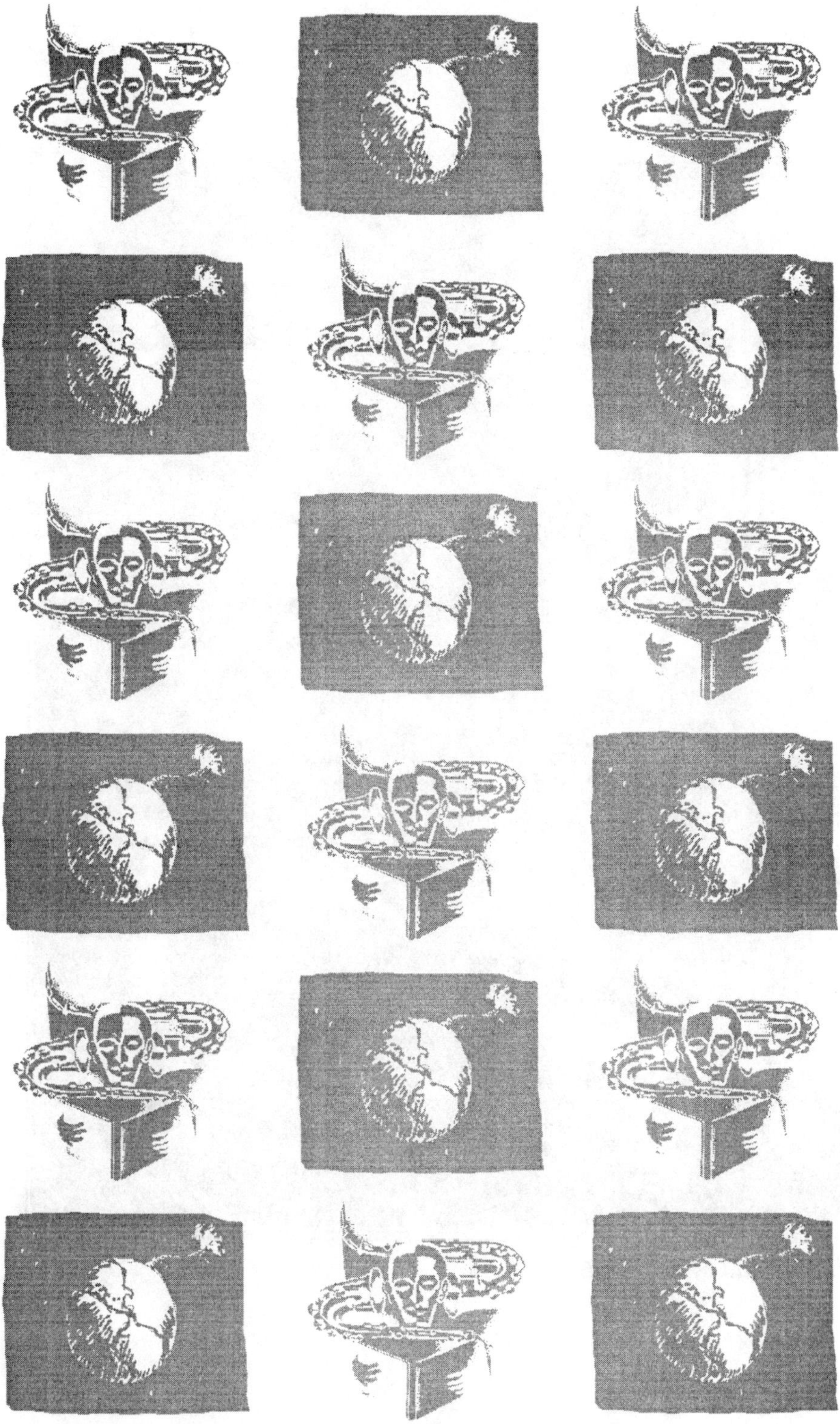

photo: Paul Miller

Music Guerrilla: An Interview with Fred Wei-han Ho

(Summer, 1992)

Miyoshi Smith

MS: Will you talk about your early professional musical back-ground as it relates to your personal/political values?

FH: I never expected to be a professional musician. I started playing the flute at the age of nine because my parents wanted me to have a well-rounded education, and part of that was to have me take up an instrument. I took up the flute because when I first saw it being demonstrated by the elementary school music teacher it seemed to be very easy—just like blowing across a Coca-Cola bottle. So I thought I could satisfy my parents and not make it too burdensome for me.

I didn't really practice much. Then at the age of 14, I was going through my male adolescence thing; I didn't want to be the only boy in an all girls flute section. So I wanted to play saxophone because saxophone is a more masculine identified instrument. I wanted to play alto or tenor because those horns got more of the solos, but I couldn't afford to buy my own instrument. So the only free instrument available from the public school band program was this big baritone because [laugh] none of the other kids wanted to carry it around to band practice—much less take it home and practice it. It was this hand-me-down baritone sax, and I took it up at the age of fourteen. It has since then become my voice; I've never taken up the alto or tenor. My identity now is rooted to the baritone saxophone.

I became involved in African American music at the same time I was going through a consciousness about myself as an Asian American/Chinese American in this society. My social and political awareness coincided with my musical growth. I think the music was just a way to express the transition I was going through. It was a way to find myself and to locate myself particularly in the struggles of oppressed peoples in this society. Music has always been part of that expression, and I became very involved in music at the age of sixteen—particularly with Archie Shepp who's in the Amherst area where I grew up. Then I went to college.

I went to Harvard University and I was quite alienated there by the Eurocentric curriculum and academic elitism. I put aside playing music. Then, when I finished college, I decided to become a construction worker.

During my periods of unemployment, I was collecting a fairly good unemployment check, had a lot of free time and I started practicing again—two, three, four, five, six hours a day. One day after working construction for two years I just decided I was happiest playing music, and with very little thought decided I would move to New York and give it a go as a professional musician. That was quite a shock for me because I came to New York without an apartment, without a job, without any contacts in the music world—just starting completely from scratch. So it was a period of paying a lot of dues. It was a lot of struggle. But I learned a lot from it. I think having a political activist organizer background helped to focus me a lot. I brought certain kinds of administrative and organizational skills that many musicians lack, but I think the main thing is that it gave me a sense of clarity and purpose in what I wanted to do. It wasn't just music for music's sake. It was music for liberation: both my own, as well as social. This would not only be my career, my artistic expression, but it would fit into the social struggle in the society. So in a nut shell that's kind of how I got to where I am today. I think I've been fortunate to be able to unite my personal and artistic and professional and political interests into one. I think too often we live very fragmented kinds of lives because we're not able to do the things that we really want to do in life—that creates a lot of alienation. I've been able to be clear about what's important to me and to pursue that—oftentimes with very little financial reward or support. That's never been important to me, but I know they're very important to a lot of other folks whether they want to admit it or not. So my music has been part of a larger sense of purpose than simply my own individual satisfaction or career.

MS: What were your ideas, plans or goals, musically, when you came to New York City?

FH: When I came to New York I had no goals as far as career. I didn't know what it meant to be a professional musician. All I wanted was to learn as much as I could and to get as much experience in as many playing contexts as possible. I think first of all being a baritone saxophonist limited my opportunities because primarily I could only work in big bands, and I was Chinese American in a music industry that was fairly segregated, mostly in terms of social cliques. I didn't fit in anywhere—because there's only a handful of professional Asian American "jazz" musicians. So I had to find my own identity. I think that's what prompted me to start my own projects, lead my own groups, and write my own music. When you don't have something you can necessarily fit easily into, then you have to create your own scene. So that's how becoming a bandleader, and becoming a composer and arranger came about. I really had no goals, and to this day I don't think very much about my career. There's not a record label that I want to be a part of for instance; there's not a tour circuit that I want to work *per se*, and I think I'm an enigma to many people.

When I was attracted to this music as a youth it was the music of struggle, you know it reflected the ethos, the spirit, of the '60s. People like Archie [Shepp] and Max Roach were inspirations to me. But a lot has transpired in this society in the last 20 years. There's a general kind of conservatism.... The so-called Classical Jazz, the New York traditionalist revivalist thing has been disappointing to me. I made this statement at the National Jazz Network Conference where I was a panelist. I said that this is the first time in the history of the music where 20-year-old musicians are playing styles that predate their births and are stuck there. I have always found the music to be fresh and vital and radical in the sense that it has always paid homage to the roots and the traditions, but every generation has had the responsibility of finding their own voice and their identity. Yet this is the first time where this generation is assuming an identity and a voice that predates their birth into this world.

So I feel like this music that has been called Jazz has been infected by the general conservatism in this society. The music business is simply about making money and packaging, and the role of artists and their creative ideas—are not important to the profit making scheme. I find that, for example, in the music business most of the A&R people are white men who don't understand what I do as an Asian American much less relate to what I'm doing. So I'm an underground artist in the truest sense in that I'm not looking for their legitimation or necessarily their support. If we can do business together fine. But I'm not looking to tailor my work or who I am to the status quo. Most of my support has largely come from fellow travelers, people who understand and believe in what I'm doing and share a part of that. So that's why you can logically explain where I get booked and who I record for and that sort of thing. I mean it's fairly clear who are the people with integrity and progressive outlook, and those who are simply parasites of one kind or another in this business.

MS: What people and musics influenced you?

FH: As a young teenager learning to play the saxophone, I studied with a studio musician named who taught me a little bit about arranging. Then I went over to the University of Massachusetts and sat in on a lot of their rehearsals and workshops. I studied with Archie Shepp for two or three years as a teenager—not saxophone, but ensemble. I played a lot of big band music: the music of Thad Jones, for instance, or Count Basie. That taught me a lot about orchestration. I would take home the parts of all the instruments and I would write each part out on a score sheet. I would study how the arrangements were put together and that's how I learned about such things as voicing. When I came to New York I got together a couple of times with Hamiet Bluiett. It was very important for me to understand how to play altissimo—above the normal range—on the baritone saxophone. But I largely just taught myself. I'm a self-taught artist. I just find the music that I really like and am moved by, and dissect it; learning how it's put together. But I think the main thing is to understand how the music fits in with your own identity.

MS: How did you develop your instrumental tone?

FH: I play baritone as my principal. It's a big horn; it has to have a big sound. But I've been trying to find a complex range of different voices in the baritone so it can be humerous, be sarcastic, be angry, be sad—the whole range of emotions that don't rely on conventional western pitches or notes. For instance, I utilize what I call broken notes: when you play a note you break the sound of it. Slap tounges. Multiphonics. These are terms that of course Western music has put forward to categorize or codify what you're trying to do with sound. Essentially you have a range of sound and it's really how you sculpt it in a lot of ways. You're given this raw material, sound. You use the physics of sound to sculpt it in a conscious way. There is a semi-conscious element to it also—in the sense that you don't prefigure everything. In fact, you try to immediately project a mood or personality when you play. That's the whole aspect of improvisation. It shouldn't be predetermined.

MS: Your orchestral works have nice movement to them. In terms of writing and voicings, how does drawing from different musics—that is, non-Western—allow you to achieve certain emotions? And how does it change the sound of your music?

FH: I have always been more attracted to the extended works, like the Mingus and Ellington suites, that speak to a kind of an epic story or narrative. I was never really that drawn to, for example, the jazz tune as a form. I liked the extended works because they had an expanded quality to them that you could deal with—kind of an historical, panoramic, epic narrative. My interest in opera, for example Chinese opera, kind of came subliminally since my father listened to a lot of Chinese opera records. At first I didn't like it because I was going through a whole assimilation trip: trying to become white and the music sounded like chicken scratching to me. But it creeped into my consciousness. The more that I became aware of my own identity as a Chinese American/Asian American, and saw how that was an identity in opposition to white supremacy and Eurocentrism, the more I began to understand music as a way to articulate that identity and sought to create a musical form that was not essentially

Western European, or even for that matter European American.

African American music represented that cross-cultural synthesis. It was through putting a lot of time into working with the Chinese immigrant community that I began to learn and acquire a sense of Chinese folk songs and to understand folk music as really a people's music about the lives of everyday common working people. It was not a conservative elite type of high art or high brow music; it was really the music of workers which was raw and poignant. There was nothing intellectualized or made into art, per se, but it was the stuff that great art draws from because the experiences and emotions are so real and vivid.

So it was a matter of acquiring the kind of story-like quality of the folk songs and integrating that into extended compositional forms drawing from a rich palette of colors and emotions that try to talk about the ups and downs, the twists and turns, of people's lives. I was trying to create music that was essentially programmatic, conveying certain kinds of themes, expressions, and feelings. Yet at the same time it was abstract in the sense of always searching and experimenting to find new relationships and combinations with musical structures.

So it's not simply programmatic from the point of view of being accompaniment to a story—but the music itself is the story through the very sound of it. My work has some very rich orchestrations that are not in Western symphonies or in the kind of straight ahead big band tradition. It almost has a film-like quality to it. It's narrative in the sense that I'm very conscious about what I'm trying to convey; it's not simply musical experimentation for the sake of musical experimentation. I'm trying to experiment from the point of view of how can I best express the complexity or contradiction of the situation I'm trying to comment on.

MS: Can you give an example of how what you just said works by citing a composition like "Contradiction, Please!" or one of your other pieces?

FH: In "Contradiction, Please! The Revenge Of Charlie Chan," I'm trying to work on two levels. On one level, I try to satirize and look at the paradoxes, the kind of twisted ironies, of bourgeois morality; the values that are professed in this society as opposed to the realities. For example, Malcolm X's very famous saying is the first section of this suite: "Democracy or Disguised Hypocrisy?" I'm really fascinated with contradictions, and it just kind of struck me that one of the more popular stereotypes of Chinese Americans is Charile Chan. He would always have this saying, "Contradiction, please," when he was taking exception to his white detective colleagues. It was a way in which he subverted the truism of what they thought was an open-shut-case. He would come to see the complexities or something else underlying it. This suite developed as a series of musical commentaries on some of these contradictions, dealing with our values in the society. I wanted to draw from a lot of contradictory musical influences; for example, the action adventure film noir soundtracks, futuristic free music, elements of Chinese folk music. I wanted to combine all these things together in a way that would musically personify these contradictions. So, that's the nature of "Contradiction, Please!"

"We Refuse To Be Used And Abused" is a tribute to largely black and Latina women hotel workers who went out on strike in New York City in 1986. It was a way for me to comment about the workers' struggles being on strike, but also it primarily was a celebration of the spirit of these women. People don't understand that these are the workers, when you go to a hotel, who clean out your toilet, who empty the trash, make your beds, wash the bathrooms and so forth. They're the completely overlooked and/or unrecognized segment of our society. Yet they have a lot of strength because they're not only domestic workers but at home they're being wives and mothers or whatever. And when they went out on strike they were uncompromising in their demands to the hotel management in this town. So I was very inspired by that spirit: that the bottom of our society is the strongest because so much weight has to be borne by them.

Yet they're given such little recognition, so I wanted to pay tribute to them. That particular suite weaves in and out of different kinds of meters. It begins in 2/4, then goes to 4/4, then shifts to 5/4, then 10/4 and back to 6/4. There are lots of meter changes. I also arranged different kinds of musical styles in it too, from a pop funk groove to twelve tone writing to modal to Eastern influences and back to swing. It is a reflection of the musical journey that I've taken—in the sense that our lives should always be about constant development. We shouldn't be stuck in one kind of style or thought; relying on our past ways. We should constantly be open to change because the world around us is changing and I'm trying to evoke that process. I'm constantly changing too. As I listen to more and more music, particularly music from around the world, I'm hearing these things and not necessarily trying to faithfully reproduce them as an ethnomusicologist would, but just simply drawing inspiration from them. I draw out little elements or ideas and incorporate that into my sense of being, my sense of consciousness. I'm trying to look at the world from an international global perspective to understand how so many different kinds of struggles are interconnected. If we're really about understanding how to change the planet we have to understand how all these different things fit together into a global system.

MS: Does working with lower end instruments allow you to get a fuller sound?

FH: I'd make that more of a sociological analogy. Because I play baritone saxophone which has been on the bottom—I've had to work from the bottom up. So I've located myself on the bottom which is always where the foundation is. Because I play baritone saxophone, I was forced to write my own music. I was really very bored with the traditional role that most arrangers have given the baritone sax, which is mostly the root or fifth of the chord. I have a lot of experience in the big band where the baritone saxophone is kind of an anomaly because, on the one hand, it's in the saxophone section, but, on the other hand, a lot of people write for it with the trombones because it's closer in range to the trombones. It kind of weaves in and out of the reed section and the low brass section. So I wanted to develop the baritone saxophone in a way that Duke Ellington did with Harry Carney: really expand its potential a lot more, and develop it a lot more in the middle and upper partials of the chord so as not to be stuck with triadic voicings—voicings simply based on major and minor thirds.

At one point in the mid-'80s I swore to myself I wouldn't use any more triadic voicings. I'm not as dogmatic about that now. But basically that was a way to force myself to find new kinds of harmonies. I never really was stuck too much with chords. I was more into harmony as a means rather than an end. By that I mean harmony was simply a way to find colors, but to find new colors you have to put together new mixtures. What I'm really after is finding those new mixtures, and not necessarily relying upon familiar or conventional harmonies.

MS: Was doing your independent label a way to get around the record industry?

FH: Let's face it, we don't make money from our records. To me it's kind of an underground product in a lot of ways. I've just become resigned to the fact that if you want my music, then you just have to come to me. It's like during the revolutionary period in China when the Red Army went to the hills of Yenan. If you wanted to hook up with the guerrillas you had to go to the mountains, right. You had to join them. You had to live the life the guerrillas lived. Same thing with my music. If you want this music, you have to come find us. You have to participate in it. I've accepted the fact that my music may not be found in record stores, but that's fine. Those who really want it will be able to find us when we perform, when we are out in public. People raise this question, "Well, what about wider exposure? Wouldn't you have more impact?" If you can still keep the same content in what you're doing, that's fine. But if you have to water down your content, then what's the purpose of having wider exposure?

When we talk about appealing to the least common denominator, the least common denominator is zero. I'm not about being at zero. It's a zero situation anyway, since we're not making money from what we're doing. So why do you have to make your content come down to zero!

MS: What changes would you make in the so-called contemporary music scene in terms of performance, distribution...

FH: I think distribution is a very difficult problem confronting independent artists. I've written about this in terms of the increasing monopolization of the mass communications entertainment industry. Even though they claim to have greater diversity, there's actually, when you look at the scene, a lot less variety in terms of different kinds of ideas and expressions. Everything has to be packaged into a 4/4 Western temperament, Western harmony framework. I think the only solution to that is going to be the collaboration of cultural guerrillas and underground artists who will first of all perform for and sell their work to each other. It's going to be through word of mouth or the grapevine that more people will find out about them. We have to kind of be foot soldiers in that respect. I think too many artists live under the illusion of the star syndrome. All they really want is to sign with a major label and then everything will be taken care of for them: their product will be in all the stores, there will be promotion and hype. But what kind of product is that? Rather than stardom, collaboration is very important to me, particularly between radical artistic voices. I'm trying to do that not only with musicians, but with artists of other idioms and disciplines.

We need to also figure it out organizationally, and this is a tough one: how can we promote and increase the circulation of our work! It requires being connected with and finding fellow believers in the business and administrative end of things. It also means finding radio people, presenters, managers, booking people, writers and critics who have integrity and consciousness. There are a few, but it seems like one of the job requirements for getting a well-paid gig is to leave that on the outside. They might find some quirky or kind of off-the-beaten-track voices or ideas, but they're not threatening the status quo. What they cannot deal with is stuff that actually threatens the basis of power in the society. So what I've come to learn is that there is no justice. Just us. We are making do with what we have. What we need to do is hook up more, not believe in the lies of the system, and be more mutually supportive.

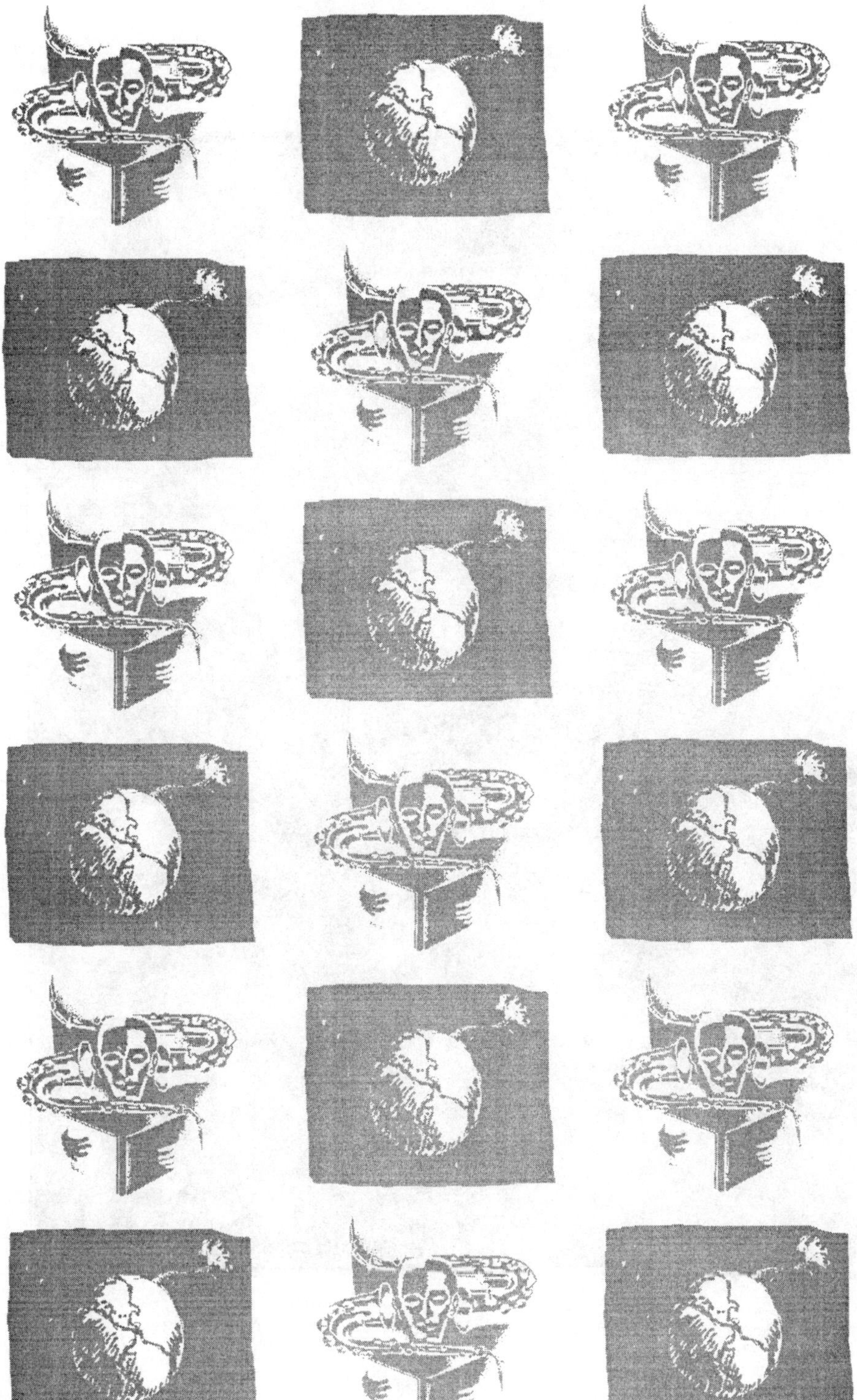

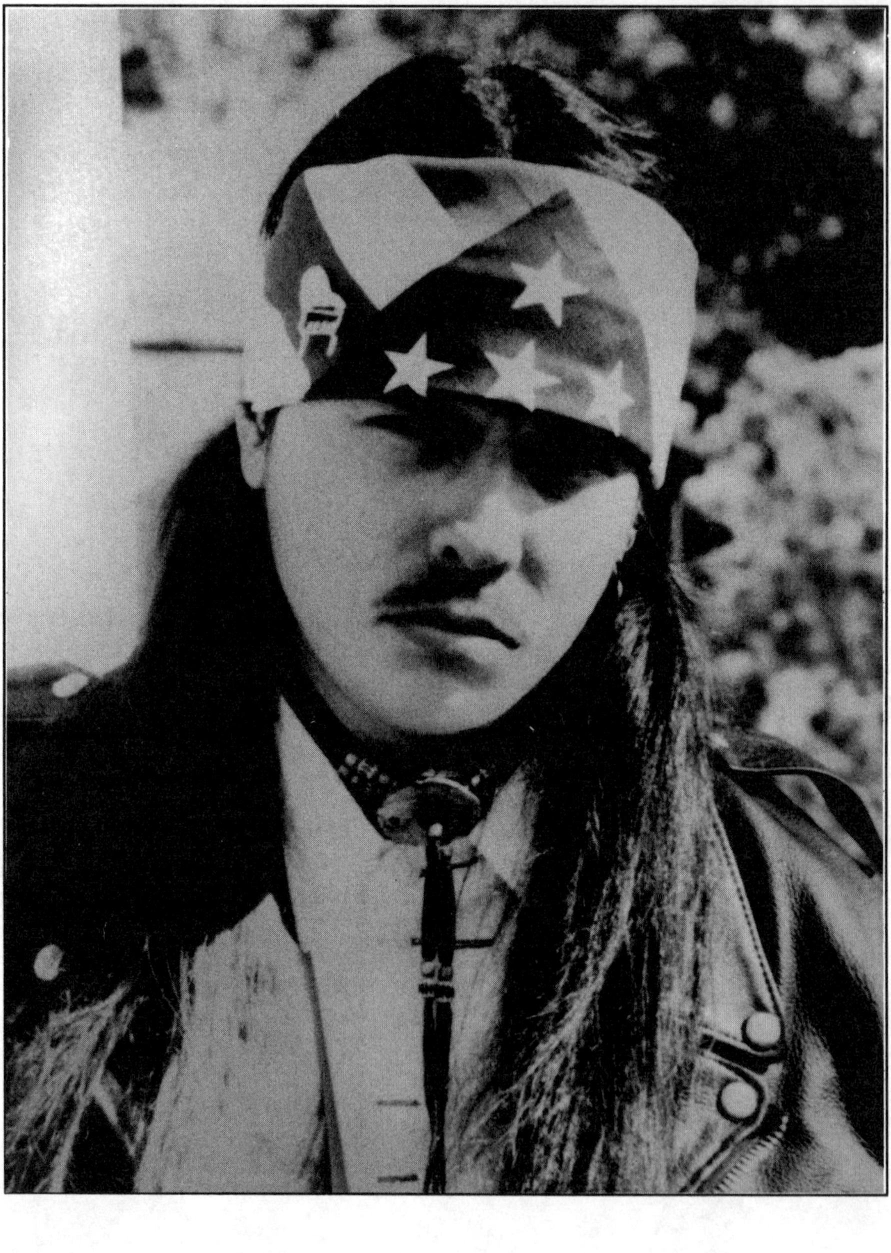

Boyz from the Rez: An Interview with Robby Bee

(August 26, 1994)

Ron Sakolsky

Time to break the silence
Time to talk about the red and black alliance
Seminole, Cherokee, ya I could go on.
Check your family tree
If you think I'm wrong
African, Native skin, both are said with pride
Two oppressed races fighting side by side.
— "Ebony Warrior" by Robby Bee

RS: You are a formally trained musician fronting a Native American hip-hop band. How did the Boyz From The Rez project come about for you?

RB: Basically, rap is poetry. So, if you happen to both be a musician and a poet then that's just more power to you. As far as the issues go that I write about, it is very easy for me because I have lived them all my life. It started when I was a kid because of being around my father [Tom Bee] and the music was always around the house. He was the leader and founder of the group XIT which was one of the first Native groups to really delve deeply into politics.

RS: Yes. Some of your father's music is being re-issued these days, isn't it?

RB: Yeah. We're doing quite well with that. We [SOAR— Sound of America Records] have it on CD and cassette. It's selling just as well as ever. Its very classic music and the issues really haven't changed very much. Native people are the forgotten people.

RS: Well, as you say, the issues, unfortunately, still remain the same, but the form of musical expression is somewhat different. It seems to me that Xit was mining a different kind of musical vein than you do. You call your music Pow-Wow Hip-Hop or Red House Swing. What are the musical influences that you incorporate in these labels?

RB: I like all styles of music. I'm one of those people that's very open minded musically. Every music has something to offer. My music is a little bit different than my father's, not so much politically in terms of what we say, but in the genre of music. The times have changed so much since rock was the genre of music everyone listened to. It was the best way to get your message across. Now the young kids today listen to a lot—rap, hip-hop, house, whatever. Plus, I think that rap lends itself to political music because of the way the form of the music is set up. Basically, you can say more in a four-minute rap song than you can in a four-minute pop or country tune because you're rapping on the beat. Therefore, you say a lot more in a shorter length of time. It's almost like a speech on a podium. I think that the form of music is very effective in getting the message across. Like anything else you can use music in a negative way or a positive way. I know a lot of kids are influenced musically. That's not to say you can blame everything on the artist, but I believe that musically you can contribute to the world just as much as a politician does. I know kids will listen to someone they admire, like a musician, before their own parents or teachers. And if they are going to listen to me, or anyone else, then I think I should make sure I have something worthwhile to say.

RS: What is it that you are trying to say? How does your message fit into your vision as an artist involved in connecting music to social change?

RB: My music is a form of social change because it brings up the issues in the first place. I always thought that half the problem in anything is not even knowing that there is a problem. I think when it comes to Native Americans, especially Native American politics, this country is in a major denial.

RS: I have a friend [Sarah Schulman] who is a novelist who calls this country the United States of Denial.

RB: Yeah, I believe that too. I'm not pro-negativity. Sure people look at me as if I'm a negative person, but I think that bringing up these issues is actually a positive step forward for all people. I don't think they are just Native American issues. I think they're human issues. Half the problem is ignorance between the races. I mean, if you don't understand one another and all you know are the stereotypes about one another then those are the things you are going to think of everytime you come across one another. When we realize that we have similarities, I think a lot of those walls of ignorance can be torn down. First of all, we have got to get people to realize that Native Americans are still here. It's not just an Old West sideshow thing. We're very much still here and the problems have not disappeared. The problems from the past are still here, in the present 'cause they've never been actually dealt with. In my music I am trying to get issues across that people might not even know about. If Leonard Peltier was a household name, he would be free.

RS: You call him "our Nelson Mandela" in one of your songs...

RB: Well, he is our Nelson Mandela. Nelson Mandela was wrongfully imprisoned, and the U.S. put pressure on the South African government but, it does the same thing. You have to practice what you preach. If you look at all the facts, it is a clear-cut case that he should be out. The problem is a lot of people don't even know who he is. I can go on a streetcorner and say the name, Nelson Mandela, and most likely seven or eight out of ten people will know who I am talking about. Yet if I said Leonard Peltier, most people would have no idea who the hell it is I'm talking about. This to me is very sad because he is a political prisoner in our own country. I see all these people with kind hearts wanting to do something abroad. Well that's great, but, why don't they look in their own country. We've got so much in this country that is wrong. So much that we could do here. I think that the average human being, regardless of race, color, creed, whatever, has got a kind heart, but I think most people in this world tend to be sheep and not shepherds. There aren't as many leaders as there are followers. If they don't know the facts, they are going to follow the wrong person. I think that if they really knew what was going on there would be more of a concern. There would be more of a rally. A lot of people are appalled once they do know. These are not things you see on the nightly news. With Mandela, unlike with Native Americans, he's got the majority in his country behind him, but what also helped him was world wide opinion that put pressure on the government to release him. They made such a stink about it. He became such a household word that they had no choice but to free him. You can look at the Civil Rights Movement in *this* country. There were a lot of non-black people involved who said this is not a color issue but a right-or-wrong issue.

RS: Aside from having a very positive message and being able to educate people and raise their consciousness on issues like that of Leonard Peltier, because of the genre of music that you have decided to operate in, you're already building an alliance between Native Americans and African Americans. Was that a conscious choice on your part?

RB: Well, another thing that freaks me out is that racism has been so effectively done in this country where they actually single out black people and Native people as two separate entities. When in reality, oppression is oppression. And, going way back to the formation of this country they treated both people the exact same way. I mean there were Native American slaves before even black slaves. Its been documented that at least one-third of all black Americans in this country have some Native American ancestry that they can trace back in their families. It's more than obvious that there is a connection there. If you look at the cultures there are similarities. Way back when, Native Americans used to adopt African Americans into the tribe. In our song "Ebony Warrior," we talk about the black and red alliance. I always knew about it, but I think there is a stronger connection there than most people either Native or black really realize. Some of the great leaders like Frederick Douglass, were black and had Native American ancestry as well. There have been lots of cases documented of Native and black situations where, when they united, they were undefeated.

RS: Certainly in your band Michael D embodies that idea of the "ebony warrior." Yet I wonder what you think about something like the Buffalo Soldier phenomenon, where oppressed people are pulled apart and turned against one another, rather than seeing themselves as having a common struggle.

RB: Knowledge is the key in everything. If you don't have the knowledge than you're nothing more than just a puppet on a string because people can then effectively manipulate you. I always tell people the less you know, the less you have to go on, the more likely you are to make the wrong decisions. What they have done in this country is to have effectively kept people ignorant so they don't even know where they came from, what their past connection is to one another. Therefore, they are easily manipulated into fighting one another, not realizing that we're in the same exact predicament and we actually are brothers and sisters. United you stand, divided you fall. I mean they did the same with Native tribes. They got one Native tribe to fight another Native tribe. They did the same in Africa where they had one African tribe fight another African tribe. It's just divide and conquer. It's a very old concept—since the beginning of time—which they have effectively used. They get people thinking about race and color instead of cause. I really don't think color. I think cause. It's different. If you think just color you become the very enemy that you're fighting. You get so involved in what you are doing that you become blinded and you become the enemy yourself.

RS: Given your intentions, how do you get your music out to all the diverse groups of people in the population. Do you play the pow wow circuit? Do you play clubs that cater to a rap audience? Do you play colleges? In terms of audience, how do you reach beyond just Native Americans and educate everybody as you suggest, not to the exclusion of Native Americans of course, who might even be a priority, but beyond them, how do you get to these other groups?

RB: Obviously when you talk politics the venues and avenues of performance where you can play are more limited. Once you become political, you become branded. Oh, no! Here comes Bob Marley! Oh, no! Here comes John Lennon! They single you out because they know the power of music. I mean, the right songs can do more than a political speech ever could in Washington, D.C. We pretty much operate like any other political group. We've done lectures at colleges and schools. We've done a lot of reservation gigs. We've done a lot of things in Europe. It's a lot more closed in this country though. For instance, Buffy St. Marie is actually on a major label with Warner Bros., but yet her music is not really easily accessible. She can't even play in this country because there aren't really venues. There are still a lot of people in this country who are in control that are totally against Native Americans coming up. It doesn't take a genius to know what was done in this country was wrong. Though you can't go back in time, you can focus on the present, which obviously leads to the future. But until they are willing to realize that they messed up, they did us wrong; then there's never going to be healing.

RS: You know, you mentioned Buffy St. Marie and I think in terms of what you're trying to do there has been an interesting kind of reciprocity on the part of Sweet Honey in the Rock who just recently released a version of one of Buffy St. Marie's songs—to express that connection between Native and African Americans on the part of African Americans. Do you see that kind of thing happening more frequently? I know hip-hoppers have been very active musically in dissing the Colombus Quincentennial that happened a couple of years ago. Do you see that kind of trend happening more often?

RB: It's fine to diss Columbus, but I'd also like to see it go into other forms as well. If I was a black person and I was playing for the Washington Redskins and I knew that my red brothers didn't like it or that it was wrong, then it would be hard for me to play. What if the roles were reversed and it was called the Washington Blackskins? The predominant race in Washington, D.C. is, in fact, black people. If they were to change the name to Blackskins, would it be allowed? I'm always telling people freedom is like a bicycle, you've got to keep pedaling, because once you stop pedaling you go all the way back down the hill again.

RS: It sounds to me that one of the things you are saying is that it is one thing to talk about Columbus who lived a long time ago, but there are issues today that need to be addressed.

RB: It's great that we talk about the past as far as keeping the knowledge of what happened so that we don't ever lose it because you don't want to backtrack. I think one thing that history is supposed to teach us is that if you learn from the lessons of the past, hopefully, you won't make the same mistakes again. So, it's good to know that stuff, but I don't think it's good to dwell on it. When they think of Native Americans, if they think of them at all, non-Natives always think of them as the past—always the past, the past, the past. A good example is Hollywood movies. It's always the Wild West. A Native American has got to be on a horse and wearing feathers. They can never put them in the contemporary realm. So that's half of it. They still have this romantic feeling of Native Americans not realizing, well like, yo, we're still here, and we're just like anybody else. A lot of people used to think when I first started that rap was just a black thing. You go to the reservation, they're very hip about what is going on. They like rap. I really don't see music as being any color.

RS: In light of reassessing past history toward making future alliances, what about the New Orleans Mardi Gras tradition of "masking Indian"—the Black Indian musical tradition which still survives in the Crescent City. To some extent that is a romanticization, but in another sense it's making clear that there is an historic connection there being addressed in the present tense. I was wondering if you wanted to comment on that one, or if you know of other situations where that kind of thing happens?

RB: I don't think there is ever a cut and dry answer in anything. There are always good things and bad things about everything. It's good to have that black/Indian connection, but I think it's better when a person of their own race is representing themselves. Yet, I think it is a positive step to have that bridge of knowledge. A lot of black people don't even know that connection, even Indian people for that matter. I know sometimes when Native people will see black people at a pow-wow, a lot of them are so ignorant that they do not even know that a lot of people are there because they themselves have a Native American ancestry, and are very curious and interested in pursuing that part of their family tree. I meet several every time the Boyz play a pow-wow that say, "Yeah, on my dad's side I'm Cherokee," or "I'm Blackfoot," or I'm this or I'm that. The problem I always have, and I always think it is funny, is that unless you are one-hundred percent Native, people don't think of you as a Native. Or, they say you don't look Native because there is a certain stereotyped way you have to look, I guess. They always have that romantic stone cut image with a sharp nose and long hair. The tribal rolls, in a way, are siding with the government. They keep, once again, unity from fully happening as far as people that are not one hundred percent Native. Maybe they're only half, quarter, maybe an eighth, whatever. That keeps them from being part of the Native world. Where as with a black person, if he is only a fourth black, then he's still black. You still have that connection.

RS: Well, obviously, growing up in a household with Tom Bee, you were able to have your consciousness raised about these issues. Were there any other Native musicians, or musicians in general, that influenced you in terms of your own kind of approach to music?

RB: Oh, man, there's just so many! Basically, I respect all that are out there because you've got to understand that for a Native musician to go out there and do it, it's twice as hard because of the fact that they don't take Native people seriously to begin with. You know, they kind of shun them. I draw from everyone—obviously, my father, his group, all the other people that my father knew at the time going back to Jesse Ed Davis. I like Buddy Redbow a lot. I thought he was a very talented person, just as talented as any other of these country people I see on the charts. For awhile I even did country radio and so I'm not just talking out of context. It's a very prejudiced thing if you ask me. If it is a white person with the same voice and the same ability, there's a lot of doors that are open, but because he was a Native, he never was taken seriously.

RS: What about someone like John Trudell? Let me explain. When I listen to his music it seems to me that he's incorporated the blues in his music in much the same way that you've incorporated hip-hop in your music—combining rock and blues in his case, and hip-hop and rock in your case, with Native music. Was he an influence upon you?

RB: He is definitely an influence on me. He is a poet. To me, Trudell is like a Native Shakespeare. The only difference between us, is once again this different generation. He comes from my father's generation when there was that blues rock connection. I love that music myself, you know I'm not just a rapper. I write all kinds of music. I'm not limited to just one style of music. I like all kinds of stuff, but for politics rap just seems to lend itself best to that. The blues is kind of like that same feeling—it was music that was born out of oppression. It was a form of release, of keeping your sanity. I call rap American reggae because reggae was born out of oppression. True hip-hop, when it first began, was all about what's going on in the neighborhood, and what was happening. It's obviously changed over the years, but, basically the same idea is there. I do have a problem with some rappers doing unpositive things with the music since I feel its such a powerful means. I think too much of it is wasted on dissing one another or talking about gangs, sex, and drugs. If you really realize the power of the medium of music I think you can bring about positive change as opposed to negative change.

RS: Just as blues is often considered to be a music of a previous generation, classic reggae these days is as well. Young Jamaicans are listening to dancehall and rap and young

African Americans seem to be merging rap music with dancehall music. At least that process is starting to happen. As someone who's been influenced by Jamaican music, particularly Marley and the reggae of the past, I was wondering if you're thinking of incorporating some dancehall into your music or is that something you don't think would be appropriate?

RB: It's hard to explain, but when I write a song it takes on a life of its own. I don't really have just one sound per se. Being that I'm a music junkie, I listen to everything. Depending on what the song is the music dictates itself. I have written songs that have a reggae-type style and flavor, but it's not something I intentionally go out and try to do. I start writing lyrics and then it just starts kind of forming from there. I am trying to incorporate more of Native sound in what I do because I want people to see the beauty of the Native culture and what it has to offer, but it's not something I consciously think about. I kind of just let it roll with the flow. It just pretty much depends on what the song says to me at the moment. If you just ate one food every day, even if it was your favorite food, you'd get sick of it really quick. I might go into a period where I listen to nothing but just reggae, and I might the next week switch and go back to rap, and the next week go off to rock and then jazz and then go back to classical for awhile. I go through stages where, for a couple of weeks I'll listen to just one thing and just get into that, live that, genre for awhile. Depending on where I'm at, the music takes a shape of its own. The same thing could happen with dancehall. As it stands now, I can't stop writing. I tend to always have a pen with me and paper. And in instances where I've run out of paper, I'll gladly use a napkin or whatever is available.

RS: Some musicians seem to have many musical influences but the music that they make is just of one genre. It seems like one of the things you are able to do successfully is to come up with these hybrid forms that really speak to more than one audience.

RB: It's not something I do consciously, it's just that I think it's good to be open-minded. I, myself, have got friends that like just one style of music, but I was successfully able to give them a taste of other styles and they totally flipped out. They were like little kids that all of sudden realized that, oh my god, this is something new! Wow! I've always been open to new things. I think you grow as a person, but also, you learn that genre has nothing to do with musical talent or ability or if it's good or not. It goes back to Duke Ellington's statement that there's two kinds of music, good and bad. You know? I've been influenced by a lot. Obviously with my father, since he was working at Motown in the '70s as a writer and producer, R&B is a major influence on me too. At the same time that I was taking classical, jazz and piano lessons I was listening to all the Motown, Stax and Atlantic sides, and whatever I could get my hands on. I really like the old R&B a lot.

RS: Well, let me ask a question that relates to your father. You record for the SOAR corporation. Can you say what those initials stand for and how SOAR fits into your work as a musician involved in social change? I know that one of the other artists on the label is Russell Means, a person that you wouldn't ordinarily associate with a particular kind of music but rather with political activism.

RB: As to my father, he learned a lot at Motown 'cause it was a minority company and he could see how they operated. Day in and day out, they had to deal with prejudice. He learned a lot, and he took those things he learned and incorporated them into this company, SOAR, which stands for Sound Of America Records. SOAR is a label of music for Native Americans. It's kind of like a way of documenting and keeping the Native American culture and music and all the heritage alive. We're like a Native Motown, if you will, with Native American artists, producers, arrangers, writers, all that. We have four different labels, SOAR is the corporation, and then you have SOAR, the label. SOAR, the label, is for all the traditional music recorded in the way that it should be. I mean, prior to us, there were, obviously other companies recording Native American music, but because we're actually Native owned and operated, that's a difference. Before us, they just thought of it as second class music and never really recorded it, packaged it or thought of it as anything but inferior. It was treated like the music that you'd find on the back shelf collecting dust. My dad came along and he was very adamant in his goal. Number one was to bring Native American music to the forefront and show people that music is music, and it deserves just as much respect as any other style of music. You can't say that jazz is not as good as hip-hop or rock because it doesn't sell as much. You can't go on just numbers. He started by not recording just any Native group, but the best Native groups and artists he could find. He treated it just like he would a pop label. A lot of people make the mistake thinking, well, yo, you're indian, lets turn on the mike, sing. He basically took it to the pop realm where he auditions people to see if they had what it takes in that particular field of music. We pride ourselves on our base of traditional music and that's the real heartbeat of America, you know, it's people, it's traditional music. We then have three other labels. The one I'm on is Warrior Records. That tends to be the more urban or contemporary, if you will, and that kind of shows people that Native Americans aren't, once again, just on horseback with feathers. We have the Dakota label, which is Native American story telling and folklore. Finally, we have Natural Visions, which is Native American avant garde instrumental music. We've actually even started getting into the jazz realm.

RS: And are you involved in the business end of it as well?

RB: Yes I am. If I was going to compare it I guess you'd say that my dad's Gordy and I'd be Smokey Robinson. He does more of the business-type stuff, my specialty is more musical. He lets me produce acts. We listen together. We critique different things. We listen to tapes. We have a lot of stuff submitted to us just like any other record label. We pick certain artists that we think are good and also fit into what we're doing or that we think we could market in the right way. We treat it just like any other company.

RS: Okay. Well let me ask you one final question. This is sort an overall question and it has to do with your larger vision as a musician and as somebody involved with producing Native American music as well. What would you like to see come about in terms of both the music and the larger society?

RB: It's going to take more than just one generation or two or whatever to get the full dream achieved. There's got to be a generation willing to sacrifice and get that ball rolling forward. Obviously, the ultimate goal would be to where Native American people are accepted in the society as people and not ridiculed and the day when they let them speak for themselves and where they're not just treated like step children, where they are actually accepted as being human beings. Now, Hollywood and the government and everyone else speaks for them and on their behalf rather than letting them speak for themselves. Native children need their own musical heroes. I think, without a company like ours there's really nowhere for a Native American musician to go because there is nowhere they are really taken seriously. However, we are more politically conscious than Motown. While not everything we do is political, with a lot of the stuff we do put out, other companies wouldn't touch it simply because they might be afraid. I always know this, if you're going against the wind you're making a difference. If you're not going against the wind and you're just following the crowd, you're not doing anything new. You're just standing still as far as I'm concerned. That's a good way to monitor your success. You're thinking, these are hard times and I'm running across a hard road, facing resistance, but that's how you know you're making a difference.

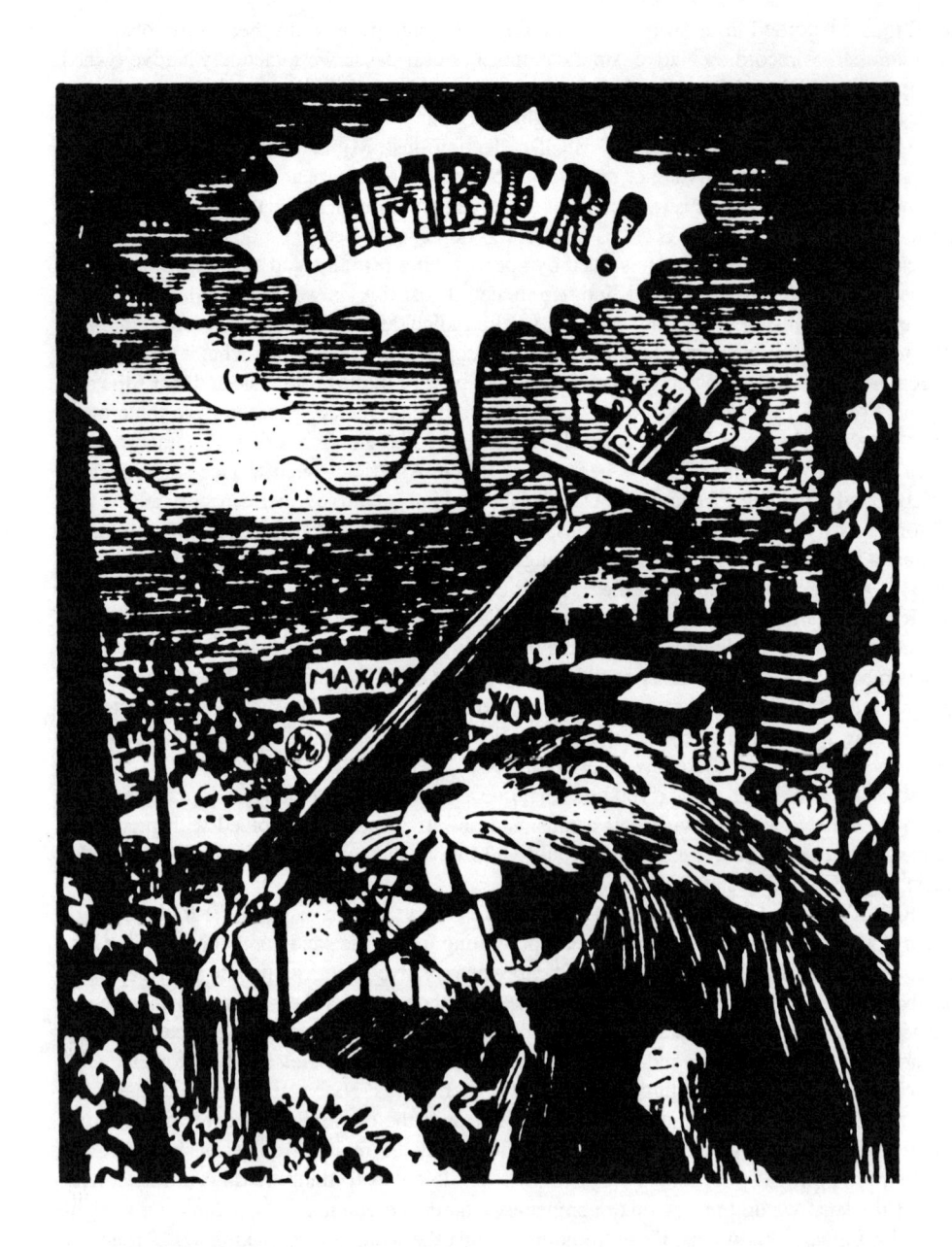

L. F. Productions

Who Bombed Judi Bari?

Darryl Cherney

Now Judi Bari is a Wobbly organizer
A Mother Jones at the Georgia Pacific Mill
She fought for the sawmill workers
Hit by that PCB spill
T. Marshall Hahn's calling G-P's shots from
    Atlanta
Don Nelson sold him the union long ago
Now they weren't gonna have no Wobbly
Runnin' their logging show
So they spewed out their hatred
And they laid out their scam
Jerry Philbrick called for violence
Was no secret what they had planned
So I ask you now...
WHO BOMBED JUDI BARI?
I know you're out there still
Have you seen her broken body
Or the spirit you can't kill?

Now Judi Bari is a feminist organizer
Ain't no man gonna keep that woman down
She defended the abortion clinic
In fascist Ukiah town
Calvary Baptist Church called for its masses
Cammo buddies lined up in the pews
You can see all of their faces
In the Ukiah Daily News
And they spewed out their hatred
As Reverend Brovies laid out their scam
Bill Staley called for violence
Was no secret what they planned

(So I ask you now)

Now Judi Bari is an Earth First! organizer
The California Redwoods are her home
She called for Redwood Summer
Where the owl and the black bear roam
Charlie Hurwitz he runs MAXXAM out of
    Houston
Harry Merlo runs L-P from Portland town
They're the men they call king timber
They know how to cut you down
And Don Nolan spewed their hatred
As Candy Boak laid out their scam
John Campbell called for violence
Was no secret what they planned

(So I ask you now)

Now Judi is the mother of two children
A pipe bomb went rippin' through her womb
She cries in pain at night time
In her Mendocino room
F.B.I. is back again with Cointelpro
Richard Held is the man they know they trust
With Lt. Sims his henchman
It's a world of boom and bust
But we'll answer with non-violence
For seeking justice is our plan
And we'll avenge our wounded comrade
As we defend the ravaged land

(So I ask you now)

Wm. Crook, Jr.

Timber!: An Interview with Judi Bari

(7 November 1994)

Ron Sakolsky

RS: What is the connection between your music and the organizing that you do. How do you see those things fitting together in terms of your life?

JB: Music is a really good organizing tool. It gives the whole thing a kind of spirit; it really fuels the movement in a lot of ways. Also, as an individual, music enriches your life. So, if a movement is going to go anywhere, there has to be some joy in it. It has to be something people want to do. I think a movement that's held together with music is way stronger, it's going to survive a lot more, inspire people a lot more.

RS: When I think of what you just said, I remember the Wobbly song tradition with Joe Hill. Meridel Leseur has said the IWW (Industrial Workers of the World) was a singing union and that was one of the reasons it was so inspiring.

JB: One of the first things that attracted me to Earth First! is that they sang. I used to work in an AFL union and also independently as a union organizer before I ever got to Earth First! or IWW. Actually, the first song I ever wrote was for a contest in the United Food and Commercial Workers (UFCW) union. I was a retail clerk then, and they were this really right wing union. They were going to have a contest for people to write a version for our union of "Solidarity Forever." I wrote a parody that was called "Aristocracy Forever."

RS: So it was the union bureaucrats that you were ridiculing?

JB: Yeah. It was the labor aristocracy. Songwriting and singing gives you a method of expressing yourself because your emotions are stronger than just words.

RS: Was this prior to the UCFW's decertification of the Hormel Workers Local P-9?

JB: Oh yeah, way before that. I was in the retail clerks union in the early '70s. I have actually led two strikes, one was by the retail clerks union and one was by the post office union. There was a quote about the AFL that I once heard in the Wobblies that I liked, and I think you can apply it to the Sierra Club as well. They said that while the AFL has seven million members and a lot of money, and the Wobblies have 25,000 members and no money, we have this wealth of verse and song. It's because only great movements that mark turning points in history inspire great music. So, there is an element of that, too, especially in the Earth First! stuff. You know, Darryl Cherney would write these satirical songs on the line while we were at the protests and they were just totally awesome songs. It really just gave it a power that was way beyond anything we could have had if we were just standing there chanting or something. The songs were funny just like the Wobbly songs. I think that is also one of the ways people are able to sustain great danger. Both in the Wobblies and in Earth First!, it was a life and death struggle and you had to be really brave to do this stuff.

RS: So people's spirits are kept up in that way.

JB: Yeah.

RS: Did you write "L-P" on the line, too?

JB: No. I wrote "L-P" while I was driving around organizing. I spent hours and hours in my car driving all over the place. So, I wrote songs while I was driving.

RS: This book we're doing has many different kinds of music and musicians represented in it. How would you characterize your music?

JB: It's definitely folk music, in every sense of the word. I don't know if this is a deprivation or a benefit, but folk music is deprived of the media way of communicating. We are like minstrels. We tell the stories of our actions in the songs. I remember one of the first actions I learned about in Earth First! was because someone wrote this epic song about it. So there also was that aspect of us using the music as a medium to tell our history to each other.

RS: Do you think one of the reasons that folk music is used so often by organizers is that fiddles and guitars are pretty portable to take around with you?

JB: Sure. That's definitely one of the reasons. In fact, I was always glad that I played the fiddle because it was so much lighter than the guitar. You know, I was just learning how to play fiddle, learning country style fiddle from some people who did that, and one of them was telling me about how in Appalachia where they developed these styles of music that people had to walk long distances in the mountains because there wasn't any kind of transportation. One of the ways they kept walking for so long was that they did these marches on the fiddle. They are similar to reels. They are really spirited. Shortly after learning them, I went on my first wilderness blockade. The first thing we had to do was hike five miles uphill to get to the cut. I had never been able to walk and play fiddle at the same time. I thought it was too hard. But, due to necessity, I started doing it. We played music the whole way up. So, I think it's more than just the portability of the instruments. It's also that the style is appropriate for the action. Darryl is a much better musician than me so he used to play all different styles. In Redwood Summer organizing campaigns, we had this cross-cultural thing where we would have the rednecks and the hippies facing each other across the lines. Because Darryl knew and could play country music, he was able to reach out to the rednecks. Some of the people that became our best logger and millworker contacts first got interested listening to the music. Do you know the song "Potter Valley Mill?"

RS: Yes, but why don't you tell me about it because not everybody reading this will.

JB: Okay. When the Potter Valley mill closed I was just beginning to get together with Darryl on workers' issues. He was writing a lot of songs about the forest and stuff like that. Actually, he wrote "Where Are We Going To Work When The Trees Are All Gone" before he met me, but most of his songs were just focused on the environmental stuff. When this mill closed down in the next valley over from me, the sense of what that was to the workers, closing the only employer in the area, meant something to me and I communicated that to Darryl. We, together, wrote this song, "Potter Valley Mill" about their closing down the mill in Potter Valley. It was a country song, and it had a fiddle part, and it was written in country style. It came out really good. We went to the local country station with it. We asked if they wanted to play it and they did. They started playing this song, and within two weeks it became the most requested song on this country station. The people requesting it were the mill workers. The station had us come on to talk about it knowing that we were Earth First!ers. One of the mill workers wives started selling tapes of it at her video store in Potter Valley. Just writing a sympathetic song was a way that we reached out and met people, that we crossed over the cultures.

RS: I think that one of the things you do so well as an organizer, is crossing over those cultural barriers. I was at one of the anti-MAXXAM actions during Redwood Summer. There was someone there who played a musical saw and I thought, this is really interesting. The lumberjack symbolism of the saw in the politicized concert context takes on a whole different meaning, yet it is a type of music that is familiar to people that are a part of the lumber industry.

JB: Yeah, but not so much anymore. They like a more modern country style of music. That is kind of like the music of their parents. People from this generation are going to identify more with being able to play the songs that are on the country radio station. Now that is where you can get people to start listening.

RS: Well, yes, of course, but it is part of their heritage. It might be old-fashioned, but doesn't it still have the country-music cachet that enables you to use it to build coalition?

JB: Well, yeah. For sure.

RS: How else does music figure into your organizing?

JB: It is helpful in making it through really terrifying times. Like after the bombing, when I was still getting death threats, and while you were probably up in Humboldt county at the Maxxam action, I didn't make it back to the front lines at all. By September, I was trying to move back here. They were still sending me death threats. One of their goon squads was the Stompers. They were going to stomp us, and they wrote a death threat that was put in my landlord's mailbox threatening to burn out me and any hippie shack on the road. What we did was write this funny song about it. I remember nights just sitting there absolutely terrified. The way we got through it is we wrote these hilarious songs. We were rolling on the floor laughing about them.

RS: You turned it around that way.

JB: Yeah.

RS: I remember when the idea of Redwood Summer was first proposed. It was to be like the Mississippi Freedom Summer. Of course, music was a big part of that as well. Did you see the musical connection right from the start?

JB: Darryl did. We did use that right away. One of the songs we did right at the beginning was "Oh Freedom." We'd say, "Oh, freedom for the land." And we'd go, "But before I'll be your slave, I'll be buried in my grave, with a shiny monkeywrench clasped in my hand." I really don't know if what we are doing here has the historical import of Mississippi Summer or not. There's somebody who goes around and does this show on labor circuits. It's called "Links in a Chain." Have you ever seen that?

RS: No, I haven't.

JB: It's a really neat show. What he does is take the same song and he shows how it's rewritten—in the civil rights movement, in the labor movement.... He traces the same song through different movements. It think that there are links in the chain between the movements. I think that the fact that the music hasn't been surviving as much as it should is one of the problems. We aren't connected to our past enough.

RS: So the way of preserving it, then, is to continue to use it and to make it topical for each occasion.

JB: Yeah. To use the songs and use them over. Make them topical for the thing you are doing now.

RS: Is part of the power of that approach the fact you are dealing with familiar tunes and that people can pick up on them right away and sing along and be part of it.

JB: Yeah. They are singable. With technology, music has become a consumer item rather than something that you do. One of the reasons that I think it is different here is because we live in the country. I don't have electricity. A lot of people I know don't. You have to entertain yourself more and you get used to entertaining yourself more if you're not so overloaded with electronic stimuli. When I lived in the city I played violin when I was a kid but I had never picked it up again. I didn't know very many people who played music. When I moved out here, so many people play music that, after awhile, you're just gonna, 'cause there's so many people doing it.

RS: It seems to have a lot to do with building community in that setting too.

JB: Oh, sure it is. The whole idea of acoustic music is more appropriate to the pace of life and the experiences here than it is to somebody in the city. A lot of our music comes from rural Appalachian mining songs. The union movement in mining has a really rich tradition of songs. Darryl and I also used the tune of "Will the Circle Be Unbroken" for our reproductive rights song, "Will the Fetus Be Aborted?"

RS: Other than in direct action campaigns, has music been a signifcant part of the struggle?

JB: Yeah, we have been contesting the Mendocino county forest rules for four years. We've stood up to whatever they've thrown at us, and we've kept coming back. Finally, we got to the last meeting and the Board of Forestry didn't even want to come here. That day we managed to outnumber the paid timber worker audience.

RS: So, they're paid to be there?

JB: Actually, what they did is they gave them a "choice" of either losing a day's pay or coming over on the company bus and getting fed the company lunch and stomping for the company. Even given the "choice," half of the workers at the Georgia-Pacific mill chose to lose a day's pay. The people who came were the right-wingers. Georgia-Pacific would create these paid, hostile mobs at these meetings. So, we stood them all down to the last day. At the very last meeting, we outnumbered them. The timber industry had run out of speakers by lunch, and we were making them listen to every hippie in the county one after the other until eight o'clock at night. Finally, when it got to be our turn, three of us went up there and we brought our instruments and we played this song, "Bullshit." Do you know the song?

RS: The Citizens Band song?

JB: Yeah, we played that song. The Board of Forestry was annoyed to be there at all much less have to listen to that. Everybody in the audience was clapping along, even the Board of Supervisors—you know, our county government people. The Board of Forestry was getting more and more annoyed. Finally, at the end, we said, "L-P's full of it, GP's full of it, the Board of Forestry's full of it," and they were trying to smile and be good sports. At that point they got really grumpy and we turned around to leave. They had already chastised us once for howling in this meeting. As we turned around to leave, the whole room howled. It was awesome! So, the final day before the stuffy Board of Supervisors, the last thing we did was a musical "salute" to them and to their whole process. That was fun!

RS: What are you doing musically these days?

JB: Well, we have a hilarious song called "The FBI Stole My Fiddle." The perfect response to the FBI. I don't do as much music lately though, because I've been working on the FBI case. It's very intense right now. You know, the FBI also stole my time to play the fiddle.

RS: What is the status of the case at the moment?

JB: We've passed all the FBI's motions to dismiss. Which means we're in the discovery phase. That's when they have to open up the documents and we get to interview them under oath. So, I've been spending the last year sitting across the table from lying, slimy FBI agents and listening to them do it. I have to tell you the best verse of "The FBI Stole My Fiddle." It's a blues song.

> "They said my strings was fuses. My bow, it was the light. Down inside my fiddle hole, I stashed my dynamite. So when I stroke my fuse strings with my fiddle bow, you'd better run for cover, because the fiddle might just blow."

By the way, the FBI has subpoenaed all of our music. In this discovery phase, not only are we allowed to discover all their stuff, but they're supposed to be allowed to discover all of our stuff. So, they just subpoenaed all of our songs, recorded or written, all of our songs that have anything to do with the defendants or the subjects we think are at issue in this case. Considering that we have songs with long lists of suspects in them, and songs making fun of death threats, we are going to bury them in songs!

Tuli Kupferberg

Shake Shake Whore of Babylon

Tuli Kupferberg

Shake Shake Whore of Babylon
Let me see your Golden Ass
Shake Shake Whore of Babylon
Let me smoke your $200 grass.
Shake Shake Whore of Babylon
Lay me on your casting couch
Shake Shake Whore of Babylon
Dream me, ream me, Make me say "Ouch!"
Hey Shake Shake Whore of Babylon
I'll do anything to be a star
Try me, buy me, break my balls, Slap my prick on Billboard walls.
O Shake Shake Whore of Babylon
Rent my soul to the Video Man
Option my axe to the Fucker-in-Chief:
The Army, The Air Force — The Banker Band
Hey Shake me, bake me Whore of Babylon
Serve my heart on a breakfast bun
Shake Shake Whore of Babylon
And then play my record again.
Shake Shake Whore of Babylon
Let me smell your Golden Ass
Buy me a mansion over poverty's highway
Shining in the silver glass.
Shake Shake Whore of Babylon
Serve my heart on a Buttered Bun
Shake Shake Whore of Babylon
And then play my record again
Play my record again
And then play... my record... again.
Won't you play it just once more...?
I'll be your best friend.

MAXIMUMROCKNROLL

ISSUE #94
WORLD WAR 3
MARCH 1991 $2

KARMA SUTRA   LA POLLA RECORDS   MR. T EXPERIENCE   LAUGHING HYENAS

Maximizing Rock and Roll: An Interview with Tim Yohannon

(18 August 1994)

Scott M. X. Turner

At the incredibly incendiary moment in the mid-1970s when punk rock[1] was born, it was split in two. And the energy that was—and is—punk flew off in two drastically different orbits. To most, the disparity between the two was undiscernible. But to those in the punk scene, or those nourished by it, the differences couldn't be clearer, nor a source of greater division between the two camps.

One was a way to make money.

And one was a way of life.

MAXIMUMROCKNROLL began as a radio show in northern California in 1977, the same year the Sex Pistols' "God Save The Queen" was Great Britain's top-selling single during the Queen's Silver Jubilee celebration. Well, it wasn't officially—the conservative firms that tallied music industry figures refused to accredit "God Save The Queen" as Number One on the singles chart, even though it far outsold everything else.

Loud, fast, melodic, passionate, energetic, destructive and vital. Anyone could play punk if they wanted to. And as soon as enough people did, the divisions emerged. Divisions that encompassed stylistic, political, cultural, technical and economic sectors of the genre.

Tim Yohannan has been MAXIMUMROCKNROLL's prime mover since its outset. In 1982, MRR debuted as a magazine for and about the international punk community. Today it publishes monthly with a circulation of 15,000. Skimpy by mainstream publishing standards, but healthy for a magazine—more accurately, a fanzine—so dedicated to its do-it-yourself punk ethic that it rejects all connection to the corporate world, refuses to use glossy paper stock, relies largely on volunteer submissions from punk writers worldwide and has a classified ad policy that dictates "40 words cost $2/60 words max for $3. No racist, sexist or fascist material."

Yohannan has learned much in seventeen years. He's still passionately idealistic about the power of punk music. But quixotic he's not: Yohannan's learned, sometimes painfully, that there are challenges the punk community is simply not up to. Instead of tossing in the towel, though, Yohannan takes aim at the brigands he sees massing outside the punk community's gates: corporate usurpation, reactionary beliefs, and any individual's refusal to get involved. "In the long run," says Yohannan, "what's important about punk is not the lyrics, what people say, but what they do."

Maximizing Rock and Roll: Tim Yohannon Interview

There is no doubt that MAXIMUMROCKNROLL is a poster kiosk for punk strategies and ideas worldwide. But how does punk measure up—culturally, musically and politically—as it approaches its third decade? Punk singer/songwriter/guitarist Scott M. X. Turner spoke with Tim Yohannan over the phone in August 1994.

ST: What do you see as the relationship between bands in the punk scene and *MAXIMUMROCKNROLL*?

It seems to me it's a case of where *MAXIMUMROCKNROLL* is supportive of the scene and does what it can to get bands self-sufficient, get bands going, but it also seems like bands certainly rely on *MAXIMUMROCKNROLL*.

TY: I guess there are some bands at a certain stage in their development that maybe would rely on it, although I think less so nowadays.

ST: Because there's a much larger 'zine scene out there, or you're losing influence?

TY: Yeah, there're a lot more 'zines and electronic media, so they're less dependent, which is good. I don't really have any desire to be the lone voice of communication for a band we think is good or we think is bad. It's nice to be able to give your opinion and not have that heavy weight hanging over your head.

ST: What groups out there—classes, different cultures—do you feel the magazine doesn't reach, and you'd like to reach out to, find some way to connect with?

TY: The limitations of who it reaches are one, cultural. In other words, most black kids would not necessarily be that interested in it if they're into black culture. There may be marginal interest from various cultural groups as in—hmmm, I wonder what that's about. But it's not going to be an ongoing interest, I don't think.

ST: Is that because punk can be fairly unchanging in its reach, or because there're a lot of other cultural sources out there?

TY: Well, I don't think punk is unchanging at all. I think it's broadened and broadened and broadened to the point of absurdity. I think that if you ask any two people who say that they're into punk what it is, you're just gonna get totally different answers. So even on the musical side there's no agreement. Never mind the cultural side, never mind the political side, never mind any other aspect of it, the business side. It's not a definable thing any longer.

So with *MAXIMUM*, we've chosen to take a fairly narrow definition and work with that. Some people have felt threatened by that because it is so narrow and feel that it's a reactionary position, or it leaves out other people. But what I think it does is it allows us to be more idealistic and it allows other people to step into the void and fill what we're not doing.

But in terms of other people and other cultures, or even in mainstream culture, sure I'd like to reach more people, but at what price? I'm not willing to do it at the price of watering down what I feel, or at the price of going to a glossy, color cover and being distributed by companies that are owned by major labels.

ST: There's that firm ethic of *MAXIMUMROCKNROLL*, that once a band passes into any kind of connection with a major label or corporate entity they're pretty much dropped.

TY: Yeah.

ST: By the way, what's your criteria of a sell-out?

TY: Hmmmm. I dunno, I guess somebody who purports to be one thing and then changes. On the one hand, for instance, take a political band that signs to a major label and then rationalizes it. That's a sell-out.

But then that leaves off the hook people that never purported to be political, and somehow they aren't criticized at all. In a way, I think they're even bigger jerks. Anybody, actually, who's born into this world at this point and doesn't develop some kind of consciousness about what the fuck is going on at a gut level—doesn't have to be an educated, erudite, well-defined philosophy. Then, if you choose to participate in it for your own individual gratification, you're a sell-out in my eyes.

ST: You're not gonna write about the band Green Day[2] again?

TY: No. Our commitment is to the grass roots. Probably 80 percent or 90 percent of what we've covered at any given point has been relatively unknown bands. We cover the stuff that we like musically, and we cover stuff that is not getting corporate attention.

ST: There's a letter in a recent *MAXIMUM* from a fellow, Simon Wood. He was talking about how uncomfortable he feels when fans come into the scene who seem to be coming from an MTV background, or from a much more mainstream or corporate background. He's very angry—he doesn't wanna be in the same room with people like that, it makes him uncomfortable. I think that's a real elitist point-of-view, and that rubs against my view of punk. It strikes me as a Pete Wilson identity-card concept.

TY: [Laughs] Well, I think it's good to have the whole range of opinions going. I think from some peoples' perspective, *MAXIMUM* is like that now.

ST: Is that because of your new policy of what you'll review?[3]

TY: Right. And I can accept the argument that in some ways it might not be very politically a good move because it's limiting. In other words, there's a tendency towards eclecticism, both musically and culturally on one hand.

Theoretically I think it's fine, but do I like the music? No. [laughs] I just don't like the music when it becomes more eclectic. So I think it's fine for people to define the extremes. It doesn't mean everyone has to agree with it. In this kid's case, okay, that's fine. I'm glad he's taking that position, and I'm glad other people are taking a broader position.

ST: That's a good segue into some of your columnists. Lately, Mykel Board has been taking heat for some of his positions.[4] In fact, it seems like your male columnists have a "cleverdick" perspective, a kind of P. J. O'Rourke style of writing, whereas two of *MAXIMUM*'s women columnists, Ayn Imperato and Christeen, are much more honest and straightforward.[5]

TY: Right now the column section is in flux. For instance, in the next issue and the issue after that you're gonna see a lot more women columnists. Most of the columnists I could take or leave. Personally, in terms of—what did you call it, "clever-dick"...?

ST: Yeah, a male, clever-dick perspective where it's more important to be hard and grizzled and tough and funny and ironic rather than just getting at the issue.

TY: Yeah, Mykel is like that. Mykel will go to any extreme to get a reaction. People are always surprised when they meet him that he's a really nice guy. And Rev. Norb, who we've added recently, maybe sorta fits that way too.[6] But then there are some of the male columnists who are down-to-earth, humanistic types like Mike Bullshit —

ST: Eugene Chadbourne?

TY: Yeah, sure. So I wouldn't make a generalization. What I wanna see is more women, more perspectives, maybe queer perspectives.

What I like, even though I disagree with the points of view that Mykel puts out, is that they're sassy, and they're in your face. I like to see that from a left perspective point-of-view too. Although it does seem, and this is a generalization, that people on the left tend to be more serious and self-serious.

ST: And also careful about the language.

TY: Right. They might be more right-on in terms of what I'm feeling, but I think they're boring. And they aren't very funny. I think humor and sarcasm and anger mixed together are some of the chemicals that make things interesting. It's a great way to get a message across, to hold people's attention, and that's some of the ingredients I liked most about early punk rock. It was very sassy and "we don't care what you think." And as things have gotten more and more "P. C." within a certain element of the punk scene, I think it's gotten very deadly boring. So even though my heart might be closer to that, I just can't read the stuff.

ST: There's that whole issue of, say, having a band that's just explosive in what they say and not very careful and insulting in what they say; well those bands almost always tend to get the press, get the attention, kick up the dust. I couldn't think of a real good example in punk, but in rap, a band like N.W.A. is gonna get a lot more attention than the Disposable Heroes of Hiphoprisy[7] did.

TY: Right. It's partly that. Just as in the mass media, people are intrigued by the outrageous. So the more over-the-top you are, the more people are gonna be fascinated with it. It's the old adage "any publicity is good publicity," and I think you could add on there "negative publicity might even be better publicity."

ST: Well it sticks with people more. Is there a point where you'll draw the line?

TY: Yeah. I'm reticent to give publicity to people whose positions are out-and-out what I would call fascist. They can go somewhere else. We'll cover a lot of reactionary stuff, especially in the record review section. But in terms of interviews and stuff like that, I don't really care to oblige them. So people can find out that these things exist through *MAXIMUM*, but I'm not gonna give 'em a lot of space.

ST: It's also possible to cover them as a news item, or comment on some piece that comes in. There's a letter in the current *MAXIMUM* from a kid who's talkin' about starting his own record distribution cooperative, in the mold of Mordam.[8] And you'd written a note afterward, saying it was a good thing, keep up, keep trying with it. I see a big difference between coverage like that and, say, items in Lefty Hooligan's column where you just cover a news item. That's a big difference to people.

TY: Right.

ST: Your aim is to try and strike a balance between heavy politics and fun music and cultural coverage. But do you feel caught between the issue of free speech and that of freedom of race, gender, sexual orientation, class? Those contradictions of upholding freedom of speech if it means giving a voice to someone offensive—an ACLU-type position.

TY: Yeah, I don't feel obliged to be everything to everybody. For instance, when we narrowed the scope of what we were going to cover musically, we started getting all these accusations of "banning, you're banning!" That's bullshit. Banning is an attempt to squelch, or to make things unavailable to the public in general. All we're doing is choosing to cover what we wanna cover. If those people get coverage elsewhere, it doesn't irk me. There's a difference between rejecting a record and banning a record.

ST: Do you think the punk scene is infused with a strong sense of politics these days? Is that in an upswing or a downswing?

TY: It's scattered because the punk scene is scattered. There are certain elements of the punk scene that are very political, there are certain elements that are absolutely not political. I would say, compared to ten years ago, it's definitely less political.

I think what's happened is that the punk scene in a lot of ways has moved to the suburbs. Some of the issues there are pretty different. And it's also gotten younger than it was ten or fifteen years ago.

ST: Do you think it's more creative? I was in Chicago a few weeks ago, and on a Friday night we went to the Fireside Bowl, a beat-to-shit bowling alley near Logan Square where they had four or five punk bands going at it. It was one of the best shows I've been to. They were great. It seems like there's more innovation on how to get things done.

TY: Innovative in terms of not the music, but in terms of the vehicles?

ST: Yeah.

TY: Yes, I think that is true. I think it's spread everywhere. What's been good up 'til now is that it's spread on its own terms. But now, with the success of so-called punk bands in the corporate world, what I'm afraid of is that there's gonna be a ballooning of interest that's gonna warp the slow, steady dissemination that's taken place 'til now. Where suddenly there's gonna be a lot of people interested, then they're all gonna disappear.

ST: It seems that even if there is a ballooning, where a number of bands get signed and there's an upsurge of interest, most people are gonna get left behind, with the result being more interest in the d.i.y. [do-it-yourself] ethic and embracing it more as a survival technique.

TY: Well yeah, I think maybe among a core of people that might be the case. But for those people that might sorta drift to it, they're drifting toward it because it's popular instead of unpopular. They're drifting toward it because there's money to be made, instead of "we're doing this because we feel like it." So the motivations of people getting involved may change. And that's a very fundamental difference.

ST: Do you think a punk band on a major label can make a difference—in terms of the number of people they reach, or do you think that no matter how many people they reach or how good their music is, that they're completely compromised?

TY: Yeah. In the long run, what's important about punk is not the lyrics, what people say, but what they do. I mean, you had The Clash as the perfect example of a band that was political, signed to a major, reached people all over the world, and didn't change a fucking thing.

ST: Yeah, I was gonna use them as an example because I wouldn't be a musician now if it weren't for them, and I might not be politically-involved either. I grew up in Greensboro, North Carolina, and there was nothing going on there when I was growing up. It wasn't until I heard The Clash—man, that changed it all around for me. That was the spur right there. In North Carolina in '78, '79, I wouldn't have gotten a hold of them if they were on a small, London-based indie punk label.

TY: Eugene Chadbourne did, didn't he? Some people will, no matter where they live. And it isn't 1978 any longer. The dissemination of independently-produced stuff is much broader, much more available. And I don't accept the argument that because some band can get their things into chain stores that is actually gonna have anything but a financial effect. As to the few people who say they maybe maintained some kind of political belief as initially contacted through The Clash—there're very few of them still around.

I think when you balance that vis-à-vis the negative impact of corporations on an independent means of communication, it doesn't add up. I just had to laugh when I read something recently that said "Green Day was one of the few left-of-center bands at Woodstock." Left of what center? What are you talking about?

To me what's important about punk is an anti-authoritarian belief. And a place for freaks. A place for those people who don't fit. It may never grow into a mass movement, and maybe it shouldn't. Maybe it should be a place for the alienated to communicate and create. But once it becomes a mass-marketable thing, then the nature of it changes.

ST: You see that here in New York with rap. Ten years ago rap was something that was so threatening here to the authorities. Every time there was a block party in the South Bronx or Brooklyn, it was a big deal. And now, who's scared of it? The PTA in Middle America for different reasons, or politicians looking for a campaign issue, 'cause they have no ideas of their own.

TY: Right. It doesn't necessarily have to just be threatening. I think what's important about it also is its integrity. That's how I view it. Twenty years ago I did expect the world to change. Now I don't necessarily expect that. If it happens, great. But that's not my m.o., that's not why I'm doing what I'm doing. I'm doing it because I want to maintain my integrity. I wanna get through life feeling good about what I'm doing and say, "Yeah, I stuck to my fucking guns." If in the process of that we can shake shit up, great! But I'm not banking on an ultimate success in order to maintain my current momentum.

ST: Do you think *MAXIMUM* preaches to the converted?

TY: No. I think that most people involved in the punk scene are definitely to the right of me. And within *MAXIMUM*, as you pointed out, there's a variety of perspectives. There's not a coherent *MAXIMUM* perspective. As the person that does most of the work I can make some attempts at yelling louder than the other people that work here [laughs]. But I don't think there's a coherent perspective. People make that generalization about *MAXIMUM*, but I think they're stark-raving mad.

ST: I would've made it based on not a left-, center- or right-political orientation, but that *MAXIMUM* seems to be very humanist. It seems to be—and you're gonna laugh—very sweet and warm, reaching out to people and saying "here's a place you can be, here's a place you can be a freak," like you said before. I definitely don't see that as a right-wing value.

TY: Okay, from that perspective I guess you're right.

ST: Have you gotten a lot of feedback from *Book Your Own Fuckin' Life* (BYOFL)?9 Is it successful, do people really get around by using it?

TY: Apparently they do. I was gonna perhaps discontinue it after this third one, just 'cause it was —

ST: A pain-in-the-ass.

TY: Not just a pain-in-the-ass. I think it was also half-assed. I got a lot of feedback from people about it at that point, when I threatened to discontinue it. Some people came along and said they wanted to try and work on it this time. So we're gonna try another one.

ST: That's good news, especially compared to the letter you ran in the back of *BYOFL*, about how hard putting it together is, how many people waited until the last two weeks before deadline to submit information. Jason [Mojica, of Rocco Publishing] wrote elsewhere that there's a whole shopping bag full of submissions that came in late and were never included. It was pretty grim. Does that kind of thing anger you about the work-ethic in the punk scene?

TY: Yeah, I have a streak in me—I'm pretty much a workaholic. When we started Gilman Street in Berkeley [see more, below] about seven or eight years ago, we fucking killed ourselves getting it going, ran it for about a year-and-a-half, and then shut it down. My feeling was this community doesn't deserve it. Why should I be a masochist. In other words it was an idea, it worked briefly, it didn't really work the way I had hoped, and I didn't really care to put in that kind of energy for something that in my opinion was gonna be compromised that much.

When some other kids came along and said they wanted to do it, and it would be somewhat along similar lines, we said "okay, great, here's the sound system, here're the keys, there's the landlord, you're in business." But it's not what I had envisioned.

So there's a streak in me where I'm always trying different projects that are pretty idealistic, and if they don't meet my level of expectation or community participation or whatever it is that I think they require, then I'll abandon 'em.

ST: What was your initial idea for Gilman Street?

TY: I wanted it to be a place that would be run by the bands and the fans. Bands would meet and figure out what the bills would be. The bands would take responsibility for the whole show, for cleaning up, for every aspect of it. I wanted it to be a cooperative effort amongst the different constituents within that community. I wanted it to be something where people could take control of something that up to that point had been like a commodity that had been something for sale.

The bands never really got it.

ST: You had put it forth to them in no uncertain terms?

TY: Oh yes, yes, yes. Meeting upon meeting [laughs]. Maybe there were individuals within a couple of bands that got it. But for the most part the bands just wanted to make music. And for the most part people just wanted to be entertained.

We tried some experiments early on where we would not announce who was playing. All we would tell people was that we were guaranteeing them a great show. The door price was so cheap—you're gonna get five bands for three bucks and it's gonna be a great show. That didn't work; people would only come for certain things that they knew.

There were various attempts at trying things differently. Theme nights of different types with varying degrees of success or failure.

ST: It's a twofold thing: needing a community to succeed, but also helping to build that community, almost a Catch-22. That's hard to find in New York, with the possible exception of CBGB. No one here goes to clubs just because the clubs are a cool place to hang out.

TY: Maybe at ABC No-Rio they do.[10] Anyway, that was the idea.

We had all sorts of interesting ideas. We had a thing called the Mind Fuck Committee whose whole job it was to think up things that would just weird-out people at the show. It was almost like theater in a sense. Something that would happen to them without them knowing what it was, that would make 'em think.

We had a South Africa Night, where when you paid your admission you got a passbook like blacks in South Africa had. You'd go inside, and then, at a certain point, we'd have a whole gang of people dressed like cops come barging in the place, throw people against walls. If they didn't have their passbook they'd be cuffed and dragged into a room. They had no idea what the fuck was going on. Chaos to make a point!

We had an open mic on stage where if someone didn't like what a band had just done or sung, whatever, they could go up there and confront 'em, right there on the spot. And that was part of the condition to bands playing there, that they had to deal with this.

ST: How did the bands react?

TY: Well, very few people availed themselves of this opportunity. There were a couple of times when it did happen, and the show would just stop dead and big discussions would take place! It was really weird. It was great! I wanted people to leave the show with their brains working. Have fun, go crazy, and also come out of there with your mind clicking instead of dead.

ST: Another good function of that is pulling down the horrible barrier between band and audience. I never fully know what to think about all that. When our band plays, we try and break it down as often as we can by challenging people, having them talk to us during the show. But so often making that attempt feels so artificial, maybe because we've been so indoctrinated about this division. Any attempt to bridge that gap can feel so artificial, and I'm not sure how to break it down.

TY: It's difficult, and I think the only way it can be broken down is if the club encourages it. In other words, the club and the band conspire to try and turn the audience into a participant. Short of that, it's always gonna seem forced and weird, I think.

ST: Certainly when you get on a little larger level, getting involved with security people, people who haven't a clue to begin with, larger club owners. You're not gonna see it on that larger level.

TY: You hardly ever see it on a small level [laughs].

So that's what I wanted to try and do. I wanted to try and create something that would have broader implications for how our community formed itself and functioned. In the end, it wasn't gonna work that way. And what they have now is good, it's still a volunteer-run place, the kids work there and help out and it's chaotic in its own way. It's still idealistic in a certain sense. But it's not exactly what I had wanted, and I didn't wanna put in the kind of energy that it was taking out of me.

ST: Let me put a devil's advocate question to you. While I agree that independence is the way to go, isn't this whole *Book Your Own Fuckin' Life*, start-your-own-label-and-distribution-network process a case of little capitalist cells in the making?

TY: Yes. Right now, it's not an argument between let's say capitalism and socialism, or capitalism and anarchism. It's between capitalism and petty-bourgeois capitalism. And that's the best that we can manage at the moment.

ST: Where do you take it from there?

TY: At this point, just being able to keep the corporate fuckheads away is the whole battle.

ST: Well, there's the whole corporate hegemony. It's not just an issue of keeping monetary exploitation at bay but thought-exploitation and the idea that you have to rely on these people.

TY: Right, but there is obviously an element within the punk scene that is more on the anarchist-cooperative kind of level.

I don't have a high degree of faith in that. I don't necessarily believe in cooperatives.

ST: Because of issues of commitment?

TY: Yeah, partly. It's too easy to come and too easy to go. Generally, younger people are not going to maintain a high level of responsibility over a long period of time. There're exceptions to that, but generally they've got all sorts of exploring they're doing in their lives and they're not just gonna take on some huge responsibility and stay with it for five years.

ST: So it can take on the feel of a Junior Achievement program.

TY: Yeah, I guess. There's a whole element of cooperatives that's too hippie-ish and too touchy-feelie for me, and the decision making is just too painful. I think that if people would just get by that and say, "Okay, the people that put in the most work should have the most say-so; there should be some kind of check-and-balance for the rest of us," I think that's more realistic. And it allows for more flexibility. It allows for things not to become too stagnant and predictable.

ST: What's the idea behind the *MAXIMUMROCKNROLL* radio show?

TY: It was actually the first thing we did. We started the radio show in '77, and we were doing that for about five years before we ever started a magazine. The radio show was our base.

I just lucked into getting a radio show on a Pacifica station out here, KPFA in Berkeley. Sorta came in through the back door. They had a very high-power signal, it reached about 80 percent of Northern California, which is great 'cause we got punk rock out to Modesto, Nevada City, Bakersfield, all sorts of places that had never heard anything like that. Bands would pop up in those places. You could see the seeds being sown, and it was really great, and it was a lot of fun to do.

With the magazine we could be more in depth and more serious, whereas, with the radio show it was more fun and music.

ST: Is the radio show still doing its job? Punk is so universal these days.

TY: Well, four or five years ago we got kicked off KPFA finally.

ST: How come?

TY: We weren't "P. C." enough. They were sorta goin' more towards the NPR direction. They were cleaning up and trying to appeal more to the middle class and stuff like that.

At that point, a local college station offered us a chance to do the show live, and we declined. What we decided was to do it in-house. Do it on tape at cost to non-commercial stations that wanted it. Now that's what we do—tape it once a week, sell it for five bucks. There's usually anywhere from twenty to thirty stations at any given time that take it.

What we're playing on those tapes is stuff that most college radio stations are not gonna have in their library. Even though maybe on some level punk or hardcore is more accepted, the stuff we're playing still isn't being heard.

ST: How do you decide what gets on the radio show? In fact, for that matter, how do you decide who gets feature articles or interviews done on them in the magazine?

TY: Radio, it's up to the individual DJs. I don't even do the show anymore myself. There're about seven or eight DJs, and they rotate every month. They pick from the library what they want.

As far as the magazine, when stuff comes in I'm in charge of the vinyl side and this other fellow's in charge of the CD side. We listen to stuff, and if it's within our musical parameters and the corporate parameters [laughs]—or the uncorporate parameters—then we'll review it. If it gets rejected, it goes into a box where it sits for a week. Some of the different columnists that write music columns can go through there and decide whether they wanna mention it in their columns. Or if somebody feels like I've really blown it they'll come back to me with the record and say, "Look, you gotta listen to this again, I think you're wrong, we should review it." Then we'll listen to it again and see. It's pretty subjective.

ST: That's fine, it's a magazine. Again, ya can't be all things to all people.

TY: Fanzine is what it is. I'm not pretending to be objective! [laughs]

ST: You have a real preference for vinyl over CD?

TY: Yeah.

ST: Why is that?

TY: I love 7"s. I think they're the best format. To me, listening to music isn't about getting stoned and lying on the floor. It's about playing something, play a track and it's like "Wow! That makes me think of this song" and you go grab it off the shelf and you throw that on, and then your buddy goes "Oh no, listen to this!" and grabs something.

To me that's the kind of energy and quickness and continuity that I like. I remember sitting around and playing records with my friends in the '50s and it was that sort of approach.

And, the fact is, I think 99 percent of the bands are incapable of making a great album. I think most bands, at best, should make two 7"s a year—at best. Maybe one. It's just too easy to make LPs or CDs. And tapes to me are not fun, unless you're just riding around in a car.

ST: You won't review tapes any more, is that correct?

TY: No, no longer. We just don't have the personpower to do all formats.

I just prefer the 7" 'cause it's quick. I like the artwork-type setup on 7"s. I don't think CD singles do the trick at all.

ST: Do you think there's an exploitation effect on consumers where CDs are involved?

TY: There's an element of it. There's always gonna be new technology and they're always gonna try stuff. There're some good aspects to that, but to me, punk music does not sound better on CD. And the argument that CDs will last forever, I don't think that's true.

Anyway, in a couple of years they're gonna come along with another technology to try and get everyone to buy everything all over again. So part of it is a scam and part of it is there's gonna be new technology. But if something comes along that can replace the 7" that's as fun and whatever, okay, cool. But it hasn't happened yet in my mind.

ST: Would you do a TV. show, say a public access program?

TY: Not interested in TV or video. It just never appealed to me. I like radio a lot. I like listening to ballgames a lot. I like that medium, and I like the print medium. Even though I'm very into computers in terms of producing the magazine, I'm really not into electronic communication that much. It just seems silly to me that you're typing away to somebody—ya better be a good typist! [laughs] It almost seems like a step backwards. "Wait, Mykel, why are we typing on these screens to each other when I could just call you! This is really dumb!"

ST: Well, 'cause it's new. See, my problem with video is that it goes against the idea of music making people think. I was in high school in the late seventies and I'm so thankful that videos weren't around then. I hear songs from back then that remind me of who I was going out with at the time, or friends, or some cool adventure we went on. These days videos tend to replace those images. You have to fight very hard against someone else's images sticking in your mind and pushing out whatever you've come up with on your own.

TY: Yeah, that's the whole argument with television, that it cuts down on the imagination.

ST: I wanna ask you first about the creeping influence of the Internet and electronic 'zines. How do you view that, and is MAXIMUMROCKNROLL gonna go in that direction?

TY: I'm not in contact with that very much, and I don't really have a plan to go in that direction. Right now I've got my hands full in various forms of communication I'm already engaged in and really couldn't do justice to anything else. I'm stretched about as thin as I can get.

ST: Do you think that sometime in the future you'll just cave in MAXIMUMROCKNROLL as a printed magazine and go electronic?

TY: Well, I could foresee a future when perhaps things would go electronically in a mass way, but we're not there yet and I don't think we're exactly close, either.

ST: Do you feel like MAXIMUMROCKNROLL follows the standards and parameters of the punk scene or sets them, or is it a mix of the two?

TY: Probably a mix of the two. On one hand, since the magazine is 90 to 95 percent dependent on contributions from the scene—most of it is not done in-house in terms of the writing—it's gonna reflect what's going on in that community. On the other hand, at times we attempt to focus on different issues or take positions that are not the most popular positions within that community. So it's a little of each.

ST: What's an example of a stance you've taken that's caused a huge shit-storm?

TY: For years we were notorious for not liking New York hardcore, during the era of Agnostic Front and all those bands that were, in my opinion, pretty neanderthal and reactionary and homophobic. We took a very brazen stand against them, and it lost us a lot of readers on the east coast. We were very unpopular on the east coast.

We've taken positions at times against the Krishnas, which made us unpopular among a lot of the Straight Edge-type people.[11] Obviously, we were always anti-skinhead. That made us popular in some ways and unpopular in other ways, and definitely [laughs] meek when we appeared in public.

Recently with this major label thing, it's a divisive thing with our position that we took with ads and what we were gonna review and our definition of what punk rock is. That has alienated a lot of people and made a lot of people very unhappy with us.

ST: That seems to me unfair. You're putting points out there as to why you hold those standards. When it comes to not liking the New York hardcore scene in the '80s, you're not just doing it because it's some petty bullshit "we're west coast, you're not", or even vaguer than that. You're giving specific reasons, and you'd think people would pick up on the thought behind it, whether they like it or not. Do people not think it through to that degree?

TY: I dunno. Some people would maybe be moderate in their reactions, some people would be more extreme in their reactions. You know, to be young is to be passionate.

The delicious thing from my perspective is that we can do this. Because we aren't making a living off it. I have a regular morning job, and that's what I live on. None of us can draw money from *MAXIMUM*. So what that means is we get to be able to say, when somebody calls up, say Atlantic, and wants to do ads, we say "NO!" And they're stunned. They don't get it. "And we don't even want your promos. Stop sending 'em! And don't call me again, please! Take me off your follow-up list!"

A lot of the bigger indies will always be calling us. Everyone's got people hired now—not only the bigger ones but some of the middle ones—to follow up. "Did you get our CD? Are you gonna review it? Do you like it?" And I just say, "Look, you're welcome to send us stuff. If we like it we'll review it, but don't call me. Take me off the computer. Please!!"

ST: What's your criteria for refusing to deal with indies? When they strike a distribution deal with a major, or is it a stylistic thing?

TY: If they're P&D'd[12] by a major, or they're major-owned—in other words, if a major is paying their bills, then to me they're a captive of the major. If Caroline or Relativity [large, corporate-owned "indie" labels] is P&D'ing them, then they're a subsidiary in my mind.

Whereas, if they're between a rock and a hard place, and the only way they can get their distribution is through one of those outfits, then I'm not pleased by that. I don't let them mention that in their ads, but we will review their releases.

ST: So you're flexible to a degree.

TY: Up to that point. But otherwise no.

ST: What's your whole outlook on the international punk scene? Okay, that's kinda broad. But just take it and run with it. Is it healthy, are there connections with punkers in the U.S.? Are they falling victim—for instance, in Eastern Europe is the punk scene there falling victim in the way that society is falling victim-to capitalism's reemergence?

TY: Yeah, to some extent that's true. And then you have your rebels that are resisting that. They resisted state capitalism and now they're trying to resist private capitalism.

That's one of the things I think *MAXIMUM* was instrumental in, helping to connect things internationally. Creating links all over the place, and that is still going on. For instance, there's a kid that works on the magazine named Devon who's in a band called All You Can East. Just through pen-paling and whatever—I mean, his band isn't even on a label, he's just put out his own releases, a couple of singles and an LP—his band has gone to Japan twice, just left now for a tour of Australia, New Zealand, Thailand, Hong Kong, Japan again. Then they're coming back, then they're going to Argentina. And he's not rich at all. He made all of these arrangements, figured out how they could just about break even, and they're doing it. It is totally awesome!

But now there is, between Europe and the U.S., a situation where it's easier for a U.S. group to tour Europe than it is for an American band to tour the States. It's gotten so pat, and Europeans are seemingly more interested in American bands than their own bands, that I think the local scenes over there have been hurt because of that.

There's a lot more communication than there ever was before between Japan and the West. And that's a really cool thing. American bands are going to Japan more frequently, and Japanese bands are coming here a lot more. That's a new wrinkle.

ST: There was a scene report from Amsterdam, I think, in a recent *MAXIMUM*. It was complaining—and I think justifiably so—about how when a U.S. punk band plays there Dutch bands have real trouble getting opening slots, and they're just brushed aside. It sounds like a star-treatment is being given to U.S. groups and the local musicians are just forgotten about. Is that a fairly consistent occurrence?

TY: Yeah, with U.S. bands going to Europe, that is the case. There are so many going that it's just inundated the place. But that's the fault of the scenes there, that the kids into it are so into just American bands, for whatever dumb reasons, that they've forsaken their own. And the club owners, the same.

It used to be much more about playing squats and things like that. Now it's much more about money.

ST: So you don't see it as a bully-American cultural *blitzkrieg*? It's more of a homegrown fascination with U.S. bands?

TY: Well, it takes two to tango. On one level you can say it's American cultural imperialism. But they're lapping it up.

ST: We've talked some about commodification of music. I think someone unfamiliar with the punk scene could pick up a copy of *MAXIMUM* and look at the tons of ads and the tons of records out and available and just think "this is the most commodified thing I've ever seen!"

TY: Yeah, yeah. It definitely can give that appearance, and to some extent it could be correct. I don't have that gut-level reaction against ads. There are a lot of people in the punk scene that do have that, both within the anarchist scene here, and in Europe, where in the past at least, there was much more of a political bent to the punk/hardcore scene. I think that's changed as Europe has become more Americanized.

Anyway, there was always more of a "you have so many ads, you're in it for the money" approach. And I can see where people could draw that conclusion about *MAXIMUM* or about the scene in general. I don't have that feeling.

As somebody who collects records, I find [the ads] indispensable. I wanna know what's coming out. And we make the ads so cheap that anybody can do 'em. For twenty bucks you can get your ad all over the fucking world. So to me, I don't see it that way. I think they're a good part of the magazine. It's a part that I think is important.

Each year, we publish our finances in April telling people what we do with all the money that we brought in and such. Hopefully, at least in terms of us, people will see that, okay, we're not in it for the money ourselves.

I could see how someone picking it up, reading it, seeing all the ads would think that the whole punk scene is a commercial thing, or that *MAXIMUM* is a commercial thing. But I think that's misleading.

ST: Is there any possibility of a move away from commodification? Or is it simply an unrealistic idea to not put out records? Maybe putting tours together where it's just music to hear, not to hold and exchange. Granted there's still money changing hands, you'd have to charge at the door to keep the tour going. But is there a shot at an eventual rejection of commodification of music?

TY: No, I don't see that happening. Now, there's a label called Sound Byte House, it's a band and a label. They put out 7"s maybe twice a year or something like that. What they do is put out split-singles with their band and another band and they mail it to people for free. All you gotta do is write in and say "I want your single."

They'll ask you after you get it if you wanna send them a donation or not. But they're not banking on it. It's sort of a compromise position. Yes, they are creating a commodity. No, they're not just selling it.

But I don't see a change as you described it.

Endnotes

1 Punk, hardcore, straight edge, hardline, garage, rock'n'roll. All young'ns of gospel and the blues, of course. Punk is more than music...it's the style, look, lifestyle and political and social beliefs of folks in the punk community. Punk encompasses hardcore and other punk-subset styles in the same way hip-hop encompasses rap (divided into new school, old school, dancehall, gangsta and others), old breakdancing moves, graffiti art, and the growing hip-hop prose and poetry school.

Punk is loud-hard-fast. It sprang up in the mid-'70s as a reaction to bloated and pretentious "progressive" rock groups of the era like Emerson, Lake & Palmer and Kansas. Hardcore emerged in the early '80s and was louder, harder, and faster still. Straight Edge rejects chemical stimulants, hardline embraces certain fascist elements. Garage goes back to the '60s, is young and organic and loose. It's all rock'n'roll, but not much rock'n'roll today is punk.

2 Green Day, an Oakland-based punk band, put out two good solid LPs on a small indie, Lookout Records, before signing with Reprise Records (part of the Warner Bros. conglomerate). Their first major-label release, *Dookie*, was one of the biggest-selling albums of 1994 and helped them win appearances at both Woodstock '94 and the annual Lollapalooza tour.

3 "Send MRR your release for review. Don't send wimpy, arty, metal, MTV corporate rock shit here... We want punk, garage, hardcore, and will review all those that fall within our area of coverage... Specific criticisms aside, it should be understood that any independent release deserves credit for all the work and money that goes into it." So it's stated at the beginning of MAXIMUM's record reviews section.

4 "Is it strange that young men rape, when laws and parents deny them legitimate sexual channels," Board wrote in one column. He was taken to task in a subsequent letter to MRR that pointed out, "Rape is not a crime of insatiable sexual desire. Rape is a crime of violence. A demonstration of power. A means by which women are kept in place.... [Board] is buying into the myths invented by patriarchy." Another Board column elicited a number of letters criticizing his account of experiences with child prostitutes in Thailand. The letters were angry with Board's contentions that "[t]hese kids are having a fun time"; that if these kids don't want to participate, all they have to do is say "no;" and that he was helping to prop up the Thai economy with his visit to a child prostitute.

5 Imperato's September 1994 column dealt compassionately with age-ism, and Christeen's, in the same issue, confronted on-the-job sexual harassment with an account of an attack she suffered at the hands of a co-worker.

6 Rev. Norb's recent column in the September 1994 issue of MRR was a several-thousand-word, foaming-at-the-mouth diatribe against Green Day because the Rev. Norb's band was tossed from a bill headlined by Green Day.

7 N.W.A. —Niggaz With Attitude—are best known for their 1988 LP *Straight Outta Compton* and one of its singles, "Fuck Tha' Police." The now-defunct band challenged police and societal violence against the African American community, but was also blatantly misogynistic and homophobic. During the controversy surrounding "Fuck Tha' Police," N.W.A. spent weeks in the mainstream media—as was the case with Ice T and Body Count's "Cop Killer." N.W.A. alumni include Dr. Dre, Ice Cube, and Easy E.

The Disposable Heroes's only LP, *Hypocrisy Is The Greatest Luxury*, took uncompromising stands against misogyny, queer-bashing, capitalism, police violence, mass-media manipulation and other political maladies. The powerful LP sank like a stone, despite successful tours, an opening slot on U2's massive Zoo TV Tour, and positive press.

8 Mordam Records, based in San Francisco, is a collective of large and small indie labels that banded together in order to distribute their records without the difficulties of using an established distributor.

9 The latest (at the time of this interview) *BYOFL*, current through 1994, is a resource guide with a "country-by-country/state-by-state listing of punk/hardcore/garage/indie bands, zines, promoters, labels, radio, video, food, lodging, etc." *BYOFL* is co-published by *MAXIMUMROCKNROLL* and Rocco Publishing.

10 ABC No-Rio, on Rivington Street on New York's Lower East Side, has been a gathering point for the punk community going back to the early '80s. Bands play downstairs while art exhibits, video showings and readings take place upstairs. ABC No-Rio has held countless benefits for everything from squatter communities facing eviction to replacing a recently-robbed band's equipment.

11 The Straight Edge punk community eschews drugs, alcohol, tobacco and puts a huge emphasis on taking back control of one's life in the face of everyday societal pressures. Washington DC's seminal '80s punk band, Minor Threat, helped spearhead Straight Edge. Other punkers dismiss Straight Edge advocates as didactic, moralistic, and no fun.

12 P&D—Pressing and Distribution. A band pays for the cost of recording an album or single, and a label will pay to manufacture the record/CD/cassette ("pressing") and get it around to record stores and sometimes radio stations ("distribution"). This type of deal may or may not include money for promotional costs such as touring, advertising, radio promotion, videos and the like.

A more comprehensive deal between a band and a label usually sees the label front a large sum of money to the band to pay for the record's recording costs (an "advance"). Then the band is forced to pay the advance back to the label when—or *if*—the record starts to sell. Until the advance is fully paid off, the band goes unpaid—much like pre-UMW coal miners who were forever in debt to the company store.

Tim Yohannan can be contacted at *MAXIMUMROCKNROLL*, P.O. Box 460760, San Francisco, CA 94146-0760. Phone (415) 648-3561; fax/modem (415) 648-5816.

Rocco Publishing, who put out *Book Your Own Fuckin' Life*, is at 2427 South 58 Court, Cicero, IL 60650.

Scott M. X. Turner can be reached at Triage Records, 199 Prospect Place, Fourth Floor, Brooklyn, NY 11238. Phone (718) 857-4607.

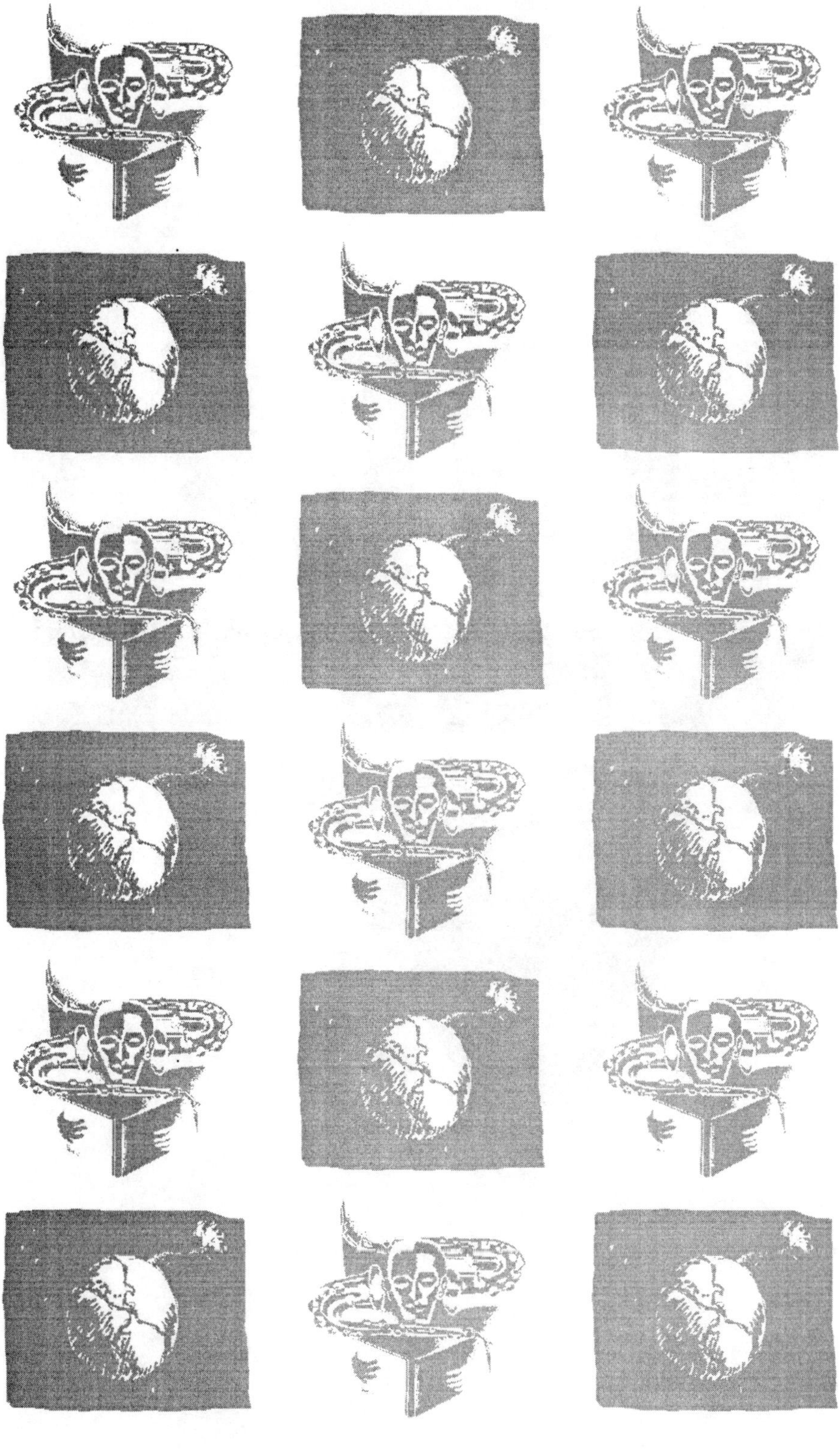

the BLACK WEDGE tour

The Black Wedge Tours:
"Take Something You Care About and Make It Your Life"

Jean Smith

"One step easier than punk! The Black Wedge is out to spread the word of how to combine poetry, music and politics and have a fun time doing it. Hardcore poems and shredding guitars, radical voices crushing sexism, militarism, poverty and conformity. The Black Wedge wants to set wild hearts and imaginations free, to release a riot of emotion—opening up a new arena for activist resistance culture."

In the early part of 1986, Mecca Normal released their first LP on their own label, Smarten Up! Records. Soon thereafter, they flew to Montréal and hooked up with Rhythm Activism; another voice and guitar duo dealing with social concerns from an anti-authoritarian perspective. While the four stood around in the basement of the Canadian Broadcasting Corporation building waiting to go on live radio coast to coast, they listened in on the segment prior to their spot—England's Red Wedge was being featured. Formed in the late '80s to support the Labor Party, the Red Wedge presented political ideas within a musical context, a showcase of musicians encouraged people to vote Labor. The Black Wedge, coming into existence that night, would encourage people to reclaim their voices, to speak out against oppression rather than rely on electoral politics as a means to solve social problems.

A phone call was made to Vancouver and a bus was secured for a West Coast tour. The tour line-up included Mecca Normal, Rhythm Activism, Ken Lester (D.O.A.'s manager, activist and poet), Dave Pritchett (longshoreman and poet) and Bryan James (a self-described "jingle man").

Leaving Vancouver after a sold-out show, the tour headed south, playing nightclubs, a bookstore, an art gallery, a soup kitchen, a record store, universities and as many radio stations as possible along the way. Our preliminary promotional work paid off, and articles appeared in many publications, including mainstream daily papers.

The show, divided into five segments, dealt with a variety of issues. Mecca Normal performed "Strong White Male," "Smile Baby," and "Women Were King"—all of which brought up sexism and male oppression. They also performed "Are You Hungry Joe?," a dialogue between Joe and the guy that stood between him and a bag of groceries at a food bank. Rhythm Activism also addressed poverty in "The Rats." Bryan James' songs were about pornography and the lure of the TV screen. Dave Pritchett's poems were mainly about disenfranchised citizens and lost love. Between songs and poems, we all talked about what we were trying to do with the Black Wedge. Sometimes it sounded dogmatic and rhetorical, other nights it was spontaneous and charming. In Olympia, Rhythm Activism's Norman Nawrocki called for a raid of the Safeway next door—it didn't quite happen, but there was enthusiasm for the plan.

As a group, the Black Wedge was grappling daily with the same concepts that we pontificated about from the stage nightly. In San Francisco, Bryan and I published a small newsletter called *Bus Tokens*. We distributed it that evening at the show. I was the only woman on the tour and Bryan is black, the rest of our tourmates were white males. In a somewhat frustrated tone, *Bus Tokens* railed against authoritarian attitudes on the bus, sexist comments and personal gripes. As a group, we presented a show to inspire people, to introduce the possibility of creating poetry that was aggressively useful and music that was stripped down to the powerful basics of guitar and voice, but as the tour evolved and people became more frayed, I became more aware that we had created a microcosm of what we were expressing opposition to. I think people who address social concerns are expected to be beyond reproach. With the Black Wedge tours and subsequent politically based endeavors, it became very clear that there was no purity in this type of work. There was no path laid out in front of us; mistakes were made, experience altered our approach. It seems like people tend to wait for a signal to start a project; the strange thing is that once you start a project. you forget about the beginning, you are too busy dealing with the stream of problems and opportunities that follow.

Holland, 1994
I am sitting outside at a cafe table in Holland with David, our traditional breakfast has arrived: salami and a white bun. I order a beer and use the salami to shine my boots.

"It seems like music and philosophy have cut themselves off from life, they ignore each other, they used to feed each other," says David, continuing our ongoing conversation.

"As far as music goes, there's an agreed upon obligation to create replicas of what's already in front of us," I say. "It seems like the one thing necessary to make something of value is the thing we're encouraged to hide. Difference. The thing that makes us different from each other."

My beer arrives, filled with bubbling amber in the slant of morning sun. I am looking at the back of the cafe wondering what the rectangular black shapes on the far wall are, I realize they are other rooms.

"Success seems to be viewed in terms of ability to imitate. Who told us to stop making up life as we go along? It's funny how we've traded political rights for consumer rights, we've been reduced to buying and selling popular concepts, guzzling approval. Who's trying to create anything?"

Prior to the Black Wedge, Mecca Normal had not toured at all. That first tour was amazing; we met poets, community activists, anarchists, feminists, people at radio stations, record-label people, fanzine writers and bands. It was incredible to drop into a community and see what was going on and, at the same time, represent ourselves. I don't think we had any idea of what was out there in terms of like-minded people. Since that first time out, Mecca Normal has done about thirty tours in North America and Europe. After the group tours, we became more insulated, preferring to tour by ourselves and play on regular rock bills as a contrast to the four-guys-on-stage syndrome.

Talking With K Record's Calvin Johnson: An Interlude

JS: *When you're interested in a band, is it the idea of working with somebody who has a similar method or vision and not necessarily a particular sound?*

CJ: Right, for instance, Mecca Normal. The first time I saw them was on the Black Wedge tour where they got together with their friends and said, "Hey, this is important, let's do it." It wasn't as if they were saying, "How can we sell this new album?" It was a tour of people and half of them weren't even bands.

JS: *You know, when I think of K, it doesn't exist in the realm of "isms." I don't think of an interest in overly politicized dogma. I see you doing things that follow some of those sentiments, like putting out a lot of music by women and being a Do-It-Yourself label, but the word from K isn't put together in a literal way. It's interesting that you were attracted to the Black Wedge, because it was very literal.*

CJ: One of my ideas, in the back of my mind, is that instead of saying that we're smashing sexism, we're trying hard not to be a macho rock 'n' roll label.

JS: *Does it ever bug you how much Mecca Normal talks about these things in literal terms?*

CJ: No, I think it's great. For me, the idea is, we're trying to create an environment where those negative things don't exist. I think for a lot of people who are making music in a political way...one criticism I might have is that they don't allow for dialogue. If you disagree with them they just turn off. I've encountered a lot of people in music who have strong political views who don't have a strong tolerance for other people's views.

JS: *They need to get out more.*

CJ: It's hard for things to change if people aren't going to exchange ideas. If they're only going to say, "If you disagree with me, then you're the enemy." One thing that's really useful when discussing issues, especially issues of repression, is to see all the different points of views and try to understand why someone would look at something as oppressive and someone else doesn't. Not to say that one person is right or wrong, but to understand why that can exist.

JS: *To want purity out of every situation is an antiquated idea. It is totally language based—having everything succinctly packaged, allowing no ambiguity to leak in at all. I don't think there is a reality where that exists.*

CJ: Extreme points of view are also very useful because so many people are trying to avoid conflict. The great thing about rock 'n' roll is that because it is a three-minute song, you can get one idea across. That's important. Artistically, it seems like so few people are doing anything interesting, taking risks, changing or adding anything. I see a lot of changes with Mecca Normal. I see you adding things and subtracting things one at a time, slowly over a period of time and it's really interesting. Whatever you're doing at any one time is fantastic. It works as a whole, it's complete, and it's not like a work in progress. That's exciting, and it's exciting to meet other people who are doing things like that, but a lot of times those people aren't well understood by the people who are just consumers of media, consumers of music. They're just like, "Oh, entertain me." It's kind of sad when people who are doing something that's different get to a point when their different thing becomes the accepted thing.

In 1987. the Black Wedge got on the same old school bus and drove from Vancouver to Winnipeg. Rhythm Activism, Bryan James and Mecca Normal were on the bill again in addition to Toronto's Mourning Sickness—"committed to destroying all forms of patriarchal power..." and Peter Plate, an agent of the spoken word, who had seen our San Francisco shows the year before and decided to join us. Responding to an ad in *Open Road*, an anarchist news journal, Nelly Bolt took on the driving and an information table with anarchist news, Black Wedge booklets and prisoners' rights information. David Lester (Mecca Normal's guitar player) set up a display of political posters at every show. Booklets containing a selection of everyone's work and a compilation tape were sent out to secure shows. One promoter in Edmonton canceled our show after hearing Peter Plate's piece "San Bernadino" in which, to paraphrase, Peter jerks off on church door handles Saturday night so his dried seed will glisten on the priest's hand Sunday morning. Konnie Lingus of Mourning Sickness brought up the rights of sex-trade workers, herself being one. Prudence Clearwater and Lynna Landstreet were the other band members. When we met up with Mourning Sickness for a Toronto show, Prudence had been attacked by a man on the street the night before. She was so strong up on stage doing her usual rant against street harassment, "Listen to me, little man," she howled down at the audience. It felt like our introspective world of touring had been interrupted by reality.

On a ferry ride across a lake in British Columbia, Peter jumped up on the roof of the bus without warning and began a poem. The other passengers tried to pretend this was not happening; people in cars actually rolled up their windows. Nelly Bolt, our driver, also got up there and did her first public performance of her poetry to a captive audience.

In '88, Peter Plate and Mecca Normal went to England to perform on the cabaret circuit. We were sandwiched between highland dancers, comics, and skits. Peter was dynamic; all his pieces were done from memory. Mecca Normal had always wanted to be either a contrast to a larger, more traditional rock band, or as part of the Black Wedge, an element within a similarly motived group. In England the other acts were entertainment, something we never wanted to be!

After the tour ended I stayed in the North of England doing solo readings and running a women's writing workshop which was set up for me by Keith Jafrate, a poet, sax player and an employee of the local council. He was running writing workshops at all different levels involving poets and people interested in improving their writing skills. Keith joined the '89 Black Wedge tour in North America. He teamed up with Rachel Melas on bass. We were joined again by Peter Plate. We toured the West Coast and in the East before the thing exploded for financial and personal reasons. That was the last tour that I know of called the Black Wedge. The name is available for other people to use to present anti-authoritarian ideas. It is meant to be an arena for people who might not otherwise be known well enough to bring out an audience. It was never meant to be a closed group that was only active for a short time.

> *Bicycles are moving throughout the city; at the end of a journey, they are left for the next person to use.*

If the Black Wedge shows themselves were not consistently well attended, we did get air time and press, not only at college stations and in leftist publications, but on national radio (Canada's CBC and England's BBC); regional glossy magazines appeared with photos and major dailies ran features. We felt that pushing our ideas about anarchism into mainstream culture was important, and we succeeded. The headlines read, "The Black Wedge spreads the word," "Anarchist poetry to the fore in war against social injustice," "Paint it black," "Black Wedge strives for the subconscious," "Feminist aggro in the Black Wedge," "Wedgies are back!"

The Black Wedge functions/agitates in the crawlspace of resistance, under the big house of capitalism.

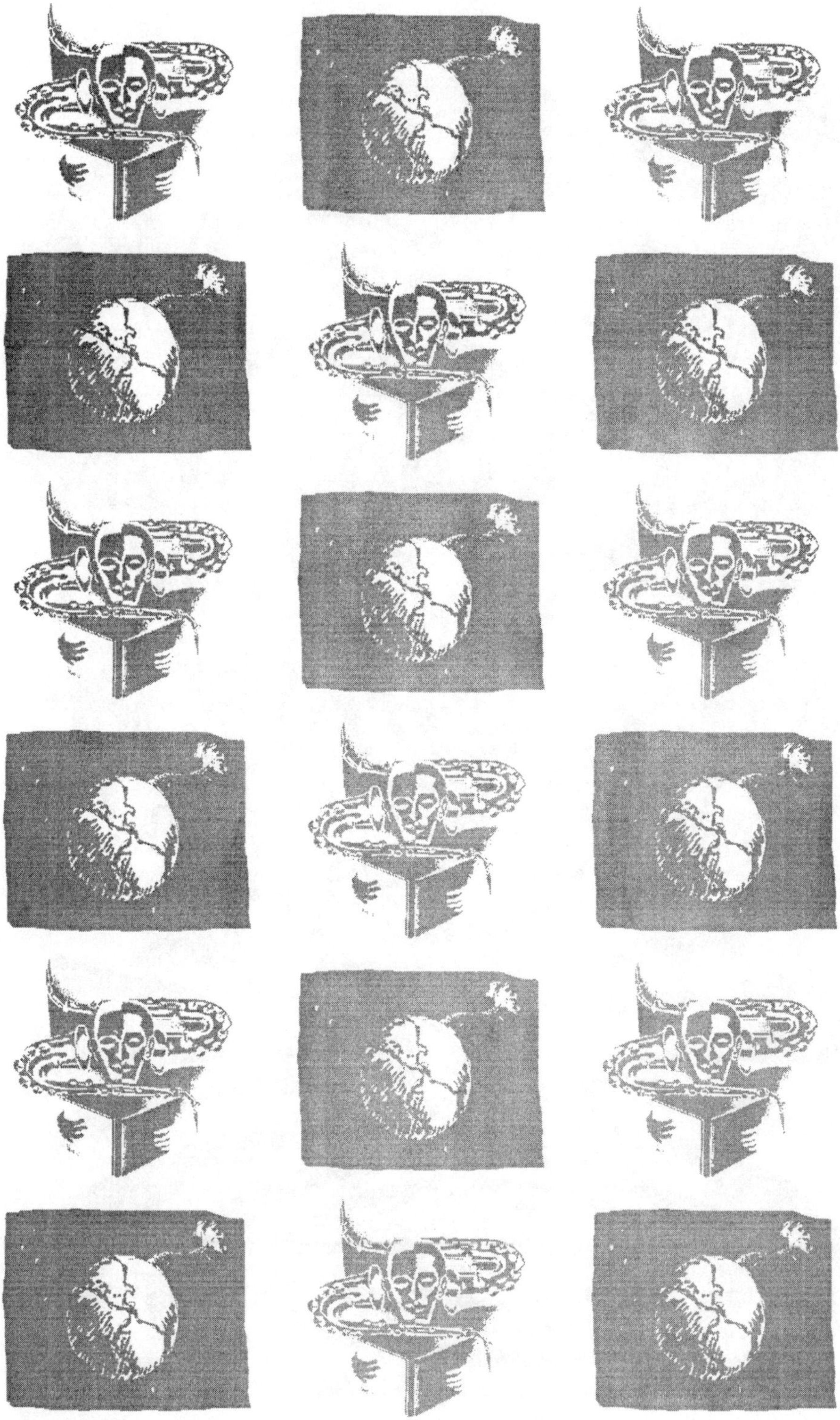

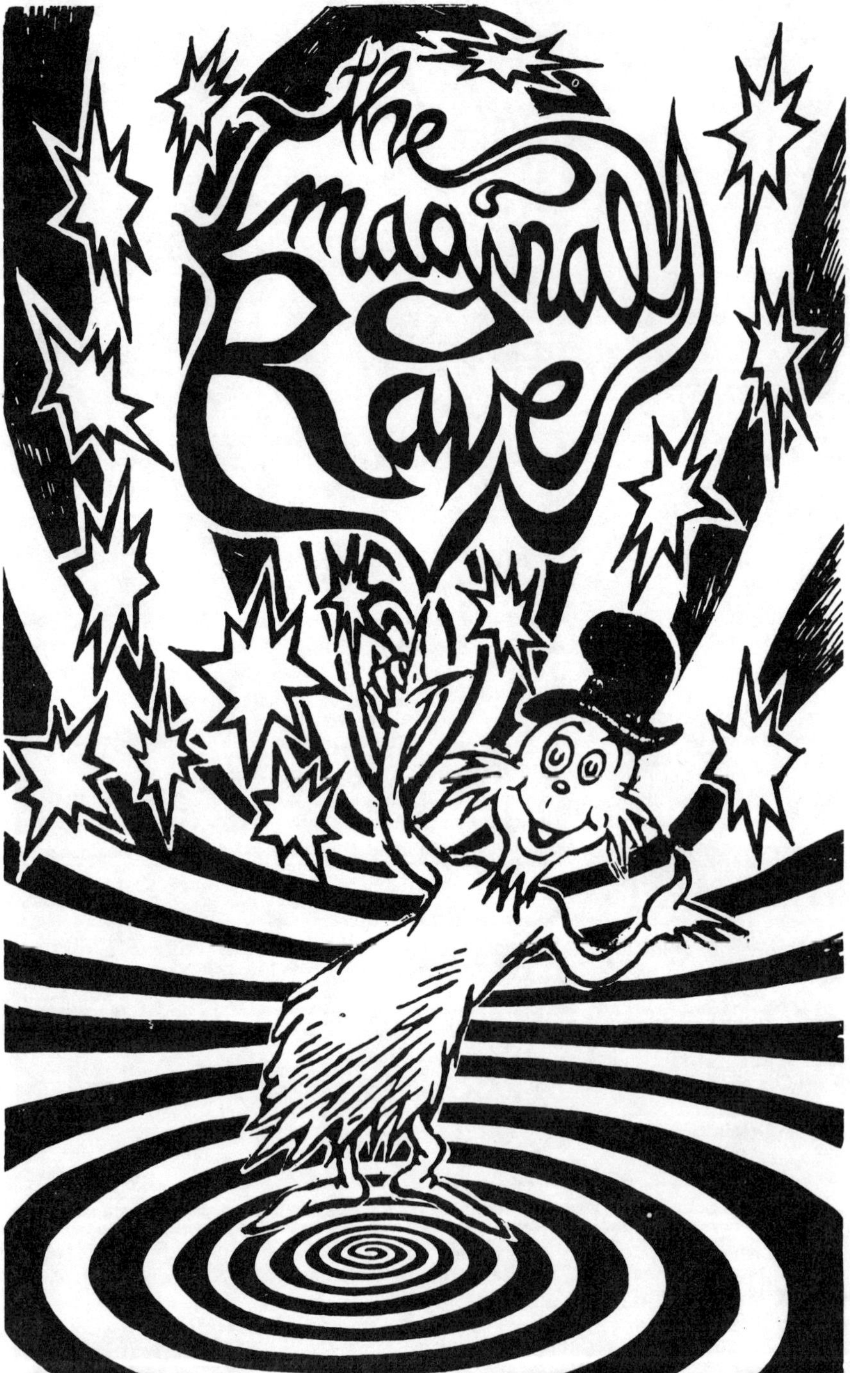
the Imaginary Rave

The Imaginal Rave

Cinnamon Twist

This is less about what raves are or aren't than about what they *might* be. So don't bother looking here for a rehash of the obvious: that raves are the latest thing in underground dance parties / about having fun / feeling good / Energy / Unity / Community...all of which *is* true, needless to say, but there remains so much more to be said, so much more to *be*!

Cut through the clouds of fashion and commercialization that wrap themselves around any major new mutation in culture. What wants to be invoked (what I want to invoke—what I hope *you* want to invoke) is that imaginal, incandescent core out of which all the smoke & noise is generated; what a rave truly can be, for some people in some situations—what it could *become;* and then, peeling away at the sides... falling off one by one, duller, flatter, greyer...and ever so much more *tame*... all those would-be and almost-raves, unavoidable byproducts of anything too real.

An old Sufi saying has it that "where there's counterfeit, there's true gold." So next time you go to something that calls itself a rave but isn't, don't just write it all off. Trust me, the real ones exist, and why *should* they be so easy to find? And after all, it's up to *you* to make them real. Alright, we already know that raves are *the* space-age tribal youth ritual, the return of the dionysian energy that first emerged in 50's rock 'n' roll and erupted in full force in the late-'60's with the intertwining of music and psychedelic drugs. But the rave current is itself only the more visible crest of something broader and deeper. It's no coincidence that it hits the States at the same time as a major resurgence of psychedelic usage. You can take the toying with neo-'60's motifs—day-glo, flowers, smiley faces, flares—as mere fashion recycling by a generation born largely post-Summer of Love. Or you can see these themes as the instinctual recovery of a project left hanging, next breath after a two decade-long lull. Or you can go even further—and why not!?—and see "the '60's" as only one recent intrusion within the Flatland of (take a deep breath now) Gravity-Bound-Domesticated-Humanoid-Industrial Civilization (got that?) of a future that is already happening, a future that beckons us towards itself and sends its echoes spiralling back through the dark and narrow tunnels of terrestrial time to make itself come true.

But only with your help, of course!

204 The Imaginal Rave

Picture a wave forming on the horizon, a big one (talking late-'50s, early-'60s): the psychick surfers coasting out there, beatniks, non-conformists, oddball academics bored with the small-town life at the shore and all its dismal soap-opera games, looking for something to carry them away into a wilder, richer world; the first swells of energy carry with them a tide of psycho-active algaes.

HOFFMAN/HUXLEY/BURROUGHS/GINSBURG/WATTS/LEARY/ALPERT/KESEY & CO., send back their first reports and manifestoes. Munching on the junk food of the gods, our proto-mutants are initiated into the mysteries of the Vortex; they glide back down to the cardboard facades of Main Street with their evocations of kaleidoscopic infinity, eyes lit with the light of alien suns. Their news answers a gnawing hunger among so many trapped within the greypastelboxroutines of the industrial-consumer-democratic hive.

More, they activate dormant circuits of the hive's nervous system, and spawn a burst of deviance, mutation: forms of rebellion less interested in disputing what varieties of greypastelboxroutines are preferable and what's right and wrong for everybody, than in setting up scouting parties for heading out to sea...

Underline the word parties.

Dosed to the gills, beatniks in existential black mutate into rainbow-hued hippiedom. Up with the Flower Children, hedonistic and "escapist"—so-called because they withdrew from the arena of domesticated primate aggro-sports known as "politics" in favor of actually learning about the infinite kingdoms within their own bodies and nervous systems.

Drop into the Haight, turn off powertrips, tune out conformism and competition.

Meltdown ensues. All the accelerated bondings through Be-Ins, Love-Ins, communes. Awash in the incense of oriental exoticism and occultist bric-a-brac, a renaissance of the spirit decks itself out in threads of psychic kitsch.

And how much can we fault them, really, if their Love &Peach trip undercut itself by becoming a denial of the Darkness; after all, they are there for us to learn from.

But just as everyone is tumbling about in the cosmic froth, anticipating revolution of millenium tomorrow afternoon at the latest, the Wave suddenly evaporates beneath them. Oops, the Earth Egg didn't quite hatch yet... just some initial stirrings. And so the children of the Vortex find themselves hurtling through the air like Wile E. Coyote, wrapped up in all their newfound lifestyles, but the vital juice is gone, and it all becomes so tame and lame so quickly, and in any case, a lot of people couldn't handle the intensity so it comes time to settle back into a safe routine, in some cases lay the ground for those who come after; & all around are the Mr. Joneses of many guises, panicked at the imminent collapse of Normalville; some take their chance to cash in on what they can of it, a lot of others are wholly freaked, and so begins a Counter-Reformation. On the one hand, a retreat from direct encounter with the Abyss crystallizes into the New Age, and on the other, it's back to the Bible, dumb drugs, white-bread, and Family Values.

And all the hipsters left posing without a clue, all the burnouts/ fuckups/addicts & victims of some invisible multi-dimensional boogeying elephant; over there in the ivy towers, the blind men scribble their learned tomes, dissecting some stray paisley footprints; but something far stranger has happened, and its awfully hard to make out just what till the next, bigger cousin of that wave starts to surface offshore.

Meanwhile even many devotees of the Vortex ascribe it to the decline in quality of their psychoactive goodies, mistaking the portal for the vista beyond (but how do you enter the vista without the portal? Hmmm... *Bethyvision!*, a distant curl of the Vortex whispers back).

Credit it all to upsurges of the Gaian mind, long-schemed scams of the giggling DNA-consciousness, or the flotsam & jetsam cast down by That Transcendental Novelty Item at the End of Time; choose your metaphors — the more the merrier; but there's a mystery-in-process that all the nice rationalistic analyses will never get at. Here I'll echo a point once made by Mr. Leary: the most subtle form of conservatism is that which views the present only through the prism of the past!

And yes (to those for whom it's not patently obvious), *it's happening again.*

* * *

At the heart of the rave is a modern, technologically-clad form of non-verbal, ecstatic communion. The ethos of openness, sharing, intimacy, touch and empathy—not to mention the pure intensities of trance itself —facilitated by the use of LSD & MDMA (hey, the fact that you have to take these things to loosen up is a sign of just how far down & lost we all are!!), in tandem with the all-night long pulsation of bodies to the same sound source, can and does create a context where layers of armoring and conditioning are shed, where those willing can find the joyful and mysterious realm of their bodies free of oh-so many enculturated ego-trips and bullshit,...while also opening the "post-terrestrial" circuits of their psyches. (Whew! Pause, rewind, read paragraph again, slowly.)

In other words, a safe space where we can be as weird as we want to be.

A collective molting ritual for the new species.

***

Or take it from another angle. Compare the rave-thing to a chemical reaction: a half-dozen ingredients (make your own list), inert & ordinary in the normal course of things. But combine them in right proportions, at the right time and place, apply the *catalyst* (& what would *that* be?) and *boom!,* you've set off an explosion, a chain reaction producing *energy, lots of it,* and in that process a dynamic that continues to transform many of the starting ingredients into new & unknown qualities. No question, of course, that skeptical bystanders can look in from the distance and reduce it all back to something familiar: escapism, consumerism, fashion parade, whatever. But we'll leave them to their nervous calculations...

***

OK, so you want a schoolbook definition of techno-*shamanism,* that catchphrase everybody likes to invoke but no one seems to be able to actually explain?

Prepare to jump levels: As the individual shaman/ess evicts demons and excises magical darts from the sick person through a mixture of magickal sound & motion, so on the level of the diseased and crisis-ridden "global village", raves aim to heal the collective body by shaking it loose of its neurotic fixations and death-fetishes.

Exorcism through Dance

Unhooking the talons and shadowy webs of control. A physical unlearning of a few thousand years worth of *bad habits.*

Learning to be at once a little more human and a little more alien.

Healer, leader, visionary, outcast: the shaman/ess' role is multi-faceted, both at the center but also relegated to the margins of the community. The use of rhythmic sound and/or psychoactive compounds are central to shamanism. The shaman/ess chants, hums, drums and dances as a way of programming her/his voyage into the "spirit realms" (a.k.a. *hyperspace*), as well as of healing the mind and body of others... all on a more face-to-face, way low-tech scale, of course.

So there, chew on that for a while.

***

It's a pretty sad but predictable fact that so-called radicals have been oblivious to this phenomenon, just because it seems to emanate out of *niteklubland;* too bad—when will they figure out that all social alienation is ultimately grounded in an alienation from the body — that realm of nature closest to us but oh-so far away. Their heroine Emma Goldman once proclaimed to the grim socialist militants of her day: "If I can't dance in your revolution I want no part of it."

And what if dance could be a modality of social change?

A heretical thought, no doubt. "Free your ass and your mind will follow," so said George Clinton. But hey, he was just another crass capitalistic rock star, right?

Not to rescusitate, however, that burdensome word, Revolution. Scratch the R, highlight the E. Quote an obscure graffito from a wall in Paris, May 1968: "This is not a Revolution but a Mutation." And say rather, *TAZ*. Temporary Autonomous Zone.

Like the TAZ, the rave is wild, nomadic, outside the maps of Power. At its best, the rave opens onto a realm of free-form behavior and perception, one in which there is no hierarchy, no leaders or followers, at most the dj and the light-show artists. (Hopefully benign—be careful who you leave your sensorium with!)...

Not unlike the Situationist International's notion of the "situation" (sorry, I just had to drag them in here!), a space of liberated interactions... but where the participants are the art and the show, the synergy between them all the event (or event horizon?). (Did the S.I., by the way, ever have anything to say about music or dance?!?) If the insurrection was supposed to realize itself in a festival, we might ask, why shouldn't the festival turn into an insurrection — an insurrection of Love?

Anyone who has been part of a *real* rave, if only once, briefly, knows that its insane, insanely beautiful ferocity is something that exceeds all the contrived parlour-games that pass for alternatives, social or political. The simple fact of this ferocious hedonism is, without words or slogans, *a refutation of domesticated existence*. So *fuck it* if most of this California rave-scene is still ensnared in niteklubism. Invade the pseudo-raves, instigate roving micro-raves. Doesn't take more than a ghetto blaster and a handful of courageous revellers to start a rave on any streetcorner or park, see how long it takes to catch... or to be shut down....

This is *our* form of protest—our style of dance is angry and combative as well as loving and celebratory. To free our bodies first from the rotting carcass of history.

And from there... who knows where we'll go?

***

Prediction: a few years down the road, the rave-scene will be looked back on as the primary networking mechanism for the tribes of star-farers.

***

Dance

If you had to have *just one* metaphor for it all to live by and through, wouldn't that just be it. The spiral dance of life... so it sounds cliched, but cliched only in words, in words....

Dance

But (& rave-friends can detour here for a sec, these are words for those who've never raved and long stopped going out to)

Dance

Dance—this kind of dance — is *freeing motion*. Not just moving to the beat, but letting the beat help you throw off all the constricted robotic movements that have been imprinted into your heart, your eyes, your ears, your arms, your ass, your dreams, by all the tricks, traumas & seductions of society; and find the *real you*. Dancing with the world, but dancing off the consensus-trance, that narrow greyout rightangle robotic updown freezeframe pseudo-reality.

Raves signal the return to Western culture of sacred dance. A dance that balances disciplines with excess, ecstasy with focus. Look at the three great monotheisms that have molded our psycho-somatic matrix: Judaism, Christianity, Islam: none of them possess any tradition of sacred movement. They have all been scared shitless of the Body, and have instituted its repression in a thousand and one subtle ways. How appropriate that the advent of a spiritualized form of movement to the center of Civilization should present itself in a totally decadent, seemingly profane form. And people wonder why raves are actively suppressed in the U.K.? Don't be surprised if it happens here too! And let's get this out of the way too: dancing on a decent dose of psychedelic is something else again: communing with the animal spirits encoded into the depths of your skin, letting them out of their millenial cages. Learning how you can be each of them when you need to be; and it's also abou learning how to fly, how to turn yourself inside out into a spinning glowing disc, though that is a little harder... and then, once we've got that under our belts, we can do it *together.*

It's been said before, but not clearly enough: UFOs R Us.

***

So what if all this prepackaged ravitis costs too much! Don't leave it to them and whine about how commercialized it all is: *throw your own*! *And mutate while you're at it!*

So some of the dinosaurs may not be happy seeing their way of life superseded, and want to stamp out those noisy critters scampering between their feet; more intelligence and greater maneuverability will be our response. Haven't we gotten sick enough of the Enemy-Production Line?

Social transmutation can be fun too, right? There's fun, safe vapid alcoholic-nicotine hedonism, letting off steam so you can return to Monday; and then there's fun that aims high, fun allied with Will.

But watch this—all those scouting parties of the future will be known by their capacity to throw great parties—and pioneer partying as a way of throwing off the legacy of the miserable Dominator culture we've all had to grow up in.

***

Ravers, look a little ways forward: have you wondered yet what happens once you're burnt out after a year or two of intensive raving, once you've lost half your hearing, the beats become stale, and the Energy has leaked away. Where, what then?

Define the rave for me.

What does the verb *to rave* really mean to you?

But first let's list all the stuff that seems to go with it: Acid/techno/deep house music; dancing from dusk to dawn; hi-tech light shows; lollipops, floppyhats, dayglo pendants, smart drinks; $15–20 tickets; zillion gigawatts sound-systems; X, acid, nitrous, 2 CB; goofy sci-fi outfits; so many inane and beatific smiles...

Shall we ask together: just what *is* the essence of a rave?

Suppose for a second that we subtract one by one each of the above elements. Stretch your imagination to the limit, and take away even, yes, even *the music;* till all we have left are the people, all those people who have found each other in this beat, in these hidden gatherings, but without the beat, just heartbeat, pulse-rate, breath... *and the exchange of love-energies* (isn't that what sex is, ultimately?)... Radiant and revelling in our unearthly beauty... so here we are: much as we adore it, do we really need the dance music to affirm our commonality, the patent fact that we are siblings of the same spiritual family who through the raves have managed to find one another and in that finding remember who each of us truly is, orphan child of eternity. Do we need to confuse the rave with the quality of our common presence, our moving-loving together; can't we take the essence of the rave, freed of all the externals we associate with it, transfer and apply that energy elsewhere, to just about anything...?

It comes down to a challenge, a challenge posed in that leap from normal space to hyperspace that kicks in when the "rave" really starts to rave: those altered moments when each of us in being truest to our uniqueness enters into a harmonious whole. Elusive as this may be, it calls out, and asks to be realized in every moment of our lives. It asks for creation, *creation of life,* for the nurturing of real communities that last deeper & longer than a few hours on the dancefloor.

All that creative energy, apply it not just to your style of dress but to your mode of *being*. Free eros & intimacy from the shackles of socially-programmed sexualities (gay vs. straight, male vs. female), from monogamy and the neurotic fixation on genital sexuality.

Turn down the volume, listen to the silence, tune in to your inner rhythms, follow the energy pulse that connects you to your Self, to others, to Gaia, to the stars.

Yes, celebrate, celebrate your arrival here at last after a long trek, but don't forget, this is only the point of departure. These parties are our loading docks and shipyards. (And don't worry, there is plenty of Work to be done, enough healing & cleaning for us all.)

Here is where we will build not just a house, but a ship, a ship of dreams, a starship. Woven out of *love. Chaos. Laughter. Imagination. Will.* & each other.

And embark; post-nuclear families setting sail out along the unwinding multi-dimensional origami strands of alternity...

Our motto:
Utopia or bust.

—The Barbary Coast, July 1992

Some conceptual map-points for the Imaginal Rave (as if you really cared! What, ravers read!?!): *TAZ*, by Hakim Bey; *The Politics of Ecstasy, Neuropolitics, Info-Psychology*, by Timothy Leary; *The Revolution of Everyday Life*, by Raoul Vaneigem; *Ultrahouse, Tekno-Acid Beat*, and *Towards Thee Infinite Beat*, by Psychic TV & others (Waxtrax Records); *The Principia Discordia*, by Malaclypse the Younger; *The Food of the Gods, The Archaic Revival*, by Terence McKenna; *The Sufis*, by Idries Shah, & any ol' record by George Clinton.

"The Imaginal Rave" is a Tribal Donut Production. No copyright. Text may be sampled and reproduced freely, but pleez give credit & contact info where possible. Copies available for $2.00 cash through the mail (or for four International Reply Coupons from abroad). Copies of Tribal Donut #1 (24 pages of hi-density chaostrophy) also available for $2.00 cash. Send all correspondence to: Tribal Donut, 41 Sutter Street, Box 1348, San Francisco, CA 94104. Thanx to Freddie Baer for Mac-assistance, and to everybody else out there helping to make this rant outdated and superfluous by the time it sees print.

Custom LP & cassette packaging by Panic Records & Tapes, Chicago, mid-late 1980's

Long Live the Humble Audio Cassette
–a eulogy

Scott Marshall

It is such a drag to be trapped in an Einsteinian time-space continuum model—Albert must have been shilling for space aliens, effectively trapping us on this planet for a few millennia. As a global inmate, I sit and ruminate on technological developments in my lifetime that have profoundly transformed our species' communicative ability. My thoughts inevitably turn to the electronic miniaturization, audio/video production, and digital-circuitry revolutions. Seen from the perspective of the "Baby-Booming" generation, ours was the first to be given these new and powerful tools of computing and communication straight out of the womb—and one of the most amazing tools was the audio cassette.

Our parents had recently experienced the life-changing revolution of wireless broadcasting. In the early years of this century, any small business from jewelry store to quack doctor could and did own and operate radio stations. The standardized audio formats of amplitude-modulated broadcast bandwidths, fully electronic recording, and 78 r.p.m. lacquer disc technologies were the primary tools. The mass-marketing of decent quality hardware, both for the professional and the home enthusiast alike, afforded anyone with enough money to fully participate in these unheard of opportunities for communication and entertainment. Better-quality home hi-fi systems even came complete with their own lathe cutting arms for recording transcriptions off the air or D.I.Y. home projects. For a few years, the means of communication was in the hands of large quantities of people. But soon, government regulation, the National Addiction® to passive entertainment, and unbridled advertising opportunities served to restrict and commodify what was once a rather egalitarian hobby-toy for tinkering nerds. Home hi-fi turntables no longer came equipped with cutting lathes.

Enter the transistor. Invented in 1948 by John Bardeen, Walter H. Brattain, and William Shockley, this new miniaturized tube-less circuitry was based on material with remarkable properties called "semi-conductors." These tiny self-contained circuits the size of your little fingernail could replace large racks of hot buzzing vacuum tubes. Transistors made overall reduction of size and cost of electronic equipment possible for the first time. The three inventors won the Nobel prize in 1956 for their work.

Enter magnetic recording tape. The magnetic recording of audio was discovered by a Danish researcher, Valdemar Poulsen, who won a prize at the Paris Exposition of 1900 for his troubles. By World War 2, the Germans had developed flexible tape-based magnetic recording emulsion, replacing the convenient, but sonically inferior, wire-recording technology. Soon, everyone from Bing Crosby to invading WW2 generals were recording their messages and product.

Enter the audio cassette. By the late-1960s/early-'70s, the advantages of the "cassette" had become clear—they were smaller, cheaper, and easier to use than clumsy reel-to-reels or 8-tracks, and un-commodifiable beyond the blank tape itself. It wasn't that the program material was ideally suited to the format, it was that their reusability, long life-expectancy, and cheap cost encouraged the liberating D.I.Y. spirit better than any other format of self-publishing. Internationally, home-tapers and tiny production companies flourished. Bootlegging of commercial audio releases soared.

And so, the crucible of the International Cassette Underground gave rise to a richly diverse and seditious stew of creative misfits with little or no commercial-music potential whatsoever. The disenfranchised from Australia to Alaska tuned into the blab line, mailing their latest cassette concoctions and/or their tiny xeroxed 'zine to each other. Some works were serious attempts at high aesthetic, with the cassette format only an inexpensive vehicle for marketing their aural visions. Others, including myself and our little Chicago collective, concentrated on developing the overall concept of the cassette as fetishized *objet d'art*. For us at *Panic Records & Tapes*, it was the limited-edition of custom hand-crafted packaging and adornments that mostly carried the concept. Our cassettes came encased in a melted-LP "fortune cookie" that as often as not, would remain un-opened and un-listened-to, out of deference to the package.

But for the most part, the thrill was in receiving a personally hand-crafted audio greeting card, (occasionally a painfully noisy one-time listening experience), that connected a Western civilization of estranged fellow travelers. By networking, connecting, corresponding, and exchanging ideas and information, we were empowering each other to think globally and act locally. Exchanging cassettes was like exchanging elaborate cultural calling-cards of information virus rather than consuming empty marketing commodity. They were labors of love for ourselves, and for our friends in the cassette-net, most of whom we would never meet or talk to in person. But yet, we were all privy to a deeper and more personal, private, and inspiring aspect of communication than mere letter writing or phone calling. The cassette/'zine/alternative radio-station network afforded a chance to otherwise divided, conquered, impotent, and ego-isolated Westerners of all ages to culturally empower themselves and create wonderfully seditious and politically charged gestures for an international audience.

Though India still utilizes the audio cassette for a variety of commercial and agitprop concerns (see Peter Manuel's *Cassette Culture*, University of Chicago Press, Chicago, IL, 1993), and the African market uses 'em as the commodity of choice; the peculiarly oddball and fringe cultures of the North Americans, Europeans, Israelis, and Australians have had a relatively brief and intense love-affair with the now-fading analog format. The distance and breadth of correspondences have been quite amazing at times, with a global community's worth of gratifying anecdotes to keep us warm as the ravages of time and age reduce us to the misty realm of memories.

Enter the music 'zine phenomena. Along with the independent audio and video enthusiasts, the Amateur Press Associations began to publish 'n' ship their spew 'n' reviews to far-flung weirdos the world over. It was the mid-1970s at KAOS-FM at Evergreen College in Olympia, Washington when a group of like-minded individuals came together to put together a music publication with international relevance. Entitled *OP*, and edited by John Foster, the new publishing venture was undertaken with a pre-programmed life expectancy of 26 issues (A issue to Z issue). Though this un-pretentious little broadside began as a simple station program guide, the ripples, networking, and inspiration it caused was immeasurable. *OP* contained a wealth of news, reviews, and interviews with the leading lights and minds of the burgeoning international independent music scene. I would opine that *OP* opened more doors of perception, brought together more widely-scattered people, and inspired more creative juices to flow than any music-based periodical either before or since.

Too soon the life expectancy of *OP* ran out. The now-'zine-dependent global community of D.I.Y. cassette and LP enthusiasts collectively held their breath for a few months and wondered what publication would fill the void. Eventually, word came that there would now be two magazines to take the place of *OP*. *Sound Choice*, published by David Ciafferdini, seemed to embody the same bare-bones no-bullshit ultimate 'zine sensibility that made *OP* so charming. *Option*, published by Scott Becker, quickly established itself as the fancy, four-color, up-scale version of the original item. *Sound Choice* valiantly survived for 5–6 years, while *Option* still shmoozes on as of this writing, indistinguishable from other glossy B.S. rags in the alt-mainstream pro-music slime-line. Stellar domestic publications from 'those days' that come to mind here in the twilight gloaming include: *File 13, Bananafish, Forced Exposure, Factsheet 5*, and *MAXIMUM ROCK'N' ROLL*.

Non-profit free-form radio stations on four continents worked in conjunction with the 'zines to create a nurturing environment for the rag-tag international community of home-tapers. For the broadcast media, one could usually count on FM airtime and play-list charting from: KAOS (Olympia, WA), KPFA (Berkely); KDAI (Minneapolis); WZRD, WNUR, and WHPK (Chicago), CKLN (Toronto), CKUT (Montreal), WFMU (East Orange, NJ), WREK (Atlanta), *Recrues Des Sens* (Bordeaux, France), and various other important college and non-profit stations. In addition, many of the North-American co-conspirators received unusual amounts of attention from OOUM, state-funded alternative FM in Zagreb, then-Yugoslavia, and a free-spirited DJ named Dinko Bazadona (where are you now?).

And then there was Robin James. One of the preeminent cassette-networkers in America, and tangentially associated with the wild-haired bunch at *OP*, James' influence and promulgation of the cassette format struck chords and found aesthetic currency in many nooks and crannies throughout the world. In a recent telephone conversation, Robin offered these observations, "My main thing was cassettes. [I enjoyed] exploring the parameters and fringes of the medium. It gave me an identity. I met a lot of people. And I didn't make a dime. But when you plugged in that little piece of plastic, the cassette became a surreal event. The audio cassette played on the idea that you were getting the same product as everybody else—a shared experience like radio. But an event would happen when you put the cassette in and played it... They were a whole different way to publish."

The Future looms upon us now—and brothers and sisters, like it or not, it's in binary code. Most aspects of "modern" life will exist for the foreseeable future, at least on some level, as digital data storage. For tech-heads, it will be a boon. And why not?! *Viva la muerte de la* U.S. Postal system dinosaur! For too long the notoriously incompetent U.S. Postal bureaucracy has restricted and constrained the free flow of written and recorded information. Thankfully, Internet conferences and E-mail now enable graphics, audio, and missives to be conveyed at speeds restricted only by modem baud rates.

For children, these days, are coming to consciousness in the Global Net. The storage and retrieval of information and data is proceeding at an unbelievable pace. This new and intimidating paradigm cannot help but offer unprecedented access to greater global communication and alternative "democratic-participant" methods of self-publishing. Already there are such harbingers of the new age as the Internet Underground Music Archive, run by two young guys in Santa Cruz, CA. For a small fee, they will digitize your musical offering, and post it on their server for all the world to down-load at their leisure. (Of course, the major music labels are freaked and outraged at the complete lack of copyright enforcement.) Various new gateways and browsers to the global Net (like *Mosaic*), are being conjured up monthly to allow greater ease at communicating with your fellow species. And while Big Brother Bureaucracy flounders around in the La Brea tar pits of a Cold War mentality, making feeble attempts at regulation and surveillance (like 1994's Clipper Chip legislation, or Internet pornography indictments and convictions); the digital paradigm-shift sails on at a break-neck system clock-cycle rate.

But let us hope there will always be time for analog circuitry and audio cassettes. The "warmer" and "richer" qualities of analog audio are deservedly well-known. Whether it's musical instrument vacuum-tube amplification or old-fashioned recording tape, the end product, cassette or vinyl, is always imbued with a mellow, sweet tonality that compact-disc technology cannot approach. Like a well-crafted oil painting, no amount of digitally-manipulated imagery can surpass the Genuine Analog Article. And by the time digital recording, computing, and communication equipment becomes accessible to absolutely everyone, that will probably be the day governments are finally able to make significant in-roads into digital surveillance.

Until that day of digital nightmare comes, we will still capture and contain our music and dreaming on an 1/8" wide strip of magnetically-sensitive plastic, which creeps along at 1 7/8" inches per second. Some of the best things in life will never be rushed.

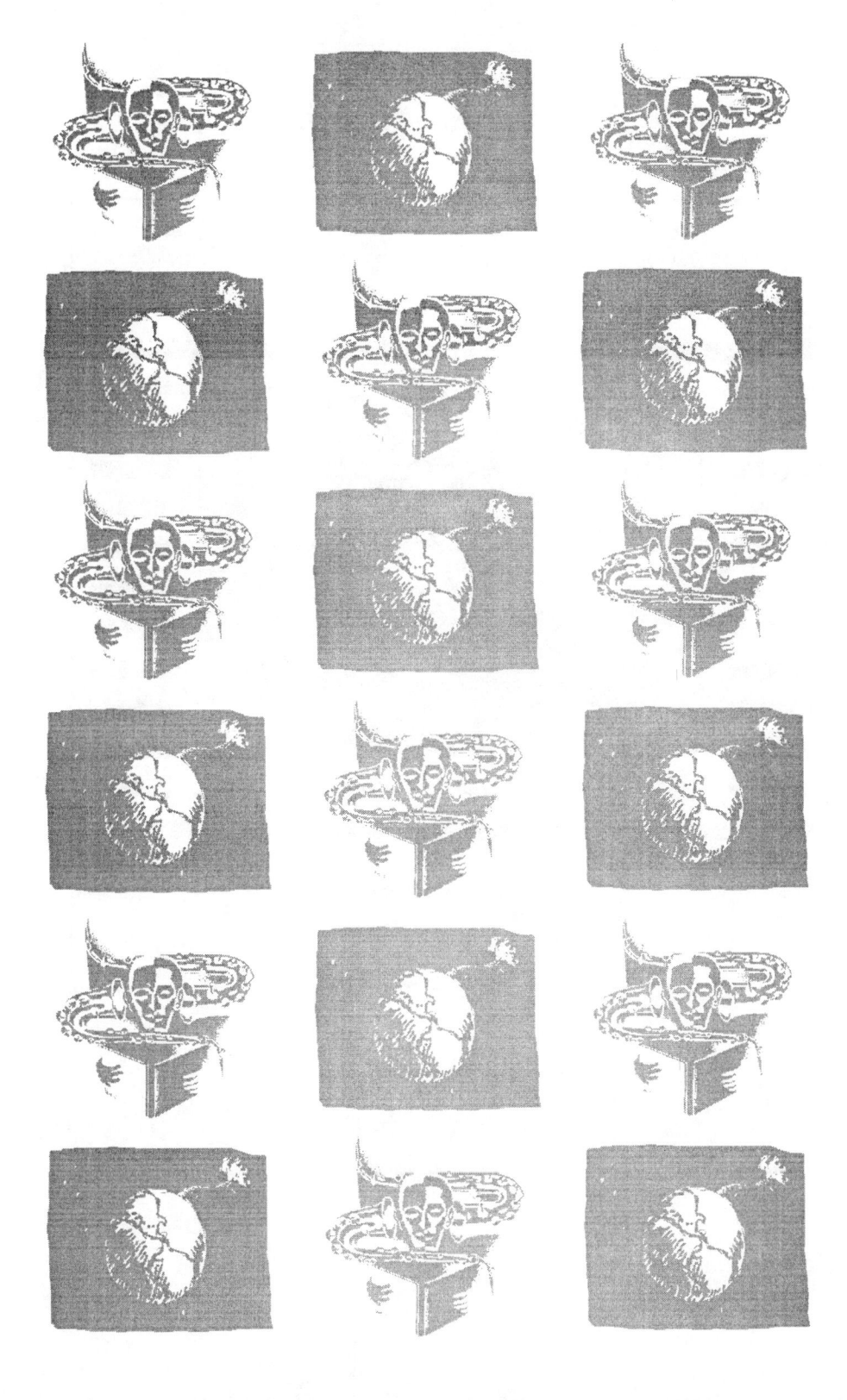

THE Grand Delusion

The Tape-beatles

Plagiarism®:
An Interview with the Tape-beatles

(1994)

Stephen Perkins

In 1994, the Iowa City-based multimedia band the Tape-beatles were asked to provide their perspective on the nature of intellectual property for a film on plagiarism which was being made by San Francisco filmmaker Craig Baldwin. Baldwin asked Iowa City art historian Stephen Perkins to interview the Tape-beatles, while his wife, filmmaker Arda Ishkanian, videotaped the proceedings. During the discussion, the Tape-beatles addressed issues which may turn out to concern anyone doing cultural work in the 21st century. An edited transcript of the interview follows, with Perkins often taking the role of devil's advocate.

Present were Tape-beatles Linda Morgan Brown, Lloyd Dunn and Paul Neff. (Ralph Johnson has relocated to the San Francisco area, and John Heck now lives abroad.) The interview took place in the Tape-beatles' Burlington Street studio, a windowless, sheetrocked, climate-controlled basement space with plenty of electrical outlets.

SP: Tell me, just what are the Tape-beatles?

LD: That's a big question. The Tape-beatles are a group of five individuals who originally got together in 1986 to pursue what we thought at the time was a new avenue of production that would make use of audio tape as an expressive medium. We felt at the time that audio in particular was a medium that hadn't been explored thoroughly by artists, and what we wanted to do was to explore it on our own terms. We were influenced by the French *concrete* musicians, such as Pierre Henri and Pierre Schaeffer, and a few other modernist composers like Edgard Varèse and John Cage. We were also heavily influenced by some pop music that had used tape effects and manipulation, such as the Beatles' work. We have a modest studio we've set up over the years. We have a lot of used equipment and inexpensive home audio equipment, nothing too elaborate.

SP: Can you talk about "Plagiarism®: A Collective Vision"?

LD: That is our de facto motto, appearing on a lot of our printed material and t-shirts. It refers to a certain cultural practice that we feel has a lot of creative potential, which is Plagiarism®. We take the works of other artists and disassemble them and re-shape them to suit our own ends. We extract meaningful bits from them and combine them with bits from other works, and create something that did not exist before, but which nonetheless has many of the earmarks and cachet of the works that it came from. It's not the point of Plagiarism® to hide the sources; in fact, we go to great lengths to point out the fact that our work is indeed plagiarized.

The "Collective Vision" part comes from the fact of others working with similar ideas, who have arrived at these ideas more or less independently of us. We felt like we came up with the idea on our own but then we found out that there were other people doing it, too. So there seems to be a place in culture for this stuff, and it seems to be popping up in different places all at once, of its own accord really, so this fact lends some credibility to our choice of this particular practice.

SP: Credibility for ripping other people off?

LD: Yes, ripping other people off—but not doing it at their expense. There's a certain ethic behind how we do this sort of thing. There are all sorts of laws and rules pertaining to how cultural work or intellectual property can be used by the people it's handed on to. And there are a lot of laws—copyright, trademark and patent laws—that try to protect the output of creative people. It seems like this is probably a good idea, given the fact that we live in a capitalist society in which ideas are treated like commodities to be consumed in much the same way as frozen string beans.

But we have come to believe that doesn't tell the whole story of what intellectual property really is. Culture is a shared experience. When someone makes a record, or writes a book, or draws a picture, and then sells it, in a sense they're selling the material support that helps the thing exist physically, transportably. But the cultural part, the part that people are really buying it for—not the physical compact disc or the physical marks on paper; but the work itself—becomes part of the consciousness of the consumer. Their minds come to "own" it in some deep sense. Maybe in some cultures selling cultural experience would be unthinkable; primitive cultures for example, where song and dance are a shared experience. Everyone participates. Here, "culture" is merely passively consumed.

PN: But you can't really say that we're trying to move people back to the idea of a shared culture such as a primitive society might have, because we commodify our work just like everyone else. We sell CDs, for example. Another way you could look at Plagiarism® is the way in which we say we plagiarize—we don't re-package old Beatles material as our own; instead we perform what we sometimes call "recombinant" techniques on them, creating what are definitely new works, made out of previously finished products. It's a collective vision because we're not the only ones doing it; we are not the first people to do this and we won't be the last. This practice of taking work from one context and using it for other than its intended purpose is as old as the hills. The only difference between us and just about any other cultural work is that we say we're plagiarizing and we make a big point of it. We hope that in doing so we can shed light on the nature of the creative process a little bit.

SP: I don't see how being honest about the activity you're involved in absolves you from the underlying criminality of it.

PN: There's nothing criminal about what we're doing. We do not consider what we're doing to be criminal or unethical.

SP: But if you were to speak to a lawyer they might have a rather different opinion on it.

PN: Well, they might, but they're lawyers. They've got a vested interest.

LD: Right, it's certainly true that we're on shaky legal ground with this sort of stuff. We recognize the fact that somebody probably could sue us if they saw an opportunity in suing us.

SP: So you haven't been sued yet.

LD: No, we haven't. But we also recognize that the practice of litigation is essentially opportunistic. People are often willing to sue, in the cultural arena especially, only if there is something to be gained. We don't have deep pockets and this protects us to some degree, in other words. We're not a likely target of litigation in any of the things we've done, mostly because if someone were to sue us, they wouldn't recoup enough capital to offset the legal fees.

In the case of Negativland, whose CD *U2* was clearly a lampoon of a popular rock group, I believe they were sued because Island Records (U2's label) was concerned that people would mistake Negativland's CD for a U2 CD, thus diluting U2's market. Negativeland was making fun of U2, but they had the misfortune of being signed to a prominent independent label (SST), and I believe that Island saw both an opportunity to quash the little bugs (Negativland) and gain financially. SST makes a lot of money as compared to other independent labels.

SP: So if the target of Negativland's lampooning was a particular band and their inflated reputations, then what is the equivalent for the Tape-beatles?

PN: Well, our scope is wider. We don't spend time going after particular people, so much as we go after some broad trend in the political and cultural climate.

LMB: American popular culture. It's basically the thing we're commenting on. The fact that everything we see and do today is marketed to us. Marketing is one of the most influential things in our culture. So I think we're making fun of how culture and cultural heroes become part of us. I think it can be dealt with more deeply. Perfect strangers have become household names.

SP: Does this activity give you power? Are you trying to keep culture at a distance or are you trying to neutralize it? One would understand that you are against these tendencies in culture, but by taking these different pieces and putting them together—

LMB: I don't know if I could say that I'm against mainstream culture; it's just an attempt to recognize what it is, to try and define it, and have some of our kind of fun with it.

LD: It's a valid point of outrage for us to say that none of us—not just Tape-beatles—are active participants in our own culture. We're encouraged to be passive consumers of culture, and discouraged from trying to make our own statements. The Tape-beatles are trying to bridge the power gap. It is an empowering act to take this kind of stuff that comes out of the pipes like running water, and using it to fit our own ends. By taking what we consider to be meaningful, telling bits of culture, and looking at them in a new context, making them seem strange, it estranges us from it and puts it under a microscope so it can be examined with something like detachment and objectivity.

SP: So you take bits from culture, recombine them, repackage them, and sell them, for another audience to enjoy?

LD: Yeah, well it would seem ironic and the point is not lost on us about what you're trying to do with that provocative observation. At the same time, it's our hope that the audience that buys our stuff will understand what we're doing. I think of our work as a kind of a virus. We have these ideas that don't have this broad appeal, but we have managed to get them out there and be heard, to infect culture with blips of our stuff. It could roll off into something big.

I've always very much admired the statement that the Velvet Underground didn't sell many records, but everybody who bought one went out and started their own band.

PN: Lester Bangs.

LD: O.K. I've always admired that kind of following that the Velvet Underground seem to have. That's the kind of thing we aspire to.

PN: We don't have any conceits about leading a revolution, digital, analog, or otherwise. I think that the revolution is—

LD: —being televised.

PN: Yes it is! Very much so, and it's probably on the radio, and on the Internet as well. The very fact that you're listening to what we're doing changes the way you listen to everything else. If you don't believe me, try it. Listen to the Tape-beatles for a week, then turn on the TV and you will hear the sounds on there in a totally different light...

I'm studying to be a librarian and our perspective on copyright causes me plenty of trouble in trying to reconcile it with my emerging professional views. The issues we're touching on are very big issues in that climate. Do we continue to hold these 19th century views on intellectual property in the face of technology which encourages us to do otherwise? Bear in mind that technology tends to motivate cultural change. So it affects what I do, certainly.

LMB: As technology advances, ideas advance with it.

PN: Do you think that technology motivates social change, or is it the other way around?

LMB: Well, I think it's both. You've got to be able to use what you know. Sometimes it goes beyond what you know, too, so you have to come up with a new set of ideas to grasp the significance and possibilities of a new technology...

Eventually, in the fine arts, you start to realize you're being bogged down with a lot of technique, and you find you've bought into a lot of things that are going to take up most of your time and thinking so you have to spend a good deal of your time alone in the studio, cloistered. I joined the Tape-beatles because I was attracted to the idea of a group working together, criticizing each other's work, being confrontational, and still working toward a common goal. The Tape-beatles were building something rather than working alone and feeling alienated.

LD: We felt that there was a collective aspect to the activity which was really worth pursuing. We did that at the expense, sometimes, of our friendship. The four of us—before Linda joined—were very aggressive and a little bit hostile to other Tape-beatles' ideas that didn't precisely match our own. I think all of us came to realize that there are ineffable qualities to the emanations from people whom you don't fully understand, and that if you begin to work with a person and the things begin to fall into place, it really enriches what you yourself are doing. In fact, I think that in the collaborative effort we've built up over time, including Linda, we've become pretty adept right now at negotiating all the little personality foibles each of us has, and working together so that something interesting comes out of it. We're all always surprised by what we end up doing.

PN: This kind of dynamic is not unique, I think. It pertains to every musical group I've worked with. I definitely think of us as a musical group—

LD: —and John and I think of it as an "art band"; and Ralph probably thinks of it as something a little different, and so does Linda. So all of those different points of view help to make it multi-faceted.

PN: Also, we're not simply a musical group. All the different products we have out make us multi-faceted. We have a CD out, some tapes, a video, film for the performance, buttons, t-shirts, and all this stuff. We are sort of a small media conglomerate.

SP: How do you think that people's ideas about the original have changed with the advent of new technology, i.e., photocopy, computer, tape-recording, etc.?

PN: There are several ways you can approach that. In one sense, ideas of the original have not changed one iota since the Renaissance. This is the legacy of copyright laws that we currently have; there are a lot of fences preventing the truly free exchange of intellectual property. These fences exist so that culture can be trafficked as a commodity. However, a lot of ideas about the original are changing because technology such as copiers and computers allow us to make very nice copies of things with very little effort. Suddenly a lot of things that were treated as originals, such as documents for example, don't really have to be treated that way because they can be copies and sent to whomever you want. In the old days, you had an accountant scribbling away at a ledger, and if you lost that ledger, boy, your business was doomed. Now everybody's got it in digital form and they can send it to whomever they want, and every day it's backed up onto disk, and we don't have to worry about it as an original anymore. And people like that.

SP: So you think the idea of the original is obsolete?

PN: What I'm driving at is that we considered originals to be so important because they were unique. Well, uniqueness is giving away to ubiquity in many parts of our life, and what the Tape-beatles are trying to do is say, "Hey, this is not just true in the business world, the research world, and the education world, this is true in art as well." Technology is motivating change in art just as it has motivated change in all those other fields. It's annoying perhaps that we still have to deal with commodification in doing what we do. The reason we make CDs and sell them is because there's no easier way to distribute our product. I think we are gradually getting to a point where people stop thinking of the song as original, something sacrosanct. I think that's going away. Commercial concerns, and others, motivate this. It's almost sneaking up on us. One day a lot of people in the music and art world will wake up to the fact that one can plagiarize, and that it's O.K.; it's just another technique. That the whole idea of the original has outlived its usefulness.

SP: Even so, do you think that still defines plagiarism as creative activity, or is it an activity that's simply more dependent upon choice and selection?

PN: Creativity is choice and selection.

LD: Creativity occurs in plagiarism, because you have to choose creatively what to plagiarize. So a person's creative personality comes in through the back door, so to speak, because they're making choices, just like conventionally "creative" artists are. So it's still a reflection of the individual's character I think.

Creativity and originality really have nothing to do with each other. But I see it more as a matter of instinct and personal conviction than as something I can put into words. [Thinks for a minute.] I mean, when someone is creative, that act does not necessarily entail making something unique and new. Baking a cake is a creative act. Your mother may have used the same recipe as a thousand other women, but it's still a creative act. So creativity and originality have nothing to do with one another. They're strongly linked in our minds, probably because of cultural conditioning.

Walter Benjamin deals a lot with the idea of the original in an essay he wrote in the 1930s called "The Work of Art in the Age of Mechanical Reproduction." The medium he was addressing in that essay was the motion picture, but I think the things he raises are really pertinent to our concerns. He defines the original as having a unique quality that no other object possesses, and he calls this quality "aura." He says that when you stand in front of the Mona Lisa at the Louvre in Paris, you experience that aura because you are aware that you are standing in front of an object that was touched by Leonardo, and it is something that has a continuous existence that spans five hundred years. The aura is what, Benjamin maintains, separates the Mona Lisa from any reproduction, no matter how perfect it may be. So we intuitively understand that when we look at a reproduction, the aura is dissipated and the spell of the aura is broken.

But aura becomes kind of a confusing issue when you start looking at the mechanical reproduction, or production, of artworks. In the particular case of the motion picture, what is it that contains the aura? When you're in a movie theatre, you're not really looking at the object; it's somewhere behind you in the projection booth. It's a technical expedient to create the moving shadows on the screen, which is the motion picture experience. These shadows clearly don't contain the aura in the sense Benjamin defined it, because they are a reproduction, mass-produced in quantity for any theatre willing to show it. If you go back in the projection booth and look at the print, you still wouldn't be in the presence of the aura because a print is just a copy of a negative, another reproduction. In addition, looking at the physical print robs you of the experience of the moving pictures, the pictures in motion, themselves.

Then if you were to go to Hollywood and look up the negative in a vault somewhere and look at that, you still wouldn't have the aura experience, in spite of the fact that you are in the presence of the motion picture "camera original." To take it even further, if you were to go back in time to attend the filming of the picture—the "pro-filmic event" as film theorists like to say—you'd miss out on the controlled situation of editing and sound mixing and the whole slough of effects that are introduced in post-production. So the aura is dissipated when you make works of art that are intended for machine presentation; and this is a predicament unique to the 20th century.

Right now we're approaching a position where the original is completely unimportant. For example, in digital recording of sound, in theory, every copy is identical signal-wise, to the source tape the copy is made from. No information or fidelity is lost in digital to digital copying of audio, or software, or anything recorded digitally. So the original has no special significance, and has no particular value.

PN: But the idea of the original is persistent, though. So even in cases where you don't have to have one, you have people who worry about it. I'm thinking, for example of the U.S. Constitution. The original manuscript is stored in a vault in the National Archives with all sorts of high-tech protection and stuff.

LD: But it has aura.

PN: But we don't need it for anything; the Constitution is reproduced in millions of school textbooks, so anyone can read it. And I think that anyone who values it at all values it for what is says, and not for what it is physically. It's valued for the ideas contained in it. It's not usually admired as a work of calligraphy, for example.

LD: That's an interesting issue. Raising this example from the non-art world is provocative, because the U.S. Constitution is an object of contemplation like a work of art, right? It's an object of reverence like a work of art; it's kind of a sacred relic. It's the repository for a set of ideas that crystalize at a certain point in time, and it's the physical evidence for that crystallization. In that sense, the Constitution does have aura. It's totally imbued with all this cultural residue that we as Americans have in our heads as well as in the school textbooks.

I think this brings us back to some of the issues we were dealing with earlier, too. The fact is that a work of culture is as important as a non-material thing as it is as a material object. We're claiming that when something comes to us through the channels of reproduction and marketing, that's work that has ideas in it. It's the ideas that are important. It's not the physical thing itself. It's not even really the music. It's what the music does to us that we're——purchasing. So the Tape-beatles are attempting to de-materialize ideas, to free them from physical shackles, and the laws and constraints around them that are modeled after laws that protect physical real estate.

SP: So you're a conceptual art band.

LD: "Conceptual Art" has a connotation of a particular movement and a particular group of works in the '60s. So clearly we're not that.

PN: On the other hand, what's not "conceptual" art?

LD: Yeah, every work of art has a concept.

SP: Maybe to be more accurate, you're talking about things having ideas attached to them that are more important than the things themselves. So when you sample from other sources;

one aspect is the joining of different sounds, but also it's the clash that comes from the ideas that come attached to those sounds. Perhaps it's more accurate to say that you're a concept band. You're playing with different ideas.

PN: That's true. We make our choices very deliberately. We are just as interested in the ideas carried by the sounds we sample as by the sounds themselves. We would be doing something very different without that. I'm sure the Tape-beatles would sound very odd to people who don't speak English, for example. Or who aren't Americans and don't understand all the references or even recognize them. I don't think that's a bad thing.

LD: The fact that ideas are channeled through these means is the most important element of artwork for me. The fact that information, culture, ideas, what have you, the objects exist simply to transport. They're supports, they're media for transporting ideas, for transporting culture into the heads of other people.

PN: Yeah, but the point I'm trying to make is that a lot of people who make art think their medium is neutral. I believe that there are no neutral media.

LD: You believe that there are no neutral uses of media?

PN: The fact that you're using a certain medium to communicate something says a lot about what you're trying to communicate.

LD: So you're saying that if we choose to make television, that automatically categorizes us as saying a certain thing.

PN: It makes it easier to do some things and harder to do others. People coming out of the same university journalism departments; some go into print journalism, others go into television. Nobody tries to pretend that these are the same thing. And the reason they're different, despite the fact that the people in them have the same training and near-identical ideologies and achieve different things, is because of the differences between the two media. This is Marshall McLuhan's basic thesis in *Understanding Media*—that however you choose to communicate affects what you're communicating.

SP: Just broadening the scope from what you've just been saying, what do you think the prospects for "cultural jammers" are when they're up against centralized media?

PN: Well, that all depends on circumstances, and what you're trying to do.

LD: "Cultural jammers" actually have an advantage, I think, over other kinds of artists. If you choose to be co-opted by the system—that's a very charged phrase—but if you choose to exhibit your paintings in a gallery and get an agent and grants and all that stuff, your opportunities for really doing incisive and far-reaching critiques of the status quo and the current social order are severely limited. I think "jammers" have a special opportunity in that they're not subject to anybody else's decisions about their work, about how that work will be displayed, or what the subject matter of that work is, or what the content or quality is. They get to do it all themselves. That's a real advantage. They're not censored by anyone, they don't preemptively pre-censor themselves to curry the favor of granting agencies.

SP: So it's a kind of marginal outlaw position.

PN: The smaller you are as a cultural unit, like the Tape-beatles, probably the less ties you're going to have, and the more freedom you'll have to do what you want. And add the proviso that the smaller you are, the less likely you will be noticed and stomped on.

LD: And the flip side of that is that your resources are limited, so you have to make the most of what you got. That ends up being good, too, because if you're being forced to think more creatively, because your resources are limited, about how best to use those resources, the chances are good that you'll think through the content thoroughly, too, to make sure you have something really good and important to say.

SP: In the late 20th century, is it possible to make art and not steal intellectual property?

PN: No.

LD: No. One of the reasons is that we live in a culture where intellectual property, and property in general, are the primary currencies of transmitting that culture.

LMB: Everything that's been thought of influences us all. We use things in different combinations to make something that's newer than what already exists.

PN: You can't think of anything without using the thoughts that came before it.

LD: Ideas don't come out of thin air. They come out of individual experience, which is shaped by the culture the individual resides in. Culture itself is a set of ideas, so if you're going to claim that you made something up out of the blue and that nobody had any influence on you, well, it seems obvious that this simply can't be the case.

PN: We don't believe we're the leaders of an *avant-garde*, because we don't believe there is an *avant-garde*. We believe that what we're doing is the reflection of a cultural trend that has been going on for decades. Plagiarism® is ubiquitous and eternal, and it is an increasing trend in the age of mechanical reproduction. We're going to be seeing many, many more manifestations of it.

SP: If plagiarism is such a widespread activity, it would seem from the notoriety that you all have gained, that you're obviously fairly competent plagiarists. One might also say that you're also very original plagiarists.

PN: We don't really think of ourselves as original. There's nothing original about shameless self-promotion.

LD: We're original only in the sense that we make works that didn't exist before we made them. I had a friend once who said about us, "Boy, for plagiarists, you guys are awfully original." That's kind of a key insight, I think.

SP: It seems to me that plagiarism as you've framed it is an activity inherently antagonistic to capitalism—

LD: It's also kind of the main project of capitalism, if you think about it. Manufacturing is something that's set up to make infinite copies of the same thing, if you're willing to broaden the scope of Plagiarism® to include copying. Manufacturing, they call it "production" when it's really reproduction, is a big capitalist project.

But you're right, we pointedly choose our way of thinking about culture to be antagonistic to the way it's typically thought of. So if people think of music as a commodity to be consumed in much the same way as frozen string beans, then we want to challenge that. We want to say that music is also something else. In its most important aspect, it's something other than simply a commodity. It's something much more.

Ralph once said something that I think is quite smart. He said that, once you start using Plagiarism® as a creative technique, the world becomes different, and can be explored anew. Plagiarism® freshens that which is stale, and re-invigorates the tired. Under Plagiarism,® the world is new. You can start exploring it again.

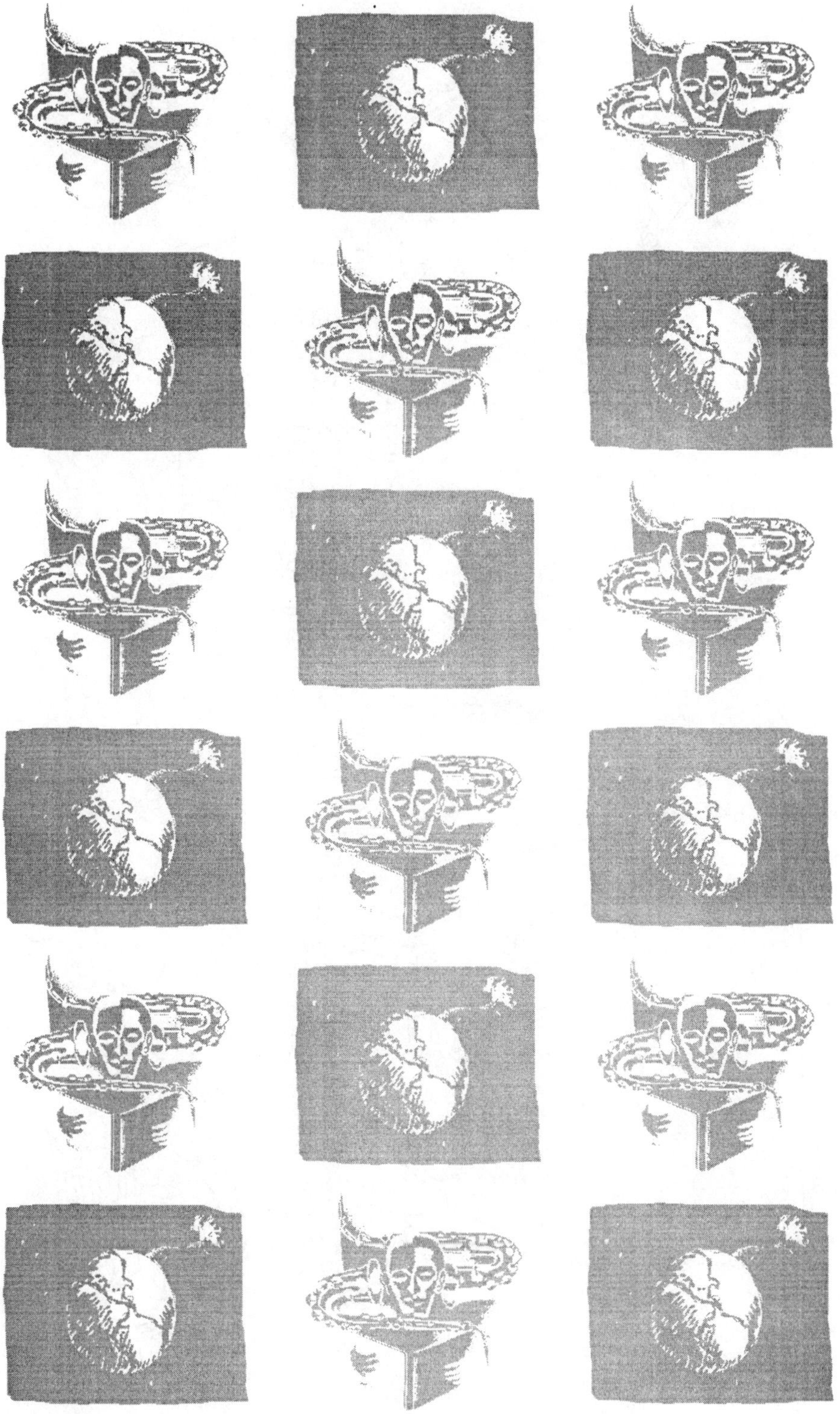

Mark Enslin

Recontextualizing the Production of "New Music"

*Susan Parenti,
Mark Enslin,
& Herbert Brün*

The Performers' Workshop Ensemble[1] is a troupe of performing composers and composing performers. In order to establish connections between art and society, we take as a point of departure the desirability but insufficiency of making concerts. Therefore, we create not only compositions and concerts, but also projects that question in art the status quo of society.

We see ourselves as working in parallel strategies: as a team of teachers who incorporate performance into our teaching, and as an ensemble of performers who incorporate teaching into our performance. While a good deal of our time is spent on stage and in working with students on performance and composition, these activities are nested within a conceptual framework of critical thinking and critical teaching.

What follows is a description of several projects engaged in by the Ensemble since it was formed in 1979, alternating with a few excerpts of pieces, and a few independent statements that indicate some of the thinking that goes into shaping the projects.

Experiments in Concert Format

Whereas "new music" is written by composers, its reputation and social significance are provided by people who are not composers: textbook writers, magazine journalists, radio interviewers, and newspaper critics.

For most newspaper readers, "new music," if known at all, has become known by its exported dilemmas. Up until the past few years, readers could read about a "new music" that was reported to be standing on one foot, separated from its listeners by a "gap." Was this gap due to the music—its difficulty, its complexity, its little known points of departure? Or was the gap due to listeners—their old-fashioned expectations, their lack of education, their unquestioned desire for entertainment? Was it due to the music that listeners couldn't talk about it? Or was it due to the listeners?

In the Performers' Workshop Ensemble, we are concerned with the dilemmas which surround "new music," and with the relationships, reported and unreported, possible and not yet possible, between "new music" and its listeners: What happens between "new music" and listeners? How does music effect listeners, and how do listeners effect "new music" in a social world?

However, our activities as composers and performers who prefer not only to write and perform "new music" but also to write its reputation, lead us to act on a premise unsupportable by the aims of the mass media. Our premise is that in a social world, things are what's said about them.

Thus, in composing and performing "new music," and in addressing listeners and dilemmas and gaps and relationships between each and all, the news of the Performers' Workshop Ensemble is that we investigate and expose an indispensable component of those relationships: language. The language of the newspapers. The language that listeners speak and comment on and mumble to themselves and copy from newspapers. The language of performers as they try to perturb a score into a performance of music. The language of composers proposing and following processes whose traces will (they hope) add to those relationships that turn acoustic chaos into a musical event.

We take as a point of departure that there exists a relationship between a crisis in the relations between "new music" and audience, and a crisis in the language about music; that it is due to the existent language about music that we can't talk about it, and not due to existent listeners nor existent music.

Thus in our programs we wish to change neither audiences nor "new music," but rather change the language that exists between them. We present concerts of music interrupted by dialogues and brief texts, some commenting on, some acting out confrontations between listeners, performers, composers, music, and the word "new." We give ourselves an imperative: to present our audiences with language, so that they can hear.

In the Performers' Workshop Ensemble we became interested in the idea of composing a performance: bringing about a performance which without that performer or group of performers would not happen. The tradition in making concerts is to leave most decisions to tradition. Composing a performance means looking afresh at the criteria used in deciding the whats, whens, wheres, and hows of performance; looking afresh at intentions. Experiments were made with inserting skits on listening between music pieces; displaying and explaining the notations of the pieces during intermissions; putting a trio by Bach for which the players had worked on bringing out its asymmetrical phrasings, next to an experimental trio from the 1940s, next to an experimental trio from that year; giving a poetry reading in which were inserted brief, seeded discussions with the audience on the performance so far; presenting pieces that include elements of satirical cabaret; offering a concert at a gallery that included a timed showing of a painting, parallel monologues comparing the viewing of a painting with shopping for a toaster, and a text piece on galleries; following a "new music" piece with a play in which the composer of the piece is touchy about how another audience member talks about the piece and the composer's friend is touchy about being called his girlfriend.

Clarinet

Piano

(End of *Backbite* for clarinet and piano, by Mark Enslin)

Both musicians freeze at end of music
Musicians bow
Audience applause
Blackout
Actors enter in blackout, applauding, & sit in a row facing audience
Musicians exit
Lights up on applauding actors
Actors begin

mark: [to sara] They didn't play the rhythm right!
sara: It sounded good to me.
mary: [to bill] Where are we in the program?
bill: Beats me.
mary: Then what was the name of that last piece?
bill: Another question that baffles the mind—I don't know!
sara: [overhearing; turning to bill and mary] That was "Backbite" for clarinet and piano. [pointing to mark] He wrote it.
bill: You wrote that piece?
mark: Yep.
bill: Ooh, glad I didn't say anything bad about it!
mary: Oh, Bill.
bill: Well, now that we've got a real live composer sitting right next to us—what do you call that type of music?
mark: What "type" of music?
bill: Yeah. That piece of yours, for instance—what type of music is it?
mark: I call it "new music," for number one, and for number two, since it's new, there's no "type" for it, yet.
mary: Well, but it's classical, sort of, right?
mark: No, it's "new music."
mary: Yeah, OK, but what I mean is, it isn't pop or jazz, so—well, what would you call it?
bill: What I think she's getting at is, well, as I see it, my girlfriend and I are part of a vast unschooled audience, who sit in a concert hall feeling like caterpillars in the midst of a grape stomping festival—
mary: Bill!
bill: —like fish in the middle of a cornfield: we float, we drift, we try to swim, we flash our fins—but we end up drowned in a puddle of mud! In other words, our basic sensibilities are so confused that we've gotta wait till the morning's newspaper in order to find out what it was we heard the night before! The problem, I feel, is that the human race is in danger of los—
mary: —losing its basic categories. I've heard this before.
bill: And that's a terrible thing! In short, all we want to know is: is it lean meats, bread products, dairy—
mary: —or vegetables?
mark: None. It's "new music," as I recall having said before, at least three or four times.
mary: Well, excuse us, we're not in the arts, that term doesn't mean much to us, alright?

(excerpt from *Touchy*, by Susan Parenti)

Listeners who occasionally find themselves listening to new experimental music frequently describe themselves as being lost. Although listeners are in a better position to declare this a problem and do something about it, composers and performers of new experimental music, who are aware of this fact, are also in a position to do something about it. Composers and performers can: (1) ignore this fact and accept as fate that listeners will find themselves lost; (2) strive to make music less new and experimental so that listeners will find themselves in familiar surroundings; (3) avail themselves of advertisers' packaging techniques that can turn anything into a familiar thing; (4) treat performance as a context for teaching—wherein being lost is a necessary and temporary state—by inventing new ways of presenting new experimental music. Response (1) reflects no interest in social change; responses (2) and (3) go along with social changes that are part of the status quo; response (4) reflects an interest in creating social change that goes against the status quo.

Response (4): treating performance as a context for teaching implies a shift of medium. A shift of medium from music to theater, for example, can be done in such a way that listeners become intrigued by experiment in music. One such project that has not yet been exhausted is Composed Rehearsals. The general assignment for composed rehearsals is to write a scene in which the concert presentation of a piece flips into a rehearsal situation. In the scene, sections of the music that present difficulties for listeners are shown to present difficulties for the performers as well; while performers grapple with performance problems, they give listeners an inside view of the piece. The scripts have to be so written that the quarrels that erupt, the glooms that descend, the debates decided by trying out different versions allow the eavesdropping listener to get an insight into the significance of a piece: to glimpse some of the alternatives chosen and something of the process of their choosing.

House Theater

Another form and forum for experiments with the format of performance is House Theater, which was initiated by Susan Parenti and Candace Walworth (a former member of the then recently split-up theater collective the United Mime Workers). House Theater has involved members of the PWE and other members of various communities in Urbana and Champaign, Illinois in the creation of a non-University, non-commercial context for mixing experimental music and political satire in a lived-in setting. A House Theater makes use of the doors, windows, stairs, porch, kitchen, bathroom of a rented house in Urbana to create a quasi cabaret atmosphere with small cafe tables, flowers, candles, coffee-can clip-on lights hooked in the frames of windows and doors, and with tea, wine, cider, juice, and snacks served in intermissions. The atmosphere, program, and performance are so designed that people might by turns be entertained by coming to an understanding about something; by seeing and hearing something not yet understandable; and by being asked to take another look at something we all understand all too well.

If you find a home with space enough for 35 people to sit; if you build 8 small tables for people to place their drinks on; if already three friends live in that home and pay rent; if you plan a program that "mixes neighborhoods," putting political satire next to "new music" and a bawdy poem next to a highbrow dance; if, inside this semi-nightclub atmosphere, you serve wine and cider and food during two intermissions; and if a weekend of five performances is followed up two months later by another program—then you have a House Theater.

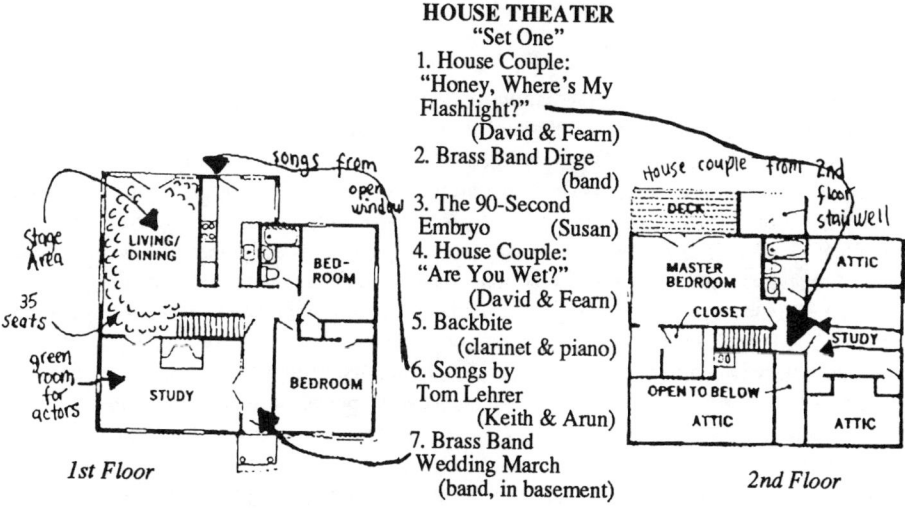

HOUSE THEATER
"Set One"
1. House Couple: "Honey, Where's My Flashlight?" (David & Fearn)
2. Brass Band Dirge (band)
3. The 90-Second Embryo (Susan)
4. House Couple: "Are You Wet?" (David & Fearn)
5. Backbite (clarinet & piano)
6. Songs by Tom Lehrer (Keith & Arun)
7. Brass Band Wedding March (band, in basement)

1st Floor — Stage Area, 35 seats, green room for actors, LIVING/DINING, BEDROOM, BEDROOM, STUDY, songs from open window

2nd Floor — House couple from 2nd floor stairwell, DECK, MASTER BEDROOM, CLOSET, STUDY, OPEN TO BELOW, ATTIC, ATTIC, ATTIC

You're invited. You walk up the stairs of an unfamiliar home. A child with a top hat greets you: "Welcome to the House Theater!" You see, amidst the knicks and knacks of a home, a small stage, some 35 chairs arranged around small wooden tables. You take a seat. You face neighbors. From the staircase, someone seems to be arguing with someone upstairs. At first confused, you realize the performance has begun. Then follows thirty minutes of more performance. Political satires make you laugh, experimental music leaves you puzzled. Your neighbor has the opposite reaction: laughs during the music, is silent and blank during the satires. You make a mental note to talk about it later. Intermission. You hesitate, but when the "waiter" who brings you your glass of wine turns out to be the musician who brought you your piece of "new music," you can't resist: a discussion with neighbor and musician keeps you busy till the lights dim for "Set Two".

By experimenting with alternatives to traditional concerts and traditional theater formats, we have been able to address many people who do not otherwise attend experimental music or theater programs. The House Theater has been particularly effective toward this end.

Working Towards Community

We ask the question "When is community?"—and initiate activities, or take part in ongoing initiatives, such that 'community' be the consequence.

The House Theater project is one such initiative for creating links that are aimed at generating community. In addition to the homemade House Theaters written largely by members of the Performers' Workshop Ensemble, there was a House Theater in 1986 called *The Society of Hinges* written by high school students who had been working with Jeff Glassman. Several students working with composer Mark Sullivan and mime Encarnita Figueroa in East Lansing brought to Urbana a House Theater program on music and pornography. Friends who had been members of Herbert Brün's seminar living in Chicago likewise brought a program discussing, among other topics, South Africa and Mozambique; students at New College in Sarasota,

Florida (where the Ensemble has been in residence a few times) have traveled to Illinois twice with House Theater programs they had written. The Ensemble also has made House Theaters with members of communities we have visited, programming pieces we brought with pieces written by our hosts: Chicago; Virginia Beach; Kassel, Germany; Los Angeles, Sioux Falls.

Some projects were initiated in a "Seminar in Experimental Composition" offered by Herbert Brün at the U of I, to which students, ex-students, non-students, and visitors were invited to bring a problem, show a piece, raise an issue, make a statement, give an assignment, answer a statement, respond to an assignment, organize an action, and engage in formulation-seeking discussion.

One of these, a project in two parts called *The Song of Art and The Nest of the Song*, was instigated by Patrick Daugherty. It introduced the idea of 'desired consequences' as the beginning of a link between composers and community activist groups. Two concerts of music and theater with descriptions of desired consequences of the pieces written by members of the seminar were performed. Representatives from each community group were invited to write descriptions of the desired consequences of their group's activities. Then each group "commissioned" one of the composers to write a piece related to a problem encountered by that group; the pieces were performed in a series of concerts later that year (1979).

Members of the Ensemble have made projects to incorporate performance into demonstrations and social activism, including, during the Persian Gulf War, a five-ring circus burlesquing the administration's attempts to justify its actions (including a "surgical strike" in an "operating theater"); tableaux protests on street corners: actors frozen in scenes commenting on the news blackouts; a "Peace Conference", during which students, members of the surrounding community, and members of activist groups met to work on a variety of issues. In 1993, when the army was displaying obsolete weapons as a public relations move, they were visited by a "Clownspiracy" which had a display of its own.

The Performers' Workshop Ensemble taught a class in the Fall of 1994 at the University of Illinois called "The Need for, and the Traces Left by Experiment in the Arts," in which students are asked not only to study technical, formal, and social experiments, but also to make experiments. This class followed a related ensemble-taught course (student–teacher ratio approximately 12 to 7) called "Composition Between Disciplines," which was offered three times between 1991 and 1993, in which relations between (1) a social critique of the power of language to determine seemingly free interactions and (2) various approaches to composition in a variety of media culminated in a student-written, -designed, and -performed House Theater.

Classes taught by the PWE have explored such questions as: If you know that many people believe a current lie, do you expose the lie, or the believers? If you want to protest a policy, practice, relationship supported by many people, when do you protest against the policy, practice, relationship and when do you protest people's support of it? If a text succeeds in expressing social criticism, what could music add to the expression without subtracting from the social criticism? Under what circumstances does a piece intended as protest register as protest? What do I do facing the desire to have an effect, on the one side, and on the other side, the danger of being choked and devoured by popularity? Music needs words more than words need music (if the words have a music, do they need another one?) How can the criteria used to locate social injustice also be consulted in writing a poem or a piece of music?

How do I begin a piece? 1. I make an absurd proposition and construct its logic. 2. I make myself afraid of the cliché I like. 3. I anticipate the nightmarish proportions to which simple data can grow.

Shall I write a feminist poem about women's issues, or: a feminist poem about architecture; a feminist poem about excuses; an anti-war poem about love of a place; an anti-war way of quarreling with my roommate; or an anti-racist way of talking to my parents? Could there be an anti-racist, anti-war, anti-fascist, anti-sexist way of writing music?

And such statements as:

Many successful works of art reflect present day reality and facts. *Affirmative output of our society.* They are successful in that they allow us to see our society, as it is embellished and affirmed by the artists and composers whom it favors.

Some successful works of art reflect the problems which maintain the system wherein they are conflicts. *Indignantly contrite output of our society.* They are successful in that they allow us to see our society, as it is heavily armed against change, under a thin coat of free thought accorded the artists and composers whom it favors.

A few successful works of art reflect the problems which assail the system wherein they are contradictions. *Affront as input to our society.* They are successful in that they allow us to see our society as if it were also another, different, society and, rather than its future, that of the artists and composers who favor it.

Even fewer successful works of art reflect the desire for, and the rejection of, our society as tomorrow's reality and facts. *Utopia as input to our society.* They are successful in that they allow us to see our society as it prevents itself from becoming what it wants to be, to see another society which helps itself to what it wants to be and its future, rather than that of the artists and composers who favor it.

No work of art necessarily fits only one of these descriptions. Every work of art, however tells composers and their audiences, whether they admit it or not, to which combination of descriptions it best fits.

No description of a work of art necessarily heeds all of the composer's intentions. Most of the composer's intentions, however, may be quite irrelevant for any description of the composition.

No composer necessarily plans to have the composition fit any particular combination of descriptions. Every composer does, however, have a share in the responsibility for that combination of descriptions which fits the composition.

In recent years we have begun a more ambitious project related to generating community, the *Summer School for Designing Society.* Under this audacious title, a 10-day summer school session was tried on a small scale in Urbana in 1992, and has since been tried in two 4-week sessions in the intentional community of the Gesundheit Institute in West Virginia 1993, and in one 5-week session in 1994 in Sioux Falls. Instead of taking the present society as given, participants are invited to give time and attention to formulating their *desires* for a society they would like to live in. Participants live together cooperatively for several weeks, and discuss, write, take classes, make classes, make performances, make experiments exploring the consequences of taking *desires* as a point of departure.

Endnote

[1] The members of the Performers' Workshop Ensemble (PWE) collective as of January 1995 were Susan Parenti, Mark Enslin, Lisa Fay, Jeff Glassman, Rick Burkhardt, Sam Markewich, Joe Futrelle, Danielle Chenowyth and Herbert Brün, whose Performers' Workshops initiated in 1979 were the impetus for our name and work.

Marcelo Lima

Part III.

Shattering The Silence of the New World Order

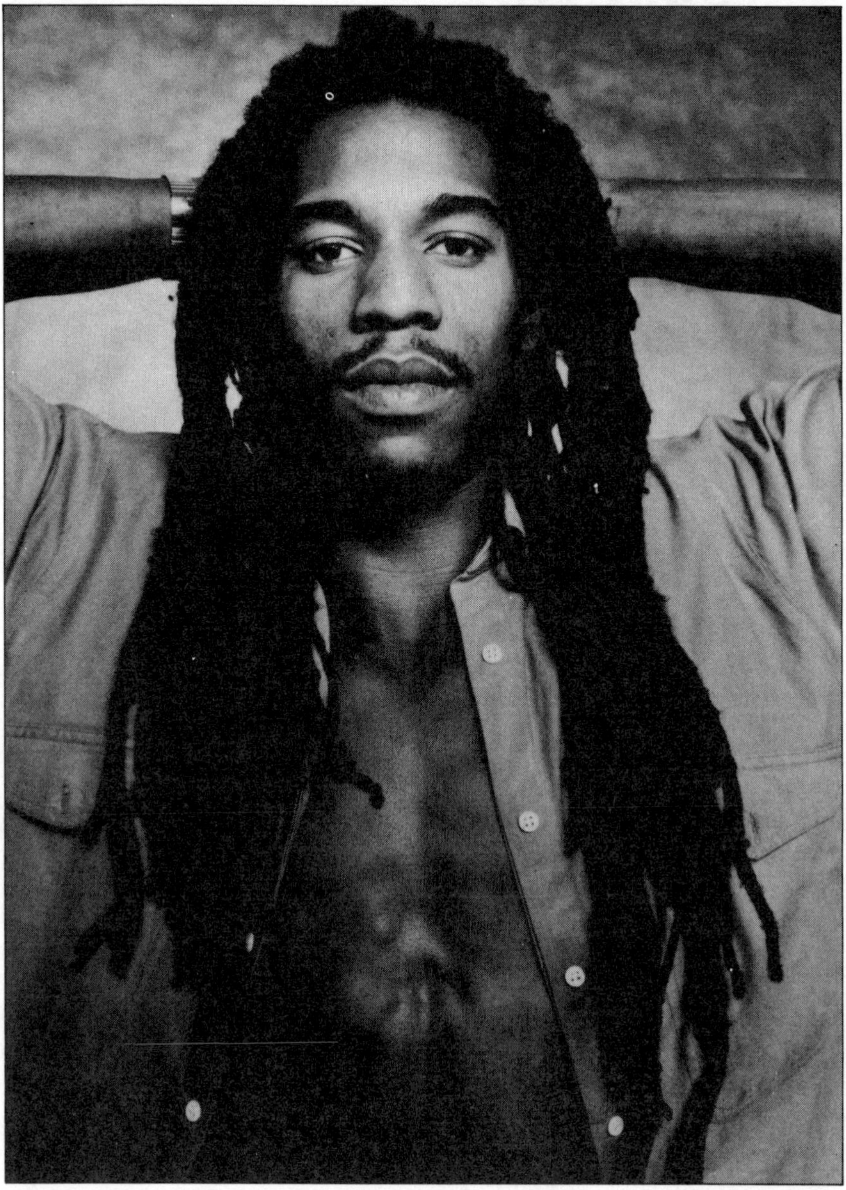

Us & Dem

Benjamin Zephaniah

Me hear dem a talk bout Unity
Dem hav a plan fe de Effnick Minority
Dem sey Liberation totally
But dem hav odder tings as priority
Dem hold a Conference anually
Fe look at de state of Equality
Dem claim dem fighting hard fe we
When we want do it Independently
De us,
Dats dose who are made fe suffer
Some are found in de gutter wid no food fe eat,
Us,
Well, we are clearly frustrated
We jus not debated when Parliament meet,
Dem,
Well dey are known by dere fruits
Dem hav many troops fe batter yu down,
Dem,
Well, Now dem hav power
But dere shall be an hour.
When de table turn round.
Us and Dem it is Us and Dem
When will dis ting ever end
Yu mus know yu enemy from yu fren

Know yu enemy from yu fren now
Face de facts, yu can't pretend now,
I write dis poem fe more dan Art
I live a struggle, de poem plays a part,
I know people, very trendy
Dem talk to me very friendly,

Us & Dem

But dey are coping
So now dem voting all dem frens in,
Do frens oppress we,
How dem arrest we
An den dem givin we Judge an Jury
When we start demonstrating
Dem hav dem prison cell waiting,
Pon de Telly dem talk fe a while
Wid fancy words an dem plastic smile,
Where Party Politricks play it's tricks
Dere is nu luv fe de old, nu luv fe de sick
Us and Dem it is Us an Dem.

Now me hear dem talk bout World Peace,
But dere's Wars at home
An dem Wars will not cease,
Not till all de Queen horses
Women an Men find a new direction
(Start again),
Politicians talk bout World economics,
But read de Manifesto
It reads like a comic,
When dem talk bout housing
Dem mouth start sprouting
Words dat fe ever an fe ever yu doubting.
If yu in doubt yu don't hav a shout
When yu talk against dem
Dem sey get out,
Some call it Democracy
I call it Hypocrisy
Dat mek me start feel Revolutionary,
When rich fashion cramps poor style
I stop an after a while I ask,
Is it me class or is it me colour
Or is it a ting I don't yet discover,
Us an Dem it is Us an Dem
When will dis ting ever end,
Us an Dem it is Us an Dem
Yu mus know yu enemy from yu fren,
I repeat again, now it's Us an Dem,
Don't pretend are yu Us or Dem,
Pick yu place from now
Before de confusion.

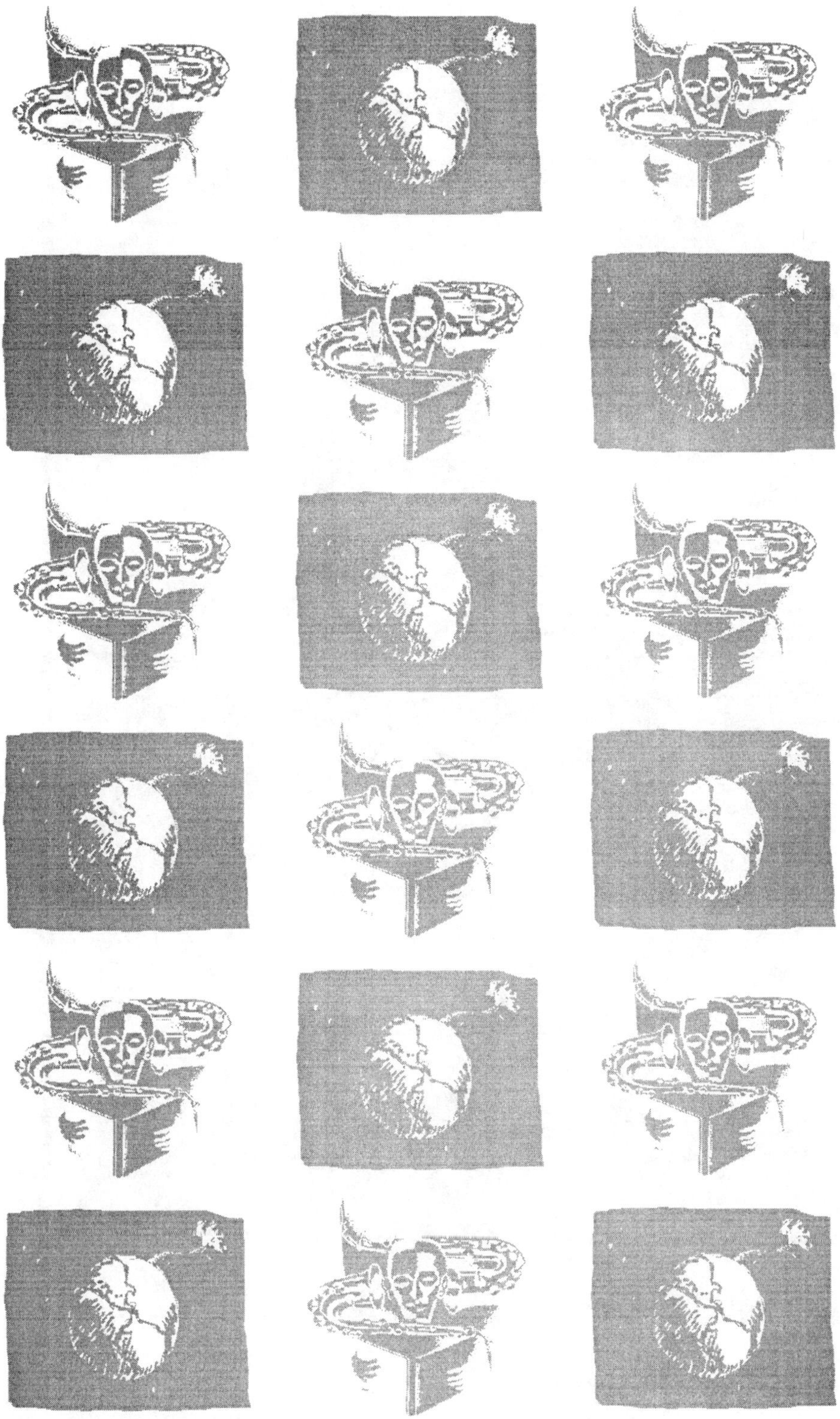

Ricardo Levins-Morales

World Music at the Crossroads

Ron Sakolsky

When Robert Johnson stood at the Delta crossroads he knew exactly the nature of his situation. The sign said, "Nigger Don't Let The Sun Set On You." The hellhounds were on his trail, and there was no turning back. He was an unwelcome stranger in the strange land of rural Mississippi, not African, no longer a slave, but not free, and his life was not worth a plugged nickel to white America. Perhaps, as Julio Finn (1986) suggests, he was calling in poetic *patois* upon Papa Legba, Haitian *loa*/divine trickster of the very same crossroads where he had originally been initiated into the Deep Southern Hoodoo spiritual tradition that explained his remarkable artistry as a bluesman.

Over 50 years later, the Neville Brothers of New Orleans in their song, "My Blood," were able to summon Jah to the crossroads ("Jah, please come to the crossroads") in a modern "hoodoo blues cum reggae" that self-consciously identified Third World liberation struggles with African-based forms of spirituality. Kenyatta Simon and Kufaru Mouton's percussion invoked "Holy Mother Africa" to "set all the people free." More recently, it has even been recorded with the Haitian musicians Les Freres Parents for filmmaker Jonathan Demme's *Konbit: Burning Rhythms* anthology of the music of Haiti. In Haitian *voudoun* (voodoo) tradition, Papa Legba is the Master of the Crossroads. Yet while the Neville's album was dedicated to "the sufferers," unlike the makeshift Texas hotel room and office building studios in which Johnson recorded in the Thirties, the production for *Yellow Moon* was state of the art Daniel Lanois.

If this sounds like a contradiction, it should come as no surprise. When the Delta blues took to the highway, and headed for Chicago, it modernized its sound accordingly, becoming the popular music of urban African Americans. Later it became a source to be plundered by white imitators and popularizers from Elvis to Eric. While this is hardly a success story, it is instructive in understanding the crossroads that World Music is presently at in the Nineties.

During his life, Robert Johnson, as an African American, was the "other," despised by white American society. Today the apocalytic blues that he played is watered down and treated merely as "exotic" fodder for the pop music machine. The blues at first escaped or repelled, and then increasingly attracted, white Americans, and that same dynamic is at work today in relation to world music. For some white musicians the cross-cultural vitality of these musical "discoveries" is used to spice up tired rock (or art music) formats from Eric Clapton to Paul

Simon to David Byrne and Peter Gabriel. Though some give back more than others, this appropriation process is just another chapter in the long history of what Charles Mingus once called "black roots, white fruits."

That all of the contradictions facing world music today should surface at each W.O.M.A.D. (World Of Music And Dance) Festival is not a criticism, but a recognition of the flagship nature of W.O.M.A.D. in relation to world music. In microcosm, W.O.M.A.D. encompasses all the issues currently facing world music as it attempts to leave the ethnic music ghetto and move further into the mainstream without giving up its roots. Born from the ashes of Rock Against Racism's late seventies consciousness-raising festivals of resistance put on by the British left, and Peter Gabriel's long-standing entrepreneurial patronage, W.O.M.A.D. had its first festival in 1982.

A key question W.O.M.A.D. raises by its very existence is whether the music of the world is to be taken seriously on its own terms by world music producers or whether it is simply to be merchandised as this year's "next big thing" with the market continuously moving on to another exotic locale and leaving the previous year's musical fad in the dust? Are the world's musical cultures to be ransacked for the entertainment of North American/European consumers in what Herbert Mattelart (1994) views as a sort of "aural tourism" that purports to be "politically correct," or are we entering a period in which global consciousness will be nourished by musical connections between cultures that transcend both cultural isolationism and cultural imperialism? The answer, of course, is that both are presently happening simultaneously.

Picture the following scene which unfolded quite spontaneously at lunch in the pressroom towards the end of a 1990 W.O.M.A.D. Festival in Toronto Canada that I covered. As two members of the *Quebecois* band Josephine sat around the lunch table sharing in some Louisiana cajun licks, a member of the Joaquin Brothers band (a Native American "chicken scratch" outfit from Sells, Arizona) joined in to be followed by members of Pura-Fé (a Native American band from New York) and the Sabri Brothers (a Qawwali ensemble from Pakistan) in what ended up as a jam on the Kenyan tune "Malaika" (originally recorded in the early Sixties by Fadhili William and the Black Shadows). The scene was simultaneously being home-videoed by the other Joaquin brother, It worked so well as both a musical jam session and a sharing of cultures that all conversation ceased in the cafeteria as the music began to build.

The other side of the coin, is cultural imperialism and dilution. Can world music, faced with cultural penetration by the transnational corporate music industry, maintain its cultural integrity while continuing to grow and to incorporate new influences and discover hybrid forms that seem compatible. For example, when Africans are influenced by rock, the borrowing is selective. While it is the neo-African elements of American popular music that are most attractive, this still leaves the danger that more complex polyrhythms will be discarded for simpler African American drum programs simply because they sound Western, which is equated with modern. Or will an exciting new cross-pollination emerge?

A related question concerns the role of the Western musician in relation to world music. Billy Bragg's presence at the Toronto W.O.M.A.D. Festival is indicative of the tensions inherent in that role. As the only European headliner in a festival primarily featuring musicians from Third World countries, Bragg had some fancy stepping to do.

Instead of appearing solo on only one occasion and attracting 6,000 people in an arena-rock style venue, Bragg played 6 separate evening concerts. Each one had a different W.O.M.A.D. opening act; ranging from Mozambique's Eyuphuro to China's Folk Artists of Shanxi, from Guinea's Fatala to India's Prahalad Natak, from the now recently deceased Sierra Leonian S.E. Rogie to the N'awlins-based Mardi Gras Indian band, the Golden Eagles. In effect, Bragg delivered his audience to these international musicians. Similarly, he announced plans of touring in the future with the Nicaraguan reggae band, Soul Vibrations, whose Atlantic coast reggae is mixed with Latin rhythms and instruments such as the timbales.

Yet Bragg was not content with simply "Simonizing" world music and leaving it at that. He also was instrumental in organizing a well-attended roundtable discussion on political expression in world music, entitled "The Rattling of the Drums"; featuring Jamaica's renowned storyteller and mother of "dub poetry" Louise Bennett-Coverly ("Miss Lou"), Ugandan political exile Geoffry Oryema, and the Ottawa-based Native American Alan DeLeary whose multi-ethnic band Seventh Fire combines reggae, Native and Latin rhythms with a punk rock edge and issue-oriented lyrics.*

To top it off, in fine "biting the hand that feeds you" style, Bragg repeatedly denounced the Molson Beer Company's sponsorship of the event at every opportunity he got. Not only does W.O.M.A.D. in England have no corporate sponsorship, but the Canadian Molson Company had just gobbled up Carling-O'Keefe and was being boycotted as the festival began for threatening to close down the Molson Brewery on the Lakeshore in Toronto and laying off about 1000 people. Bragg, leading the charge, had, by the end of the festival, stirred up such a hornet's nest that the Molson name was loudly booed at the free gala final performance which featured all participating artists on stage.

This incident brings up the larger question of the context in which world music is marketed. In this regard, we can certainly distinguish world music from world beat. As Joe Boyd of Hannibal/Carthage Records points out, "Both of these terms are marketing devices which were invented to give retailers a bracket to sell records, but 'world music' is the more encompassing term with 'world beat' being primarily sold as dance music."

Randy Grass of Shanachie Records is proud that it was his company that came up with the concept of world beat, and he has actively promoted it by supplying labeled divider cards to the record retailers and, in a recent venture, distributing the *Beats of the Heart* world music film series on video. For him, "World beat is exciting because it is a combination of musics that haven't been done before. It's a fusion of pop with ethnic traditions—ethnopop. Traditional music is exciting with its raw melodic and rhythmic energy, but there are limitations as to who can enjoy it in its pure form. With world beat there are new pleasures to be had with production compatible with contemporary pop music and so it reaches a wider audience." Witness the international disco mania for Ofra Haza culminating in the sampling of her wailing Yemenite vocals by hiphoppers Eric B and Rakim in the '80s. World music, on the other hand is a less restrictive term than world beat, though it is still not as pluralistic as the less catchy but more accurate, "musics of the world," it includes traditional, classical and popular musics.

However, "ethnopop" is a misleading term in some ways. As Bill Nowlin at Rounder Records sums it up, "It is only ethnic from our viewpoint. It depends on where you are. Why is Zaire producing world music, but the U.S. isn't? This is an ethnocentric viewpoint which is based on the idea that we are here, and everything else is world music." In this sense, while world music is a better term than the more obviously ethnocentric "non-Western music" which explains the music of the world in terms of what it is not, rather than what it is; the term world music is still problematic in that its connotation continues to situate the rest of the world in relation to the West. Ultimately it can lead to the creation of the kind of synthetic Global Village ambiance present at the 1993 W.O.M.A.D. one day tour of the United States that led *Village Voice* reporter Richard Gehr (1993) to label it "Ethnopalooza."

---

* See the "Rattling of the Drums" chapter in this volume for a fuller treatment of this event.

Yet even though the current vogue for world music might be a little trendy, Nowlin is hopeful that it is a good trend because it shows a renewed interest and pride in immigrant roots and an appreciation of other cultures rather than a Fortress America attitude. Similarly, if the multicultural nature of American society is recognized then it becomes possible to identify world music enclaves in the U.S. in the *zydeco* of Louisiana or the Tex-Mex *conjuntos* of the Southwest. According to Real World Records recording artist/founder and W.O.M.A.D. father figure Peter Gabriel, "I genuinely believe that the arts and music in partnership, are a great vehicle for opening doors and allowing for some understanding between people...there is a mood of isolationism I find quite disturbing which is running alongside the increase in racism and rise of the right wing in various countries. It is very dangerous because I think that it is much easier to abuse people when there is some distance between you and them, when you don't feel a connection with them and cut them off and they are treated as 'them' and not 'us.'"

For Gabriel, W.O.M.A.D. provides an arena for cross-cultural musical encounters between artists and audiences and among artists themselves. He downplays problems of appropriation, and seconds Ugandan musician Geoffry Oryema's desire to break down the walls of "Musical Apartheid" and Senegalese superstar Youssou N'Dour's criticism of the "New Ethnographers" who oppose the mixing of "traditional" and "modern" sounds in contemporary African music as inauthentic and would like to keep African music securely locked into a stagnant folkloric prison. (*Worldwide*, 1992)

As to the future, what role will the major labels play in relation to all the musical ferment? According to Joe Boyd, "Problems arise when Third World musicians twist themselves out of shape to meet American market demands. At Carthage/Hannibal, we make marketing decisions after the recording is done. I'm fine with the majors including world music in their catalogs if their interest is genuine, but usually there's a flurry of interest among a few execs which force prices up and two years later the records are remaindered. If an independent record label like ours wants to reissue them it is very costly."

A related issue for the future of World Music is whether festivals like W.O.M.A.D., can avoid the trap of what Galena Chester and Tunde Jegede (1987) define as the presentation of "patronizing global glimpses without a hint of the conflicts and struggles in the world." While simply celebrating diverse cultures in a vacuum of exoticism without acknowledging the political context of the music is a dead end, focusing exclusively on victimization and oppression presents other problems of omission. It is only the process of building on the creative tension between the two that will take us deeper into both.

Another political question is that of audience. The audience is obviously becoming an international one, but what is less apparent is that it is also becoming more ethnically diverse. W.O.M.A.D. is not now an exclusively countryside camp-out affair as in its origins. The recent Golden Gate Park venue in San Francisco drew 100,000 people, and, like Toronto, was located in an urban venue so it attracted a more varied audience in terms of race and ethnicity. While an urban festival is less enveloping, this diversity adds a new dimension. In Toronto, the "ticketed" and "non-ticketed" stages made it possible to see almost all of the performers free of charge and so democratized the availability of the music. The festival then becomes a sharing not just between musicians, but between those who were in attendance as an affirmation of their cultural identities and those who sought to learn more about cultures of which they are not themselves a part (not that these categories are necessarily mutually exclusive).

World music is a music whose time has come. The real question is not whether world music will continue to gather a larger following, but rather, what will be the terms by which world music will relate to the current dominance of Western pop. Will it be assimilated? Will W.O.M.A.D.'s big name rock acts booked as bait to lure the unsuspecting concert goer to discover musics from other parts of the world merely overshadow the very artists their presence is designed to highlight? Will Barnum and Bailey hucksterism or cultural integrity prevail? Will it have a separate but parallel existence? Will vibrant new musical combinations emerge which respect the integrity of their foundations? World music scholar and distributor, John Storm Roberts (Original Music), is fond of quoting his journalist grandfather P.B.M Roberts in such situations. "Show me a prophet and I'll show you a fool," said P.B.M., "but," as grandson John notes, "there does seem to be a permanent trend toward world music, developing slowly over many decades, constantly seeping in like the tide through the marshes." That the tide will both transform the marshes and itself be transformed is a given. What the nature of those transformations will be is still unclear.

Bibliography

Broughton, Simon, et al., eds., *World Music: The Rough Guide* (Penguin, NY, 1994).
Chester, Galina, et al., *Silenced Voice: Hidden Music of the Kora* (Diabeté Kora Arts, London, 1987).
Diamond, Jody, "There is No THEY There," *Musicworks* No. 47 (Summer 1990).
Eno, Brian, "Why World Music," *Whole Earth Review* (Spring 1992).
Erlmann, Vert, *African Stars: Studies in Black South African Performance* (Univ. of Chicago, Chicago, 1991).
Feld, Steven, "Notes on World Beat," *Public Culture* (Fall 1988).
Finn, Julio, *The Bluesman: The Musical Heritage of Black Men and Women in the Americas* (Quartet Books, London, 1986).
Frith, Simon, ed., *World Music, Politics and Social Change* (St. Martins, Manchester 1991).
Garofalo, Reebee, ed., *Rockin the Boat: Mass Music & Mass Movements* (South End, Boston, 1992).
Gehr, Richard, "W.O.M.A.D.," *Village Voice* (Sept. 21, 1993).
Goodwin, Andrew, and Joe Gore, "World Beat and the Cultural Imperialism Debate," *Socialist Review* (July-Sept. 1990).
Lipsitz, George,*Dangerous Crossroads* (Verso, NY, 1994).
Malm, Krister, and Roger Wallis, *Media Policy and Music Activity* (Routledge, NY, 1992).
Manuel, Peter, *Popular Music of the Non-Western World* (Oxford, NY, 1988).
Mattelart, Herbert, "World Music and You," *The Baffler* (June, 1994).
Marre, Jeremy, and Hannah Charlton, *Beats of the Heart* (Pantheon, 1985).
Roberts, John Storm, *Black Music of Two Worlds* (Morrow, NY, 1974) and *The Latin Tinge* (Oxford, NY, 1979).
Seeger, Anthony, "Singing Other Peoples' Songs," *Cultural Survival* (Summer 1991).
Various Articles, *Worldwide: Ten Years of W.O.M.A.D.* (W.O.M.A.D. Communications Ltd., 1992). (This volume includes a Peter Gabriel interview with Thomas Brooman, and Yousou N'Dour's article "World Music or A World of Musics?: An African Perspective").
Various Musicians, (W.O.M.A.D. panel discussion in Toronto), "Rattling of the Drums," *Cultural Democracy*, (Spring, 1990).
Wallis, Roger, and Krister Malm, *Big Sounds From Small Peoples* (Constable Books).

Interviews

Joe Boyd, 1990.
Bill Nowlin, 1990.
John Storm Roberts, 1990.

Left to Right: Billy Bragg, Louise Bennett-Coverley, Rob Bowman, Geoffrey Oryema, Alan Deleary. Photo by Bonnie Rubenstein.

The Rattling of the Drums:

Political Expression In World Music—

W.O.M.A.D. Forum, 12 Aug. 89, Toronto, Ontario, Canada

RB: Hi. My name is **Rob Bowman.** I'm from CKLN, 88.1 FM, a community radio station in Toronto. Welcome to W.O.M.A.D. — a World Of Music, Arts and Dance. Those of you who have been down for the last three or four nights for the W.O.M.A.D. Festival have been very lucky to see just an incredible array of diverse talents from the various cultures all over the world. We've been very privileged to have this in our city. I think we're very, very lucky.

Hopefully this forum will also enrich all of our lives and we'll have a lot of fun with it. It's called "The Rattling of the Drums—Political Expression in World Music." Perhaps I should amend that title to "Political Expression in World Arts." W.O.M.A.D. is more than just music. Though music is certainly a focus, a number of our participants up here have done things in other arts as well as music. Toward that end, let me introduce the participants in the panel.

Allen Deleary (AD) is a Chippewa Indian who is based in Ottawa, originally from Detroit. He leads a group called Seventh Fire. His previous incarnation is in Thom E. Hawke and The Pine Needles, and Art and Soul. Virtually everything he writes and all the material he performs is politically-based. His group is basically a "Who's Who" of cultures. They're from Nicaragua, and Ecuador. There's a Canadian in the ensemble. There's also a Mohawk Indian, as well as Allen. So it represents a diverse group of people.

Geoffrey Oryema (GO) is originally from Uganda. He's a refugee at the moment who's been living in Paris for the last 12 years. He plays guitar as well as *lukeme* (thumb piano), *nanga* (a seven-string harp-like instrument) and flute. Geoffrey writes a variety of different material, and much of it political.

Billy Bragg (BB) is a gentleman hailing from Barking-Essex, a suburb of London. Billy came of age in the midst of the punk explosion, started a solo career in the early eighties, and much of that career has involved singing songs that addressed a number of political issues.

And last, but in certainly no way least, is **Louise Bennett-Coverly (LB).** Louise has performed for over 50 years. She hails from Jamaica and has dominated much of the entertainment within that island—as a storyteller, prose writer, poet, musician, and collector of folklore. Two generations within that country have grown up with "Miss Lou" as part of their daily diet. That's amazing! With people I've spoken to that I know from Jamaica, as soon as I bring up her name, a friendly smile just envelops their face and they remember their childhood. They remember hearing her on the radio and reading things in the newspaper that she wrote. She has really affected a big, big part of what goes on in Jamaica. With her, as I understand it, politics has been connected to giving cultural validity to what she calls *JAMMA* language—Jamaican English, Jamaican dialect, Jamaican talk, call it what you want. Otherwise it would have died.

I've told you a little about the four participants. I think they should tell you a lot more about themselves—who and what they are, how they were politicized, and how they incorporate that in their art. So I'm going to start with a three-part question. At what point, for all of you did political things start becoming important and at what point did you become politicized? What were the catalysts for that? What were the events that made you realize that there was something definite in life that you had to address. Within the context of your life and your art, what are the issues for you? Who wants to be first? All right, you're on Billy!

BB: Fair enough. Well, I came into politics relatively late. I didn't do anything political at all until I left school at the first opportunity when I was 16 in 1974. I didn't go for further education. I worked in a variety of dead end jobs. I have to say that the person who made me political, the inspiration for all my political thought, is Margaret Thatcher. That's the truth! By end of the late 70s, there wasn't really that much difference between the Labor and Conservative governments in Great Britain. They were both committed to at least keeping the welfare state—the state was an integral part of consensus politics in Britain.

Then Thatcher came into power and she began to dismantle the welfare state, and this began to affect me in a number of ways. The things I'd grown up taking for granted—free education, free health care—were threatened and the rattling of the British sabre came during the Falklands War in 1982. It was Thatcher's reelection in 1983 that first began to bring together the humanitarian thoughts I'd always had and bring them into a specific political focus. the great catalyst for all this, and I think the political catalyst for my generation in Britain was the miner's strike in 1984 and the struggle to defend the Greater London Council, who were the left wing Labor city council for London. The GLC was committed to spending money on art that reflected the cosmopolitan make-up of the city of London. So they would be bringing in a lot of the kinds of acts that W.O.M.A.D. has been putting on this week, and subsidizing it heavily.

So it was getting involved with them, and then getting involved in the political struggle in defense of the National Union of Mine Workers and their jobs, that made me really think out my stance. That was what brought me to the conclusion that I was, in a broad sense, a socialist. I continually scrutinize and evaluate and express the ideals of socialism in the broadest sense, not from a dogmatic ideological background, which puts so many people off, myself included. I mean, going to Labor Party meetings in Britain is really BORING—committee after committee after committee...

My politicization process came about through reading and conversation with people and listening to other people's ideas, both from within the left and outside the left—if we have to even call these ideas left-wing. I would call them humanitarian ideals about equality and understanding. To bring that together is to really find out what socialism means.

Socialism all over the world is being redefined. Obviously it's being redefined in the [former] Soviet Union and places like that, but those of us in the European left also have to rethink the dogmas—the Leninism, the Marxism—that have left us unable to compete with a capitalism that always goes for the lowest common denominator, moves incredibly quickly and continues to come at us from all angles. It is important for me to continue listening to other people's ideas, both from within the left and outside the left, listening to people on the Christian left, listening to people on the feminist left, to bring their ideas together, to redefine what socialism means.

Some people would say we're stuck with, I would say we cherish, the ideals of equality, so that when one of us moves forward, we all move forward together, but that sometimes does make socialism a bit of a monolith. So what I would like to commit myself to doing, is to evaluate and to discuss through my music, through discussions like this, and through writing articles, through any means of communication: what socialism is, what socialism means and what socialism can be for the next century.

LB: Me? I didn't even know I was being political at all. I tell you something. All of a sudden I realized when I was a little girl, when I was a child, the thing that bothered me was that we didn't sing Jamaican folk songs in school. When I was a child, I said, "Why can't we sing our songs?" In those days, everything that came from the Jamaican was discouraged, or it was bad. People were saying that, "You have bad hair." If it's curly like mine, it's bad. And they say, "Your color bad." "You talk bad." Now this was terrible. I say, "No, everything couldn't be so bad." No. These people that I knew and loved, the people who had always been kind and good to me, all had this "bad hair" and "bad color." I said, "No. This can't be right." So I didn't believe the part about the hair. I didn't believe the part about the color. So I said, "The part about the talking can't be right either." It must be wrong too.

I used to go to bed every night with an Anansi story. I used to think of the Anansi stories and songs as my lullabies. All these stories had songs and they were telling about this tricky spiderman who could turn himself into anything he wanted. You could go to school, and all of us schoolchildren knew about the stories. We would take them outside at recess time, but we couldn't go into school and talk them. "Anansi stories in school? What? Oh no! You hear about Cinderella?" I didn't know. I just thought, "Why should this be?"

Then I knew I wanted to write down things and they said you had to write in the formal language—the standard language of the day. We were taught to read and write in it, and we could read and write in it, yes of course, but we had another language which was strong and full of life, and full of the things that were happening around us. I started to write first about sitting underneath a palm tree dreaming and all them things. But you know, I wasn't getting it until I went on a tram car one day. I was just between thirteen and fourteen and this was what they call a market tram. The market women sat at the back; the four last benches were relegated to the people who were bringing in the food. They'd sit at the back with the baskets and things. Anybody else could sit at the front but the market women couldn't go with their baskets. That didn't have anything to do with color or bad hair but it was just that the baskets might tear somebody's stocking or something. So they'd say, "Well, basket people go to the back." Well, these people they sat at the back. But I tell the truth they didn't like it if anybody who could sit at the front come and sit at the back because if the tram car was full and they couldn't get a seat in the back they couldn't go in front if there was a seat in front, they couldn't take the basket up there. So they didn't want to see anybody who could sit up front come and sit in the back. But you know, who took this seriously, after all? This day, I wasn't fourteen yet, but I was a little portly. I was going to see a movie. I had on me dress, I didn't have on school uniform. I was going on the tram car, the front seats were full so I just jump on one of the back seats and the market woman said to another one, *"Pread out yourself, one dress woman a come, pread out."* Everybody just spread out their aprons and things all over the seat: no seat in your attire.

I said, "My god." I went home and I wrote the first set of verses in the Jamaican language: "Pread Out Yourself Dear Liza." I went to school and I said this for the children in school and they were the best people, they could tell if it good or bad. Them say, "Yes Louise man, write another one." So that was where they started. In my verses I always just talk the truth about what's happening and if it turned out to be political, I say like brother Anancy, "I don't take responsibility for how this thing turn out."

Now there are what people call the "Young Dubbers," the "dub poetry" movement which is going on in the Caribbean and especially in Jamaica. We have a lot of people now writing in the language. On stage, you'll find that in most of our songs and stories, most of our writers are now writing plays in the language. And that is a change, a great change. If you start something, you've got have the courage to keep yourself responsible for that change. And the whole way of doing that is not to stop. You just keep on. If you believe in what you're doing, you keep on. And then, well, hopefully you see the fruits of your labor. No, the drums have never stopped in the hills but there were times when the drums weren't in town at all. The drums were sort of barred from town. Today, you have the folk songs, the traditional dances, and everything being recognized every year at the independence festival.

As to the role of women, we are not "Adam's Rib" in these things. Women are the backbone.

GO: I became sensitively tuned to politics in 1971, January 25th. What happened was something I never thought I could see in my life. My late Dad happened to be in politics as such but my surrounding was full of that: like certain evenings I could hear my Mom and my Dad and somebody else discussing some political issues and I would tell myself, "What is this party business, what's the Uganda People's Congress, what's the Democratic Party, what is the Conservative Party?" In Uganda, we have one major problem, tribal differences, that is the major problem today. That's what's blocking ways, that's what's hindering progress in many African countries. To cut the long story short, 1971 came like bombshells. I saw truckloads of human flesh. This is what I mention in one my compositions. I almost passed out and then soldiers I'd never seen before, those were mercenaries, they broke into the house and got my Dad. They were treating him like a little boy, just a toy. I saw that. Sometimes it still haunts me. Then Amin shuttered the economy. The economy went to zero. He had no ideology whatsoever. He talked of reconstructing the country, and the so-called program, Economic War. Well the economic side I could understand, but the war bit I couldn't understand. People compared him to Hitler, but with Hitler I think there was declared war. With Amin there was no war supposedly, so I don't know who he was fighting.

So all my compositions then began to mold up on that very point, the politics of Uganda, people disappearing and abuse of human rights. That's how it all started and I'm still at it. Governments have changed and we are still talking about democracy. My definition of democracy is: "Would you like to take my seat?" That to me is democracy. When it comes to guns then, it becomes very undemocratic. In 1986 another government came in through some revolution and they are still talking about democracy. Well major problems cropped up, tribal problems and religious problems. There were three main political parties, the Uganda People's Congress (UPC), the Democratic Party (DP) and the Conservatives. Now, to become a member of the DP you have to be a Catholic. To be a member of the UPC meant you were a Protestant. This problem is still going on, the speed is almost faster than the speed of light. So through my music I'm trying to talk about that, trying to put that message across with the hope that someday some change will take place, but not by use of guns. If you inject pressure into an oppressed society then with time we hope to change things in Uganda.

Everybody is scared about talking about it—musicians in Uganda have been slaughtered. When my father was assassinated by Amin in 1977, they wanted to get me because I was in theatre. I was one of the pioneers of the first professional troupe of its kind in East and Central Africa. It was called Theatre Limited. Amin did not realize that my plays were political, even though he attended. He would say, "Ah very good." He didn't understand the text until somebody told him he was stupid.

AD: Well I guess to begin, I look at it and say, 'Where did your political start come from,' and I say, "Well, I was born with it. My parents were born with it. My grandparents were born with it. My great-grandparents were born with it." I am a Native person of this country—and I don't mean Canada, I mean North America—I have no boundaries. We live in a country that, for my people, has been under a state of siege, since good old Chris Columbus sailed the ocean blue. For that reason, I feel there's always been a constant pressure, a 24-hour state of siege. I have to look at it from that approach. I was born into a political situation. I grew up in Detroit. My father was an ironworker. A lot of Indian men used to do iron work in the big cities. And we were a part of that. People ask me what kind of Indian I am. Hey, I'm an urban Indian. Really, I'm a Chippewa.

I had to fill out these alien cards every year that say, "What are you? Negroid? Caucasian? Asian? or Other?" I got "Other." Indian other. Other Indian. So I think it comes from there. Growing up in an Urban environment, you go, "What kind of hunting am I going to do here? Where's the feathers, beads, and shiny objects here? What do I go hunting for? How do I maintain my lifestyle?" You have parents and extended family who say, "You are who you are. Your grandparents were Chippewa. Your parents before them were Chippewa." They've been under constant pressure. You realize that.

As a youth, I got into thievery, actually, growing up in the trade. But after a while, I got out of that, and I went into university. I like to write. I think the power of words is just fantastic, and I always liked to write poems and little things like that. I started out doing the "feathers, beads and shiny objects" kind of poems. That's one element of it, and as a Native person you try to maintain that traditional element of it in your vision. I grew up in a city, but then I'd go visit my grandparents. I'd go stay with them summers. I'd look at the living conditions for them as I was growing up and I'd say, "God, this is a state of squalor." I'm thankful I grew up in the nice golden suburbia in Detroit, but then I believe in the extended family, and I'd look at all of my relatives and I'd say, "Wow. Things ain't right here."

My good buddy who I met at university and am partners with musically allowed me the opportunity to start fitting conscious lyrics to the music. We took it from there, and we now play in a band called Seventh Fire. The name comes from our prophecies. The Seventh Fire is a time before the Eighth Fire. The Seventh Fire is the catalyst for the Eighth Fire. The Eighth Fire, can be either a good renewal or a bad renewal, contingent upon our collective consciousness. Within my generation I see people coming around and starting to get back into their traditions, and young people getting up and saying, "Yeah, I'm really sick of this. I ain't going to take it no more."

For me, yes I'm at that point, I'm sick of it and I ain't going to take it no more, but I don't want to do it with an approach that leaves out the majority cultures because that's not the society we live in today. I believe I live with everybody on this Turtle Island and, musically, I think it's a conscious effort to make people aware that we are here together. There are certain people, not only mine—women, blacks, you name it, who are under a state of siege and suffer all kinds of oppression through sexist and racist systems that are set up to dictate how our life will be. You go to my community, and you've got 80 percent unemployment. You've got people on welfare. My reserve is down river from Chemical Valley. We can't fish there. You can't hunt muskrat anymore. What do you do? Go on welfare and kill yourself or drink yourself to death.

A lot of the music we do, we do with violent overtones. It's not to condone it, but it's because there's internal violence in our communities which is directed at ourselves, and that's really counterproductive. Through music, if you can force people to think—youth especially—and direct their energies to other targets, that is really relevant. Make your own external targets. Don't do it to yourselves.

RB: As you can see by the opening statements by all four of our participants, they come from very different contexts. I'm curious. Once all of you became politicized, and once you started becoming aware and active within your art; you started confronting ideas, systems, actions, activities that others obviously have extreme vested interests in protecting, whether it's Idi Amin, the Jamaican school system, Margaret Thatcher, or whether it's the American-Canadian government. Once you started actively expressing your beliefs through your art, what sorts of pressures were brought to bear on you to either (a) cease and desist, or (b) moderate what you were saying in one way or another.

GO: There is a certain amount of fear because once you're on the boat or the train, you start being pressured. I'm talking particularly about family members because when you've become a driving wheel then they will start asking for your family members, be it a sister or an uncle or a brother. These are some of the threats I have been receiving over the years. My family mainly left in 1977 but 1979 saw the fall of Amin and it was so obvious that things were going to brighten up and the "Pearl of Africa" would shine again. Thousands perhaps, from all sorts of fields, came back to Uganda. In June I was hoping to go back, but then the end of June there was another *coup d'état*. Some people became refugees twice or three times. I couldn't understand. So I received threats then saying if you don't shut up we shall get one of them. It really scared me, scared the life out of me. I changed a bit. I kept quiet, I shut up for two years but then things went on, tribal differences were so—it was an open issue. If you were a Northerner—I am a Northerner—if your name starts with the letter "O"—you're in trouble. If you belong to the UPC, that meant you were an Acholi: you were in trouble. So for two years basically, it was like mountains just raising up. I thought, "To hell, there's a tribe being persecuted to which I belong." Then I thought, I am proud of what I am, I am proud of what I'm doing. In Paris, I give numerous concerts. (The threats) returned, but now it's open, and I am willing to continue.

RB: Allen, Miss Lou, or Billy? What sorts of pressures did you feel? Were pressures brought to bear at all to get you to moderate what you were saying and stop doing the kind of work you wanted to do?

BB: Not intensely, not like towards Geoffrey. Trying to deal with the multi-national record corporations and media, there are incredibly subtle pressures used. They're very, very subtle. Quite honestly, if you're making music that is in anyway political, if you're just playing it in some little corner to a group of people who agree with you; you're wasting your time. You've got to get out there and get your ideas across to people who disagree with you.

The music industry is very, very inviting. No matter what you're saying, they'll find a way of marketing it. If it's salable, they'll dress it up. Radical rock does sell. The Clash have proved it, and all the Woodstock stuff was marketed. Girls are in this month. Who are we going to have this month? Oh, it's Tracy Chapman. It's just the industry pigeon-holing everybody. But at the same time, I think it's a very positive movement that a woman like Tracy Chapman can work within the racist, sexist music industry without going to the lowest common denominator which always, for women, has been the exploitation of their sexuality. So the subtle pressure is to not be taken over by what their vision is. You must come to some sort of—I hate to use this word—compromise between what you want to achieve and what they want to achieve.

If this had been a political forum in Great Britain attended by any of the Left and I used the word compromise, they probably would have hissed me off stage for saying it. I happen to believe politics, and specifically democratic politics is based on compromise. Politics is another word for compromise in a democratic system—not the kind of compromise like the Labor Party compromise in England which upsets everybody—but a fair and equal compromise. If you're not doing that, you're forcing your ideas down on people.

I personally took part in "Red Wedge" in Britain, which was kind of like Pop Stars for Socialism or Artists United Against Thatcherism. We worked specifically with the Labor Party, not because we were Labor Party members, or even, in some cases, Labor Party supporters. That wasn't the criteria. The criteria was that we were against Thatcherism. For us in Britain, of all the things we want to address—anti-racism, economic freedom, our role in NATO, environmental issues—none of our goals are going to be achieved until we've gotten rid of Thatcherism. I must underline it's not personal because I don't believe in the personalization of her. She is merely the top of the pinnacle. We have to totally get rid of the whole idea of Thatcherism and monetarism in Great Britain. So in that aspect, Red Wedge's coming together did, at least in the music press, begin a debate about those issues. And now there's other specific initiatives around to bring the troops out of Northern Ireland and stuff like that. All of us working in isolation can achieve things, but working together, I do believe we can achieve bigger things, and it's good to have some interaction between artists from different cultural, sexual and social backgrounds working together. I think it's a positive thing.

RB: Billy, you've been very lucky from what you and your manager were telling me from the beginning because of the contracts that you fortunately had the savvy to know how to sign.

BB: No, no, no. No one wanted to sign us to a long-term contract to start with. So we were lucky that the next time we came to do an album, we already had the strength of having proved ourselves.

With a little band that's just starting out, if a record company comes in and says, "We'll give you $100,000. Sign this for the next 20 years"; it's incredibly tempting. You're on the dole and you just want to get going. You're frustrated and you know you can do something. So we were lucky in that it was the other way around. I was lucky to get in there with a one-album and short publishing deal. So when I went back with the next album, I was able to get rights back off the first, but that's not the usual way it goes...

RB: I think of Bob Dylan's first contract, which was a long-term contract. On his second album, with "Talking John Birch Society Blues," Columbia Records said forget it.

BB: Capitalism is not about choice. Capitalism wants monopoly, naturally it wants monopoly, and the record industry isn't some charitable institution where nice people rise to the top. It's the same as any other industry. What sells is the lowest common denominator and that's what they want you to be.

RB: Okay, Miss Lou and Allen, pressures brought to bear on either one of you with regard to moderating what you were doing?

LB: When I started, a lot of people felt that the Jamaicans would never be able to talk again. They might as well close the schools. There were a lot of people who were very adamant about killing the dialect. "We have got to kill this thing," they said. Even some Jamaicans, they love the language, but they're just a little dubious about whether this is respectable. I was fighting for the respect of our language. *"I don't know how dem can seh Jamaican language is corruption, yet dem English language is derivation derived from the Norman, French, and the Latin and Greek. When we derive from dem, it's corruption, but yuh see de unfairity."* Very early I had to compromise a bit to get my work published. There's always pressures.

RB: Okay, Allen. Pressures that were brought to bear upon you.

AD: I probably imagine the federal governments attitude about our band is, "It's a flash in the pan and hopefully it will die out."

RB: Wait till you get that CBS Records contract...

AD: But like with what Miss Lou and Geoffrey Oryema said, sometimes the pressure is brought to bear form within, from within my own people. You know you got the fat chief going, "Well my people are starving, do you think you should really be saying that?" I can't deal with that. I can't really care about that because he's already elected his path himself, to jump right into the system that is set up for him, and I work my hardest to speak outside of that forum. Most of the pressure comes from within because a lot of our organizations, the communities, are spoonfed because it's a federal responsibility, because they signed those agreements and they have to honor those commitments. In a lot of my lyrics I talk about the situations in communities, about the welfare states in communities. You might get someone from within going, "You know you shouldn't say that, you're biting the hand that feeds you." I can't overly concern myself with that.

BB: How do you feel about being part of a festival that's got corporate sponsorship from a company that's just closing down breweries all over Canada. Here's this month's copy of *Now*, which has a whole big splash on the festival on the front cover, and then you turn to about page 48 and there's a full-page ad from the Molson Brewery Union saying why people should be boycotting Molson brands of beer. So all of us are having to deal with those kinds of compromises. I support W.O.M.A.D. I want to be part of W.O.M.A.D. W.O.M.A.D. does whatever it feels it has to do to get its gigs on down here, but as artists what we have to do is make it clear that they may be sponsoring festivals like this, but they certainly don't buy our acquiescence. I make clear statements from the stage—and I've been doing it every night—about corporate sponsorship and union rights.

The first night we had a very interesting discussion. Well, it wasn't really a discussion, it was a one-off heckle. It was one of those inspirational one-off heckles that helps you get across what you're saying It's my feeling that the reason why Molson is having to go around and buy out breweries like Carling and O'Keefe is not because they just like buying places to play monopoly, but because they have to do this to compte with the American beer corporations now that the free trade deal has gone through. So I'm saying this one night and someone in the audience says, "Yeah, but American beer's cheap." So the choice seemed to be, for Canada, do you want trade union rights or cheap beer?

As artists, we can not be intimidated by the hand that is feeding us. We must make clear statements. In that way, we're not allowing a company like Molson to look cozy and good-time, and we still can be on the side of something that I personally feel is very, very important, which is this festival. We have to make sure that we clearly understand not only what Molson-W.O.M.A.D. implies, but what it means to us as artists when we interact with our audience.

Yet while I think we have the responsibility to try and do things, you can't follow the audience home and see what they do politically. You've only got so far to go. I don't think you should be going that far with them, but I think one of the most important things you can do is, not allow the audience to use you to take their responsibility away for changing the world. If the audience wants to change the world, then it's your duty to focus that desire, but to reflect the responsibility for change back on them. You can't let them think, "Well, I've done my bit. I've bought my Billy Bragg LP—I've done my bit for democratic socialism in North America." So I think our role as politically engaged artists is to provoke questions in people's minds and to provoke debate. We must be part of the alterative media that's not giving the views reflected in the news page. Our press at home is exclusively right wing now. It's owned by a very, very few rich individuals, and it more or less parrots what the government says on all but a very few issues. I think our role is to bring people together, to focus their anger, to focus their frustrations, but in the end, to reflect it back on them.

QUESTION FROM AUDIENCE: I wonder how much you all feel that you're preaching to the converted?

AD: I think in a large circumstance, in some of the shows and the benefits we do, we're pretty well preaching to the converted, but there's also that little minority that comes in just because of curiosity. We can plant a seed and a concept in a person's head. If they come and they just dance, then maybe something will click a little while later on. That's one of the things I can do. Above and beyond that, hopefully the converted audience gets larger.

BB: That's what you're trying to do You can't just stand at the door and say, "Do you agree with Bill's politics?" If you say "Yes," then alright, you're not coming in. In the end, for the people that do come, the people that do agree with you, you're hoping that if they come for one specific issue they feel strongly about, you can open their eyes to other issues. They see that you're not just a single-issue person which is particularly important, not so much in Canada, but in the U.S.A., where so much of the political activity is not around a Left socialist kind of broad labor movement, but on single-issue politics, Your duty as a performer is to tie together all the threads. You can't have strong feelings on racism or strong feelings on sexism, you can't feel strongly about what's happening in South Africa, without having strong feelings about what's happening in your own town. So in that way, we're not preaching to the converted. What we're attempting to do is make a community of the converted, to bring the converted together and show them what they have in common.

If you believe that revolutions begin, not in record shops, but through a raising of consciousness, then yes, popular culture can play an important part, not on its own, but with other catalysts in society, in eventually bringing about social change. So don't think we're preaching to the converted. We're trying to provoke and inspire and focus people who have similar feelings to our own to go out and think about broader issues. The amount of your political worth is not commensurate with the number of buns you put on seats. That's really important, because there's times when you obviously feel like you're peeing into the wind and nothing's changing and no one comes along.

But I'm sitting here next to Miss Lou, someone who's had a very, very long career, who said earlier that you just have to keep going and keep going and keep going. I'm sure there's been times when Miss Lou's popularity came to a plateau where she thought, "What direction am I going in?" But while she was doing this, in the middle of her career, there were people coming through directly influenced by her work, like Bob Marley, who were carrying on that whole expression of Jamaican culture in a global sense, and through listening to Bob Marley, I came to respect the culture of Afro-Caribbean people in Britain. Miss Lou has influenced people for generations rather than just on a short term pop star basis. So through Miss Lou carrying on and carrying on with what she was doing, the ramifications are huge.

An excerpt from this panel discussion first appeared in the Spring 1990 edition of *Cultural Democracy* magazine, the national publication of the Alliance for Cultural Democracy. We print it here in expanded form with their consent. Another excerpted version later appeared in the 1991 (#49) edition of *Musicworks*.

OFF
THE
PAGE
INTO
THE
STREETS

DUB
POETRY FESTIVAL INTERNATIONAL
MAY 8-15 1993   TORONTO, CANADA

Dub Diaspora: Off the Page & Into the Streets

—Toronto, Ontario, Canada
(8-15 May 1994)

Ron Sakolsky

For those dissatisfied with Reggae Sunsplash's continued neglect of the dub poetry idiom, this Toronto gathering of dub poets from throughout the world (the culmination of two years of planning) was indeed a revelation. So unheralded are dub poets at Sunsplash that, according to Adugo Onuora, at the 1991 Festival, they were actually paid *not* to perform on the originally contracted "Night of Consciousness." Aside from the more internationally known poets Mutabaruka and Oku Onuora; the scheduled appearances of Yasus Afari, Cherry Natural, Nabby Natural and Durm I were canceled at the last minute by Sunsplash organizers and the poets were literally left waiting in the wings backstage. The official rationale of time restrictions belied political silencing of reggae dissidents as was evidenced by a three hour wait for the band Third World to begin the next set.

In contrast, the Dub Poetry Festival International showcased the most conscious and rootsy dub poetry from all over the Caribbean, North America and England in venues throughout Toronto that ranged from the streets to high rises to community centers, to art galleries and to university settings. Formats for these events were a mixture of panel discussions (in which the distinction between panel and audience quickly dissolved into an egalitarian sharing), poetry readings and musical performances.

While not all the artists represented would call themselves dub poets in the strict sense of the term, the dub poetry concept ultimately proved inclusive enough. As Ras Mo (Domenica) put it, "In Domenica, we don't find the term 'dub poetry,' but rather 'peoples performance poetry.... In the Eastern Caribbean when you say 'dub,' people relate it to Jamaican reggae and dancehall DJs, but I have nothing against the term because 'dub poetry,' 'performance poetry,' 'rhythm poetry' and 'rapso' are all based on the same form from different islands." Moreover the influence of dub poetry goes beyond the African presence in the Caribbean. An active participant in the Festival was Allen DeLeary of Anishinabe origins who flatly stated, "The African diaspora doesn't apply to Indian cultures," but talked of how reggae and dub poetry influenced the music of his band Seventh Fire. Moreover, South African dub poet Mzwake Mbuli confided to the audience in a heartfelt aside during his exuberant, hard as nails performance at York University's Underground Club, "I *am* because of *you*. I drew my inspiration from the Caribbean."

Of course, it makes perfect sense that dub poetry should come full circle in Africa. As Mutabaruka (Jamaica) elaborated, "The commonality is not jazz, reggae or even dub, but the African oral tradition—though they take we outa of the country, they never take the country outa we." This placing of the origins of the tradition in Africa offers a refreshing change of pace from all of the endless discussions about which came first, dub poetry or rap, that can sometimes degenerate into an esoteric debate about how many angels danced on Kool Herc's turntable. Accordingly, the Festival brought together griots from all parts of the African diaspora. As Oku Onuora (Jamaica) put it, "This Festival is a grounding between brothers and sisters." It was a chance for many to meet and greet their counterparts from other parts of the world, and for others to reunite with old friends and comrades, and the spirit of sharing was often intense—both in terms of areas of agreement and disagreement.

As Ras Mo observed, "It was a time to thrash out a number of issues in terms of not only form but content." The two most controversial content issues to be thrashed out over the course of the Festival related to sexism and homophobia. As to the former, not only dancehall slackness, but the Rasta ideal of the "African Queen," were challenged by some of the sisters. In regard to the latter, Sister Jean Binta Breeze (UK) questioned the virgin/whore dichotomy imbedded in the Queen concept, while still recognizing its difference from the pampered protectiveness of the Eurocentric pedestal. Though she directly confronted her male dub poet counterparts, it was never done with hostility. As she said, "I challenge sexism with such love that men will have to deal with me." In marked contrast to all the paeans to African queens and princesses, Breeze offered her musical anthem to the strength, independence and unbounded sexuality of "Caribbean Woman" to a very appreciative audience at her Opera House performance. Later, as Cherry Natural (Jamaica) succinctly put it, "I'm Rasta, but I refuse to be the 'weaker vessel.'" As to the men, one of the most attuned to the issue of sexism seemed to be Michael Pintard (Bahamas) who, in a dramatic appearance after being hospitalized a day earlier, read a poem of solidarity with women which extended to the intimate level of their menstrual cycles.

Partly in response to Buju Banton's dancehall record calling for violence against gays, ahdri zhina mandiela (Canada) urged the formation of coalitions with the gay and lesbian community based on a recognition of mutual oppression. As she said, "We must give people the space to exist as who they are." Accordingly, she specifically includes gays and lesbians in the lyrics of her poem "african by instinct" which she performed on stage with her little daughter belting out the choruses. Yet, the issue of gay rights was by far the most controversial, with some present considering homosexuality immoral, refusing to accept gays as equals, and others denouncing their appropriation of the tactics of the civil rights movement. As Mutabaruka said, "Not every oppression is the same oppression. I am a black nationalist." In the end, Flo O'Connor (Jamaica) had the last word when she explained that while Caribbean people living in Toronto may have different priorities than those living in Jamaica, "Just because we don't take up a cause, doesn't mean we are not concerned. Ultimately, you must deal with it in your own heart."

Aside from such emotional moments at panel discussions, the poetry performances themselves provided their share of emotion. Sister Breeze's spirited reading of four poems by the late Mikey Smith (the martyr of the dub poetry movement to whom the Festival was dedicated) not only surprised those who expected her to do women's poetry (thus expertly turning the tables on her male protagonists), but her deep feeling for these poems and her obvious grief at the loss of a revered fellow poet, led to a rousing ovation with many people visibly moved to tears.

Later in the week, she performed her new poem written out of the experience of the Festival entitled "Skin Teeth Don't Make It Right" in which she reflected on the differences aired among poets at the Festival and the male posturing which often accompanies the espousing of deeply held values. In it she directly challenged Mutubaruka's earlier African essentialist statement that "if you bring a cow into a pigsty, it is still a cow." Finding it lacking in an understanding of the complexity of the situation, she offered her more nuanced interpretation of historical events by playing off Mutabaruka's often stated connection of the struggles of Africans and Native Americans in this hemisphere with these lines: "Cow and pig don't mix/But Arawak and maroons did." In arguing for a more cosmopolitan interpretation of Africanness, she later said, "Yes, we are Africans, but we must be free to be Africans anywhere in the world." As Clifton Joseph (Canada) noted in another context, "Repatriation doesn't necessarily mean going back to Africa—the African diaspora has come home."

Mutabaruka for his part gave his concert poetry performance without musical accompaniment. In his extemporaneous remarks in between poems, he "marveled" at the way in which racism works in the music industry, "Shabba has never hit with reggae music, but only a hip hop Americanization of Jamaican lyrics over American rhythms, and a white youth like Snow, who has never been to Jamaica, has carried the Jamaican language to number one in America." He further chided Nelson Mandela for "talking too much" to the untrustworthy apartheid regime then in power. In a similar vein, Oku Onuora did an uncompromising rendition of "Bus' Out" which shook the rafters with the sound of revolution. This was in turn echoed by the ringing of Brother Resistance's (Trinidad) bell during his rapso set.* Christian ("Ranting Chako") Habecost (Germany) provided comic relief with an hilarious satirical take on the stereotypical white Rasta wannabe entitled "Blacker than Blackman" that was warmly received with much laughter at his Ital Performance set.

So, in spite of the no-show of British-based dub poetry luminaries Linton Kwesi Johnson and Benjamin Zephaniah, the Dub Poetry Festival was a rousing success in terms of who did come and what they contributed to the proceedings. Even some publicity problems were pulled out of the fire by (appropriately) a word of mouth grapevine campaign which assured the performers of good sized audiences at all venues except the out of the way York University campus whose own large Caribbean student population was not in evidence since classes were out of session.

As to the city of Toronto itself, it proved to be an excellent location for an event of this nature. As Lillian Allen (Canada), herself the organizer who had originally conceived of the Festival and a dub poet in her own right, said to me in the St. Christopher House kitchen where a (down) home-cooked meal was being busily prepared for the evening's poetry performances, "In Toronto we already constitute a diversity of dub poets. We're all from different backgrounds and countries, a microcosm of the international."

The organizers' stated goal for the Festival was: "to illustrate the social, aesthetic, political and cultural scope of dub poetry and to develop its potential as a highly creative and culturally responsive art form with the capacity to both articulate social needs and generate energy for social change." Perhaps no one better exemplified these goals than Mikey Smith. As Oku Onuora, in reflecting on the death of his fallen brethren put it, "Mikey might be dead, but the Festival continues his work."

Word soun still ave power!

---

*A lengthy interview with Brother Resistance is included elsewhere in this volume.

Carol Genetti

Nanny

Jean Binta Breeze

Nanny sidddung pon a rack
a plan a new attack
puffin pon a red clay pipe
an de campfire
staat to sing

while hog a spit grease
pon machete crease
sharp as fire release
an er yeye roam crass
ebery mountain pass
an er yeas well tune to de win'

an de cricket an de treefrog
crackle telegram
an she we er battam lip fi decode

an de people gadda roun
tune een to er soun
wid a richness dat aboun
she wear dem crown
pon er natty platty atless head

an ebery smoke fram er pipe
is a signal fi de fight
an de people dem a sing
mek de cockpit ring
an de chant jus a rise, jus a rise
to de skies
wid de fervour of freedom

dat bus up chain
dat staap de ceaseless itching
of de sugar cane

We sey wi nah tun back
we a bus a new track
dutty tough
but is enuff
fi a bite
fi wi fight

an ebery shake of a leaf
mek dem quiver
make dem shiver
fa dem lose dem night sight
an de daylight too bright
an we movin like de creatures of de wile
we movin in a single file
fa dis a fi we fightin style

an de message reach crass
ebery mountain pass

we sey wi nah tun back
we a bus a new track
dutty tuff
but is enuff
fi a bite
fi wi fight

life well head
mong de wattle in de daub

eben de dankey
a hiccup
in im stirrup
for de carrot laas it class
so muh mek no one come faas
eena wi business
dis a fi we lan
a yah we mek wi stan
mongs de tuff dutty gritty
dis yah eart nah show no pity
less yuh falla fashion
home een like pigeon
an wear dem number like de beas
but wen yuh see er savage pride
yuh haffi realise dat

wi nah tun back
wi a bus a new track
dutty tuff
but is enuff
fi a bite
fi we fight
dutty tyuff
but is enuff
is enuff

so mek wi soun de abeng
fi Nanny

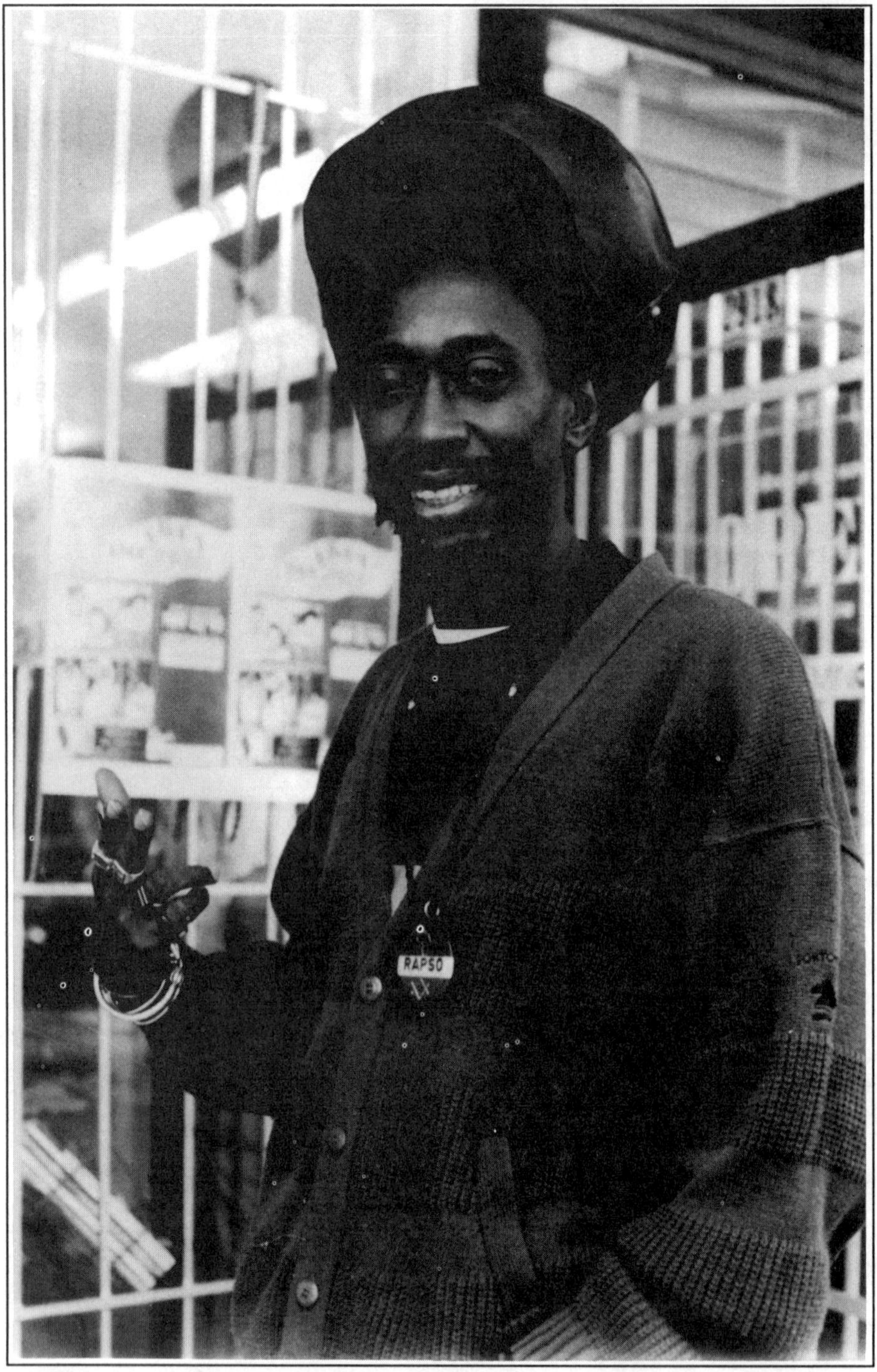
RAPSO

Rapso Rebellion: An Interview with Brother Resistance

(Feb., 1992 at The Uprising Culture Shop, the People's Mall, Port of Spain, Trinidad)

Ron Sakolsky

> "RAPSO... de rootical redemption of ancient African tradition in the Caribbean de poetry of kaiso
> RAPSO... de voice of ah people in de heart of de struggle for true liberation and self-determination
> RAPSO... de power of de word, de riddum of de word..."
> —Brother Resistance

RS: Brother Resistance, you were there when rapso was first originated. What was this new form about for you?

BR: Well, at the time it was in a way simply recreation, because it was something that we used to do in the community, where the drummers and the steel band players and the poets came together just to ease the frustrations of life. So it was just a way to free up yourself.

RS: You've seen it develop over the years. It has a real political edge to it now. How did that come to be part of the music?

BR: Well, we have to look at the period in which the rapso expression form come forward. The years 1969-1970 were like a watershed in the political history of Trinidad-Tobago because at that time it was the strongest moment of the mass movement. It was a movement for true independence, for cultural liberation, and for self-determination. Rapso come out of that general vibration that was taking place in the country at the time. This is the experience that helped to forge and nurture the development of the rapso. Over the years the rapso artists have remained consistent to that beginning and therefore their works directly seek to take from the people and give back to the people. Rapso has become the voice of the people.

RS: How does the De Network Rapso Riddum Band provide encouragement for people to come in and develop their talents?

BR: The band is just like one part of the community. The whole community arises and the music is one part of that whole thing.

RS: How does the Uprising Culture Shop fit in? What's the part that the store has in promoting creativity and community?

BR: It's sort of like an outlet for cultural books and crafts.

RS: How do you choose the books that are in the store? There's an incredible selection of books that you don't find in the average bookstore in Port of Spain. What kind of books are you interested in having here?

BR: Basically we try to sell books that will help people fill up themselves with material that is easily readable so they can educate themselves. Most of these books are to help themselves and their families. Much of the music here serves the same purpose.

RS: Earlier, I was talking a little bit to some people who said that the People's Mall itself is in jeopardy. There is some talk about tearing this very shop down. Do you think that is likely to happen? I'm wondering if the very spot where we're talking now will be here in a few years.

BR: The People's Mall represents an institution, one of the first real foundations for African people, and for who I call street people, right, people at street level, to do effective business. It is the only location right here in the center of the city where we could set up and pull ourselves together on an economic level. In the beginning there were no shops, there were just rows of tables and stores. As we progressed, we built shops. So if anything has to replace what we have here, it will simply be the People's Mall in a stronger and more powerful infrastructure right here in this same location.

RS: I want to talk to you about your song "Big Dirty Lie." You know, one of the things that has happened in the States in 1992 [the year of the interview] is the movement against the Columbus Quincentennial, to question who Columbus was and to point out how genocidal his visit was, and I'm interested in knowing what's happening here in that regard.

BR: Well, the same thing is taking place here in the sense that they're trying to set up at the official level some sort of celebration for the coming of Columbus and the coming of Europe. At the street level, or the grassroots level, we have just come to a vibration where we are trying to put up some resistance to this celebration. So in we own way we decide to put a piece together within the rapso vein, right, that would really define where we stand and make a statement against this whole celebration of this 500 years business. It is time we erase the untruths of history. It is time we made the proper correction, and let the children know what the true history is about.

RS: I noticed when I was looking at some of the different Carnival *mas* camps around town, that there were a number of them that deal with the theme of Columbus or the theme of 500 years, yet very few of them offer a critical point of view on that history. Have you been able to hook up with any of the *mas* camps who might be inspired to take a more critical view?

BR: The *mas* band coming from this community, The People's Mall, has chosen the theme, "Columbus Lie." We believe in action. Instead of complaining, we take positive action to deal with the problem of that situation. Basically the front sections of the band portray, first of all, the First Peoples of this hemisphere who were present before the coming of Columbus. So, therefore, we glorify the indigenous Indian population of South and Latin America. We feature the coming of Europe, but we feature them in a different light. We feature them as what they really stand for, you know, a crew of gangsters and pirates coming to the Caribbean. So in our poetry we reflect all these kinds of things, the coming of the ships and people's reaction to that. So when we finish it up there will have been a total dramatic portrayal of that period of history, putting it in proper perspective so that those who are alive may see it. All the others were here before Columbus. Columbus is in the last section of the band, according to how he came; last.

RS: Are you doing anything with the African presence in the Caribbean?

BR: Yeah, the African presence, all that is before Columbus. Columbus come last.

RS: I want to talk a little bit about Carnival. I'm originally from Brooklyn. I've been to the Brooklyn Carnival, but I haven't been to Trinidad before. I understand that for the last few years, but particularly this year, there is some controversy that most of the music that's coming out is "jam and wine," and not enough "truth and rights." What do think about that? Is that an issue for you? What's the right mixture there?

BR: It's an issue for me, but from a different perspective. I have no problem with the artists putting forth whatever they put out. It's Carnival and this calls for a certain amount of celebration and a certain amount of revelry and excitement.

RS: Right.

BR: From ever since I was small, I look at the music as here to generate this excitement and keep the atmosphere in that happy way. So nothing is wrong with that as far as I am concerned. The problem I see is with the media, the radio stations, and the promoters. They concentrate and play almost exclusively this music of abandon, this music of have a good time, because they have been trying to establish that Carnival is not about a people's reality, that Carnival is not about a celebration of diverse culture, but Carnival is have a good time, Carnival is color, Carnival is just everybody jump up and tumble down and everything, right? They've been trying to establish that for quite some time.

Now what's happening is that this music that they've been promoting, right, they find out a lot of people object to, but too often people focus their objection on the artist and not on the media that is bringing the music to them. But if you listen to the amount of material we have that deal with serious issues, that examine political situations, that look at the society in different ways; this music has not been aired. It has not been brought to the public. This music has been stifled for a number of years now. So you find that it is a problem that is created by the media itself. People are hearing to a great extent what they hear on the radio and television. A lot of people don't go to the calypso tents, for instance, where they could get this music live and direct. So, therefore, as far as I'm concerned, the radio has a direct responsibility to play the full spectrum of the music, whether it is "jam and wine" or political commentary. By hearing the full spectrum, people would then know for theirself exactly what is the full content of the calypso that is present for this particular Carnival.

RS: We have the same problem in the States. One of the reasons community and liberation radio stations exist is to make music available to people that wouldn't ordinarily be available. In that same regard, is there any kind of radio that exists on the island that will play the spectrum? In the States stations have had to go and do it outside of the legal boundaries. Black Liberation Radio, where I live in Springfield, Illinois, and other microwatt stations, exist in spite of the government. The government tries to shut them down. Is there anything here on the island, other than the major networks that are reluctant to change?

BR: Unfortunately, there is not. All I can say is that our organization has made attempts to get together a broadcast license, but so far we haven't been successful. One or two other organizations have tried, but again, have not been successful. So we find what they do is create a number of radio stations, grant licenses for a number of other radio stations and they all have more or less the same policy or format. The content is guided first of all by foreign interests, and secondly they play the local music or the music of Trinidad-Tobago and the Caribbean.

RS: Getting back to the music itself, where do you see rapso poetry going? What's the direction for the future?

BR: Well, for the future I think, first of all, on the international level we need to establish the fact that rapso poetry is an art form coming out of the Caribbean, and is as valid a form as the African-American rap, or dancehall from Jamaica, because it is one family, right? The other thing is that when we look at the future of rapso, we look towards the youth. We see a lot of young people becoming interested in the work, trying to get involved in rapso, experimenting and coming to us for advice and that kind of thing. Rapso has become more and more powerful and is able to completely express the sentiments of the people in such a way and with such a force that it would be heard and must be reckoned with. There are alot of young people coming up and they are writing, and are interested in, rapso poetry. It is a question of getting the facilities and so on to record them and/or to have them published.

RS: What about the connections between the African American experience and what is happening in other parts of the African diaspora. What are the connections for you between rapso and dance hall, dub poetry, and African American rap? How do you see those connections in your mind?

BR: I see it on two levels. In the first instance, when we talk about the foundation of that oral experience, we need to look at the experience of the African griot. That was the same experience that was transplanted across the oceans to this part of the world. So that is the first thing, that they come from one foundation, one base, and so therefore it is family. I also look at it from a more recent perspective. I look at it as an art form that comes out of the belly of the people, that comes from street-level. They look at political, social and economic issues with a street eye, you know, and from that level we can see that the rapso, the dub poetry and the African American rap are coming from exactly the same corner, really.

RS: Directly rising from the grassroots.

BR: Yeah, that's right.

RS: While it ends up in some cases getting merchandised by the big corporations, at least that's happened with some rap music, there's always the grassroots level that keeps generating new material. I'm wondering how you get distribution, get the word out, get airplay, get your music in the stores and make people aware of it, without falling into the corporate traps that exist that would make the music less direct? Does the Riddum Distribution Network have any strategies for doing that? Do you have any ideas on how to handle that situation?

BR: It's something we've been looking at for a number of years, and to some extent it is a little bit frightening, except that as far as we are concerned there wouldn't be a compromise, so therefore there won't be a problem. Things might take a longer time to happen if the commercial viability of the music wouldn't be as great as it is, but we fully believe that, once we stick to what we're doing, if a major corporation is interested, then it would have to take it as it is or they don't take it at all..

RS: Right.

BR: So any corporation would have to deal on that level even if it's rough economically, but we have to live life without controls, otherwise it wouldn't make sense really. At the other level, there will always be worker solidarity, picket lines, strike camps. There will always be that level of mass activity and out of that there will always be Rapso Man. There will always be that one or two persons or that one or two generations in times to come who don't have anything to do with the recording business. They just have a vibe and they express theirself in a rapso kind of a situation.

RS: So it's not necessarily a general song about freedom, it's the specifics of that particular struggle.

BR: That's right.

RS: And they're both there. Both the general and the specific.

BR: Yeah.

RS: Creating that balance means to be able to have something that can be internationally recognized because of its generality, and something that's very specific at the same time.

BR: That's right.

RS: It seems that the people I've seen who have come and gone at the store here during this interview are people who view this place as a kind of community center. People come here because there's something here that's special. If you had to define what people gravitate towards here, what would you say that was?

BR: I would say that it was a cultural meeting point for all the artists from Trinidad-Tobago. So when you want to find somebody, you come here to find them. If somebody come from Africa, you leave a message for these artists; you stop in here first to find out what's happening.

RS: To connect people with one another...I guess that's where you get De Network Rapso Riddum Band and the Riddum Distribution Network names.

BR: That's right.

RS: It's different than the radio networks that are "up there," broadcasting down. It's the network from the grassroots. Who is part of this network?

BR: Besides the practicing rapso artists, like Brother Book, we find a number of the mainstream calypso or soca artists being influenced by the rapso in terms of their musical style and in terms of directly doing Rapso pieces. People like, for instance, David Rudder, and the [then] Reigning Monarch Black Stalin, who has been a tremendous source of inspiration for our movement all through the years. He recorded a rapso, called "Revolution Time," on a recent album.

RS: Well, it sounds like you have had a seminal influence on these other musicians, they're able to integrate Rapso into something that's part of their style. You acknowledge them. Do they acknowledge you? Do they acknowledge the rapso movement as a source for some of their material?

BR: Well some of them do, but a number of them don't. Some people say, we hear there's such and such an artist and he sounded like you. We say no, he sounded like the rapso, not like us, because that's not our thing. It's a national art form. The people are doin' the rapso because the music has been kept down in much the same way as any vibration from the people has been suppressed, whether it be calypso, reggae, or the steel band movement. They always have to put up a struggle in order to come forward and take their rightful space.

RS: There are all of these links in the network that go throughout the Caribbean Islands. Will there be a time soon when you'll come together in one place? Is there any idea of possibly meeting, physically meeting, in one place and discussing the movement, exchanging notes, songs, poetry; a festival perhaps, or at least a gathering of some kind?

BR: Yes, we have been discussing the idea and trying to put it into motion. What happened is that it was expected to take place this year (1992) with the Carifesta celebration which is the Caribbean Festival slated to take place in Trinidad. Since Rapso and the oral traditions would be a focal point of Carifesta, we would have invited all these different rapso artists and practitioners of the oral tradition to gather in one place. There would be two levels planned, the academic level and the performance or workshop level. So far, though, we have had some difficulties with Carifesta, so we don't know exactly when it is taking place. But there are also some plans in motion for a meeting of all kinds of rapso and dub poetry artists in Canada, under the direction of Lillian Allen, who is a dub poet. That is supposed to be taking place in October of this year in Canada somewhere. We kind of keepin' an eye on that situation with a view to being represented out there and being a part of this historical event.*

---

* This event did take place May 8–15 in Toronto. It was called the *Dub Poetry Festival International (Off the Page Into The Streets)*, and was a spirited gathering of dub poetry artists, including Brother Resistance and Karega Mandela, from all corners of the African diaspora. See the "Dub Diaspora" chapter in this volume for a more detailed account of this event.

RS: You mentioned some of the problems with Carifesta. Why has it been put on hold? What's going on?

BR: I think it's at two levels, really. One is the obvious economic strain to host a festival of that size, for as they say, it would take a few millions to really put it together and have everything in place in a proper and organized manner. But the other level is even more disturbing because I have a distinct feeling that the organizers at the governmental level don't see the importance of that cultural communication, the importance of that assembly of Caribbean people through their art and culture. They can't see how it is viable in a businesslike way or where it is refreshing and a tonic to the Caribbean as a region. They don't see these things. In a sense culturally they are blind, because they have been affected by the foreign culture. They have been affected so that now they can't even see the importance and the beauty of theirself engaging in cultural expression. I think this is the main problem which will affect us not only in Trinidad, but on any of the islands where they try to keep it now. That same problem will crop up because of mental bondage. The colonial experience has already killed the fire in the cultural movement as far as they are concerned, because they don't know what's happening on the ground.

RS: You mentioned Lillian Allen. What about other women rapso and dub poets like Miss Lou (Louise Benett), Jean Binta Breeze and Sister Latifa?

BR: A lot of young women are interested and are following in the steps of these established women. I think that it is a very good thing for the movement. Even though you find that the majority of practitioners is men, it's because, as I was mentioning before about the experience of the struggle out of which it comes forward, the expression of what we are in this part of the world has always been seen as like a man's thing, right? But in recent years we have begun to acknowledge the contribution of the women warriors to the struggle. So when you see a woman coming forward in the rapso movement and the dub poetry, it is very, very good. It also paints a picture for a beautiful future for the movement.

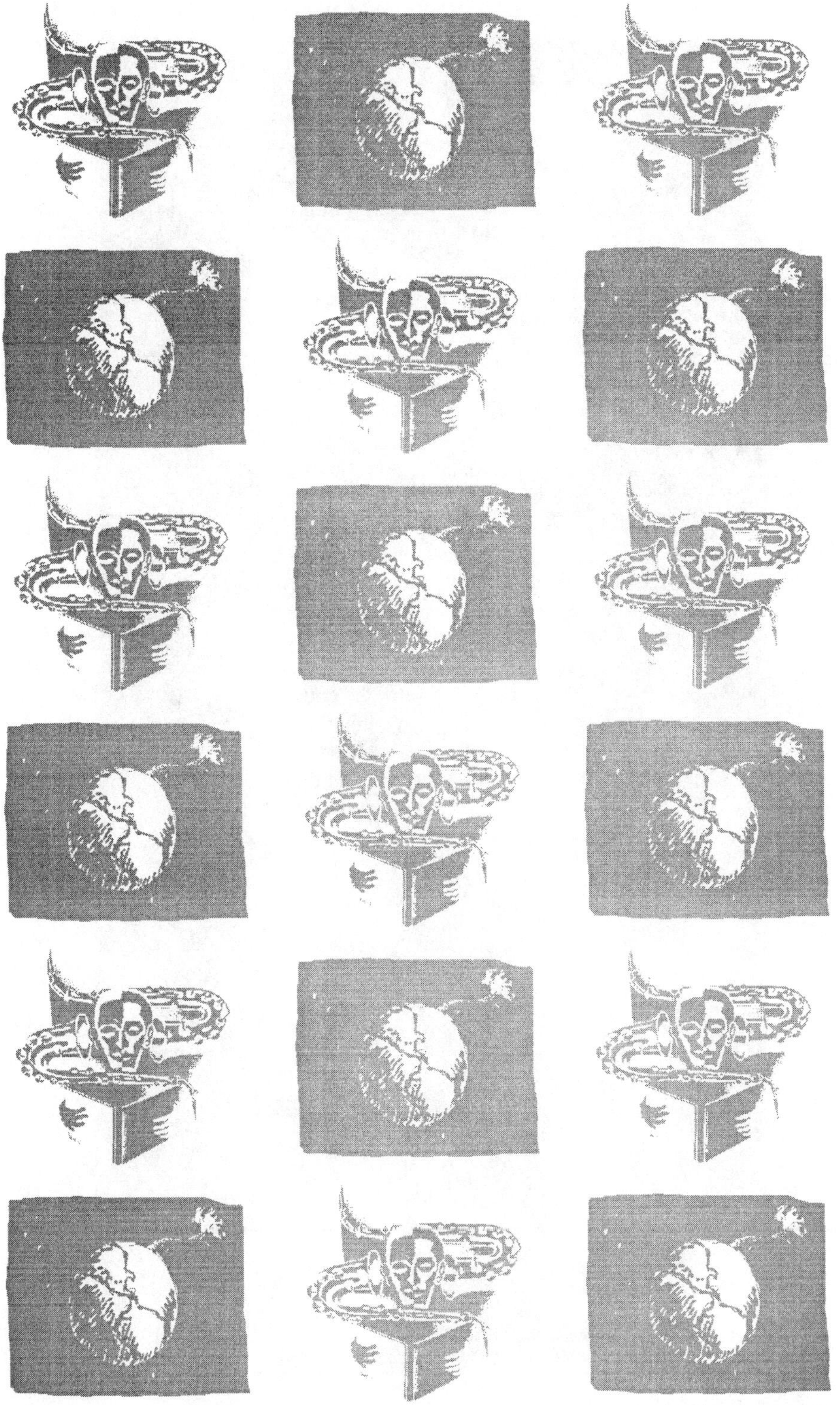

Photo: Chicago Dzviti

Thomas Mapfumo —The Lion of Zimbabwe

Sheila Nopper

Thomas Mapfumo acquired the name Lion of Zimbabwe in the 1970s when his music became a primary weapon in the liberation war of his country. For the people of Zimbabwe, Thomas is worthy of the same respect as Malcolm X, Mahatma Ghandi and Bob Marley; he is a freedom fighter, a revolutionary who continues to speak out for human rights in his country and throughout the world.

When Thomas Mapfumo first began to sing his songs in Shona, the language of his people, they laughed at him—a legacy of the spiritual devastation that colonialism inflicts upon a people. But this was in the early 1970s, just prior to the rise of the liberation war in Rhodesia—a liberation war that would win the people's independence and establish the birth of the nation of Zimbabwe in 1980.

Prior to the 1970s, popular music in Rhodesia, as Zimbabwe was known then, came from other cultures, with lyrics sung in other languages: English, Lingala, Swahili... but never in Shona. After experimenting with all kinds of music from jazz to rock 'n roll to rhumba, in 1970 Thomas decided it was time to play music from his own culture in the language of his people, who comprise 80 per cent of the country's population. "I had grown up to be a big man now," Thomas recalls "and I'd been chasing after all these types of music which were not my music; it was not from our own culture. This music, *chimurenga*, came about in 1972 when I started writing revolutionary songs. This music had no following at all because people thought it was ancient music of those who actually died a long time ago. They didn't know that was their own culture they were trying to throw away."

Chimurenga is a Shona word that means resistance, revolution or struggle. The first *chimurenga* of the Shona people was fought from 1890 to 1897—seven years of resistance against the invasion of the white settlers who then defeated the Africans and occupied their land. The white supremacist government then began the systematic oppression of the indigenous people. The next uprising started to brew in the 1960s, and by 1972 the Freedom Fighters were organized and armed resistance began. This second *chimurenga* was also fought for seven years but this time the people won their liberation. On December 21st, 1979, the Rhodesian Army surrendered to the Freedom Fighters and the people of Zimbabwe were free to rebuild their country.

As a youth growing up in the country, Thomas was influenced by the folk music of the *mbira*, an ancient African instrument that is the heartbeat of daily traditional Shona life, as well as the vocal and lyrical styles of the spirit mediums. "*Mbira* music," Thomas says, "the instrument *mbira*; it's not just an instrument. It's very sacred—something that has to do with our spiritual world." Chartwell Dutiro, one of the *mbira* players in Thomas' band, The Blacks Unlimited, learned how to tune and play the *mbira* when he was only five years old, before he started school. It was very spiritual, Chartwell believes, for him to be so entranced by the music of this instrument at such an early age. "The *mbira* is an African ancient instrument," Chartwell explains, "that is almost like a piano. It is some metal pieces that are placed on a wooden board and there are about 22 keys, which are tuned in the major keys of any scale that you might want to use. There are about three scales involved and you use three fingers to play this instrument. There is also a metal piece that is placed behind it. In the old days people used to put some shells there but now we are using bottle tops to make a vibration when you play.

"In our culture you play this instrument when there is a ceremony going on all night. There will be drums but the main instrument is the *mbira* so that the spirit mediums will be possessed and then the spirits talk to the living people of whatever is happening in the community or within the country. This is very important for the Shona people because it's not easy for a living person to talk to God. We believe in our culture that we have to talk to the spirits and then the spirits will talk to God. So it's very important for us to have this instrument so that we can communicate with the spiritual world."

Recognizing the significant role of the *mbira* in his culture, Thomas worked with Jonah Sithole, his guitarist at the time, to transfer the rhythm patterns and melodies of the *mbira* to the electric guitar. He later included one, two, then three *mbira* players in his band. Chartwell remembers the events that led to him joining the band. "When I finished my school in 1972, I started studying my music, my rudiments and theory of music in a western way, so that I could correspond my music with the royal schools of music in London. I did that for almost eight years and when I was satisfied with my musical background, considering the western side of it, I then approached The Blacks Unlimited; I actually approached Brother Thomas. And with the kind of background I had, he automatically considered me and I was one of The Blacks Unlimited. I respect that and I like it that way." This blend of traditional Shona music with western instrumentation put Thomas Mapfumo in the forefront of contemporary African music. His lyrics promote equal rights and justice and his *mbira*-focused music stimulated the ancestral spirit within the people to stand up and fight for their rights.

The relationship between spirituality and politics in Shona culture grows out of the historical links between their language and *mbira* music. By reviving both the use of Shona in his songs and the traditions of *mbira* music, Thomas acknowledged the value of their cultural roots. He stirred up an intrinsic wisdom within the people to feel proud of their ancestors, their history and themselves for surviving in spite of the oppressive conditions imposed upon them by a racist government.

The power of the *mbira* to mobilize the people was even recognized by the ruling white government. "A long time ago the music from the *mbira* instrument was not allowed to be recorded on our radios so it was very difficult to commercialize *mbira* music," Thomas explains. "But when the war broke out people started realizing who they were; they started looking for their own identity, and then we got the support we were looking for. This music was supported because people were fighting a war, a liberation war, and the music was political, very subversive to the government of that day which was oppressing the people."

During the peak years of the war, from 1976-80, Thomas Mapfumo and The Blacks Unlimited traveled extensively throughout the country and were never harassed. Although Thomas clearly identified himself as a freedom fighter, people in various political positions loved his music—the soldiers, the guerrillas, and the police. His lyrics were often written in metaphor and innuendo so that people were not always aware of their hidden meaning. Chris

Bolten is a close friend of Thomas' and is also his sound engineer. Referring to Thomas' lyrics, Chris says "His songs are very deep. The way they're used in his language, it's like poetry really, and most of his songs have double meanings. He could be saying, 'beware of the snake in the grass,' but what does he mean? Is there actually a snake in the grass or is he saying in metaphor that you've got to be aware of a particular situation in life?"

The following verse from *Shumba*, a song Thomas recorded in Zimbabwe during the liberation war, illustrates his use of metaphor to communicate with comrades in the struggle:

Gwindingwi rineshumba inoruma vakomana.
Ndoita muteka teka ndoenda nechitima.
Mbudzi Haivhuirwe pane vanhu vatereri.
Vanotora mafuta vozora maoko.

In a thick forest there is a lion that can eat.
I'm walking like a lion.
You don't skin a goat where there are a lot of people.
They will take the fat and rub it on their hands. *

"The first two lines describe the guerrillas prowling in the dense bush," explains Chartwell. "No one knew officially what they were up to or where they were but children were sent out to report on their location so there was widespread awareness of their movements. The second part of the verse is a Shona parable. Animal fat is the most valuable part of a kill due to its ability to soften and soothe the skin. Like the antlers of a deer or a moose—goat fat is the trophy. The literal translation means, 'I am a guerrilla fighting in the bush for the freedom of the people. If you hear what I am doing, don't boast about your knowledge because the enemy will hear and will run away with the information and all will be lost.'" Even though the literal translation differs from other possible interpretations of the metaphor, Chartwell claims, "The image remains the same: 'Keep secret the things that are valuable.'"

Although Shona was not the language of the white Rhodesian government, there were Shona people who supported Ian Smith's regime. When they translated these lyrics, the government became suspicious of Thomas Mapfumo's popularity. "When Brother Thomas started singing about the revolution, about people going to war and all these problems that we faced during the struggle," says Chartwell, "they (the government) felt that if his music is heard by a lot of people, the situation will be more aggressive." Thomas recalls his arrest, "Eventually I was put into detention; for three months I was there. Well, that didn't bother me because I was a freedom fighter. I was fighting for our freedom."

In the end it was his clever use of words that enabled Thomas to be released from his three month prison detention during the revolution. The white Rhodesian government was unable to challenge the claim by Thomas that his songs were based in traditional Shona culture and they let him go. They did, however, try to discredit him by first requiring him to play at a rally for Bishop Muzorewa, one of the black leaders who was negotiating an internal settlement with the government that would allow black people to vote but deny them access to key positions of power. "We were actually not part of that," says Thomas. "We were for the people and we were for those who were fighting from the bush, fighting for the genuine independence. When we went to Bulowayo we sang our revolutionary music and people didn't like that. They asked questions, why we were still doing this type of music, and I told them I didn't have time enough to compose the music to suit their situation since I was in detention... Well, they accepted that; we got away with that one.

"The next morning there was a picture of me in the newspaper standing side by side with Bishop Muzorewa, to make it look like the band was supporting the internal settlement, to confuse the people. Those who thought we had sold out well, there are so many jealous so-in-so's in this country, I mean in the whole world, people who didn't want to see us progress, who thought it was now their chance to victimize us and wipe away our popularity and make us look like we never fought for no freedom."

The plan for an internal settlement, however, was soon destroyed. In 1980, the people of Zimbabwe gave the leader of the Zimbabwe African National Union, Robert Mugabe, 67 per cent of their votes. Their independence ceremony took place in April, 1980. Although Thomas Mapfumo and the Blacks Unlimited were invited to perform, their cultural work was not recognized. The man who had created the *chimurenga* music that inspired so many people to be proud of their heritage and to continue fighting for their liberation was made to wait all night. "We went into the stadium at eight o'clock," Thomas recalls, "and ended up playing the next morning at five thirty! You can just imagine, after every other band had played. All those people at the top, the government officials, they had gone home. They didn't actually want to hear about us. It's because they were associating us with Bishop Muzorewa. To us, though, when we were made to wait so long, that was victory to us. We played for the right people; we played for those who fought for the liberation of the people, and we also played for the youth. And we said we are not going to complain." He pauses and then, with passion, says, "We were not going to apologize to anyone because we believed in ourselves. We are Zimbabweans. And we were entitled to some rights as citizens of that country. And though they were trying to victimize us, we never looked back. We carried on singing about freedom. Maybe they thought that since they were the government in power, and we had supported them during the liberation struggle, we were going to kneel down and say 'Well, ah, can't you forgive us because we played at Bishop Muzorewa's rally?' What they are forgetting is that we went there and we played our revolutionary music!"

Integral to and interweaving with the rhythms and melodies of the *mbira* are the yodelling, hypnotic vocal styles Thomas has mastered—vocal styles that express so passionately the emotion of the lyrics he has written. Like so many people feel after the experience of a *chimurenga* concert, Chris Bolten "didn't understand what the words were about for a long time; I just liked the music and the way he sang." Chartwell Dutiro explains further, "Music is a universal language. There is some music that I don't understand the lyrics but, when I listen to the instruments of the music, I can be in a different situation after listening to the rhythm pattern of it. I think also it's very important for us to sing in our language so that we can express ourselves better."

The English language, in its acceptance of ambiguity in speech, is not aligned with Shona culture. In the Shona language, for example, there is no word for coincidence. The concept is not part of their culture. The "coincidences" referred to in Anglo culture have a meaning in Shona culture—there is a reason for everything. Perhaps the ancestors were trying to forewarn you of some danger, reprimand you for some false deed or guide you to someone who will teach you an important lesson. The value of language in keeping people oppressed has been well known and used by colonizers throughout the world to oppress indigenous people. Beatings were frequently the consequence endured for speaking their own language and, in more severe cases, part of their tongue was cut out. By denying people of a particular culture their mother tongue, the colonizers systematically diminished their self-esteem and fragmented their group identity. This enabled the oppressors to divide and conquer the people and thus significantly reduce the potential for organized resistance.

Thomas Mapfumo continues to sing about the struggles that people must confront and overcome in life. "There are a lot of people suffering all over the world," Chartwell explains. "We went to London, to Europe and we also traveled in America, and I always see all these suffering people. And so our music is for the poor, it's the voice of the poor wherever people may be suffering." Thomas continues, "We (The Blacks Unlimited) are freedom fighters, and we are fighting for the poor people who sleep in the streets, people who don't have jobs, people who don't have accommodation and people who are killed for no good reasons, just because somebody wants some political power."

In spite of the prevalence of injustice throughout the world, Thomas Mapfumo still has a vision of hope and progress. "When we are home we have our own independent record company called Chimurenga Record Company that is run by me and the other members of the group," he says. "We are trying to set up a studio where we would make The Blacks Unlimited a studio band. I'm going to scout for young singers I'd like to record using my label, Chimurenga Music. If I am lucky enough we are going to expand this label and next time we'll be doing distribution ourselves all over the world. This is what I'm aiming for. If the record company is a success then we would have gone over some hurdle," he says laughing, "The middle men we call them—yes."

Thomas continues to write about the struggles people face in his country, in the world and in personal relationships. "*Hondo*," talks about the injustice of war:

Hondo isu takairamba kare...
Kuno famba varombo
Vapfumi vachisara...
Kuurayana kwakaipa mambo...

We said no to war a long time ago...
Only the poor get killed
and look, the rich survive....
Killing each other is evil, oh Lord...*

Mukondombera is a song about AIDS, warning brothers, sisters, mothers and fathers:

Kubata bata muchiregera...
Hoyo wauya mukondombera
Mukasatya munopera...

You better stop your mischief...
Beware AIDS is here
If you're not careful, you'll perish...*

"We are not for any political organization," Thomas concludes. "We are for the people. All what we want to see is the good treatment of the people progress in our society regardless of where people come from, who they are or what their colours are. We are for the people and we are happy to work for the people and that's the way we must stay."

---

* All translations are by Chartwell Dutiro, who has temporarily left the band—and Zimbabwe—to study in England and the United States. He made a five year commitment to learn sound engineering and how to manage a recording studio and international distribution. Upon completion of his studies he will return to Zimbabwe to, once again, join The Blacks Unlimited and work toward making Thomas Mapfumo's vision a reality.

Amy Cordova

Latin Music in the New World Order: Salsa & Beyond

Peter Manuel

It is now thirty years since bandleader Johnny Pacheco founded Fania Records as a fledgling Latin record company, contracting the up-and-coming New York dance bands and distributing his records to area stores via the trunk of his car. By 1970, with the input of entrepreneur Jerry Masucci, Fania had turned the New York Latin beat into the soundtrack for the Latino pride movement that spread from Spanish Harlem throughout the urban Caribbean Basin. As salsa, Fania's name for its product, went on to become the popular music of choice for some ten million Latinos, its trajectory can serve as an index for much of what has happened in Spanish Caribbean culture as a whole over the last three decades. Far from existing in a hermetic world of dance clubs and record studios, salsa's style and and its role in Latin culture have always been conditioned by a variety of changing factors, including demographics, socio-economics, the workings of the music industry, interaction with rival music styles, and, as we shall see, the emergence of a new political order.

Salsa, like rock, was in its own way a product of the turbulent 1960s. Of course, much of sixties youth counterculture was a white middle-class phenomenon; minorities, indeed, were still hoping to attain precisely the house-and-two-car suburban American dream that scruffy bourgeois teens were symbolically spurning. But the decade's spirit of questioning and mobilization also took hold among minorities, including New York City's more than three million Latinos—primarily Puerto Ricans, or "Newyoricans." Opposition to the Vietnam War united whites and minorities, and the very economic progress made by blacks and Latinos at once empowered them and heightened their sense of ongoing discrimination. Most importantly, Latinos were inspired by the Civil Rights and Black Power movements, and the size of their own communities in Spanish Harlem and the Lower East Side ("Loisaida") had reached a critical mass that was ripe for cultural and socio-political self-awakening. In the wake of the Black Panthers, the Young Lords mobilized Newyoricans to demand fair treatment and better social services. But the most significant development of the era was a new sense of pride in being Latino. For the first time, Latinos on a mass scale rejected the Anglocentric assimilationism which had led so many to feel ashamed of their language and culture. The model of the Civil Rights movement, the new interest in "roots," and, indirectly, the still-smoldering Puerto Rican independence movement made the barrio a cauldron of militant assertiveness and artistic creativity.

The new social consciousness called for a new musical movement, which could at once embrace Puerto Rican tradition, while capturing the spirit of the barrio in all its alienated energy and heightened sense of self-awareness. Fania Records, with a combination of entrepreneurial skill, aggressive marketing, and energetic talent scouting, rode the crest of the socio-musical moment, explicitly linking in its promotional efforts the fresh, new sound of the New York Latin bands to the buoyant spirit of the barrio. Curiously, perhaps, the chosen musical vehicle was neither stylistically new nor distinctively Puerto Rican; rather, it was essentially Cuban-style dance music—especially modern versions of the *son*, which had dominated Cuban music since the 1920s. In the early decades of the century, the *son* had emerged as a medium-tempo urban folk idiom featuring vocals backed by sextets or septets of guitar, the similar *tres*, trumpet, bass, and light percussion. In the '40s, the *son* was further Afro-Cubanized by the use of *congas* and faster tempi, while at the same time incorporating more horns and sophisticated, jazz-influenced harmonies and arrangements. It was the brassy, sophisticated, mature *son* of the 1950s that became the stylistic backbone of what came to be called "salsa."

However superficially paradoxical, the choice of Cuban dance music was in many respects quite natural and logical; this music had long flourished not only in Puerto Rico, but in New York City itself, which had, indeed, been the crucible of some of the most vital developments, including the big-band mambo of the fifties. To some, labelling this music "salsa" seemed artificial, especially in the case of artists like Tito Puente and Celia Cruz, whose musical styles had evolved twenty-five years before the term was coined and applied to it. To Cubans who knew that many of Johnny Pacheco's hits were simply note-for-note renditions of Cuban records of the 1950s, the use of the rubric "salsa" seemed like an attempt to obscure the music's Cuban origins by capitalizing on the US embargo and the quarantine of the island's bands and recordings.

But if Cuban music constituted the backbone of salsa style, Newyoricans had resignified the music in a way that largely justified the adoption of a new name, however commercial in origin. As the music become reborn as a symbol of Newyorican, and by extension, pan-Latino ethnic identity, its Cuban stylistic origins, like those of the *rumba* played by street drummers throughout the city, became essentially irrelevant. While Cuba was remote and isolated, salsa, in the words of the KXLU radio program, was the *alma del barrio*—the soul of the barrio.

Despite the reliance on Cuban rhythms and forms, salsa has been far from stylistically homogeneous. Bandleaders like Pacheco and Pete "El Conde" Rodriguez have perpetuated a *típico* (loosely, "traditional") style of old Cuban bands like the Sonora Matancera, using a conjunto with only two trumpets; their music, although not original, still retains its freshness and vitality. Most mainstream bands have cultivated a more modernized sound, adding more horns and more jazz influence. Representing the salsa vanguard have been, among others, arranger-pianist Eddie Palmieri, former teen prodigy Willie Colon (contracted by Fania at the age of fifteen), and Ruben Blades, perhaps the most talented of the lot.

Blades is to some extent in a class by himself, both because of the quality of his music, his broad socio-political vision, and the fact that he has devoted much of his time and energy to non-musical pursuits. After spending his youth in Panama, in 1974, he forsook studying law for music, and soon distinguished himself as a gifted singer and composer. In 1984, he returned to legal studies, earning a M.A. from Harvard, while enjoying a modestly successful acting career. In 1993–94, he returned to Panama to lead his leftish-greenish Papa Egoro party in an impressive, although ultimately unsuccessful bid for the presidency. His former collaborator, Willie Colon, is similarly broad-minded, and recently ran (also unsuccessfully) for Congress in the Bronx on a platform of reformist community activism; as he puts it, "Sometimes writing a song is not enough." It may seem remarkable that given their ongoing involvement in other fields, their occasional LPs are invariably both commercially successful as well as critically acclaimed. But perhaps it is precisely their breadth of interests and talents that has lent their music its wider conceptual and aesthetic vision. As C.L.R. James wrote, "What do they know of cricket, who only cricket know?"

Although salsa can be said to have originated in the New York barrios, it was an international genre from the start. While Puerto Ricans constituted the core, even in New York both performers and audiences were of diverse backgrounds. Aside from older Cubans like Machito and Mario Bauza, one could mention the Dominican Johnny Pacheco, the Panamanian Blades, the Argentine pianist Jorge Dalto, and, for that matter, Jewish-American arrangers Larry Harlow and Marty Sheller. Most importantly, salsa, in connection with the heightened sense of pan-Latino identity, soon spread throughout the Hispanic urban Caribbean Basin. Aside from the regional bastions of Puerto Rico and the Dominican Republic (not to mention Cuba), salsa established strong roots in Venezuela and Colombia, with enclaves of fans and performers in Mexico City, Lima, and elsewhere.

The case of Venezuela is representative. By 1970, salsa, whether performed by local or foreign groups, had become the favored music of the Caracas' lower classes, who related as much to its infectious rhythms as to its barrio-oriented lyrics. The local, predominantly white bourgeoisie tended to disparage salsa as *música de monos*—monkey music—just as in Puerto Rico, affluent, Yankophilic rock fans *(rockeros)* deprecated salsa lovers by the similarly racist term *cocolos* (loosely, "coconut-heads"). But by the mid-'70s, salsa had won over Caracas' middle classes as well, and Venezuela, buoyed by the rise of its own superstar, Oscar d'León, had become the biggest single market for the music. Neighboring Colombia has since emerged as a new international hub, generating its own star acts, Grupo Niche and Joe Arroyo.

Salsa has never been predominantly a political music or a form of protest song. Rather, it is quintessentially dance music, designed to be performed live at clubs, weddings, and open-air concerts where Latinos of all ages, races, and ethnicities mingle and enjoy their own artistic creativity as dancers—very often, virtuoso dancers. Accordingly, most salsa songs have always dealt with the timeless topics of sensuality, romance, and praise of the music itself. (Women are rare both as performers and industry personnel, and of course, in dancing, it is the man who leads; nevertheless, salsa lyrics, though benignly *machista*, display little of the crude and blatant sexism found in reggae, calypso, and hardcore rap.) Yet despite salsa's primary function as dance music, in its most vital period—the late-'60s and early-'70s—a significant minority of its lyrics were overtly socio-political in their own way.

The songs of Ruben Blades are particularly distinctive in the ways they confront, rather than obscure. social reality. For his recording of the anti-imperialist *"Tiburón"* and his denunciation of US hostility to Cuba, he earned both progressive credentials and death threats from Miami Cubans, who banned his music from local airwaves. The most characteristic of Blades' songs, however, rather than being explicitly political, are vignettes portraying the vicissitudes of *barrio* life via epigrammatic character studies, typically at once humorous, critical, and empathetic. His *"Juan Pachanga"* portrays a narcissistic *guapo* whose indulgences in wine, women, and song fail to mask his inner loneliness and alienation. *"Te estan buscando"* depicts the plight of a naif who has run afoul of barrio loan sharks. In "Pedro Navaja," a sort of existential snapshot of barrio life, a petty gangster and a hooker shoot each other, for reasons which are unexplained and irrelevant. "Pablo Pueblo" depicts the joyless tedium of a proletarian worker's life:

> A man returns in silence from his exhausting work
> His gait is slow, his shadow trails behind
> The same barrio awaits him, with the light at the corner,
> the trash in front, and the music emanating from the bar...
> He enters the room and stares at his wife and children,
> wondering "How long does this go on?...
> He takes his broken dreams,
> and patching them with hope,
> making a pillow out of his hunger,
> he lies down, with an inner misery.

In a lighter vein, Blades' *"Numero Seis"* describes the experience, familiar to all Spanish Harlem residents, of waiting for the number six subway. Steering clear of the extremes of political sloganeering and sentimental soap-operas, Blades' songs at once entertain and enlighten, validating *barrio* life in their attempts to make salsa, as Blades puts it, "a folklore of the city."

Blades' sometimes collaborator Willie Colon has specialized in depictions of the darker side of barrio life, portraying its lurking malevolence with an ambivalent mixture of fascination and social-realist indictment that foreshadows gangster rap. While "Juanito Alimaña" non-judgmentally depicts a swaggering thug, Colon's 1973 *"Calle Luna Calle Sol"* warns:

> Listen mister, if you value your life,
> stay out of trouble or you'll lose it...
> In the *barrio* of *guapos* [strongmen], no one lives at peace
> watch what you say or you won't be worth a kilo
> Walk straight ahead and don't look sideways.

By situating salsa squarely in the Hobbesian world of the *barrio*, such songs illustrate how the genre was indeed much more than recycled Cuban dance music. Salsa was in this sense far removed from Cuban songs about quaint and colorful Havana, or from the innumerable nostalgic Puerto Rican *boleros* and *jíbaro* (peasant) songs romanticizing the idyllic and forever lost *campesino* life. The songs of Colon and Blades, rather than providing escapist sentimental fantasies, showed creative Latinos confronting their social situation and literally dancing their way through adversity. Much of their vitality, indeed, derives precisely from the spirit of exuberant affirmation—via style and language—in the face of socio-economic marginalization.

Via such an orientation, salsa became linked with a sense of international Latino consciousness. While salsa in general implicitly affirmed and embraced Hispanic ethnicity by the use of Spanish language and Caribbean rhythms, many salsa songs from this period were explicit in their celebration of Latino pride and unity. Conjunto Libre's *"Imagenes Latinas"* is typical:

> Indians, Hispanics, and blacks, we've been mixed into a blend
> with the blood of all races, to create a new future...
> From Quisqueya to La Plata, from the Pampas to Havana,
> we are blood, voice, and part of this American land
> Whether in the land of snow, or beneath a palm tree
> Latinos everywhere struggle for their freedom...
> This is my Latin image, my new song
> To tell you, my brother, to seek and find unity.

The first decade of salsa's youth—roughly 1965-75—was in many ways the most vital era of the genre. Songs about *barrio* life and specific subways intimately grounded salsa in the local and immediate, while at the same time, its calls for pan-regional Latino unity made it dynamically international. Meanwhile, salsa's affirmation of barrio identity reflected not only an acute awareness of adversity, but, more importantly, a fundamental optimism about the future, both on local and global levels. In the USA, the signs of progress were manifold. The Young Lords had pressured New York administrators into providing the *barrio* with social services, the Vietnam War ended, the economy was expanding, colleges were adopting multicultural curricula, and progressive domestic policies were enacted by a series of White House liberals (including, by today's standards, Richard Nixon!). Internationally, the Latin American left, despite ferocious repression, thrived underground, animated by the Cuban model and, indirectly, by the Soviet and Chinese blocs, which by their very existence suggested the possibility of alternatives to American imperialist hegemony. Salsa songs like Ray Barretto's *"Indestructible"* conveyed the fundamental optimism of the era:

Take your destiny in your hands,
Surge ahead, my brother, with the help of new blood
If your soul feels weary,
Think that anything is possible
Because the new blood is an indestructible force

In the 1980s, however, changing conditions led to a retrenchment of salsa's exuberant spirit, stylistic vitality, and commercial growth. With the advent of Reaganomics and its massive transfer of wealth from the poor to the rich, the purchasing power of minorities declined, and salsa record sales slumped accordingly. Latinos recognized that the progressive and militant sixties and seventies represented not the dawn of a new era, but an aberrant chapter now eclipsed by a triumphant and jingoistic resurgence of the right. On more immediate levels, salsa was paradoxically marginalized on the airwaves by the belated interest that the major record companies were finally taking in the Latin market; for the majors, rather than promoting what they perceived as an ethnically divisive and socially unsavory salsa, pressured radio stations to air common-denominator romantic ballads *(baladas)*. Julio Iglesias seemed to rule over Ruben Blades in the very homeland of salsa. Meanwhile, Latino pride notwithstanding, it was natural that many second- and third-generation Hispanics were forgetting their Spanish, assimilating to hip-hop culture, and coming to see salsa as old-fashioned.

Another sort of challenge to salsa was posed by what musicians refer to as the *"merengue* invasion"—a phenomenon which cannot be understood without some discussion of the Dominican Republic and its own music history. Within the Hispanic Caribbean, the Dominican Republic had suffered a somewhat isolated and inhibited cultural development. For their part, Cuba and Puerto Rico had been closely intertwined as the twin colonies of Spain until 1898, and since the early twentieth century Puerto Ricans had adopted much of Cuban popular music, especially the *son* and *bolero*, as their own. Cultural ties were somewhat weaker with the Dominican Republic, which had been independent since the early 1800s. Throughout the subsequent century, the evolution of a creole, national culture remained hampered by poverty, political chaos, and an ongoing denial of the country's African-derived heritage. Socio-political stability came only with the US occupation of 1916–24, which laid the foundations for the despotic dictatorship of Rafael Trujillo (1930–61).

One of the very few positive aspects of Trujillo's regime was its fostering of a national music culture centered around the *merengue*, a lively dance genre in fast tempo. Part of Trujillo's populist image involved promotion of the *merengue* of the Cibao valley, previously spurned by the urban elite. Under Trujillo's patronage and control, the Cibao-style *merengue* became the national dance, whether played by rustic accordion-based *perico ripiao* ("ripped parrot") quartets or by large saxophone-dominated ensembles influenced by swing-era big bands. Yankee commercial music, along with American business, was largely kept out of the country, and with Dominicans discouraged from emigrating or even traveling locally, Dominican musical culture flourished in its own isolated, regimented way.

The CIA-sponsored assassination of *"El Benefactor"* in 1961 inaugurated a new chapter in Dominican history. On the one hand, the US invasion of 1965 reinstalled the Trujillo elite, under the leadership of Joaquín Balaguer, Trujillo's former right-hand man. With the exception of an inconclusive eight-year interruption, Balaguer, now 87 years old, has continued to rule the country and perpetuate the grotesque socio-economic inequities of his mentor's regime. On the other hand, in keeping with the wishes of his masters in the White House, Balaguer opened the country to foreign (primarily American) investment. As multinationals like Gulf & Western bought vast tracts of land, hundreds of thousands of uprooted peasants flooded into shantytowns, especially in Santo Domingo, whose population doubled between 1961 and 1970. Along with the foreign businesses came foreign record companies and their music—rock, schmaltzy *baladas*, and salsa—putting local *merengue* on the defensive.

Merengue's relation to salsa is somewhat contradictory. Salsa, as we have seen, was an international genre, and in the D.R., as elsewhere, it functioned as a symbol of Hispanic cultural resistance to *gringo* Coca-Colonization. At the same time, however, Dominicans perceived salsa as something foreign—Cuban and Puerto Rican—in relation to the *merengue*. Most Dominicans blithely enjoyed all of the various competing musics, but for *merengue* musicians and cultural nationalists, a musical war was going on for the hearts and ears of the Dominican people. To make a long story short, the 1980s saw the triumph of a modernized and revitalized *merengue*, which, guided by bandleader Johnny Ventura and others, successfully marginalized its competitors. Moreover, the *merengue* went on to invade salsa in its own heartlands of New York and Puerto Rico. Throughout the eighties, hardcore *salseros* watched with dismay as their favorite clubs and radio programs switched to *merengue*, with its trivial lyrics, elementary choreography, simpler harmonies and rhythms, and the gimmicky antics of its performers.

To a large extent, the *merengue* has been personally carried abroad by the flood of Dominican emigrants pouring out of the country, and especially to New York City. Whether legally, or via flimsy boats plying the Mona Passage to Puerto Rico, Dominicans have poured into the USA to escape poverty and repression at home and seek a better life. Dominicans in New York, who now number over half a million, have "taken over" Washington Heights, in the process revitalizing the neighborhood's service economy and distinguishing themselves by their willingness to work hard for little pay. Thus, the Dominican bands undercut the salsa groups, and many young Latinos, intimidated by the choreographic pyrotechnics of veteran salsa dancers, feel more at home with the simple two-step *merengue*. Meanwhile, as happened with other Caribbean musics, the *merengue* world's center of gravity shifted to New York, with its music industry infrastructure and concentrated population, leading bandleader Wilfrido Vargas to refer to the city as "a province of the Dominican Republic." *Merengue* has now become an international music in its own right, and to complicate the geo-musical map further, Dominican bands in Puerto Rico and New York are now having to compete with Puerto Rican *merengue* bands. Meanwhile, Dominican music as a whole has acquired greater sophistication and professionalism. This trend is especially evident in the music of Juan Luis Guerra, whose output encompasses sentimental, if tasteful love ballads, socio-political commentary, and searingly danceable *merengue* and salsa.

As of the mid-nineties, the salsa-*merengue* war appears to have cooled off, and *salseros* seem to feel that the situation has stabilized. A portion of the salsa audience may have been irretrievably lost to *merengue*, but many Dominicans have also replenished the ranks of salsa fans. Nevertheless, the Dominican immigration has reconfigured Latin music culture. For one thing, New York Latinos can no longer be thought of as primarily Puerto Rican, and Dominicans naturally take umbrage at the persistent habit of salsa singers and emcees to try to turn concerts into celebrations of Puerto Rican identity. Further, although salsa is now more international than ever, it will not be able to rule as the chosen vehicle of Latino unity, but, in the spirit of multiculturalism, will have to share the stage with *merengue* and other musics.

Among these "other musics," mention must be made of a newcomer to the scene, namely Latin rap. The emergence of Spanish-language rap has been an inevitable development, with young urban Latinos in New York and elsewhere mixing with their Afro-American neighbors and adopting hip-hop fashions. As reggae, rap, and salsa radio programs crisscross the Caribbean, and satellite dishes bring MTV to the entire region, Latin rap has emerged as one more dynamic hybrid in the margins and interstices of the music world. Like salsa, it is an international genre, with branches from Los Angeles to Puerto Rico, and performers from all over the hemisphere. In an age where the borders and interstices of cultures are the sources for so much artistic creativity, the Latin rap of performers like Vico C and Gerardo is self-consciously eclectic, reveling in mixing Spanish and English street talk, and reggae, hip-hop, and Latin rhythms. One may argue whether its audiences constitute defectors from the salsa scene, or whether it is bringing would-be hip-hoppers back into the fold of Latin culture. What the phenomenon makes clear is that any sort of Latin musical unity will now have to take place within a widely diverse musical spectrum.

Amidst all this proliferating hybridity, what has happened to salsa in the last decade? On the one hand, salsa still enjoys its stable niches on the radio and in the club network. The big record companies have even invested in salsa, deciding that it has some commercial potential after all. At the same time, the genre seems to be in a sort of holding pattern. Struggling to retain their audiences, most salsa performers remain stuck in the unremunerative, expoitative club scene, with little hope of breaking into the crossover World Beat markets. Most significant has been the emergence of a tame, commercial, Salsa-Lite style which has marginalized the more innovative and dynamic substyles. By the late-'70s salsa, whether in New York or Caracas, had largely abandoned its portrayals of *barrio* life and themes of Latino solidarity in favor of sentimental love lyrics. Of course, salsa is not the first art form to have to confront the dual and often incompatible functions of being educational, or alternately, escapist entertainment. Some people may always prefer fantasy to social realism, and many Latinos who dress up to go dancing in plush salsa clubs don't want to hear songs about *barrio* murders—that's what they're trying to get away from. For its part, since the mid-'70s the music industry has tended to direct salsa away from its barrio orientation, to make it into a more bland, depoliticized pop—ketchup rather than salsa. Since that period, most of what has been promoted on radio and records is the slick, sentimental *salsa romántica* of crooners like Mark Anthony, rather than the more aggressive, proletarian, Afro-Caribbean *salsa caliente*. The change is also reflected in the fact that most of today's bandleaders are not trained musicians and seasoned club performers like Willie Colón, but cuddly, exclusively white singers distinguished by their pretty-boy looks and supposed sex appeal. Most of them, like Jerry Rivera, are studio-bred creations of the commercial music industry; in their occasional live performances, they cling timidly to the recorded versions of their songs rather than improvising freely, hoping to compensate for their musical limitations by extravagant smoke, lighting, and stage effects. Unfortunately, as salsa grows ever more trivial, it continues to lose the interest of *barrio* youth—precisely the people whose creative input could revitalize it.

While music industry trends and art forms to some extent have their own internal logic, salsa's course seems to reflect broader developments in the socio-political order at large. Salsa was born in the sixties and early seventies, which were a period of protest and mobilization linked to rising expectations. Domestically, the economy was growing, blacks and Latinos were discovering the exhilaration of mass mobilization, and the right wing was on the defensive. In the Caribbean, newly independent West Indian countries were optimistically confronting imperialism, and the Cuban Revolution was flourishing. Salsa embodied the moment's affirmative and sanguine spirit in its unabashedly proletarian flavor and hymns to Latino solidarity.

But those days are decades past, and we are now in the older, wiser, and more cynical 1990s. Internationally, the Latin American left is decimated, the Cuban Revolution is collapsing, and with the Sino-Soviet alternatives defunct, the American flag flies unchallenged. Domestically, the progressive gains of the seventies have been largely unmade by a triumphant Reaganism, scarcely dented by a nominally Democratic president. In the New World Order, to sing songs of revolution would be like spitting in the wind, and popular music throughout the hemisphere seems to have retreated into sensuality, sentimentality, and lumpen nihilism. Accordingly, roots reggae's messianic fervor has given way to dance-hall's glib crudity, the *nueva canción* movement has fizzled, nihilistic gangster rap rules the ghettos, and mainstream salsa has withdrawn into a commercially safe formula of soap-opera lyrics and diluted rhythms. It remains to be seen whether a postmodern pan-Latin culture can again presume to challenge *Pax Americana* in song and action.

Recommended Listening

Cuba compilations: "A Carnival of Cuban Music: Routes of Rhythm" Vol. 1 (Rounder); "Cuba Classics" Vols. 2 &3 (Luaka Bop/Warner); Salsa: "Ruben Blades: The Best" (Globo/Sony); Willie Colón & Hector Lavoe, "Vigiliante" (Fania/Musica Latina International); Dominican Republic: Juan Luis Guerra, 4.40, "Bachata Rosa" (Karen); Pochy y su Cocoband, "La Coco es la Coco" (Kubaney).

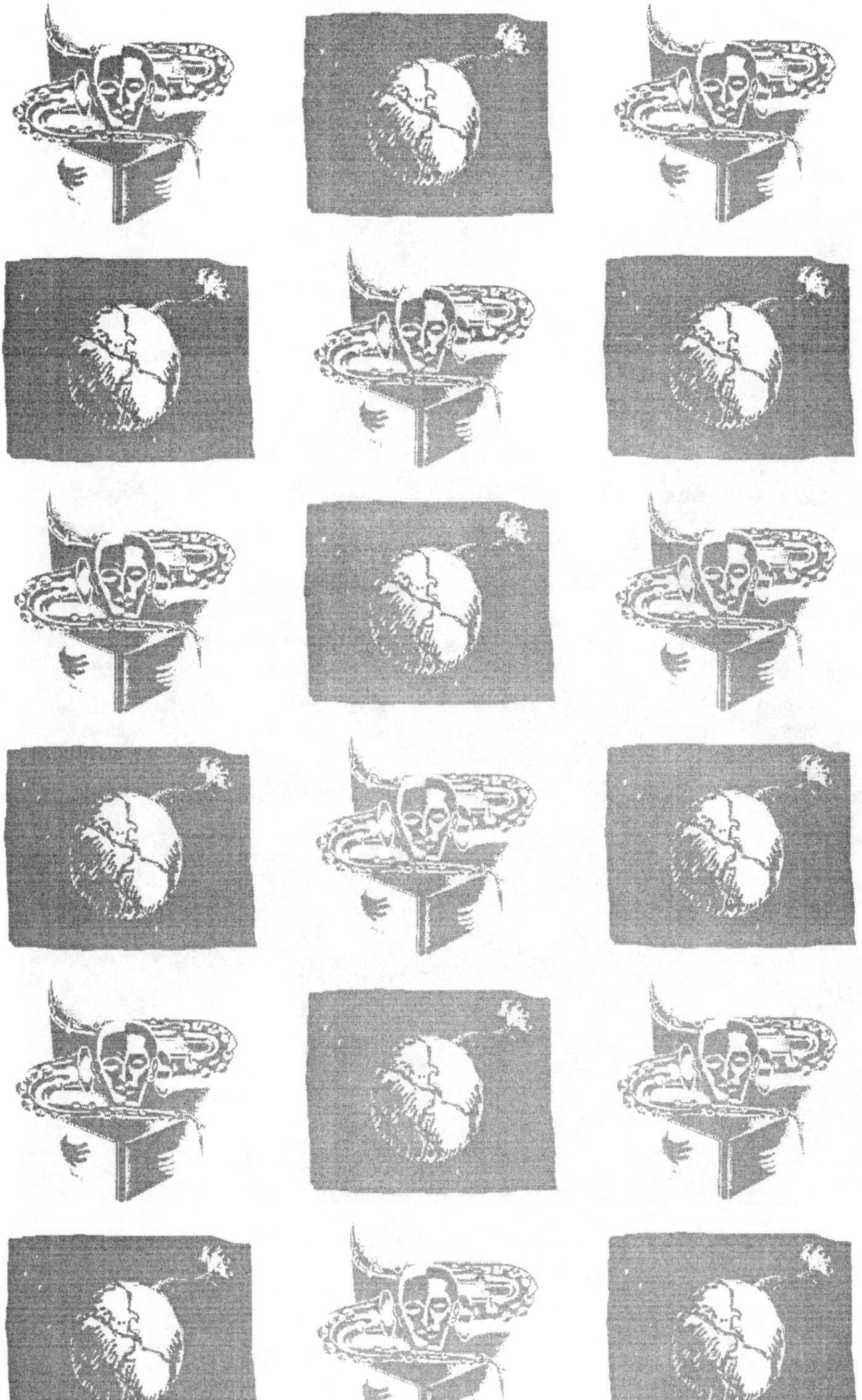

Celina González (r) and Idania Diaz (l) in front of Celina's Santa Bárbara altar. Photo: Ivor Miller.

The Singer as Priestess: Interviews with Celina González and Merceditas Valdés

(La Habana, 1993)

Ivor Miller

Celina González:
Queen of the Punto Cubano

Drummer Iván Ayala[1] grew up in New York City listening to the music of Celina González.* As a child in the 1960s he was brought to Puerto Rican *espiritista* ceremonies, where instead of using drums, practitioners would play Celina's records to invoke the spirits. This is one way that Celina's music and the dedication of her followers have blasted through the U.S. embargo against Cuba that has deprived us of some of the planet's most potent music, art and literature for over 32 years. Iván's experience shows the ingenuity of working people in maintaining human connections that are essential to them, in spite of governments that would keep them separate. Hailed as musical royalty in Colombia, Venezuela, Mexico, England and in Latin USA, Celina has, until very recently, been kept out of the U.S. market.[2]

Cuba has long been a mecca for African-derived religious and musical traditions, and Celina's music taps a deep source. It is at the same time popular and sacred, danceable and political. By using the ancient Spanish *décima* song form to sing about the Yoruba deities *(orichas)*, she has become a symbol of Cuban creole *(criollo)* traditions. A pantheon of *orichas* are worshipped in the *Santería* religion, which is used by practitioners to protect humans from sickness and death, and to open the way for peace, stability, and success.

During the 14 month period that I spent in Cuba from 1991–1994, I had often heard Celina's music on the radio, TV, and even at a concert/rally for the Young Communist League (UJC), where the chorus of "Long live Changó!" (*"¡Qué viva Changó!"*) was chanted by thousands of socialist Cuba's "New Men" at the Plaza of the Revolution.[3]

Celina is a major figure in Cuban music and cultural identity. Her 1948 song *"Santa Bárbara"* was a groundbreaking event in modern Cuban music, reviving Cuban rural music

---

*Written and translated from Spanish by Ivor Miller and edited in collaboration with Idania Diaz and Jill Cutler. Interview by Idania and Michel Diaz and Ivor Miller, December 14, 1993, in the home of Celina González in Havana, Cuba. Thanks to Karin Barber for help with the Yoruba glossary, and to Mirta Gonzalez and Guillermo Pasos in Havana. Italicized words can be found in the glossary at the end of the interview.

(*música guajira, el "punto cubano"*) for a national and international audience, and infusing it with Afro-Cuban creole spirituality. Celina is herself a *"guajira,"* (country girl) and is fiercely proud of it. She grew up near the Sierra Maestra, the mountainous region in eastern Cuba where many slave rebellions, the War of Independence, and the Cuban Revolution were fomented. She has been an ardent supporter of the Revolution, and also of the *guajira* culture in which she grew up. During the early years of the Cuban Revolution, the public performance of religious songs was prohibited, and Celina withdrew from singing *"Santa Bárbara"* for over twenty years.

It was the 1987 publication of the famous Castro interview, *Fidel and Religion*,[4] that prompted her to sing for *Changó* again, and soon after this began the current explosion in *Santería* initiations. She is an important figure in today's religious revival.

I first met Celina González and her son Reutilio Jr. at an intimate concert they gave at the old Spanish Castilla de la Fuerza at the port in Havana Vieja. She had just finished singing *"Santa Bárbara"* without microphones, accompanied by acoustic stringed and percussive instruments. I was astonished at the strength of her inspired voice and charged from the energy she manifested. Reutilio Jr., also charged from the music, eagerly signed and gave me a poster of himself and his mother. After a long conversation in which we exchanged ritual status and lineage information (he a son of *Ogún* and I of *Changó*), he gave me his home phone number and asked me to call in four days. His mother was to receive *Babalú-Ayé* the following day, and would be occupied for the three-day interim.

In Havana, December is a busy month for parties and ceremonies. December 3–4 is the celebration of *Santa Bárbara/Changó*, with thousands journeying to the church in Párraga, or making their own ceremonies at home. December 16–17 is the pilgrimage to El Rincón, the church of *San Lázaro/Babalú-Ayé*. I arrived at Celina's home in the morning of December 14, accompanied by Idania and Michel Diaz, afficionados of Celina's music and fellow Guantanameros. Celina graciously welcomed us, and we ended up talking for over four hours and made a 90-minute taped interview.

Behind the front door of her simple house sits *Eleguá*. In the other corner is a huge *Ogún prenda*, above which hangs a long machete, and next to this a portrait of Fidel (the warrior) in uniform. Celina had just received *Babalú-Ayé*, whose altar is next to *Ogún*. On a Soviet-made TV to the left of *Babalú* sits a framed gold record she received as an award. At the far side of the room stands a wooden painted statue of Santa Bárbara, four feet tall, and framed with Xmas lights. On the bureau next to her is a small statue of *el Niño de Atocha*. It is here that Celina holds court. We distributed ourselves onto the hard wood rocking chairs in the room, and a young male godchild *(ahijado)* served us coffee. A female godchild came in, a doctor, and talked about green medicine (herbology directly related to the curative practices of *Santería*). After two hours, all visitors but ourselves left, and we sat with the Queen of the *punto cubano* as she talked about her music and her religion.

When we arrived, Celina made it clear that she never lets anyone photograph her *Santa Bárbara*, because it might make the *oricha* angry. But by the time we left, she invited us to take group photos in front of *Santa Bárbara*. She is a lively and generous woman of 65, godmother *(madrina)* to a large spiritual family, and has earned the respect of many in her *barrio*, her island, and abroad.

IM: Was your family religious?

CG: Both my mother and grandmother were devout Catholics; they weren't *santeras*. They had what all the rural people in Cuba have: an altar with *Santa Bárbara, la Caridad del Cobre, la Virgen de Regla* and *San Lázaro*. The only thing my mother worshipped was this altar. I respected her very much because she was very saintly, if she saw a sick person she'd cure them, and never asked anything for her work.

My father was also Catholic. I often go to church and give masses for my dear ones and my spiritual guides.

I've been a poet since I was ten years old. It is a gift. Words come easily to me, I don't know if it could be some poet that accompanies me as a spirit. I work a lot in octosyllable (a type of *décima*), and when the feeling comes to write, words often come in this form.

I've been a seer since I was a little girl. I developed my vision alone, because my saints and my ancestral spirits wouldn't let anyone near me. Above all it was *Santa Bárbara* who said, "Nobody can touch you until I say so. I am the one who has to choose." It is for this that I respect her so, and for this that I waited so long to *make saint*.

IM: Where were you and your husband born?

CG: My husband Reutilio[5] was from Guantánamo Province. He was born in San Antonio Redo, known today as El Central Manuel Tames. I was born in Jovellanos, la Nueva Lisa, in Matanzas Province. My parents moved east to Santiago de Cuba when I was a young girl. Four years ago when they paid me homage in Jovellanos, I met my family that stayed there.

Reutilio and I met in Santiago de Cuba. Without any formal schooling, he played the guitar more wonderfully than anyone I've ever heard. His music brought people to their feet. In that time one had to be an artist! If you weren't, the audience would throw tomatoes at you in a minute. But our two voices made an impact, he was the second and I the lead. And we dedicated ourselves to working together. We were inseparable as lovers, as a married couple, and as partners in art.

We began to work the Oriente radio network in 1947. We arrived in Havana on November 2, and were hired for one week by the radio station *Suaritos*. By the end of the week we had composed the number *"Santa Bárbara."*

Before composing the song, Santa Bárbara had appeared to me twice in dreams. She asked me to sing for her, she said if I didn't I would not succeed, and if I did I would travel the world. When I made the song, it became a hit in Cuba, and from there we became famous around the world.

She also told me that I was going to enter into *Santería*. But many years passed until I was initiated in 1959. I was initiated as a daughter of the holy *Virgen de Regla, Yemayá*.

IM: Did Reutilio influence the themes of your music?

CG: In the first song of *Santa Bárbara* no, but in the others yes. When we saw that *"Santa Bárbara"* was a hit, and that she conceded to me all that she promised, he and I began to co-author songs. He made the music, and I made the words.

I don't know why, but the first song for *Santa Bárbara*, I had to make in *décima*, except for the Yoruba phrase *"Que viva Changó"* (Long live Changó) in the chorus. Thanks to her, to God, for all that I have, also *maferefun Yemayá*.

IM: Who is your godfather in *Ocha*?

CG: My godfather in *Ocha* is Jaunelo Ortega, *"Changó Dina."*[6] He lives in Miami. I always ask *Changó* to help him and give him health, he was very good to me. He initiated me at a young age, 34 years ago. He made me an initiate of *Yemayá*, and *Changó* is my father. He belongs to the lineage of Nicolas Angarica.[7] The first godchild of Nicolas was my representative at my *Ocha* ceremony. She is a beautiful lady, an initiate of *Yemayá*, and sings beautifully to the *Oricha* and ancestors.

IM: How does your training as an *espiritist* and *santera* influence your performance style?

CG: I never look at the audience. I concentrate so much that at times I feel afraid, because

I have lost my senses at times, especially when I sing for *Santa Bárbara.*
When I am on the stage I am not me, and I feel it. I am uprooted, I feel that it's not normal, that it's supernatural, because I don't look at the audience. I have dancers, above all one that dances for *Yemayá,* and at times I distance myself from her. One day, during the performance I was dancing and dancing and I said "Ay, *Yemayá* is going to come." I told the dancer, "Girl, go on over there," and I went to the other side of the stage, and began to look at the audience because if I didn't, *Yemayá* would have mounted me for sure.

IM: Has your religious practice ever affected your ability to work in Cuba?

CG: Nobody has ever given me problems, because these are private matters. For example, if you wanted to make a religious ceremony, it was your own business. The Revolution was never opposed to the religion of Yoruba origin.

I light a candle every year to la *Virgen de Regla, Santa Bárbara, San Lázaro,* and to *las Mercedes.* I have a church right here in my house. Nobody has come to say, "Listen, don't do this," and my door has always been open and many visitors come.

However, when you would try to sing for the saints on TV they would tell you, "No." Be careful, because I don't mean to say that the government was opposed to this. Fidel came out with the book *Fidel and Religion,*[8] and has never been against Yoruba religion. Those were other people who said, "No, you cannot do this." I know a lot of people who threw away their saints. But when I began to sing again for *Santa Bárbara,* all the other musicians began to sing for the saints. Now everybody sings to *Changó.* Although before many people hid their saints, now everyone is a *santero.* Never in my life have I seen so many *santeros* as now. Why is it that now everyone is making saint? And this is when it costs more, before it was almost free.

I never threw away my saints, or denied that I was religious. *Santa Bárbara* has always been in front of my door, and will be here until I die. I have never denied to anybody that I am a *spiritist,* a *santera,* and that I go to church. I respect God over everything, because my religion is clean, it doesn't harm anybody. As my mother said, "Don't harm anybody, and nobody will harm you."

IM: Did you have to develop as a *spiritist?*

CG: I've had many proofs. One of them is my granddaughter who's been in the States for 22 years. She left as a young girl, and she made saint over there. Her mother, my daughter, was trying to call me by telephone so I could give my blessing to her ceremony, but she couldn't get through. The day that we communicated, I asked her, "Did your daughter Cecilita *make saint?*" And she said, "Yes, how did you know?" And I told her "I dreamed that I came to a throne."[9] The throne was that of *Obatalá,* and when I saluted it I said *"maferefun Obatalá, maferefun Obba."* And she told me, "May God bless you! This is the saint that my daughter made, *Obatalá* is her father and *Obba* is her mother." Although they have made saint, and are far away, my children contact me when they're going to take a new step in the religion.

IM: Of all your children, has Lázaro Reutilio been the only one to carry on your art as well as your religion?

CG: No, my other son is a *babalao*; he has an orchestra, and is a professional musician. He has lived for many years in Miami.

IM: How is your religion expressed in your songs?

CG: We don't sing in the Yoruba language, but in Spanish so all the Spanish speaking peoples will understand. For example, *Santa Bárbara* is in octosyllable. *La Caridad del Cobre* is in *décima.* The song of *la Virgen de Regla* isn't in *décima.* I composed it with a little bit of Yoruba.

Sometimes I put in a few Yoruba words. For example, in the Church she is known as *Santa Bárbara,* but in *Santería* she is *Changó.* I have a song to *Obatalá,* who is the blessed *Virgen de las Mercedes* in Catholicism. Also we made a song to *Eleguá* that's been recorded throughout the world. The Church knows him as *Saint Niño de Atocha,* others call him *San Roque.* Thus *Eleguá* is represented in the initiation room as either a child or as a man.[10] *Ogún* is known as *San Pedro,* but he has many avatars, such as *San Juan el Bautista* (St. John the Baptist) or *Santiago Apóstol.* And *Ochoosi,* who is the great hunter, is known as *San Norberto.* Because where he points his arrow, it hits the mark. We have songs for all of them, including *Yemayá,* who is my guardian angel, My *Yemayá* is called *Asesu.* Also the holy *Virgen de la Caridad del Cobre,* who is *Ochún.*

Reutilio and I also dedicated a song to *San Lázaro,* and apart from this, I have my own song for *San Lázaro.* The latest song I wrote, that I'm going to record, is a prayer to *Oyá, Jecua-Je Yansa.* For her, I made a beautiful song.

We have songs for all the saints, but in our own style so that everyone can interpret them. Because you can speak a Yoruba word to a *santero,* and he'll understand you. But an *aleyo,* no. An *aleyo* is someone who doesn't have *Ocha.* And then if *aleyos* don't understand what you're saying, why are you singing to them? I sing not only so they'll dance, but also so they'll understand what I am manifesting. I want my songs to communicate, to move the public.

IM: Have you had success outside of the country?

CG: In Colombia, they named me "The Goddess of Colombia." When I come on stage, everyone asks for the song *"Santa Bárbara," "San Lázaro," "El Hijo de Eleguá,"* (The Son of Eleguá) *"A Francisco"* (To Francisco). Francisco is a *Congo* (a guardian spirit) of my godfather *Changó-Dina,* who initiated me, and to this spirit I made a song that is called *"A Francisco."*

In England they call me "Queen of Country Music." The group that went to England with me is *Campo Alegre,* and they were well received. There was a lot of excitement, with lines and lines to see our show. The newspapers said that people there are saturated with electric music. They became very excited with our music. They came to the stage to see the *bongos,* the drums, the *marimba* of Mario Oropesa (may God keep him in glory, *Ibayen bayen tonu*). The music of the lute[11] was emotional to the audience. The *tres* also called a lot of attention.

IM: Which group are you working with now?

CG: I have a group that's called *Piquete Cubano.* It's traditional creole music, and the musicians are young, something that makes me happy. It's directed by Bárbaro Torres, who is considered at this time to be the best lutist in Cuba, because Raúl Lima died, master of country music on the lute. The second master was José Manuel Rodríguez, who we also had the misfortune to lose.

We present a show that is primarily country, my son Lázaro Reutilio is presented as a songwriter and soloist. Afterwards we perform the music of Celina and Reutilio. Then we sing some Yoruba based songs and close with popular music where Reutilio Jr. sings *boleros* and *guaracha.*

We interpret country music like it is. I don't argue with the younger people, because everything evolves, and logically young people want to be creative. For example Liuba María and María Victoria have wonderful voices, María Victoria sings country music beautifully. But I continue interpreting my music in the manner of Celina and Reutilio, accompanied by my two sons and my group *Piquete Cubano.*

Our music comes from the *Mambises* that struggled for Cuban independence. Because of this Reutilio and I made the song *"Yo Soy el Punto Cubano"* (I am the Punto Cubano), that says "I lived in the hills, when the *Mambi* battled, with a machete in hand." They took the *tres,* the lute, and they sang on the savannas or in the hills where they fought for Cuba. Why has this tradition died?

Why don't they teach young children in elementary schools, who have such good voices, how to work with country music without deforming it? One can put in new things. Logically everything must evolve, respecting the origins. They should know in what way *"el son"* is not *"el son montuno,"* because the latter is country.

IM: Has there been a festival of country music in Cuba?

CG: There has never been a festival of country music in Cuba. A short while ago there was a festival in Varadero where Pablo Milanés[12] was the only one to remember to bring country music. He invited my group and me. My respect to master Pablo Milanés, and for this I love him like a son. Also I admire Silvio[13], because he respects my music, and composed a very elegant song entitled *"Guajirito Soy"* ("I am a *Guajiro*"). Our roots must be respected. We have roots in China, Spain and Africa, but our own country music must be celebrated. Why is there no festival of country music?

Every region in Cuba has its own music. For example, in Oriente one has *la guajira de salon, el son montuno,* and *el punto campesino,* that have many tunes. In the central part of the country including Santa Clara and Santi Spíritu they play *las espirituanas*; in Camagüey, las tonadas *camagüeyanas*; in Matanzas, *las tonadas matanceras y los puntos cruzados*; in Pinar del Río *las tonadas carbajal,* that are the same as the original tunes from Spain. In la Isla de Juventud (the Isle of Youth), *el sucu-sucu*. Why aren't these roots celebrated in a festival of country music?

Today cooperatives exist, new houses made of stonemasonry, but one mustn't forget *el bohio* (the palm thatched houses), nor the country serenades that the rural people have for entertaining themselves.

(Ivor Miller's interview with Merceditas Valdés follows.)

Merceditas Valdés, left.
Photo by Ernesto Javier.

Merceditas Valdés.
Photo by Ernesto Javier.

Merceditas Valdés: "the Little Aché"

Merceditas Valdés[14] was the first singer of popular music to bring Yoruba-derived music and liturgy to Cuban radio and television.* She sang with Obdulio Morales, whose orchestra is reputed as the first to utilize *batá*, the family of three drums used in Yorubaland and in Cuba for ceremonial music. Valdés worked for many years with Fernando Ortiz, a scholar whose writings were devoted, among other topics, to the African-derived music and ritual practice of Cuba.

Beginning in the 1960s, governmental pressure kept Valdés from singing *oricha* songs for over twenty years. Yet when she was allowed to sing again, she recorded five albums, called *¡Aché!*, numbers 1–5. These records have helped create a revival of Yoruba content in all genres of Cuban popular music. Initiates of *Santería* use her records in ceremonies when drums are not available, and even to warm up the atmosphere before the drummers arrive.

Both Merceditas and Celina claim to be ardent revolutionaries and openly religious, and both have lived for years with the pressure not to sing sacred songs. However, each has been received differently by the listening and dancing public. This may have to do with their life styles, their skin colors, and the content of their music. Castro and other Cuban leaders have from the beginning put the Cuban peasant *(guajiro)* in the forefront of the interests and values of the Revolution. Celina is from the rural part of Oriente, where the Revolution started, and sings about peasant revolts. Her music, no matter what the theme, is danceable to a wide public. Merceditas is from the city of Havana, and sings mainly devotional music, not directly related to the Revolution. Her music is danceable only to those who know the specialized movements of the *orichas*. Merceditas had no children, while Celina, who had five children, was seen as a stable person and a good mother. Merceditas, whose skin is dark, who sings in Yoruba accompanied by *batá* drums, was seen as belonging to a marginal part of Cuba that identified itself as part of an African Diaspora. According to some, the CCP (Cuban Communist Party) repressed the identities and activities of black Cubans as an interest group.[15] Celina, whose skin is light, who sings *guajiro décima* songs in Spanish, was seen as an authentic "creole" *(criollo)*, the mixture that the Revolution upheld as "truly" Cuban (100% Cuban). Celina's musical style fits well within the ideal image of Cuban nationalism, the *mulata*, often represented as a harmonious blending of African and Spanish peoples (ignoring the violence of slavery, rape and continued prejudice). Merceditas's style, "pure" Yoruba and urban, seems to defy Spanish influence and ignore Cuban peasant music.

When Merceditas speaks of the musical aspirations of Gilberto Valdes, the research of Ortiz, and their celebrations of "Cuban culture" and its African roots, this must be seen in the context of a new nation, recently emerged from slavery and struggling to emerge from colonization. Performances of black Cuban music were courageous acts of cultural activism highly polemic in their day. Alejo Carpentier writes that in the 1920s "Rural music was held up [by racists] to counter the Afro-Cuban music, as a representative of a white music, more noble, more melodious, and cleaner [both acoustically and metaphorically].[16]

Putting aside their unequal reception in the political sphere, it is in their performance styles where Merceditas and Celina seem to share commonalities. Both women speak of their public performances as acts of private devotion. Although they use a proscenium setting, they concen-

---

*Interviews with Merceditas Valdés in her house, Vedado, La Habana, July 30, August 4, and August 12, 1993. By Idania Diaz and Ivor Miller.

trate on the *orichas*, not on the audience, and Celina speaks directly of possession states during performance, while Merceditas hints at it. The West, infamous for its body/mind split, and Sub-Saharan Africa, famous for the union of body/mind/spirit through possession (the divine "mounting" a devotee), seem to meet and dissolve in the concerts of these two women. Like hot bitter coffee poured over white sugar, they fuse to create a potent Cuban brew. Using a proscenium stage, they infuse this given audience/performer split with the presence of the orichas.

When I heard Merceditas perform in Havana with the group Yoruba *Andábo*, she began by praising Fernando Ortiz, who remains a hero in Cuba. She said:

MV: As a Yoruba singer, I was born in the house of Don Fernando Ortiz, with guidance from the *batá* drummers Oru Batá, Jezús Pérez, and Trinidad Torregrosa, founders of the National Folklore Group. I am proud that he was my mentor—the third discoverer of Cuba, ethnologist and folklorist Don Fernando Ortiz.[17]

Merceditas invited us to her home several times to talk about her life and music. She spoke about her family heritage and her faith as a source for her music. She also spoke about Ortiz's relationship to Afro-Cuban ritual practice.

When we arrived at her apartment, I was held back by Idania Diaz, who was in front of me. She pointed to the white powder lying before the door. The dust was left by Merceditas as part of a *santería* style cleansing *(limpieza)* of her home. After the floors are cleaned with prepared water, a portion of it is cast out the front door with egg shell powder *(cascarilla)*. This clears out the negative energy accumulated in the house, yet visitors must avoid the powder to avoid the negative power *(osorbo)* it contains. Stepping over the dust, we entered the doorway opened by Merceditas. She seated us in front of her altar for *Ochún*, goddess of sweet water, and generously shared with us her experiences.

MV: I am from Havana and am an initiate of *Ochún*. My Yoruba name is *Obi Numi*, which means "the union of two waters."[18] I'm grateful to all the *orichas*, and I live to adore them, yet the *oricha* I like to sing for most of all is *Ochún*.

I sing this music with sweetness, and this is what has kept my audiences coming. When I am performing a song I think that I am looking at the deity, at the *oricha* in front of me. Although it may be my own fantasy, I really cherish the idea that in the moment of performance I am singing for the *oricha*.

I come from a religious family. My grandmother was a descendent of Africa. She was delirious in her affection for me, and taught me to handle herbs for their medicinal properties as well as for their use with the *orichas*.[19] She was called María Salomé, and was initiated in the African way.[20] My mother Pilar was an initiate of *Obatalá*, and was initiated while I was in her womb. Because of this I say that I was crowned before birth, and my later initiation for *Ochún* was actually only a confirmation of my original crowning. When she died, my mother had more than 40 years of experience as a *santera*.

Every Sunday in the house of my grandmother they made a *rumba (rumba de cajón)*, and we all danced and sang. Her house was in el barrio de Cayo Hueso in Centro Habana.[21]

My birth as an artist was in a program called "the Supreme Court of Art" *(la Corte Suprema del Arte)*, when I was twelve years old. I won first prize with *"Babalú-Ayé."* Later I began to sing popular music: *guaracha, son, guaguancó* and *rumba*.

When the maestro Obdulio Morales[22] was forming his orchestra, he was looking for a voice to sing Yoruba music. They tried me out and I began to work with him. It wasn't easy for me to sing in another language. In 1943, we began to audition for work in various radio programs, and the only station interested in this music was a very small one owned by a Spaniard called Lauriano Suarez, they called him *"Suarito"* [thus the name *Radio Suaritos*].

When I began to sing this music, in the 1940s, there were many problems, because it was the first time that it was broadcast by radio. Many people, especially the *santeros*, thought that I was desecrating the music, but after a while everything calmed down.

Obdulio Morales was the first to bring *Lucumí* music to a symphonic orchestra. He was a musician of high caliber; he was the director and the arranger of his music—he prepared everything. His orchestra came to be a society of [Afro] Cuban folklore. He and his family were religious but he never was initiated into *Santería*. In the orchestra those that played drums were all *santeros,* the chorus members were not. Obdulio was advised by Jesús Pérez and Trinidato Torregrosa, who played drums in the orchestra.

Our first work was a success! At this time the only program listened to in peoples' homes on Sunday, from 7 to 8 PM, was mine: "What's up at home?, Merceditas with *Batá* Drums" *(¿Que pasa en casa?, Merceditas con los Batá)*. The drummers *(bataleros)* were Trinidato Torregrosa, Jesús Pérez, and Raul Perez Nasaco, who all taught me to sing in Yoruba. They were my consultants and worked for many years with the Contemporary Dance company *(Danza Contemporanea)*. Jesús Pérez played the great *Iya* (mother) drum; he was an excellent player. When the owner of the radio station Cadena Azul learned of our success, it was a great blow to him, because we had auditioned for his program and he didn't give us a contract!

Doctor Fernando Ortiz[23] listened to us and later contacted us. At the time, I was 17 years old, and I began to teach classes with him, along with many other drummers and musicians. During this period we presented many conferences in the grand auditorium of the University of Havana; we worked very closely for three days a week. I sang Yoruba songs habitually, but I also sang *Arará, Iyesá* and *Palo* in the conferences of Oritz.

As Juan Marinello[24] has said, Dr. Fernando Ortiz was the third discoverer of Cuba, because he spent his life researching the African and folk Cuban roots of our music. He would go to Africa annually to be nourished by these roots; he often went to Nigeria, and it was with all this information that he gave his conferences.

When he realized the success he was achieving with us, he told me: 'Merceditas, from now on, I'm going to call you "my little *Aché*" *("mi pequeña Aché")*.

He was not an initiate into *Santería*; yet he had many presents from the different African kings that he had visited. In one room of his house he had a beautiful throne made with precious stones like malachite. He didn't show this room to everybody. He also had a lovely throne given him by the king of Ife.[25] In it were two pillars carved to depict the stages of a man from birth until death, with the body of the person studded in pearls, rubies and diamonds.

He had another throne with the *orichas* rudimentarily carved from wood. It was filled with gold-bordered cloth; he called this room his "little treasure."

He was from the middle class, and had a good upbringing because his parents were rich. He was an only child, he studied in the best schools, he founded a society dedicated to the research of Yoruba culture and called it the Society of Afro-Cuban Studies *(Sociedad de Estudios Afrocubanos)*. He was its president and published a bimonthly journal that documented the history of the different *orichas* and their particular *patakines*.

I felt content at Ortiz's side. He supported my radio program, and appeared at the radio station to listen every date that a saint was celebrated.

As he was aging and getting sick, in 1957, he retired from the university and was interned at the rectory of doctor Clemente Inclán. At this time we gave the last memorable conference in the university auditorium. Many important figures were there, like Alicia Alonso, Alberto Alonso, Wifredo Lam, and all the martyrs of Humbolt[7] who at that time were living underground [involved in clandestine activity against President Batista]. The house was packed, and this farewell to Don Fernando Ortiz was one to remember.

It was a day to remember because many of the students who today are martyrs came to the conference, and the police began to circle the auditorium in their cars. They came up to Fernando and I, and told us "if anything happens, don't run or leave for the streets," and we moved to a room at the side of the auditorium. They told us, "there is a person here we are trying to capture," but luckily nothing happened.

The Cuban Revolution triumphed in 1959, and I began to work in the program *"Palmas y cañas"* (Palm Trees and Sugar Cane), of which I am a co-founder with Celina González, to whom I give my respects. In this program we interpreted *guaracha* music, and the rural people gave me the name of *"la salsosa"* (the saucy one).

I have never sang for *Santería* ceremonies, nor for other sacred parties in private homes. I don't like to go to ceremonies, because when I've arrived everybody is having a good time and singing, yet when they notice my presence, everything stops and people ask if I'll sing. When I go to a party, I want to enjoy myself like the rest. I want to be treated like anybody else, and for this reason I haven't been to a sacred party for years.

I passed a period where I couldn't sing Yoruba music because certain people said that this was backward, that the music would effect the children in a bad way. In this epoch, from the 1960s until recently, I was partially retired. Then the religious revolution began, and now everyone is a believer. Many people have the appearance of having just been initiated into *Santería*, but in reality they were hiding their beliefs until now. I have never negated my religion, because Afro-Cuban practices are our roots and are our music. Today, the majority of Cuban musicians sing for the *orichas*; even Pablo Milanés has incorporated *batá* drums into his group.

In this moment our music is flowering and making the world aware that our roots are integrated into Cuban popular music. One can already see how many groups are using *batá* drums, and this gives me much pleasure. Many people are interested in this phenomenon and value the introduction of *batá* drums into modern music groups. This [Afro-Cuban musical and religious] revolution will continue because there is no one who can stop it now.

I would like to have a successor, and when I see that young people today are interested in this music I am happy, because I've always been of the opinion that Yoruba music has the same value as any other musical genre. All the years that passed without my singing Yourba music I spent quietly awaiting the moment when we could again publicly sing for the *orichas*.

Conclusion

Due to changing government policies and a devastated economy, Cuba (and especially Havana) is currently undergoing what many Cubans have described to me as a religious explosion, where thousands are being initiated into *Santería*.

Among other sources, practitioners are getting inspiration for their faith from popular music, where many of the leading figures are *santeros* and *babalaos*. Along with Celina and Merceditas, there is Adalberto Alvarez, a *babalao* whose song *"Y que tu quieres que te den"* was a smash hit in 1992. Its chorus line stated: *"Voy a pedir pa' ti, lo mismo que tu pa' me"* (I'm going to ask [of the *orichas*] for you, the same that you ask for me). His 1993 music video (*"Que te pasa mami"*) made a point to show him wearing a green and yellow beaded *Idé* (sacred bracelet) for *Orula*, the *oricha* who reveals human destiny through divination.

While *Santería* has existed for hundreds of years, practitioners have until recently kept their identities secret. Today one can see white-clad *Iyawos*, and hear ceremonial *batá* music in all parts of Havana, revealing the active African heritage of Cuba.

Santería is often used as a way to help practitioners succeed in their endeavors. At a time when the government can't provide basic foods for most Cuban people, many are turning to *Santería* with better results. As I witnessed in Celina's home, the religion helps build community, which often leads to the sharing of food, especially during ceremonies.

Artists help us make sense of the present, and sometimes give us the shape of things to come. In this extraordinary moment in Cuba's history, artists like Celina, and thousands of *Santería* practitioners are suggesting that Cuba's future lies in finding local solutions for its troubles, based on Cuban models, and not from those of its former colonizers: Spain, the United States, or Russia.

But above all, the experiences of Celina and Merceditas give us insight into the historical process of syncretism and the integration of creolized practices into Cuban popular culture.

Endnotes

1 Iván is a member of the Ayala family of Puerto Rico, who are famous as *bomba* and *plena* musicians.
2 See her 1993 release, Celina González, *¡Que Viva Changó!* (Qbadisc QB 9004), containing several of the songs mentioned here (although the original recordings from 1948 are much richer).
3 Ernesto "Ché" Guevara (d. 1967), hero of the Revolution, who was for a time Minister of Industries and the president of the National Bank of Cuba, hoped for the "appearance of the 'New Man,' the Cuban of the future, who would see his labors not as a dull, boring obligation but as a joyful contribution to the welfare of his society. Material incentives would soon become the debris of the past." In a 1965 publication *(Man and Socialism in Cuba)* he wrote: "One of our fundamental ideological tasks is to find the way to perpetuate heroic attitudes in everyday life.... To build communism it is necessary to change man at the same time as one changes the economic base." How ironic that the heroic attitudes of the "New Man" might be inspired not only by Marx, but also by *Changó,* the ancient Yoruba king turned "god of thunder." Quoted from Robert E. Quirk, *Fidel Castro*, (New York: W.W. Norton, 1993): pp. 520, 522.
4 Here Castro expressed his opinion that religious belief could be complementary to revolutionary struggle, as exemplified by Latin American Liberation Theology. Within a few months of publication in the Spanish original, *Fidel y la Religión* "had been bought by a million Cubans, one-tenth of the entire population." Harvey Cox, Introduction to *Fidel and Religion*, (New York: Simon & Schuster, 1987): p. 17.
5 Reutilio Domínguez. Died 1972.
6 At the time of initiation, *santeros* receive a Yoruba name related to their *oricha*.
7 Nicolas Angarica (1901–76) from Perico, Matanzas, was an important figure in the development of *Santería* in Cuba. He played the sacred *batá* drums, and directed a *batá* group to play for *Ocha* ceremonies in Havana. In 1955, he wrote what is reputedly the first published instruction book of divination for *santeros,* which has been reprinted: Nicolas V. Angarica, *Manual del oriate (religión Lucumi)*, (Miami: Ediciones Universal, 1979).
8 *Fidel and Religion: Castro Talks on Revolution and Religion with Frei Betto.* (New York: Simon & Schuster, 1987).

9 The *Santería* altars constructed for special ceremonies, like the week-long initiation period, the anniversary of an initiation, or a drum ceremony, are called "thrones."

10 *Elegúa* is represented as such during the *Itá* divination.

11 The Cuban lute (called *laúd*) is an offspring of the lute, with as many as twelve double strings.

12 Pablo Milanés. Composer, singer and guitarist, born 1943.

13 Silvio Rodríguez. Composer, singer and guitarist, born 1946. One of the creators of the Latin-American "new song" *(nueva canción)* movement.

14 Merceditas Valdés, born October 14, 1928.

15 See Carlos Moore, *Castro, Blacks and Africa*. (Los Angeles: Center for Afro-American Studies, UCLA, 1988).

16 "*A lo afrocubano [los adversarios de lo negro] se puso entonces lo guajiro, como representativo de una música blanca, más noble, más melódica, más limpia.*" Alejo Carpentier, *La Música en Cuba*. (La Habana: Editorial Pueblo y Educación, 1989): 274.

17 "*Merceditas Valdés nació como cantante folklorista de la casa de Don Fernando Ortíz, que ya Uds. lo saben, que lo han leído mucho y se ha hablado mucho, con asesores de los bataleros Oru Batá, Jesús Pérez, Trinidad Torregrosa, fundadores del Conjunto Folklórico Nacional. Yo me siento orgullosa de que haya sido mi mentor—el tercer descubridor de Cuba, etnólogo, folklorista que fue Don Fernando Ortiz.*" August 7, 1993, at El Convento de Santa Clara, Habana Vieja.

18 "Union of two waters" is not a literal translation from Yoruba. One translation is "Born inside water," or "we give birth to one inside water," which follows Merceditas' story of being crowned while inside her mother's womb (see below). Translation by Professor Frank Arasanyin of Yale University. ["*Abi Numi*": "A" is "we"; "*Bi*" is "to give birth to, to bear something;" "*Ninu*" is "inside;" and "*Omi*" is "water." Many Yoruba names are full sentences condensed into short phrases.

19 *Santería* is first and foremost a system for healing, and most of the herbs used in its practices are for healing purposes.

20 Merceditas is referring to a practice brought by Yoruba slaves that has been transformed in the development of modern *Santería*. An initiate today will be "crowned" with their *oricha* protector *(angel guardiano)*, and "receive" several others in the ceremony. In the tradition practiced by her grandmother, the initiate was "crowned" by one *oricha* and received only *Eleguá*, the messenger.

21 Cayo Hueso was a working class neighborhood famous for its *rumba* musicians and *Santería* practitioners.

22 Obdulio Morales. Orchestra director and composer, born 1910. Director of the National Folklore Group *(el Conjunto Folklórico Nacional)*.

23 Fernando Oritz. Ethnographer, lawyer, archeologist, linguist and historian (1881-1969).

24 Juan Marinello Vidaurreta, (1898—1977). Professor emeritus at the University of Havana. One of the most award-winning Cuban writers of the century. See Juan Marinello, *Ensayos* (La Habana: Editorial Arte y Literatura), 1977.

25 *Ife*, or *Ilé-Ife* in Nigeria, is the sacred city for Yoruba peoples.

Bibliography

Abiodun, Rowland. "Understanding Yoruba Art and Aesthetics: The Concept of Ase." *African Arts*, 27, 3 (1994): 68–78, 102–03.

Angarica, Nicolas V. *Manual del oriate (religión Lucumi)*. Miami: Ediciones Universal, 1979.
Brown, David H. "Thrones of the Orichas: Afro-Cuban Altars in New Jersey, New York, and Havana." *African Arts*, 25, 4, October, 1993: pp. 44–59, 85–87.
Carpentier, Alejo. *La Música en Cuba*. La Habana: Editorial Pueblo y Educación, 1989.
Castro, Fidel. *Fidel and Religion: Castro Talks on Revolution and Religion with Frei Betto*. New York: Simon & Schuster, 1987.
Gerard, Charley and Marty Sheller. *Salsa!: the Rhythm of Latin Music*. Crown Point, IN.: White Cliffs Media Company, 1989.
Martínez, Mayra A. "Merceditas Valdes, Cantar Siempre," *Revolución y Cultura*, No. 133–134, 1983, pp. 63-66.
Miller, Ivor and Idania Diaz. "Celina González: The 'Queen' of the Punto Cubano," *Lucero: Journal of Iberian and Latin American Studies*, 5 (1994), pp. 9–19.
Orovio, Helio. *Diccionario de la Música Cubana: Biográfico y Técnico*. La Habana: Editorial Letras Cubanas, 1992.
Ortiz, Fernando. *Nuevo Catauro de Cubanismos*, Editorial de Ciencias Sociales, La Habana, 1985.
Quirk, Robert E. *Fidel Castro*, New York: W.W. Norton, 1993.
Roberts, John S. *The Latin Tinge: the Impact of Latin American Music on the United States*. Tivoli, NY: Original Music, 1985.
Weinstein, Norman. "Celina González, ¡Que Viva Changó!," *The Beat*, Vol. 12, No. 5, 1993, pp. 68–70.

Discography

Aché II: Merceditas Valdés. EGREM, 1988.
Orishas: Merceditas Valdés. EGREM, 1989.
Homenaje: Jesus Perez in Memoriam. Conjunto de Percusion de Danza Nacional de Cuba, EGREM, 1987
Santero. Celia Cruz, Mercedes Valdes, Caridad Suarez, Coros de Obdulio Morales y Alberto Zayas, con los Tambores Bata de Jesús Perez. Panart (Venezuela), 1987. [Original 1950s].
Celina con Frank y Adalberto. Celina Gonzalez/ Adalberto y su Son. EGREM, 1987.

Glossary

Aché	Authority—the power to make things happen.
Ahijado	Godchild. A person guided through the many rituals of *Santería* by a godparent, or *padrino/madrina*.
Aleyo	"Unconsecrated," someone not initiated into *la Santería*. Literally "stranger", or "visitor."
Apetebi de Orula	A woman who has received *La Cofa de Orula*. An *apetebi* may assist *babalaos* in ceremony.
Arará	A Yoruba-derived ritual practice originating from the Yoruba of present-day Benin.
Asesu	One of the avatars of *Yemayá*.
Babalao	An *Ifá* diviner, a male priest initiated into the branch of *Santería* called *Ifá*. (*Babaláwo* in Yoruba).

Babalú-Ayé/	Babalú-Ayé is the *oricha* of pestilence, which he can spread or cure.
Asujano Asollí	Asujano Asollí is a praise name. In Yorubaland known as *Soponnón*, the deity of small pox. Syncretized with *San Lázaro*.
Bembé	A large ceremonial drum, and also a ceremony where this drum is played. A Yoruba term.
Bohio, el	A palm thatched hut. *Bohio* is a Taino Indian name for house or mansion; it was their name for Santo Domingo, the center of their civilization before the Spanish invasion. (from Juan José Arrom, personal communication, 1994).
Caridad del Cobre, la	The patron saint of Cuba. See *Ochún*.
Changó	*Oricha* of lightning, truth and sex. Master of strategy and tactics. Syncretized with *Santa Bárbara*. In *Yoruba, Sangó* is deity of lightning.
Cofá de Orula, el	A three-day ceremony performed by *babalaos* where a female "client" is ritually linked with *Orula*, the *oricha* of divination. This ceremony conclusively determines which *oricha* is the "owner" of the "clients's" head. There is a corresponding ceremony for males called *La Mano de Orula* (Hand of Orula).
Congo	A spirit of an African ancestor from the Congo River Basin.
Décima	Poetic form used in various Cuban and Puerto Rican genres, originating in 17th-century Spain. The *décima* consists of ten-line verses in rhymed octosyllables. The rhyme scheme of the *décima* is as follows: first line with the fourth and fifth; the second line with the third; the sixth line with the seventh and tenth; the eighth with the ninth. (From Gerard, *Salsa!*, p.124).
Ebo de Entrada	A divination performed by *babalao* to determine a "clients" spiritual preparedness to become an initiate of *Ocha*. Ebo means offering or sacrifice.
Eleguá	*Oricha* of beginnings, of the crossroads, of chance and indeterminacy, and of endings. *Elégbara/Esu* in *Yoruba*. Syncretized with *el Niño de Atocha* and *San Roque*.
Espiritista	See *spiritist*.
Guaguancó	A form of *rumba* in a mid to fast tempo. Danced by a male and female couple and involves the man's efforts to seduce a woman. See *Rumba*.
Ibayen bayen tonu	Part of a Yoruba prayer for the ancestors.
Ifá	The *oricha* of divination, also the name of the classical Yoruba divination system. *Ifá* is also known as *Orula* or *Orunmila* in Cuba.
Itá	The divination component of an initiation ceremony.
Iyesá	In Cuba, *Iyesá* is a Yoruba-derived ritual practice with distinct drums, song, and dance. In Nigeria, the *Ijesha* are a Yoruba sub-group.
Maferefun	Yoruba word meaning "give thanks to."
Make saint	See *Ocha*.
Mambises	Cuban fighters that included many Africans, freed and enslaved, and their descendants who fought in the War of Independence from Spain (1895–1898). The word has origins in the Congo River basin of West-Central Africa [*KiKongo*] (see Ortiz, *Nuevo Cataruo de Cubanismos*,

	pp. 336–337).
Mano de Orula, la	See *Cofa de Orula*.
Mo dupué dupué	I give thanks. In Yoruba, *mo dúpé dúpé*.
Moyumbo	*Moyumbar* = to pray. Daily prayer of *santera/os* asking for the health and blessing of all ritual lineage members. In Yoruba, *mo júba* = I give homage, I respect.
Niño de Atocha, el	See *Eleguá*.
Obara	Number six in cowry shell divination *(diloggún)*, where *Changó* speaks.
Obatalá	*Oricha* of purity, longevity, and creation *Obatalá* is believed to be owner of the head (or destiny) of all humans inhabiting the planet. For this reason having one's head ritually consecrated to *Obatalá* can never be harmful.
Obba	*Oricha* symbolizing marital fidelity. She is the eternal love of *Changó*, and inhabits the cemetery.
Ocha	The main initiation ceremony for *santera/os*. *Ocha* is a shortened Yoruba term for *Oricha*. In the *O[ri]cha* ceremony, the *oricha* is "made," or "crowned" on the head of the devotee. Thus the term " make *Ocha*" or "make saint." The guardian angel is said to be "made," while the other *orichas* are "received."
Ochoosi	*Oricha* of intelligence, of the hunt. Syncretized with *San Norberto*.
Ochún	*Oricha* of sweet water, love, beauty, wealth and lavishness.
Ogún	*Oricha* of iron and war. Syncretized with *San Pedro, San Juan el Bautista*, and *Santiago Apóstol*.
Oluo Oni Oni	An elder *babalao*.
Oricha	Deity.
Oriente	The eastern-most province in Cuba, from where Celina and Reutilio derived their musical inspiration.
Orula	*Oricha* of divination. See *Ifá*.
Orúnmila	See *Ifá*.
Oyá	*Oyá* is *oricha* of wind, tornadoes, transformation and the *Jecua-Je Yansa* cemetery. *Jecua Je Yansa* is another of her names. In Yoruba, *Yansa* means mother of nine.
Palo (Palo Monte)	A Cuban religion of Bantu/BaKongo origins with dance and drum ceremonies.
Patakines	Stories. Legends of the Yoruba *orichas* recited in divination.
Prenda	A consecrated iron cauldron used to house *Ogún*.
Punto Cubano	Traditional country music that includes distinct regional genres found throughout Cuba. A *Punto* group is composed of a guitar, the *tres*, the *triple*, the lute, the *clave* and a *guiro*.
Rumba	Afro-Cuban party music that includes percussion, dancing and commentary on everyday life. Performed by an ensemble of three *conga* drums, *palitos* and *claves* with a lead singer and chorus. Three forms of *rumba* are the *guaguancó, columbia* and *yambú*. (from Gerard, *Salsa!*, p. 127).
San Juan el Bautista	See *Ogún*.
San Lázaro	See *Babalú Ayé*.
San Norberto	See *Ochoosi*.

San Pedro	See *Ogún*.
San Roque	See *Eleguá*.
Santa Bárbara	See *Changó*.
Santera/o	An initiate of *Ocha*, a branch of the *Santería* faith.
Santería	A Cuban religion based in Matanzas and Havana that has origins in Yorubaland (today know as Benin and Nigeria).
Santiago Apóstol	See *Ogún*.
Santo	*Oricha*, see also *Ocha*.
Spiritist	One who can "see," "receive," and work with spirits of the dead.
Tres	A nine-string Cuban guitar crucial to *guajiro* music. It is made up of three groups of doubled or tripled strings, and played with a plectrum.
Virgen de Regla, la	See *Yemayá*.
Yemayá	*Oricha* of the ocean, of nurturing, the bringer of all life on the planet.
Yoruba	While there are distinct groups of Yoruba peoples, they comprise one of the largest ethnic groups in Africa. Their homeland is in Nigeria and the Republic of Benin. Yoruba is one of the "major" languages of Nigeria.
Zapateo	Danceable country music based on the same principals as the *Punto Guajiro (Punto Cubano)*. The *Zapateo* is of Andaluzian origins and spread widely throughout Latin America in the 18th century. It is still played and danced in rural Cuba.

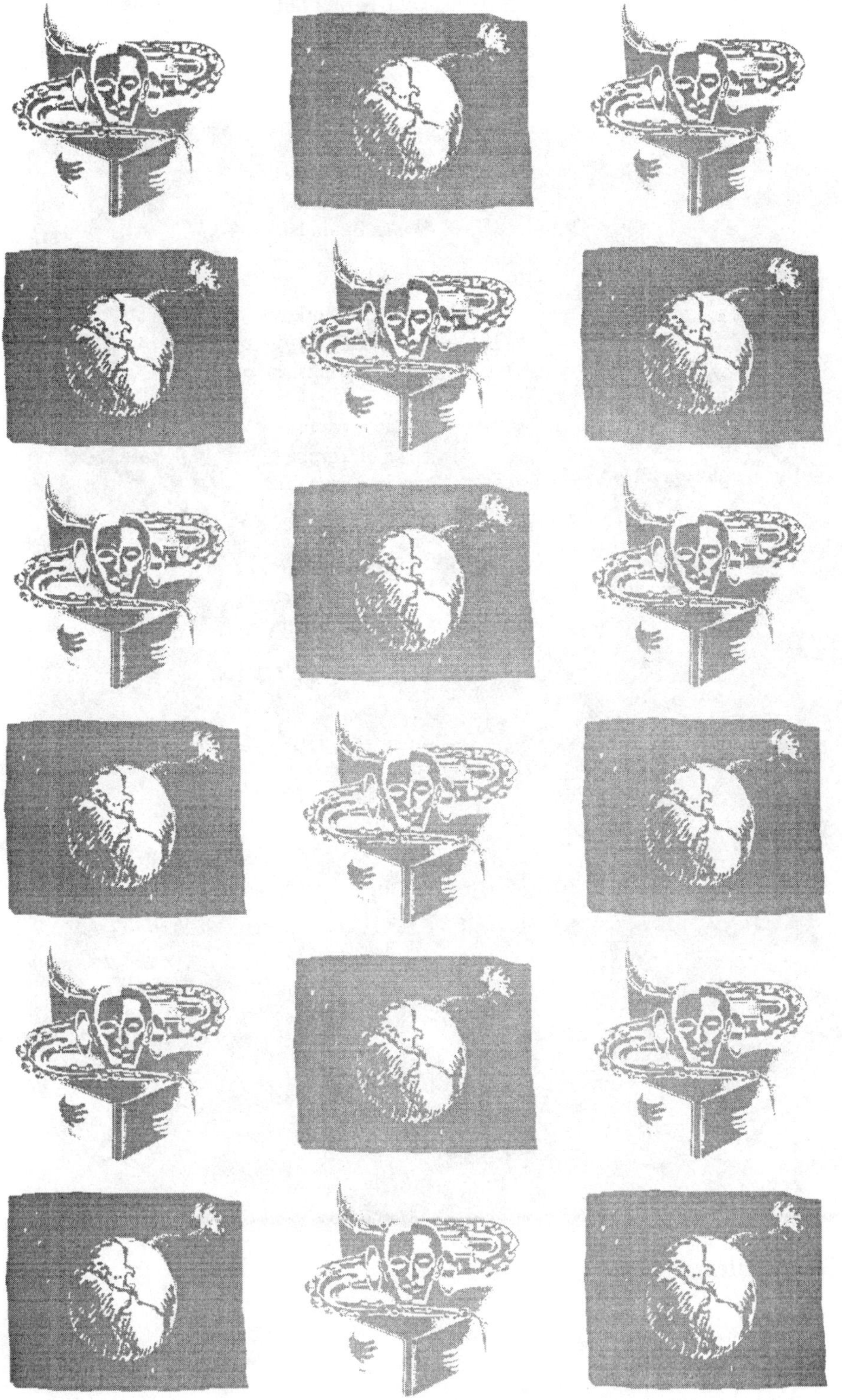

Wendy Allen

Craft, Raft, and Lifesaver: Aboriginal Women Musicians in the Contemporary Music Industry

Jilli Streit-Warburton

Music performed by Australian Aboriginal women is an effective and age honoured means of negotiating identity. It provides an avenue through which musicians can explore and precipitate change. For Aboriginal women living in a society shaped by a white, male hegemony, music is like a raft that ferries them through the hazards of the mainstream. For many, it has also been a lifesaver, keeping alive important knowledge and raising spirits. Above all, it is a craft which carries the prospects of a "bran nue dae."[1]

In Queensland, there is a piece of furniture which is presently enjoying an unprecedented popular revival. It is called the "squatter's chair." A squatter's chair is a large easy chair with wide arms and pieces of wood which can be swung around to the front so that tired squatters can rest their legs. In the past, they were generally found on the shady verandahs of sprawling Queensland homesteads. Now, most people aspire to have one.

In terms of the symbols of hierarchy, the squatter's chair has implications similar to the *Akubra*[2] and the *Japara*.[3] All are richly imbued with androcentrism and the myths of Australia's colonial settlement. The squatter's chair has always belonged to the ruling class, and so represents a seat of power. It is an unsurpassed icon of the imperialist nostalgia on which, like the squatter, Australia's dominant ideologies rest. Historically then, colonial conquest is the source of the mainstream paradigms which have shaped the Australian social landscape for the last two centuries.

Caught in the undertow of the main current, Aboriginal culture has for generations been swept into the quiet waters at the edge. Despite efforts at "building bridges"[4] and launching cultural projects, Aboriginal artists have found that the mainstream runs deep and is lined with rocks and cliffs.[5] In this era of Mabo,* which is marked by changing attitudes to Aboriginal land rights, concepts such as origins, ownership and identity, formerly assumed to be fixed in time and social space, are being re-examined, reinterpreted and in some cases reinvented.

At the first National Aboriginal and Torres Strait Islander Women's Music Festival, held in Sydney in December 1992,[6] one of the performers said:

---

*A 1993 High Court decision that struck down the legal fiction of *terra nullius* in relation to Aboriginal vs. settler land claims, and decided cautiously in favor of Aboriginal land rights.

"As Aboriginal women musicians we not only share a past history, we also share a present reality and a future intent."

Indeed, this formulation, which locates people in time, and links them through the memory of shared experience with past and present, is often expressed by Aboriginal people as being very important. For example, Aboriginal writer, Philip Morrissey, called his contribution to the collection *Aboriginal Culture Today,*[7] "Restoring a Future to a Past."

Defining what it means to be "Aboriginal" has occupied the European population since the beginning of settlement. Up until now *Aboriginality* has been defined for legal and administrative purposes in at least 67 different ways. This obsessive search for an appropriate characterization of *Aboriginality* reflects the ambivalence of the dominant culture with regard to the indigenous population.

Aboriginal writer Marcia Langton[8] says that for her:

"...Aboriginality is not just a label to do with skin colour or the particular ideas a person caries around in his/her head...such as Aboriginal language or kinship system. 'Aboriginality' is a social thing...not a fixed thing. It is created from our histories. It arises from the intersubjectivity of black and white in a dialogue."

During the 19th century, evolutionary "scientists" defined "Aboriginality" in terms of genetic inheritance. In the 1930s and 1940s, attitudes, such as those of Tindale,[9] which were reflected in his research and writing, were grounded in eugenicist assumptions about miscegenation, and ultimately led to policies of social engineering. They under-pinned the White Australia policy, and later the policy of "assimilation." Up until May 1967, Aboriginal people were formally excluded from citizenship and were not counted in the census. Requests for constitutional amendments had been refused 24 times by public referendum. In 1993, 1.7% of the population of Australia identify as Aboriginal.

The current definition used by the Commonwealth is based on High Court opinion and is a social, rather than a racial, one. It stipulates that an Aborigine is a person who is a descendant of an indigenous inhabitant of Australia, identifies as Aboriginal, and is recognized as Aboriginal by members of the community in which he or she lives as an Aborigine. Many Aboriginal musicians I have talked to feel comfortable with this definition.

Marcia Langton[10] clarifies that, while it is possible to speak of different cultural origins and different Aboriginal societies, there are pervasive commonalities in Aboriginal life across the continent. The most important of these is the Dreaming, which was described by Stanner[11] as a "cryptic, symbolic and poetic "philosophy" in the garb of an oral literature." Central to the Dreaming, and therefore, to Aboriginal life is the performance of song.

Perhaps a useful way to conceptualize Aboriginal music is as a number of different, but overlapping styles, ranging along a continuum. In this model, the processes of adaptation and obliteration lead to new syncretized forms of musical expression, so that each style reflects the specific circumstances which influenced its production and its reproduction.

Ethnomusicologist Cath Ellis[12] suggests that Aboriginal music can be meaningfully divided into two categories, which she describes as *tribal* and *non-tribal,* and which, according to her research, are interconnected. Ellis says that:

"Modern tribal music deals with altered conditions of daily life and describes, in traditional form, contemporary patterns of behaviour...new composition is taking place within the tribal idiom in the form of contemporary Dreaming songs...(pre-contact) tribal songs have gradually disappeared with the destruction of tribal society and the removal of Aboriginal people to missions and reserves. ...Europeanized Aboriginal music has broken the tarries of tribal divisions and tended towards a pan-Australian tradition."

Ellis concluded that the introduction of a variety of European instruments such as harmonicas, accordions, banjos, acoustic and electric guitars, was critical in developing non-tribal music and in stabilizing the use of Western intervals and meter in Aboriginal music performance.

Aborigines confined on missions were taught Christian sacred music suitable for congregational singing. Ellis suggests that "Aboriginal people were comparatively receptive to sacred music because of its function as a form of ritual communication with the powers of creation." Those employed on stations came in contact with Country and Western as well as European folk music traditions. As Aborigines drifted into urban areas, mass media influenced their musical forms and currently, all modern genres can be found in Aboriginal non-tribal music.

Patterns of *tribalized* song, in the geographical area researched by Ellis,[13] are, she maintains, so distinct that it is possible to trace prehistoric patterns of migration, by mapping the diffusion of different song styles. "Traditional" Aboriginal music is normally magical, commemorative or educational. Magical and commemorative songs are performed in connection with the mythological realm of the Dreaming.

There are three main types of educational songs. The first group can be typified as primarily *ecological*. They are designed to enhance the fecundity and health of the flora and fauna on which the group depends for its subsistence, by tapping into the power of the Dreaming. These are generally referred to as *increase songs*. The second type are songs that are concerned with social control and moral codes of behaviour; and the last group are those that deal with life events. These include songs sung at birth, healing songs, love songs to attract sexual partners, and songs used in mortuary rituals. The imbrication of interlocking musical elements creates an intricate complex, which invokes the appropriate mythological associations and ensures the release of the powers, around which the entire community is structured. In the political economy of the Aboriginal culture, status and power are endowed through music. Knowledge about music is knowledge about the physics and metaphysics of survival, in other words, about life in its entirety.

Contemporary Aboriginal music, (that is, "non-tribal" music), also often referred to as *Aboriginal rock*, exhibits features which link it synchronically with world events and world music. It is also linked to ancient elements of "tribal music."

We see, for example, young Aboriginal women singers adopting the looks and panache of Tina Turner, a performer who is widely regarded in Australia as a prototype for black female musicians. We note, too, the "dreadlocks" of Aboriginal reggae fans tucked into red, black and yellow Rasta hats. And listeners are quickly alerted to Aboriginal rock music, because it invariably identifies itself with an indigenous instrument, most prominently *bilma* or *yidaki*,[14] or *didjeridoo*.[15]

Like other indigenous musics, Aboriginal music has existed mainly in the margins. It has served as a dynamic adaptation to hostile circumstances, and has helped ease the adjustments necessary to survive the changes triggered by colonization, and absorption into the global economy. In Australia, these "changes" have included total dispossession and widespread genocide. More recently, they involved the institutionalized kidnapping of children, which persisted up until the 1970s, in accordance with the federal policy of "assimilation."

Contemporary repertoires contain many songs lamenting the loss of children who were taken into state custody against the will of their natural parents, simply on the basis of their

Aboriginality. "Run Daisy, Run," by young musician Leah Purcell is a moving example, she sings:

"Run Daisy Run!
They were the last words
Her mama did say;
Run to the highlands
Run through the scrub,
Well, just run,
The white man, he's ridin' high.

...She was just a little girl
Indigenous to the land,
She was happy, she was home,
She had a family, never alone.
And then the day came,
The tribal winds had blown,
The spirits, they hid in sorrow.
The white man on horseback, he came,
To take the children away."[16]

The affective sound of rock and its mass appeal makes it a potent site for the construction of a positive cultural identity in the face of oppressive alien values. As Mckenzie Wark[17] comments, "Pop music matters because it provides a repertoire of images, words and moods through which young people interpret the world." Because Aboriginal rock is "pop music," it has the potential for creating a power base of resistance and voice for demanding change.

A 1993 first draft paper on employment strategies for Aboriginal and Torres Strait Islander musicians, issued by The Australian Music Industry, says this:

"It is clear that (popular music) can be one of the greatest weapons for Aboriginal Australians in our struggle for recognition. It can get into white Australia's lounge rooms, their cars and if utilized properly, can be instrumental in changing attitudes across the board. From a young Aboriginal's perspective, music enhances self esteem—seeing Aboriginal and Islander performers on video and on TV generates their sense of self worth and their sense of cultural comfort."

Without doubt, part of the difficulty Aboriginal musicians have getting their message into white Australian lounge rooms is the pervasive negative stereotypes which inform the way things Aboriginal are perceived and represented. A particularly virulent example is the picture of the "drunken Abo." Baneful images depicting Aborigines consuming excessive amounts of *grog*, or inebriated on alcohol bought with social security cheques, abound throughout the media. Drunkenness remains a well-worn explanation for the highly disproportionate arrest rates of Australian Aborigines. I suggest that the image of the "black drunk" constitutes an icon which stands in a binary relationship to the metaphor of the "squatter's chair." Langton,[18] proposes that the notion of the "drunken Aborigine" is a myth of origin which has existed in Australia since the beginning of settlement when Bennelong was first "tamed" with alcohol. The myth gives verity to the presumed fact of white superiority in relation to consumption of alcohol—which was (and remains) the archetypal "proof" of white superiority. Langton adds that, "the proposition being racist is not amenable to information which contradicts it."[19]

Aboriginal musicians state that drunkenness is consistently cited as a reason for not hiring them for gigs or putting them under record contracts. The "intoxicated derelict" is a convenient image which fits neatly into the sociological theory of "the culture of poverty." The logic of this theory displaces responsibility onto the Aboriginal people for the destruction of their society and the tragic living conditions which have resulted from the loss of their self-sufficiency. In this context, it is no surprise that Aboriginal musicians have struggled to find a niche in the mainstream market.

In his study of social power and musical change in Zimbabwe, John Kaemmer[20] speculated that, in a given society, it is the arrangements of power which strongly influence decisions concerning the kinds of musical events that occur. Furthermore, he proposed that it is the developing regularities in these decisions which constitute the major process in determining the nature of the resulting musical culture. These observations appear to be an accurate description of the situations in Australia.

For Aboriginal musicians, career pathways in the music industry have proved particularly elusive. Even the most cursory survey shows that this cannot be due to lack of talent. The explanation must lie, therefore, as Kaemmer suggests, in the arrangement of power.

Country singer Jimmy Little, who has been singing for forty years and has "thirty six albums and two generations of rock'n'rollers and country music fans behind him,"[21] only had his achievement recognized in 1994, when the Australian Country Music Festival in Tamworth inducted him into its Roll of Renown. Little admitted that his first reaction was, "Why me? Not yet, it's not my time... I was looking at reaching 50 years in the business, before I got this recognition."[22]

The Australian Music Industry, 1993 Employment Strategy, notes that:

"Despite the success of Yothu Yindi internationally and nationally the industry in general has been slow to pick up on the potential growth at the professional level. Archie Roach, Scrap Metal and Kev Carmody have made some in-roads into the mainstream. Many other bands who have been together for many years are hovering around the entry point."

The Torres Strait Island group, The Mills Sisters, for example, who have been touring Australia since the early sixties, have only, in 1994, released their first album, *Frangigani Land*.

"(But) if the local industry has been tardy, the international interest persists. Yothu Yindi have signed a record contract with an American company. Djaambi have spent more time touring internationally than they have in their own country. Joe Geia toured more extensively and for better money in the last six months in Europe."

The tourist industry, on the other hand, is demonstrating increasingly that it sees Aboriginal culture as a valuable commodity just waiting to be packaged for export. A front page article of the national newspaper[24] recently underlined this. It connected stark and naked indigenous beauty as a compelling tourist attraction. The article, which spilled on to page two, shows an image from a tourist advertisement shown on Tokyo television.[25] The picture is split horizontally in two. The top section shows a fresh young Japanese woman, dressed for sightseeing and wearing a broad-brimmed sun hat. Behind her, the now famous rock band, Yothu

Yindi, are performing the song *"Djapana,"* "dressed" for their stage *corroboree* in white body paint and big smiles. Below is a panoramic view of Australia's long-famous natural feature, Ayers Rock, its name printed in English beneath it. Japanese script down the left hand side spells out, *Australia Wonderland*. Linked by the references contained in the pun on rock, these images explicitly identify Australia as a wonderland by virtue of the Aboriginal "rock" which lies at its geographic heart and, by extrapolation, its cultural center. Contemporary Aboriginal rock music is shown as a natural extension of ancient Aboriginal wisdom and ritual, for which Ayers Rock[26] is cast as the literal and symbolic site. Following this advertisement, there were 15,000 enquiries from would-be Japanese tourists to Australia. The attraction lies in the notion that a visit to Australia is synonymous with ecological and spiritual awareness, and with the acknowledgment of indigenous land rights and social justice.

All of these features are fashionably expressed in the music of Yothu Yindi. The article quotes an interview with Tony Virili, the regional director of Tokyo's largest FM station, who says:

> "Until recently, people here thought Australia had a history of 200 years. Now they hear Yunupingu (Yothu Yindi's lead singer) on prime time radio talking about things that happened 40,000 years ago—the history, music and beliefs of an ancient culture—and modern issues like the environment. Yothu Yindi... represent ecological awareness and a kind of consciousness about important issues that more people here are also voicing."

For Aboriginal musicians the implications of international fame and local ignominy are truly ironic. On one hand, they are forced to gain recognition overseas before they can get exposure at home. On the other hand, touring overseas means making compromises—going commercial and commodifying their act. This implies making the music more palatable to mainstream tastes, and manipulating text and images so that the messages ultimately become defused and the music denatured.

Although Aboriginal women musicians are confronted by all these conditions, their music includes another dimension. Not only does it reflect the specific knowledge drawn from their experiences as members of the indigenous minority, but also as women, in a largely patriarchal society. These factors differentiate their music from that of their white sisters as well as from the music of their black brothers.

Aboriginal women's music includes a range of styles, from lullabies to laments to caustic protest songs. The acapella group Tiddas, has recently released two albums. The first, entitled *Inside My Kitchen*, was an important breakthrough. It was the first album released by a women's group identified as Koori.[27] The word *Tidda* is widely used by Aborigines and translates as sister. Many songs sung by the Tiddas reflect a concern for the issues of sisterhood, but come, they claim, not from the feminist movement, but from the heart.

It is interesting that this album was not produced by a record company, but by Paul Petran of the Australian Broadcasting Company. His reason was that he liked the music and wanted to play it on radio, but the record industry had not considered it of sufficient commercial interest to record, so he had to produce it himself.

The album mainly explores environmental issues and Aboriginal identity. The song "Spirit of the Winter Tree," for example, employs the image of eternal renewal, suggesting the immanent efflorescence of Aboriginal culture. Like many contemporary Aboriginal songs, it speaks of "the land of my people's Dreaming" and contains elements of lament as well as inspiration. In this song, Aboriginal culture is metaphorically likened to a deciduous tree left "naked under the winter sky," but the tree:

"Still holds her head up high;
She maintains her dignity;
For the spirit in the land,
Gives back a sense of identity, of identity.

For it is from this land that my people,
Gather their strength of identity.
For the land is our mother who'll hold us close;
Like the tree,
You take from us our children and our ways;
You try to force your values on us,
Treating us like second-rate citizens."

The song is resolved with the affirmation that the spirit is growing stronger with each new day, and that, like the tree, you'll never take our spirit away... we will... adapt and still maintain our sense of being:

"We will not wear the mask of another culture
And pretend we are somethin' else."

The analogy is that Western culture has been imposed, like a freezing winter that strips the landscape bare, but now slowly and inevitably the seasons are changing, and "the spirit in the land" will reawaken the culture.

The second album called *Sing about Life* deals with a wide variety of subjects including, love, separation, freedom, sisterhood and death in police custody.

Another singer/songwriter of note is Toni Janke. She has been called Australia's Tracy Chapman. She sings with a powerful voice and accompanies herself on acoustic guitar. With the assistance of The Australia Council for the Arts, she has just released her first album[28] of original material, under her own label. Her songs are typically emotive, and her lyrics usually have many layers of meaning. The song called "get outta my car," brings into sharp focus the gulf which separates most of the white population, from the reality of a large section of the indigenous one. The song begins:

"Have you ever seen the problem on the back step of ya door,
I bet ya never had the urgency of bein' cold and poor,
Do you even know why people die,
Have you ever cared enough to cry...

Have ya ever had to worry 'bout where you're goin',
Your fate, your life, your own existence.
Have you every complained for bein' hungry.
Did ya ever wonder why you were born who you are?"[29]

Janke sings her song as an interrogation of the white majority who stand accused for neglect. But perhaps the stridency of Janke's song is because she has trained and worked as a lawyer. On the other hand, she is not alone amongst Aboriginal women musicians in her criticism, nor is it the only theme, by any means, that she explores in her music—which as her album title suggests, comes from her heart.

White colonists arriving in Australia brought with them a culture which had as its intellectual foundation a belief in Christian evangelism and Divine Providence. They also had centuries of experience as slave traders, taking Africans, who had been captured, or sold by Arab traders, from the Gold and Ivory coasts in West Africa, or from Mombassa and Zanzibar in the east, to the American colonies. Justification for this was found in Christian dogma, which perceived the world as stratified. Whites at the top, blacks at the bottom.

Later this law was given 'scientific' credence by the *Natural Law of the Survival of the Fittest*. Austrlia's isolation, had left it with a great array of unique flora and fauna. From the evolutionist's perspective, Australia was a museum, the size of a continent, and Darwin's theories appeared to be particularly relevant.[30] Aborigines, like the other primitive species of the continent, were ranked as "living fossils which had survived, through seclusion, in this remote part of the world."[31] With the opening up of the land, however, their extinction was considered inevitable.[32] James Barnard, in his opening paper to the Australasian Association for the Advancement of Science in 1890, said:

"It has become an axiom that, following the law of evolution and survival of the fittest, the inferior races of mankind must give place to the highest type of man, and that this law is adequate to account for the gradual decline in the numbers of the aboriginal inhabitants of a country before the march of civilisation."

From the outset, civilisation brought doom to the "primitive" Aborigines. It brought disease, drink, drugs and demoralisation, and it firmly entrenched the we and they; the great divide of difference.

Marianna Torgovnick[34] has observed that:

"The West seems to need the primitive as a precondition and a supplement to its sense of self: it always creates heightened versions of the primitive as nightmare or pleasant dream...Primitives are our untamed selves, our id forces—libidinous, irrational, violent, dangerous. Primitives are mystics, in tune with nature, part of its harmonies."[35]

"Primitive" has always been, and continues to be, a consuming source of fascination to Western imaginations. Photographs and articles reproduced earlier this century, in "scientific" publications, support Torgovnick's assertions. They display an unself-conscious preoccupation with the uncontaminated and exotic beauty of "primitives," both men and women.

Women, however, are subject to far greater scrutiny from the "scientific" gaze than men. Falk[36] recently pointed out that the line between "scientific" and pornographic use of photography is not always easily drawn. He cites the case of a study by German anthropologist C. H. Stratz, *The Beauty of the Female Body* (1898), which aimed at detecting the universal *golden scale* of female beauty. In fact, Stratz simply compiled a vast archive of naked women from various exotic cultures. Falk says, "the book went through several printings, and surely not only due to 'scientific' demand."

That native women are constructed by the colonial fantasy as "sex slaves," or as solicitous (and by extension promiscuous), by virtue of their bare-breasted beauty, can amply be illustrated by reference to the literature of the period, both "factual" and fictional. Moreover, current mainstream images of black and indigenous women, are still frequently locked into this fantasy. Images which connect black women and lust, continue to be pervasive, undoubtedly because they speak to (and for) the people with power, and the men with the money to consume them.

The advertising campaign for the 1993 album by Nigerian born singer, Sade, called *Love Deluxe*, is a case in point. Sade, (who is now British) is pictured in the advertisements and on the album cover, naked to the waist with her head flung back and eyes closed. An expression of ecstatic pleasure flows across her chiselled and exquisitely featured face. The impression is extremely sculpturesque, reminiscent of highly polished ebony, inferring, perhaps that the woman as well as her craft, reflects an image which has been constructed as a work of art. Whether Sade colluded or was coerced in the creation of this representation is not clear.

However, if you are not convinced about what is being sold by the picture, then the words say it all. This is "no ordinary kind of love," indeed not, this is "Love Deluxe," so come on and "wrap yourself in it," it implores, with phallic suggestion, to its listening/buying public. Here, "yourself" (the public), is firmly constructed by insinuation as male/subject/agent, and "it," (the music), becomes the sexualised object, the "exotic" female. "Wrap yourself in it" can be read as an invitation to get it on, or rather, "put her on." Her music and her sexuality are conflated to the extent that we are no longer certain which is which, or if there is any difference.

Although Sade is not Aboriginal, the assumptions manifest in this kind of promotion affect colonised black women universally. These experiences are part of Aboriginal women's "shared past history," and their "present reality." Many Aboriginal women singers express their desire to control the way they are represented and the repertoires of a large number of singers assert their intention to resist the forces of sexism and racism, in the name of a self-determined future.

"Freedom" is the title of a song released during 1993. It was written and recorded by singer/songwriter Kev Carmody, together with the Tiddas. The chorus is a strong affirmation of intent; they sing:

> "We say freedom, freedom will come... welcome freedom
> Justice, justice will come... welcome justice
> Freedom, equality, justice are one,
> If we resist then justice and freedom will come
> Freedom will come"

The second verse is assertive:

> "My being's my spirit
> The land is my law
> The industrial savages
> Keep the oppressed so poor
> Resistance will break the stealth eagle's claw
> Peace is much more than the absence of war"

The driving rhythm of the chant, and the lyrics throughout the song are characteristic of much contemporary Aboriginal music. Part of the chant goes:

> "The manchild... the Motherearth
> The land, the law, the living sun,

> The creatures and the living plants
> All cry out as one... they chant freedom"

The final verse is filled with hope:

> "Reach out for peace
> Embrace human love
> Our global brothers and sisters
> Shed generations of blood
> Freedom will triumph... justice endure
> When we struggle united, against every war"

Ruby Hunter is an articulate and respected singer/songwriter with a rich background of experience. She recently signed a contract for the production of her first solo album called, *Thoughts Within*. This contract with Mushroom Records has been described as a "musical Mabo," because it includes a clause which allows for the specific cultural circumstances which affect Ruby as an Aboriginal woman. Ruby's songs are mainly narrative, and frequently extremely empathetic. For example, she sings, "sister, I know how you feel, sister I know you're hurtin', I know for certain how you feel, I know its real."

Sometimes her music is simultaneously sad and strongly affirmative, such as the powerful song "Black Woman."

> "Black woman, black life
> Domestic violence, what a life
> A change goina come my way."

Because Ruby is backed on this record by her well known husband, and award-winning Aboriginal singer, Archie Roach, she finds herself constantly obliged to negotiate with the media to get coverage for her own achievement. A poignant example of this is an article published in the national newspaper. The article entitled, "Ruby draws on experience to change classroom image,"[37] was accompanied by a photograph of both Archie and Ruby together. Although Archie is only briefly mentioned, (the substance of the text is really about Ruby), the photo shows Ruby standing not only behind her man, but completely out of focus.

An analysis of the music of Aboriginal women, suggests that they are keenly aware of the need to smash the stereotypes and overcome the obstacles that litter the gender/race course. A notable effort was the first National Aboriginal and Torres Strait Islander Women's Music Festival, held in Sydney, in December 1992, which aimed to bring musicians from around the country into touch with each other.

The International Year for the World's Indigenous People, a democratic South Africa and burgeoning interest in the music of Timbuktu (that is, in music at the "end of the western world") is opening space for the message in Aboriginal women's music to be broadcast. Listening to the music, it becomes increasingly clear that it is an art as well as a skillfully fashioned craft. It is also the raft by which Aboriginal women are venturing to navigate the rough white waters of the mainstream, and it is the lifesaver which rescues the present so that a future can be restored to the past.

Endnotes

[1] *Bran Nue Dae* is the title of a musical by Aboriginal writer Jimmy Chi and members of the Aboriginal rock band, Kuckles, all of whom live in Broome, a town in northwestern Australia. It was first performed in 1990 at The Festival of Perth, and has since toured the Eastern states of Australia, enjoying wide critical acclaim. The story lampoons dearly held notions of racial identity with an amusing twist of irony, and plenty of hope for a bright future.

[2] A broad brimmed hat made from rabbit fur felt, worn by drovers (cowboys) in outback Australia and currently very fashionable.

[3] A full-length coat made from "oilskin" and worn earlier by whalers operating in the Southern Ocean. This coat, like the *Akubra* is experiencing a revival. Both are symbols of the tough pioneering life, and infer "true masculinity."

[4] The Building Bridges Association was a cultural support project for the National Coalition of Aboriginal Organizations, which was started in late 1987. In 1989, a double compilation album was released, through CBS Records, called *"Building Bridges—Australia Has A Black History,"* featuring many bands including, No Fixed Address, Coloured Stone and Yothu Yindi.

[5] John Castles (1992); in his article "Tjungaringanyi: Aboriginal rock" says..."white encouragement of the category of 'Aboriginal music' as a reconnection with and expression of a prior Aboriginal community continues to hold a dangerously essentializing potential. Aboriginal musicians must steer a course between the cliffs of essentialization on one side and assimilation on the other." in Hayward, P. (ed.) *From Pop to Punk to Postmodernism.*

[6] For a succinct review of this event, see Streit, J. (1993) "With Open Eyes: Aboriginal Women's Music" in *Perfect Beat* Vol. 1, No. 3, July 1993.

[7] Edited by Anne Rutherford (1988), Dangaroo Press—Kunapipi.

[8] Langton, M. (1993), *"Well, I heard it on the radio and I saw it on the television..."* pp. 31, Australian Film Commission.

[9] Tindale, N. and George, B. (1939) *The Austrailian Aborigines,* republished in 1982 for The National Museum of Victoria Council.

[10] Langton, M. (1981) "Urbanizing Aborigines: The Social Scientists' Great Deception" in *Social Alternatives* pp. 21, Vol. 2. No. 2.

[11] Langon, M. (1981) Op. Cit., pp. 21.

[12] Ellis, C., Brunton, M., and Barwick, L., (1988) "From The Dreaming Rock to Reggae Rock", in McCredie, A. (ed.) *From Colonel Light into the Footlights: The Performing Arts in South Australia from 1836 to the Present,* pp, 151-172.

[13] The Pitjantjatjara lands of northern South Australia.

[14] These are idiophones, or clapsticks, used as a percussive accompaniment to the usual range of rock instruments. Seed rattles and rasps are also included sometimes.

[15] An aerophone, between one and two meters in length, and made from a Eucalyptus branch hollowed out by termites.

[16] This is a small section of the whole song, which was obtained directly from the artist, and is due to be released in the future.

[17] Wark, M. (1993) "Women of Musical Substance" in *The Australian* national daily newspaper, 7/4/93.

[18] Langton, M. (1993), "Rum, Seduction and Death: 'Aboriginality' and alcohol" in *Oceania* 63, pp. 195–205.

[19] Langton, M. (1993), Op. Cit., pp. 199.

[20] Kaemmer, J. (1989), "Social Power and Musical Change Among the Shona," in *Ethnomusicology* Vol. 33 No. 1, Winter 1989, pp. 31.
[21] Vercoe, P., "Renown at last for a little bit of country" in *The Australian*, national daily newspaper, 24/1/94.
[22] Vercoe, P., (1994), op. cit.
[23] Australian Music Industry, *Aboriginal and Torres Strait Islander Employment Strategy 1993*, pp. 10.
[24] Carruthers, F., (1993) "Aboriginal Rock Brings Back Japanese Tourists," in *The Australian*, national daily newspaper, 30/4/93.
[25] The 30 second TV commercial which cost $7,000,000, was screened 700 times over a 3 week period in Tokyo. It was supported by newspaper and magazine advertisements. The venture was a response to market research which indicated that the Japanese are curious about Australian Aborigines.
[26] Now more correctly called Uluru.
[27] Koori identifies Aborigines from the south of the continent. In the northeast, Aborigines call themselves Murris.
[28] An album called *hearts speak out*, released by Toni Janke Productions at the end of 1993.
[29] Transcribed from Toni Janke's CD, *hearts speak out*, 1993.
[30] Australia's northern capital was named in honour of Charles Darwin.
[31] McGregor, R. (1993) "A Doomed Race: A Scientific Axiom of the Late Nineteenth Century", in *Australian Journal of Politics and History*, Vol. 39 No. 1 1993 pp. 14-22.
[32] Refer to G.W. Stocking, (1968), *Race, Culture, and Evolution,* The Free Press, New York, pp. 110-32.
[33] Quoted by Russell Mc Gregor, 1990, op. cit.
[34] See Torgovnick, M. (1990), *Gone Primitive, Savage Intellects, Modern Lives,* University of Chicago Press, Chicago.
[35] Torgovnick, M., 1990, op. cit., pp. 8-9 and 244-246.
[36] See the article by Pasi Falk, "The Representation of Presence: Outlining the Anti-aesthetics of Pornography" in *Theory, Culture and Society,* Vol. 1-0, 1993, pp.1-42.
[37] By Fiona Carruthers, in *The Australian*, 19/1/93.

Bibliography

Australian Music Industry, *Aboriginal and Torres Strait Islander Employment Strategy* 1993, First Draft.
Carruthers, F. (1993) "Ruby draws on experience to change classroom image" in *The Australian*, 19/1/93.
—(1993) "Aboriginal rock brings back Japanese tourists" in *The Australian*, 30/4/93.
Castles, J. (1992) "Tjungaringanyi: Aboriginal rock," in P. Hayward, (ed.) *From Pop to Punk to Postmodernism: Popular Music and Australian Culture from the 1960's to the 1990's*, pp. 25-39, Allen and Unwin, NSW.
Ellis, C. J., Brunton, M., and Barwick, L. M. (1988) "From the Dreaming Rock to Reggae Rock" in McCredie, A. (ed.) *From Colonel Light to the Footlights: The Performing Arts in South Australia from 1836 to the Present*, pp. 151–172, Pagel Books, Norwood SA.
Falk, P. (1993) "The Representation of Presence: Outlining the Anti-aesthetics of Pornography," in *Theory, Culture, and Society,* pp. 1–42, Sage, London.
Kaemmer, J. E. (1989) "Social Power and Music Change Among the Shona," in *Ethnomusicology,*

Winter 1989 pp. 31-45.
Langton, M. (1981) "Urbanising Aborigines: The Social Scientists' Great Deception" in *Social Alternatives* Vol. 2 No. 1 pp. 16-22.
—(1993) "Rum, seduction, and death: 'Aboriginality' and alcohol" in *Oceania* 63, pp. 195-206.
—(1993) *"Well, I heard it on the radio and I saw it on the television...,"* The Australian Film Commission.
Morrissey, P. (1988) "Restoring a Future to the Past," in A. Rutherford, (ed.) *Aboriginal Culture Today,* pp. 10–15 Dangaroo Press, Sydney.
Streit, J. (1993) "With Open Eyes": Aboriginal Women's Music—A Review" in *Perfect Beat: The Journal of Research Into Coontemporary Music and Popular Culture,* Vol. 1 No. 3, July 1993, pp. 86-90.
Stocking, G.W. (1968) *Race Culture and Evolution,* The Free Press, New York, pp. 110–32.
Tindale, N. and George, B. (1939) *The Australian Aborigines,* republished in 1982 for The National Museum of Victoria Council.
Torgovnick, M., (1990) *Gone Primitive, Savage Intellects, Modern Lives,* University of Chicago Press, Chicago.
Vercoe, P. "Renown at last for a little bit of country" in *The Australian* 24/1/94.
Wark, M. (1993) "Women of Musical Substance" in *The Australian*, a national daily newspaper.
Waugh, D. (1993) "Back to the Future" in *Time Off,* 12/5/93.

Discography

Alice Haines, *One Law,* 1993 Alice Haines, Australia Council for the Arts.
Kev Carmody, with the Tiddas and Mixed Relations, *Freedom,* 1993, Festival Records.
Leah Purcell, "Run Daisy Run," unreleased at time of writing.
Mixed Relations, *Love,* 1993, Polygram music.
Ruby Hunter, *Thoughts Within,* 1994, Mushroom Records, Melbourne.
The Mills Sisters, *Frangipani Land,* 1993, New Market Music, Melbourne.
The Tiddas, *Inside My Kitchen,* 1992, *Sing about Life,* 1993, Phonogram Records.
Toni Janke, *hearts speak out,* 1993, Toni Janke Productions.

photos: Tripp Mikich

Paalam Uncle Sam: An Interview with the members of Musika and Musicians for Peace

(Spring '91)

Tripp Mikich

In the spring of 1991, I traveled to the Philippines as the guest of the Philippine Educational Theater Association (PETA) and BUGKOS (National Center for People's Art and Literature), an inter-island network of progressive cultural organizations. I had worked with PETA several years before on a good will tour of the US following the collapse of the Marcos' dictatorship, and was now traveling to the Philippines as a long-time friend, and great admirer of PETA's theater work and sophisticated development of cultural organizing as a tool for social change and political struggle. I traveled also as an Executive Board member and representative of the Alliance for Cultural Democracy, a U.S.-based organization of cultural activists and organizers.

At the time this interview was conducted, the Aquino government had already passed the high point of its popularity. Having risen to power on the waves of the "People Power" movement that had toppled the Marcos dictatorship, Aquino and her government were coming under increasing criticism and scrutiny for a deteriorating human rights record, a failure to curb military abuses and end the civil war, a failure to implement serious economic and social reforms, especially true land reform, and Aquino's personal failure to keep her promises and take a strong stand against the continuing presence of the U.S. bases.

On the other side, the Left was still struggling to regain mass support lost in its failure to join the snap elections that had set the stage for Marcos' overthrow. While an important organizational factor in the mass street demonstrations of People Power, this failure had been a serious blow to the left's broad support. Following Aquino's rise to power, there had been a brief truce and hope that negotiations between the new government and the National Democratic Front and New People's Army might bring an end to the long civil conflict. But this period was rapidly followed by new assassinations of key student and labor leaders, increased disappearances and vigilante attacks against activists, and increased military activity known as the "total war" strategy used against NPA forces and civilian villagers in various regions, notably bombing attacks against "suspected NPA strongholds" in the Marag Valley in northern Luzon and in Mindanao. In 1989, peasants marching for land reform were fired upon by Aquino's soldiers near the presidential palace and several were killed. Known as the Mendiola Massacre, it marked the end to any hope of peace or negotiation.

It was against this backdrop that I met with members of MUSIKA, an inter-island organization of musicians and cultural organizers created to develop, record and promote progressive and people's music, and MUSICIANS FOR PEACE (MFP), a newly formed organization of working musicians, created to support musicians around their own economic and social issues as well as develop musicians' support for other sectoral (women, workers, peasants, students, etc.) struggles.

This interview took place in March of 1991 in a small office shared by several organizations in a suburb of Manila. The following is an edited version of that interview. In some cases, where speakers could not be identified from the recorded materials, I have used MFP (Musicians for Peace) as a generalization. Otherwise, all material is directly quoted.

Participants included:

Noel Cabangon, in charge of production, marketing and promotion programs of MUSIKA, and member of BUKLOD, a popular progressive duet whose Bob Marley-inspired song "Tumindi Ka" or "Stand Up," could be heard at rallies, concerts, and meetings throughout the country while I was there.

Jess Santiago of MUSIKA, poet, singer and songwriter, whose beautifully moving song "Halina" became one of the anthems of the anti-Marcos years and has been translated into several other languages around the world.

Pendong Aban Jr., well-known music figure, former member of ASIN and founder of ANG GRUPO PENDONG, an ethnic-fusion and rock band.

Chickoy Pura, elected chairman of MFP, and lead singer and founder of the JERKS, a punk influenced progressive rock band.

Lito Crisostomo, also of ANG GRUPO PENDONG.

Herber Bartolome, musician and full-time singer-songwriter, who helped popularize the "Pinoy rock" genre.

Rom C. Dongeto, the other member of BUKLOD, and also of MUSIKA.

Angela Veras, educational and training officer of Musicians for Peace (MFP) and bass player of the JERKS.

Joe Villabella, PR officer of external affairs for MFP, member of ANG GRUPO PENDONG.

TM: I would like to find out what progressive music is in the Philippines. What progressive music means, both in terms of groups like Musika and MFP and what you're trying to do, but also, what kinds of messages, what kinds of themes, and what kind of elements are going into the music.

HERBERT: You cannot learn that from simply having this kind of discussion. You should learn it by attending some cultural activities.

TM: I hope to do that.

JESS: Musika came into being as a response to a need for a more systematic and coordinated way of conducting music activities in the country, especially during the late 1970s when martial law was still in place. Some progressive musicians came together and decided to organize Musika, with the purpose of helping promote "People's Music" and coordinating the activities of other similar musicians and cultural workers around the country. From 1979, Musika served as an organization of musicians and an institution at the same time. Later, in 1986, we decided to make it more of a resources/services institution, which means we try to support all activities concerning "People's Music."

In essence, we try to have various music groups become more active in campaigns for our people's struggles. We also do some documentation, publication, and research, and of course, we try to establish links with similar groups in other countries.

We help organize music groups, facilitate and initiate symposia and lectures, hold music writing workshops and conferences, and recently we've come out with a publication called NOTES. We hoped that it could be a quarterly journal, but because of financial restraints, we could only make it an occasional publication. We also went into tape production, and have recorded a collection of songs from the Visayas, which is in the central Philippines, and also a tape of songs from the Cordillera, an indigenous mountain region in the northern part of Luzon, because part of Musika's work is to gather and collect songs from all over the country and propagate those songs. We used to run a very small and modest four track recording studio which took us ten years of work to set up, but before we could get it into full operation, it burned, along with all the materials we had, including audio, print and video documentation of all our activities of the past 10 years, and our library of rare albums and records.

TM: When you talk about "People's Music," what are you referring to?

JESS: Well, generally speaking, "People's Music" refers to the kind of music that's supposed to serve the people's interests. That's a very general definition, because we believe that "People's Music" is what cannot be defined exactly. We don't want to spend too much effort trying to define what "People's Music" is because we would rather participate in the creation of it. Perhaps later the people themselves will say whether this kind of music we are trying to create can be considered their music. As far as Musika is concerned, we believe that music should serve the interests of the people and that music production and creation should generate people's participation.

TM: Is it primarily because of its content that particular music is defined as "People's Music?" Is indigenous music considered part of the "People's Music" movement in the Philippines?

JESS: Yes, of course. Very much so.

MFP: "People's music," as it grows, develops social consciousness and becomes the social voice for the people. The lyrics are very political, and they are a way of awakening the people to the truth of whatever is happening today. The songs help that, but also the music in itself, the pure music without the lyrics, is a sort of musical heritage. Like the music of Pendong Aban who plays with Grupo Pendong—the kind of music that is part of our musical heritage and is something we hold very dear. We combine that with lyrics that are part of the social conditions, the time in which the music is played, and the combination gives a very strong, very powerful voice for the social consciousness of the people.

HEBER: I want to qualify some things, because when you say "People's Music," it doesn't mean the form of music is from the people. Mostly the music in the Philippines we copied from foreign music, except for some groups that really try very hard to promote "our own," We say "our own" because it's very old, like the musical influences of Pendong's group, or Joey Ayala and other groups that use ethnic and indigenous music and instruments combined with modern forms. But most music that you hear here in our country, especially on the radio, is foreign music. The listeners are brainwashed by this kind of music. Most Filipino radio listeners think this is popular because it's always being played. But actually it's being paid for with payola from the recording companies. Even so, personally, I choose to use this kind of music, pop and rock, as a form. Because only through this music can you get that kind of listener's attention.

You only use the music as a form or vehicle to put in the content that you'd like to communicate. I started during the late sixties. I was more into rock-influenced kind of music, because it's this music that youth listens to. So we put Filipino lyrics to it and call it "pinoy rock," Filipino rock music.

I cannot say it is 100% Filipino music I use. I am very frank and honest telling you that I deliberately use influences of foreign music in my own songs for the purpose of getting the attention of the youth who are into this kind of music. I believe I can only step forward from where we are standing right now. I cannot go back to searching for what is the true Filipino music when even the definition of that is debatable. And I cannot go forward into avant garde music where my audience would be very few. So I select what is the music being listened to by the majority of youth and the majority of Filipino people. Then I use that as a vehicle to put my message across. In the process, when I put my own language, my own dialect, my native tongue into this kind of music, the influence of foreign music becomes lesser because the sound will be dominated by our language, which is our very own culture. The sound of the word is music. That's the very root of music. The melody or beat that we're forming are just parts or elements of the song. You're just using them to draw attention, like the elements of an electric guitar. The words we use are very powerful. When the people hear Tagalog, one of the dialects spoken here, especially when you talk about their problems, about what they are, who they are, when you try to situate them in your song, then they listen. Then you must be careful that what you say is true, and that it can really help them.

TM: What is Musicians For Peace (MFP) and what is it doing?

CHICKOY: MFP is a loose coalition of musicians. We have so many problems regarding the plight of musicians, that's why we've decided to form an organization. Our first priority is to go around the city for awhile and make some survey of all these musicians who are playing in what we call beer houses, what we call club musicians, because they're always on the losing end. You know, the ones who are being exploited, they're the most underrated musicians here. We'd like to get those people together and maybe we can come up with some programs regarding their plight.

TM: It sounds almost like what the Musician's Union in the U.S. tries to do.

CHICKOY: Yeah, but we also have programs like workshops, because we have to really come up with music that has something to do with our culture, so our programs are all about the cultural contribution of the musician, especially here in the Philippines.

TM: What do the workshops try to do?

CHICKOY: We have so many poets here who write in Tagalog [majority dialect spoken in the Philippines]. So we try to get all the musicians, especially those musicians who are in the clubs, together with these poets, because the musicians in the clubs do adaptations of American music, rock and roll. I think we have to really guide the musicians, especially those in the clubs, and let them know we have our own culture.

TM: Has this effort been successful?

CHICKOY: Yes, we have tried it, and I think there's so much promise in it. I think there's a resurgence of Filipino music lately. It's a good sign.

NOEL: I think the re-establishment of MFP is a manifestation that the musicians are now aware of their role and their participation in society.

TM: When was MFP founded?

CHICKOY: About a month ago.

NOEL: It actually came about after a series of workshops with Musika and discussions about the plight of musicians and their present situation. Basically, musicians who are working in folk or pub houses are not really developed in terms of their skills. So when we had these discussions regarding the plight of musicians, the musicians themselves decided to put up an organization of musicians, since there's no organization that's actually existing that's really concerned with these issues. And not only the plight of musicians, but we also emphasize skills and the development of their craft.

TM: What is the difference between Musika and MFP?

JESS: Musika is an institution. A lot of musicians want to get involved with Musika, but we cannot take them in because we are supposed to be a center. But these musicians still want to do something, because they are getting more interested in improving their craft and getting more involved with the political struggles of our people. So they decided to organize themselves through MFP. MFP is one of the groups that Musika services.

The other reasons for creating MFP include pressing national issues that have to be addressed. These are environmental issues, human rights, and the economic crisis. There has to be an organization of musicians that can stand and address these issues. And also the issue of the dominance of foreign music on the airwaves. That's what Heber was talking about earlier. About 90% of radio programming that Metro Manila is bombarded with day in and day out is foreign music, especially American Top 40, and some European mix.

TM: Let's talk about the music. About how you're using it and the forms that you're using.

PENDONG: Grupo Pendong's music is a mixture of ethnic sounds of the Philippines and popular rock and roll. We use foreign forms, and we also use our own music. We fuse this with ethnic instruments. But our use of ethnic instruments is very minimal. We realize, as Heber said, that these are not very popular forms yet, at least as far as the kind of audience we are trying to reach now is concerned. Because of years of bombardment by foreign songs, our youth has been brainwashed by Western music. So we go one step at a time and use what is available, what is popular, and at the same time we like to introduce— reintroduce I mean— the indigenous music of our land to our youth and to our people. They have been robbed of this heritage because of the influence of Western music, so we are trying to reintroduce it, to let them be aware that there is such a kind of music and it can be used very creatively, not only to the minority, but also to the majority, of people.

This indigenous music is very popular amongst the tribes which use it, that it is a part of. But over the generations that music has almost been killed. In fact, it's ironic, because many people when they hear this indigenous music, especially the contemporary youth, they think it's Chinese, or it sounds Greek to them. In fact, they laugh at it. That's how far the western influence has crept into our culture, to the point where we laugh at our own and our own becomes alien to us. At the same time we are also realistic. We cannot be purely ethnic in our music because our main purpose is to disseminate our message of hope and our message for peace through our lyrics.

TM: What about the other groups here?

ALL: Jerks!!!

CHICKOY: The Jerks actually started as a punk rock group and still is. We used to play together in Olongapo, near the American bases. The band has been together for 11 years. It started in 1979. The only difference now is we're using our native tongue. We used to play a lot of Rolling Stones, the Clash, the Doors and all that, but we had to have a means of communicating with our brothers and sisters. We used to do our original songs in English, but we can only reach a very small percentage of people that way. We got isolated in the big cities. But now when we go to the provinces, you know, they just open their mouths and look at us. And sometimes, especially when you're playing at breakneck speed, rock and roll and all that, there's no way to be understood by the people in the provinces. So I think the best way is to really have a transition from English to native tongue. Not just to bring the message through, but culturally I think that's the best way.

When we started playing, we were following the sentiment of British punk, destruction and all that. But it doesn't relate to us. The situation is completely different here than in England or anywhere. We have enough trouble here. So I think what we are after now is peace. We have to have some peace here in our society. So that's what we're doing. We contribute some of our opinions and what we think about the society. Most important is that we have to tell the truth about what is going on in our country. So we are very careful about this because a lot of people are listening to us every time we play at clubs. Those people are watching you, listening to you, and they believe you when you say something. So I think we owe it to them to tell them the truth.

TM: Give me an example of what one of your songs would talk about.

CHICKOY: Well, I wrote this song about the colonial mentality. It's called *"Reclamo."* It's kind of a reggae song. *Reclamo* means complain. It deals with something most of our people are having trouble with. Most of them, they complain, and then they're thinking they'd rather be somewhere else than here. And so all their lives they go to school, they build their careers, and then think about migrating to the United States or Europe or somewhere else. But they could have done much better here. They could have helped in shaping a better society. *"Reclamo"* is all about that. The "Brain Drain."

TM: I noticed in Patatag's music, because I confess that Patatag is the only music group from the Philippines I'd been exposed to before coming here on this visit. On their first album, released around 1986 or 87, a lot of their songs were heavily influenced by the Latin American "New Song" Movement, especially the songs of Victor Jara, which I was amazed to hear sung in Tagalog on that album. In a more recent album of theirs, *Batang Clark* (referring to Clark Air Force Base) that sound has changed. There is less of the Latin American "New Song" Movement influence and a more unique, and I would guess, more directly Filipino sound. It seems from our discussion that this change has been happening for a lot of Filipino musicians and music groups. What's happened in the last few years that's begun to make such a noticeable change in the music that's being created? What's caused this change to take place, both in the country, and in the musicians and musical field?

NOEL: Maybe you should ask Jess, because he's translated a few Latin American songs. Maybe he can talk of the influences of Latin American music on the struggles of the Filipino people.

JESS: While it's true that some songs, some progressive or nationalistic songs from the Philippines were inspired by some Latin American musicians, it doesn't mean that those songs have become "Latin Americanized." Rather, it has grown out of our concern, our desire to learn from other people's struggles. And it's the spirit of international solidarity. We believe that the struggles of the Latin American people are also our struggle here, in the same way that the problems faced by Filipinos are problems that have a direct or indirect connection with the problems of the Latin American people.

But in terms of musical form, it shouldn't come as a surprise because the Philippines was under Spain for centuries, so the Spanish influence on our culture, especially on our music, has been there for centuries.

Now, what you said, you observed some changes in terms of musical forms. I think one of the reasons for these changes is that the number of musicians that are socially conscious has grown because of the growth and development of the people's struggle in the Philippines since the Marcos years. More and more musicians have gotten involved politically. The more musicians you have writing songs about our people, the more varying exposures and different tastes in terms of musical forms. So those who are into rock finally wrote songs about issues that are confronted by our people and they used rock. Those who are into indigenous music, they started writing songs using indigenous elements. I think another reason for this of course is the growing number of venues for discussions on music and its relation to our struggle, so that more experimentation is being done now.

TM: What other musical influences have had an impact on the development of "People's Music" in the Philippines?

JESS: Before and during the period marital law was imposed, the kind of progressive music that we had here was mainly martial in tune, sloganeering in content. It was because our music then, our nationalist music, was very much influenced by the Chinese revolution. And also because the national democratic movement in the Philippines was still in its early years. So naturally it had to look up to some models. The martial music that was being produced then was a necessity because there was a need to propagate and educate about ideas. Ideas like imperialism, feudalism, bureaucratic capitalism, were all new words, new terms, new concepts as far as our people were concerned. So martial songs played a big role in propagating these ideas, these concepts. And then when martial law was declared, all the mass rallies and demonstrations where you could once hear these songs being sung or played; martial law put an end to all that. There was a long lull. You could hardly hear any songs that you could call progressive. Except for the songs that were written by groups and musicians like Heber and his group Banyuhay, and Asin. That was the mid-seventies already. So that period in our history forced our musicians, not only our songwriters, but poets as well and other artists, to be more inventive, to be more creative to circumvent the very restrictive laws during that time. Songs came about that were very poetic. Instead of sloganeering the songwriters used poetry, used metaphors. And the people were hungry for songs that talked about the concrete experiences that they met with every day, like "salvaging" (assassination or disappearance) or summary executions of people, and the strikes and militarization and all that.

Slowly, more and more songwriters started writing songs about these realities. Because mass rallies and mass actions were still prohibited, concerts, mainly on school campuses, became the logical venue for this type of music. I think groups like Banyuhay and Asin played a very big role in bringing these types of songs to the various parts of the country, because they organized concert tours during the mid-seventies featuring these kinds of songs. They had a big advantage then because they were already very popular. Their popularity was also a gauge of the dirth of material that talked about the realities of the time. Of course, they could not be too radical in their lyrics. They had to compromise to reach more and more people.

It was then that poets became songwriters. I myself had started out writing poetry. Then finally I thought I might as well write songs also, because I thought there was a great need for more songs about the realities, about the experiences of our people which were not being carried by newspapers or radio or TV.

So then these people started writing songs and playing these songs in concerts and union meetings, on picket lines, and for intermission numbers. You can imagine how these songs—you may call them underground or whatever—these nationalist songs, these progressive songs, became popular even without the help of radio or TV. Not even a recording! But because people wanted these kinds of songs, they needed these kinds of songs, they would go to concerts, bring along a small tape recorder, tape the concert, and try to learn the songs later when they got home. After learning the songs, then they would play them themselves and teach the songs to other people. So people's songs, or nationalist music in the Philippines, went through a whole process. Later, when even the military could not do anything about it anymore, we were able to hold concerts of just progressive songs and musicians. So we started out by just singing songs about social concerns, moral issues, not even political yet. From there we were able to sing songs about even the most politically charged issues.

TM: The history you've just given is very good. What changes have occurred recently? What effect has the end of the Marcos dictatorship and Aquino and the "People Power" movement had on "People's Music" in the Philippines?

JESS: I would say that "People's Music" in the Philippines is still addressing the very same issues that we were addressing when Marcos was still around. As far as themes, as far as topics are concerned, not much has changed. If there were changes that happened, they were changes for the worse.

TM: And in terms of "People's Music"?

JESS: In terms of production, for instance, cassette tape production of songs, there's been greater activity during this past five years of Cory's term. And that is no thanks to Cory. People had been waiting for this type of song. So now when this kind of music is being produced, of course, people still want to have these recordings. But just as it was during the time of Marcos, these songs are not being played on the radio. These songs are still being played during concerts, during rallies, mass actions, and all that. Some of the most progressive groups during the Marcos time have been able to record their songs, and even sell the records to some established recording companies.

HEBER: If [you ask whether] the "Peoples Power" or government of Cory Aquino has helped or not helped Philippine music, if your question is regarding progressive music, that's one answer. But for Filipino music in general, I think the government of Marcos helped better than Cory Aquino. During Marcos' time, Marcos had an annual pop music competition, and most of the Filipino composers tried to participate, although only a few could actually realize it. And this competition was annual for nine years. Cory Aquino's government is not too helpful in promoting Filipino culture in general. But the music in general was being promoted during the Marcos years because they prompted radio stations to play at least four Filipino songs every half hour. There's still that law, but it's now being violated by the radio stations. But what has happened during Aquino's government is that we are more free to group ourselves and discuss these things and also more tapes by progressive groups have come out.

CHICKOY: Although we have relatively more freedom to organize and to record our songs and to do those sorts of things, the problem still remains that they're not being played on the air. What use is a song if it's not being played? My perception is that these radio stations, even the record companies, are practicing self censorship. They're afraid of the political implications of airing these kinds of songs, although they record them.

HEBER: But that's at least one step forward beyond no recordings at all. I think what Chickoy was trying to point out is that the recording companies here, the big recording companies, their main interest is to earn money. They're businessmen and don't care about our culture. Why don't they promote our songs? Because it would only do to promote that album if they can make money. But since they are also afraid of being criticized by the military or the government, it might be perilous to their agreements, and they would rather promote other songs than these.

JESS: Don't get confused by this growing number of tape productions. That is no thanks to the government. Credit should go to the musicians themselves and the people's organizations who have financed these productions.

NOEL: Since we've been doing a lot of talking, maybe we should hear some songs, a sample of the "People's Music."

At this point, a guitar was passed around and each of the groups and musicians played songs from their repertoires. Later that evening, we all met at a local club, where the Musika and MFP musicians, as well as others not at our interview, grouped and regrouped themselves into various musical combinations, singing anthem-like workers' hymns and hard rock songs about "this is not the USA" and "Paalam Uncle Sam" (Good-bye Uncle Sam) to a crowded, hot, smoky, dance-between-the-tables crowd. In the coming weeks, I would cross paths again with these new friends as they sang at Earth Day rallies in Manila, played clubs in various parts of town, sang off the back of a truck in the city plaza of Baguio, and played till the early hours of the morning in the center of a tiny village deep in the mountains of the Cordillera.

Throughout the Philippines I continued to hear their songs, sung by the children at a special summer camp for internal refugee children and "victims of the armed conflict" at the Children's Rehabilitation Center in Manila, at a center for street children called Bahay Taluyan in Manila's "red light" district, at a union hall in Davao City in Mindanao where I listened to a group of worker-musicians from a striking electrical plant rehearse songs for an upcoming Mayday rally, and by students in the back of a jeepney on their way to a tribal gathering in the north.

In my last week in the Philippines, I would travel two days by jeepney with Grupo Pendong and others from Musika, MFP and PETA to a remote Cordillera village where we spent three days with hundreds of tribal and indigenous people, listening to their songs and *ganzas* (brass gongs), sharing their dances, and listening to their tales of struggle, each of us in turn offering music or dance or poems from our own cultures in solidarity.

While in the Philippines, there was not a day I spent nor a place I went in which the music of these friends, this "peoples' music," did not frame, brighten, expand, or color my experience. To these friends, these cultural workers, these artists, I give my thanks and deepest gratitude for sharing a small part of their culture, their people, their friendship, their music, with me. I only hope this serves as a small thanks in return.

Left to Right: Edward Blackwell, Royal Hartigan, Freeman Kwadzo Donkor, Abraham Kobena Adzenyah. Photo: Robert Lancefield (originally appeared in Percussive Notes, *April 1993)*

Playing Other People's Music: An Interview with Royal Hartigan
(21 Sept. 1994)
Fred Wei-han Ho

Royal Hartigan did his doctoral work in world music at Wesleyan University in the Eighties, and he is currently finishing his first book, *West African Rhythms for Drum Set* (Drummers Collective, Inc./CPP Belwin, Miami). He performs as a percussionist with his own group, with Fred Ho and the Afro Asian Music Ensemble, and with Juba.

FH: What led you into studying and playing world music percussion traditions?

RH: I found many of these traditions to have very complex, highly refined musical elements—more sophisticated than European art music. Not only are these traditions and rhythms more complex, but they are more emotionally intense and involving. Roland Wiggins [a professor of African American music] talks about three levels of making music: 1. The Technical—the nuts and bolts; 2. The Grammatic—how the technical elements are put together in composition and improvisation; 3. The Semiotic—the spirit behind the music. The last is ultimately the most important. I've been overwhelmed by the spirit and feeling of Ghanaian West African drumming, Javanese *gamelan, solkattu* and the vocal rhythms of South India. These traditions and rhythms reached deeply inside me. They were kindled when I was a Peace Corps volunteer in the Philippines in the late–1960s.

To me, American culture feels like a wasteland, except for small pockets, such as the African American church. In another culture, like the Philippines, the people open their whole soul to you the minute you're with them. It's a completely different way of life. Yeah, I play and love [the music of] Beethoven, Stravinsky, etc., but it does not affect me in the deep way that other traditions do. Every sound, every movement, every note...everything and every single aspect I heard in music from Africa, India and Java filled me with emotion, feeling and connection, which is quite a feat since I'm not from any of those cultures. It influenced me so much that it drew me to the music. I guess you can say the music is a means by which I'm contacting something deep in those cultures and in myself. So it's not just that I want to play a lot of hot licks on an African drum.

FH: You're a white Irish American. How can white American artists have a non-exploitative, but comradely relationship with various world traditions? Is that possible, and how?

RH: There are people who will say that you cannot. That if you are not from that culture, then you can never, ever understand that culture enough to pick up an instrument, nor do you have the right to do that. As soon as you even try to do that, no matter how well-intentioned

331

you are, you're a colonialist. And some say that's true of the drumset in the African American tradition for a non-African American person. That might even be true. I don't know. I'm not God. It could be true. I hope that it isn't. I tend to think that it may not be. I think it's not what your skin color or ethnicity is, but what you really do, objectively. This is not only my opinion, but the opinion of people who are masters in those cultures, such as Max Roach, Archie Shepp, Abraham Adzenyah and Freeman Donkor, who have welcomed me. That's part of their culture. There have been many instances where they've been open and given the music to others. Paradoxically, that's one of the reasons why [the music] gets ripped off so easily because the people from those cultures are very open and giving. I do think there's a way to go about it, at least for me, that I've worked out personally.

Firstly, I believe in never doing music of any culture until I've studied it for many years, and, if possible, have lived with the people for a long time. Given the limitations for me being from a low-income, blue collar, working class background, I don't have the money to go and do that in all instances, but I've found ways to do that, to live with the people as much as possible, to try to understand their cultures as much as possible, and to feel it. You need to do more than understand it, because you can understand it and still rip it off. You must feel it, commit to it and feel connected to it, and feel like you'd give yourself up for it if you had to.

Secondly, you must demonstrate your commitment by working your heart out to play it with integrity and with those players. The goal is to be accepted by those players, playing with integrity inside a village of that culture. It's not whether you can play it correctly, but whether you play it with integrity, and see if the people accept you and tell you so. When they tell you that, you can feel good about what you're doing.

Thirdly, when you want to perform that music, I would suggest that you don't do it unless you've performed in an ensemble of that culture, led by a master of that culture. You should seek permission from a master to use any elements of that culture, and when you use them, use them in a traditional way. For me, even though I may be able to technically, I don't feel comfortable with playing traditional cultural elements—whether it be melodies or rhythms or using instruments—in a way that isn't very close to the tradition. There's something I feel about the instruments themselves. Their sounds have to do with a way of life, and I'd be somehow misusing, misdoing what that instrument represents by not playing it on its own terms in its own cultural setting. If there is some variation, say, from a traditional rhythm, I would do it in the way a traditional musician would do it, based on my long years of studying what a traditional musician would do.

Finally, there is the issue of compensation. Anytime you perform with compensation, you have to think: Well, do I have a right to that compensation and should I at least share it with somebody from that culture or give it all to that person from that culture and let them decide how much I should get. In America, when we get into compensation, we get into copyright—property ownership. Then you have to say well, whose is it? If it's the traditional rhythms and elements, music and scales of that culture; it is theirs. In an ideal world, we wouldn't have to say that. Maybe in a perfect paradise, everybody's music would be everybody else's, and we could all share freely. But unfortunately, this world ain't a perfect paradise and we have to think about ways to show respect to cultures that have specific time and space.

FH: How do you acknowledge ownership and how do you distribute compensation?

RH: Ownership should be acknowledged verbally, whenever possible. If there's a published book, it's got to be done in the book. On a record, it's done on the record cover and notes. It's cited everytime you see something. As to a piece of music you're transcribing, most of these cultures are oral and it's inappropriate to write the music down. but if you're doing it for an educational purpose, in a book, then you need to cite that. If there's a copyright involved, I'd give the copyright to the people from the culture. Now, we get into a grey area when it's a drumset adaptation of something. In a situation where the drumset isn't from that culture—say, a West African or Javanese culture—but one is using an element learned from that culture, then I think you have to split it 50/50. Since it's the music and content from that culture that is being transformed, in my own way, for example, I'm then some kind of part-author in it, so 50/50 seems logical to me. But if it's strictly traditional, then I feel it has got to go all to the person from that culture, and let the person decide.

FH: Aside from publication and recording, what about performance?

RH: Let's say if I was to be in a concert of music from the Philippines, or to organize one, we couldn't have the concert without at least having a Filipino master artist leading an ensemble. That'd be the bare minimum. Ideally, it'd be a master leading the ensemble of Philippine musicians and maybe I could play in it. I would never represent Philippines musical culture without a master artist being there. It seems foolish when you think about it: how could anyone do that if there wasn't somebody from that culture. Any public performance of a world tradition is a cultural representation, since music is an expression of culture.

FH: What about when you play your drumset in a jazz band and it's not about portraying an explicitly traditional music, but is your own creative playing drawing from different traditions, i.e., the creative usage of world music.

RH: There's a gamut of ways you can do that. You can play very close to the original, even using indigenous instruments, but it's not in that context. Let's look at a piece we do in the Afro Asian Music Ensemble, "An Bayan Ko." I'm playing a traditional piece, *"Solog,"* with permission, but it's obvious since I'm only playing the *kulintang* [8 pitched gongs], that it's not in it's traditional context because there'd be three or four other instruments with people playing along with the *kulintang* (e.g., there'd be an *agung* [deep gong], a *babandir* [time keeping gong], and *dabakan* [wood-carved drum]). There's no question that when I play, it's not a traditional set up, but it's a traditional piece played completely in the traditional way. We must acknowledge the master verbally and in the program. And if there was a lot of money made at that concert, I feel like I should give most of it to the person that taught me. Unfortunately, we never have any concerts that make big money. We usually only make enough money to cover my expenses, so it's not feasible to return that.

The next level from totally authentic tradition to authentic tradition without the context would be using a traditional instrument in a non-traditional way, which I don't believe in doing, so we can eliminate that. As I see it, to just playing anything I want to on that instrument is disrespectful and wrong, and I don't feel comfortable doing it.

The next step would be using the traditional elements but not the instrument, which would be, say, the rhythms, but I'd put them on drumset. In this case, I think I should still acknowledge, and if there were big money, compensate, the master artist(s) to some extent.

FH: What about creative usage where boundaries are blurred or merged, e.g., taking West African rhythms and playing them on Chinese percussion, or vice versa—the more experimental usage where it no longer becomes explicitly associated with one particular tradition, as it could be a merger of different kinds of influences. If you studied with a master and paid them for educating you, isn't that sufficient?

RH: First, I don't think education in those other cultures is what we think of it in the West. Education isn't simply that knowledge is a commodifiable object that can pass from one person to another. I think education in the traditional cultures is an imparting of a way of life that isn't just a transfer. It's a commitment between both people to investigate the culture and way of life being taught—it's a life-long process like with the *gurus* and *sushiyas* of South India. You can't think of it as a transfer of a finite amount of things. It's an opening, really, of a relationship that involves a mutual commitment and responsibility on the part of the learner to respect and show his/her love of that culture and teacher by only doing what is right in terms of how the students see the culture. In the Philippines example, if Danongan Kalanduyan shows me some rhythms, even if I've adapted them to drumset in such a creative way that only someone like him would know that it's a Philippines rhythm, I still think that should get mentioned and compensated. That's because it's something that still comes from tradition. Even if it's not obvious to other people—it's true and obvious to me, and that's the only person that matters in this regard. Compensation must go to the people and/or to the teacher. If the teacher has died, then you find a way to give it to the people, or another custodian of that culture. For example, Freeman Donkor passed away, so in terms of the book I'm currently writing, I will give his share to his family. If there was no family, or no one person to deal with, I'd find a way to donate it to the village where he lived in Tsiame, Ghana, or a nearby village, so it goes to the Ewe people where he was born. It's not clearcut, but there is always a way you can do that. If it gets to be a lot of money, then the more the responsibility.

As to the second part of your question, about taking a highly creative and open approach to, say, Chinese opera instruments but playing an African rhythm on them—merging traditions. I frankly have a problem with that. I feel it disrespects the Chinese instruments and West African instruments to do that. I have no reasonable explanation, I can't tell you why. The only thing that I could tell you would sound unbelievable. So I'll tell you. I believe most instruments of the world have a spirit, a repository of reality that by its very sound is a representation of a people's way of life. As such, it cannot be altered; it has to be respected for what it does, what it sounds like and is, as if it were a person, because that's the way the people of that culture think about it. If masters of two cultures wanted to do [cross-cultural experimentation], then that's a different story. But especially since I'm not of those cultures, I feel particularly that's some kind of special thing that cannot be violated, which it would be if I were to use it in a manner that while it might be well-intentioned, was not in its traditional way of operation.

FH: Yet through time, various instruments have travelled as a result of human travels and had different kinds of contacts with new forms and new things that have evolved simply because of artists who wanted to try different and new things. For example, the drumset is not an African instrument. It is particular to African America. Does that mean a white American could never do something different on the drumset that is not within the African American tradition?

RH: Boy, that's a big question. Let me give you an example. Tajikistani musicians used North Indian styles on *dumbek* when they heard the *tabla* players of North India. They wanted to make their drumming much more complicated and intense. So now the Tajikistani *dirbigali* drum is played much more virtuosically then it used to be. That change was instigated by the people who were the masters of drumming in that culture, so therefore they have the right to do whatever they want. But I'm not a master artist in any culture, I'm not a member of the cultures that I play instruments from, so therefore I feel hesitant to do those kinds of innovations.

FH: But what about African Americans who took a French instrument, the saxophone, and they changed it?

RH: Theoretically, that's not wrong. But remember: an instrument is often tied to a sacred ritual and a way of life. Not all instruments are. You can't make a clear case—you could argue it, but I don't think it's true—for people to regard the saxophone in the same way as Javanese *agung gong*, Chinese opera gongs, Philippine *kulintang*, and West African *apentemma* and *atumpan*, which are considered as sacred by the people in those respective cultures. The saxophone does not have the same importance to the way of life of, and ritual significance for, Europeans. I don't think the saxophone, created in Europe, ever had that. Similarly, I don't think tympani has it. Interestingly, the drumset only has it among certain people. It doesn't have it universally. Take the drumset. Although its major developers have been people in the African American tradition and, in my opinion, its highest artful usage has been in the African American tradition, it wasn't originally only an African American instrument. It was assembled by people of all backgrounds that played in stage shows, primarily black and white. Never in the drumset's history was it acknowledged as exclusive property of one culture. In my opinion, the progression in the drumset styles of playing and its deep spiritual sophistication and growth have been almost universally due to the creativity and genius of African American master drummers. That doesn't mean there haven't been great Euro-American drummers that have contributed. No. Yet, the great majority of innovation, deepening and spiritualizing of the drumset has been done by African Americans. You'd have to say it is an American instrument whose greatest and deepest innovations have come from African Americans. They have spiritualized the drumset, and the sax, for that matter. I'm an American, so I have a right to play it and innovate on it.

FH: What about French people? Do they have a right to play on and innovate upon an American instrument?

RH: Yes, except for certain very restricted areas in the African American tradition. The drumset doesn't have the same kind of ritualistic and deep connotation about a way of life that would be very specific, say, like an *apentemma* of West Africa. The drumset, I hasten to add, is considered by myself, a non-African American person, to be a very sacred and spiritual instrument, but maybe not in as completely literal a way as you find in an *apentemma* and *atumpan* among the Ashanti people of Ghana, West Africa. Yet there is in the drumset a real personification. I hear many drummers talk about their instruments as if they were a person's kids. I feel that way sometimes myself. Even though it's not as specifically and intensely as ritualistic and sacred an instrument, it has come to be transformed into a much more special instrument than say if it were to be played by European symphony players. It really does have a significance, but not the same kind as you would find in many Asian, African, and indigenous cultures. [The drumset] is not quite as unsusceptible to being changed. Since it's an American instrument, and not as ritualistic, then I think it's open to anybody to deal with it. America is a culture that says about itself that there isn't any deep, ancient significance to be found in it, at least not yet. So since American culture is open by its nature, then its instruments are open too.

FH: We both oppose cultural imperialism, the outright theft and misusage of musical cultures, but the world is changing rapidly, with far greater cultural contacts happening at an explosive rate. Prior to two centuries ago, you didn't have globalized contact between various areas of the world. Now you have access and contact throughout the world. Your point is to do that with authenticity and integrity. But what is an allowable creative license and artistic experimentation? Is it wrong to blend Philippine rhythms and jazz? We've discussed the problems, but let's address the potential vastness that seemed to attract you to understand world music and to be fluent in many musical languages to enhance your artistry and creative vision.

RH: I don't think there's a problem, for example, of taking an indigenous Philippines rhythm and playing it on the ride cymbal. My Filipino teachers have said, go right ahead. It's not a problem for them. The only exception being ritualistic music, for example, Ewe cult music—I'd never touch that, unless I was playing in an Ewe group in Ghana and they asked me, and gave me permission, to play with them. I'd never play those rhythms outside of that context. I believe it'd be wrong to do so. If it's a rhythm or melody, as long as you've gotten permission to use it, it's OK, but, that doesn't mean you can do anything you want with it. It think it goes farther than that. I think you have to use it in a way that gives respect and integrity to the tradition. If I was to use [sings an African song], I'd have to use it in a way that was right musically, logically and spiritually. I'd never use that song in a pop thing, in a commercial, in any way that wasn't 110% serious, committed black American music. It'd have to make sense musically, technically, spiritually, emotionally, text-wise, instrumentally, and in terms of occasion, performers, and medium of performance. I'd never use it in writing or playing studio-generated elevator music or airport music. You couldn't put it in there. So on all these levels, it's got to be right. I know people are afraid in the last decade of the 20th century to talk about right and wrong, but I think there is stuff that's objectively right and wrong.

FH: You're teaching world percussion traditions, trying to spread what you got from it all to others. Where do you see this going? Do your students share your internationalist views and outlook?

RH: Musical reality mirrors social, economic and political realities of the world. Each culture is not the same. Each culture has its own unique thing that is deep and sacred and spiritual and enriching for human life. To be denied these things is criminal.

Music departments and presenters need to show the music of the world equally if we are to survive in this world by understanding different peoples. We need to respect, be open to, care for and understand other people and feel their way of life. We can't do that unless we live it, go to another culture and live in it. That's the first step. Live with the people at their level—their material poverty but their spiritual wealth. Music is one of the greatest ways to connect with people, because it's the repository of knowledge. The music, dance, and song is the repository of a people's culture, history, genealogy, way of life, belief system, expression, social interaction, communication, love... all of it. You'll never do it the way they do, but to participate in their music, dance and song brings you a real deep appreciation of their culture. Once you feel these things, you'll become open and sensitized and at least respect other cultures and maybe play in a number of them with integrity. To have an understanding of the world, I think this is the most important way to do it. It should be the function of media and educational institutions to do that on every level—public school to university. It's a necessity. But what do we see: music departments that are 90% European, and if you're lucky, you may get 5% of what is called Jazz/African American music. And, if any, 1-2% world music. We need to totally reverse this situation. In every department, there needs to be a number of traditions of which European music might just be one. There might even be departments with no European music. Unless this happens, we won't have cultural equity and the musically expressive equity necessary for world equity. Freedom and equality mean nothing unless we have economic, social, political, cultural and spiritual freedom and equality. You can't get that by lip service, but only through living and doing it. Unless we have institutions and governments that reflect this, the world will remain a big plantation.

Students and other people are hungry for world music. If only schools, the media and big institutions did this, people would be more open, intelligent and wanting to take part is these traditions. That's the answer.

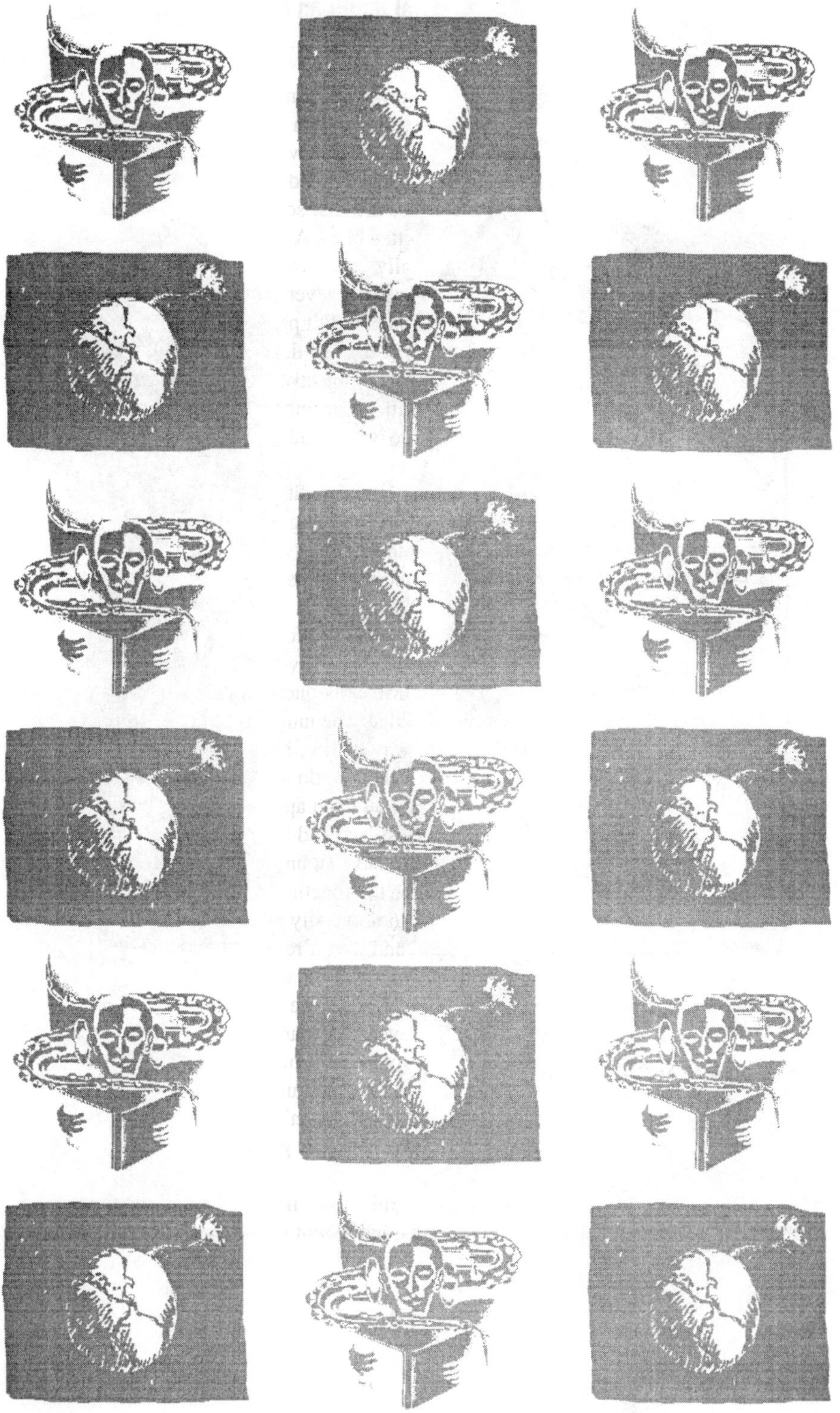

Michael Schwartz

Singing Other Peoples' Songs

Anthony Seeger

When my wife, Judy, and I were doing field research among the Suyá Indians in Mato Grosso, Brazil, we all sang together a lot. Between 1970 and 1982, the Suyá learned many of our songs—just as they had learned the songs of more than 10 "foreign" cultures before we appeared—and we sang theirs. They modified the words of "Michael Row the Boat Ashore" to "Wai kum kraw...," which means "Something's coming that stinks." We probably did equal injustice to some of their texts, but they said that we sang pretty well, for non-Suyá.

I recorded their music on the best reel-to-reel tape recorder I could take to the field. In the 1980s cassette tape recorders were everywhere, and the Suyá taped our singing just as we had previously recorded theirs. I traded blank tapes for their recordings of their ceremonies and collected more in one month than I could have in eight months of my own recording. For Judy and me, singing was one of the few things we could do that the Suyá appreciated as at all skillful and enjoyable; for them, learning our music was the continuation of a traditional pattern of learning new musical forms from monsters and captives that began in mythical times. And it was fun for all of us.

When the Suyá suggested I make a commercial recording of their music, however, we had other concerns. First, we needed to decide what other people should not be permitted to hear—and therefore what should not go on the recording. Second, we had to try to protect the Suyás community rights as artists and composers. Addressing the first concern was easy: they decided what should be excluded and I made selections and sequences from the rest that would make sense to a non-Indian, Brazilian audience. I reviewed the entire project with them before publication. The second concern, however, was not so easy to settle. On the back of the LP *Música Indigena: A Arte Vocal Dos Suyá ("Indian Music: The Vocal Art of the Suyá")* (Tacape 007, São João del Rei, 1982), we published the following in block capital letters.

THIS RECORDING WAS MADE WITH THE KNOWLEDGE AND APPROVAL OF THE SUYÁ. THE SELECTIONS ARE ARTISTIC PRODUCTIONS OF THIS SOCIETY. ROYALTIES WILL BE FORWARDED TO THE COMMUNITY, AND MUST BE PAID. THE UNAUTHORIZED USE OF THESE RECORDINGS IS PROHIBITED NOT ONLY BY LAW, BUT BY THE MORAL FORCE AGAINST THE EXPLOITATION OF THESE ARTISTS. (Free translation)

It didn't work. Although I arranged for generous royalties to be forwarded to the Suyá, we did not control the further use of the recordings. The Suyá chief was staying in our house in Rio de Janeiro when we heard, to our immense surprise, a Suyá song played behind an advertisement for Rio educational television. I looked at him with considerable concern, and he grinned and said, "It's beautiful, everyone is hearing our music." I was relieved, and also glad that all the Suyá had agreed on what went on the recording. They would not have been amused by certain songs receiving a similarly wide hearing. The next time I heard Suyá music on television was not so benign, however. But they didn't see the program; I didn't make a copy of it; I had no money for an entertainment lawyer (neither did the record company); and we didn't pursue it. Had we explored the matter, we would have found little help in existing copyright law.

A New Awareness

Ten years later, I am directing Smithsonian/Folkways Records at the Smithsonian Institution in Washington, DC. I produce dozens of recordings each year, many of them non-Western music, and I control the use rights of more than 2000 recordings. I am concerned about musical rights from at least five slightly different perspectives: as a musician, as a researcher, as a coproducer with an indigenous society of a commercial cultural product, as a record company director who has to match cost to income within the current structure of the entertainment industry, and as a member of a copyright committee of the International Council for Traditional Music (ICTM), which is preparing a document that gives a cross-cultural perspective on music ownership to counteract some of the international law being considered in this area. These different perspectives can lead to very different positions on music ownership. Each of these perspectives represents the view of a large number of individuals.

As a musician, I think we need to recognize that most musicians take musical ideas and transform them. Because almost every performance is a creative event, I worry about the effects of existing laws that inhibit live performances and restrict the exchange of musical ideas. There is a distinct possibility that more laws will further inhibit live, creative performances.

As a researcher, I am concerned about the perception that "someone is getting rich on our music" and the effect it has had on music research. It can be very difficult to study a community's music today because individuals and groups, sometimes with justification, are suspicious of strangers carrying tape recorders. Because graduate students are insufficiently aware of the ethical issues their recordings may raise, they do not obtain the kinds of information and permissions in the field that will enable their recordings to be used afterward. In fact, very little money is made on most research-based "ethnographic" recordings; they generally sell relatively few copies and usually have to be subsidized to be published at all. Inflated expectations based on news items about the multimillion-dollar contracts of Michael and Janet Jackson, however, can make even legitimate royalties seem like a deceit.

As a coproducer of a recording with the Suyá Indians, I wonder at the freedom with which Brazilian television has used this group's recordings as background music—a policy that would be rigorously policed if the music were performed by, say, the Beatles, but which cannot be policed when it is "only" performed by the best living Suyá musicians.

As the director of a small record company, I am sensitive to these ethical issues; but I also have to produce recordings that can compete in price with other recordings in a given market. Small record companies go under or get absorbed by larger ones all the time; there isn't much room for financial error. This means that I cannot allocate much more money to artists and songwriters than other companies do if I want to make enough from the recording to pay for the production of the next one. It means I do not have the time or staff to individually research the rights to every song on every recording; instead I rely on the opinions of the artist, compiler, or publishing companies. It means that whatever laws are put into effect must be reasonably simple for me to understand and they need to have concrete mechanisms to make it easy for me to obey them.

As a member of the International Council for Traditional Music's committee on musical copyright, I hope that the United States and Europe will not impose, without some modification, their individualized, popular-music-fueled concepts of music ownership on the rest of the world through international conventions. We need to examine the shortcomings of existing systems, especially with respect to the rights of communities and vernacular artists to benefit from any commercial exploitation of their arts.

Ideal laws will not protect musicians or ensure compliance. What we need is a new awareness of the issues of musical ownership and the ethics of intercultural music use—something akin to the ecological awareness that encourages individuals to change their attitudes and provide concrete means through which they can change their daily practices. Recycling, for example, works best where people are not only convinced it is a good idea but are also provided with convenient ways to put it into action. the same kind of awareness and convenience needs to be created for intellectual and cultural property.

Who Owns—And Who Controls—A Song?

The music business today is a large, complex, transnational, and highly profitable industry. Its procedures tend to serve the interests of popular music, established professional musicians, and its own structure. Policies benefit artists most when they are represented by aggressive lawyers; little is given away that is not demanded. A recent book, *Hit Men: Power Brokers and Fast Money Inside the Music Business* (Dannen 1990), presents a fairly grim but not unrealistic picture of the industry.

In capitalist societies, attempts to extend the definition and market approach applied to tangible property in all spheres of life are a logical extension of the economic system. Here we should expect music to become "property." The incredibly complex US copyright law is a logical extension of a number of features of the entire society. Yet capitalist societies are not the only ones where musical rights can be clearly defined. In many indigenous societies individuals, social groups, and communities may also have clearly defined rights and obligations to music and oratory. Among the Suyá, for example, a song belongs not to its "composer" but to the person who sings it aloud for the first time. Entire ceremonies are controlled by one or the other moiety, which must be consulted and freely give permission to the other moiety to begin a performance.

US music copyright is based on concepts of individual creation and ownership that ignore community rights to music. "Traditional" folk songs, music controlled by a moiety, and most music from indigenous societies are considered to be "in the public domain" because they are older compositions. No songwriters' royalties are usually paid on these songs. The current music copyright system only protects recent compositions; a song may be copyrighted for the life of the composer plus 50 years. The publishing company that owns the Beatles' "Yesterday," for example, receives nearly six cents for every recording sold that anyone else performs the song on, plus money from radio play, plus money every time it is used in films, videos, and on Muzak tapes. The Suyá, by contrast, receive nothing for any of those uses of their *"Agachi Ngere."*

The real issue is not the music industry in itself, but the economic and cultural exploitation of one group by another group or individual. A publishing company probably doesn't care whether the Suyá sing "Something's coming that stinks" to a copyrighted melody on the banks of the Suyá Missu River in Mato Grosso. But under existing copyright law, there is nothing illegal about taking a piece of "traditional" music, modifying it slightly, performing it, and copyrighting it. When music is owned by indigenous people, it is seen as "public domain." If it becomes popular in its "mainstream" form, though, it suddenly becomes "individual property." The song brings a steady income to the person who individualized it, not to the people from whose culture it is derived. Many Jamaicans feel that Harry Belafonte "robbed" them by copyrighting and earning revenue from arrangements of traditional songs. In spite of some efforts to the contrary there certainly have been injustices (see Wallis and Malm 1984).

Even when there are good intentions, royalties are not always easy to distribute. Sometimes the problems are internal, sometimes they are related to international affairs, and sometimes they are complicated by unorthodox claims of authorship. I was unable, for example, to set up a direct account for Suyá royalties because they had no formal legal identity and therefore no income tax number; as a result I have had to bear the expense of income tax on all the royalties I forwarded to them. The lack of US ties to Cuba made normal publishing payments to the original author of *"Guantanamera"* impossible for some time. *"Wimoweh"* (also popular under the title "The Lion Sleeps Tonight") was copyrighted not by the composer but by a South African record company (a fairly common state of affairs in music publishing). My uncle, Pete Seeger, went to a considerable effort to locate the composer's widow in order to pass to her, rather than the South African record company that copyrighted the song, some of the proceeds from her late husband's hit—something he felt was important, but was not required by law. In these cases, the US copyright law functioned and the publishing companies collected money; but it was difficult to make payments to the appropriate people even when desired. These kinds of problems tremendously complicate rectifying the ethical problems faced by all parts of the music industry; with respect to the music of indigenous peoples, these problems are multiplied one hundred fold.

Changing the Laws

Artists' sensitivity to these issues is increasing. They are giving much more attention to crediting traditional artists, even though the laws themselves have not changed. While I know of no payments to the Juruna Indians by the Brazilian popular singer Caetano Veloso, who used a Juruna flute melody on one of his albums in the 1970s, Milton Nascimento worked together with the Union of Indian Nations and the National Rubber Tappers Council, and his album *Taxi* is part of a campaign to support the Alliance of Peoples of the Forest. The copyright law has also been used for charitable purposes. Realizing that the song "We Shall Overcome" would probably be claimed by some "arranger," members of the civil rights movement decided to copyright the song and had the proceeds go to the Highlander Folk School, which had been the center of civil rights organizing. Because the song was a slight rewrite from an old hymn, "I Will Overcome," no individual felt slighted and the considerable income has benefited the school.

In most countries there is no legal recourse for traditional societies upset about the use of their music. A few countries have special laws protecting all music. The United States is among the most reluctant to consider changes in the copyright law which would give broad rights to intellectual property for "traditional" rather than individually created culture. Currently, the United Nations Educational, Scientific, and Cultural Organization (UNESCO) and several other international agencies are formulating proposals for a more equitable definition of intellectual property and the nature of its authorship, ownership, and control (see Posey). The emerging recommended legislation will probably be similar to that covering visual designs and other art forms.

Some interesting success stories have stemmed from imaginative responses to perceived injustices. The Music Performance Trust Fund (MPTF) was set up to support live musical performances: record companies contribute a certain percentage to it from the sales of their recordings (which were perceived as a threat to live performance when the "jukebox" replaced the barroom musician), and the MPTF funds pay musicians who give free public concerts. The Rhythm and Blues Foundation, in Washington, DC, was formed to provide support for aging rhythm & blues musicians. Major record companies have donated considerable sums to the foundation, which uses the money to support older African American musicians who benefited little from their popularity while their record companies made millions from their recordings. Certain musicians have taken steps to ensure that local communities receive some profits from their music. There is no reason why the Suyá Indians cannot both protect the parts of their repertory they wish to keep to themselves and reap the same rewards as other musicians from the commercialization of those parts they wish to share.

Musical rights are complex, and protecting musicians and indigenous people from exploitation will not be a simple task. The current copyright law is complex and ill serves many constituencies; but changes in it will threaten business interests, and they certainly will fight broader interpretations. Increased protection will require a considerable realignment of power and responsibilities.

A Plan of Action

The solution to the problems of music ownership is not simply a broader set of laws, but a real rethinking of the issues, a realignment of control over materials from companies to individuals and communities, and the establishment of practical mechanisms for achieving what we may believe to be desirable. Here are some observations.

1. New conventions must respect local traditions of music ownership. If a "traditional" piece is considered to be owned by a group or individual, that ownership must be translatable into some kind of international rights over the sound. Different classes of such rights need to be clearly defined in order to establish quickly the appropriate use.

2. Any new conventions must be more than a set of laws. We need easy and effective ways of ensuring that payments can be made and will reach the appropriate parties. Simply writing ideal laws will not assist recording companies and other media to direct funds to the appropriate place.

3. While certain nations would like to collect the royalties from indigenous music themselves, in many cases this will not be a satisfactory situation for those communities. Indigenous groups and local ethnic communities often find themselves in opposition to the central government. Whatever collection system is set up should assign rights on a local level rather than as "national patrimony" to be absorbed by a state.

4. Musicians, researchers, and record producers all need to be more aware of the rights

and sensitivities of the peoples whose music they adapt, research, and produce. This is happening slowly. I am constantly surprised at how many people have simply not thought through ethical and legal issues in their musical activities.

5. The general public as always, can prod individuals and companies to act more responsibly by asking them about their stand on the issue and protesting what they consider to be inadequate recognition of the rights of indigenous peoples to their art.

Endnotes

Dannen, F. *Hit Men: Power Brokers and Fast Money Inside the Music Business.* (New York: Times Books, 1990).

Posey, D. "Effecting International Change," *Cultural Survival Quarterly,* Vol 15, No. 3, Summer 1991.

Shemel, S. *This Business of Music.* (New York: Billboard Books, 1990).

Wallis, R. and K. Malm *Big Sounds From Small Peoples: The Music Industry in Small Countries.* (New York: Pendragon Press, 1984).

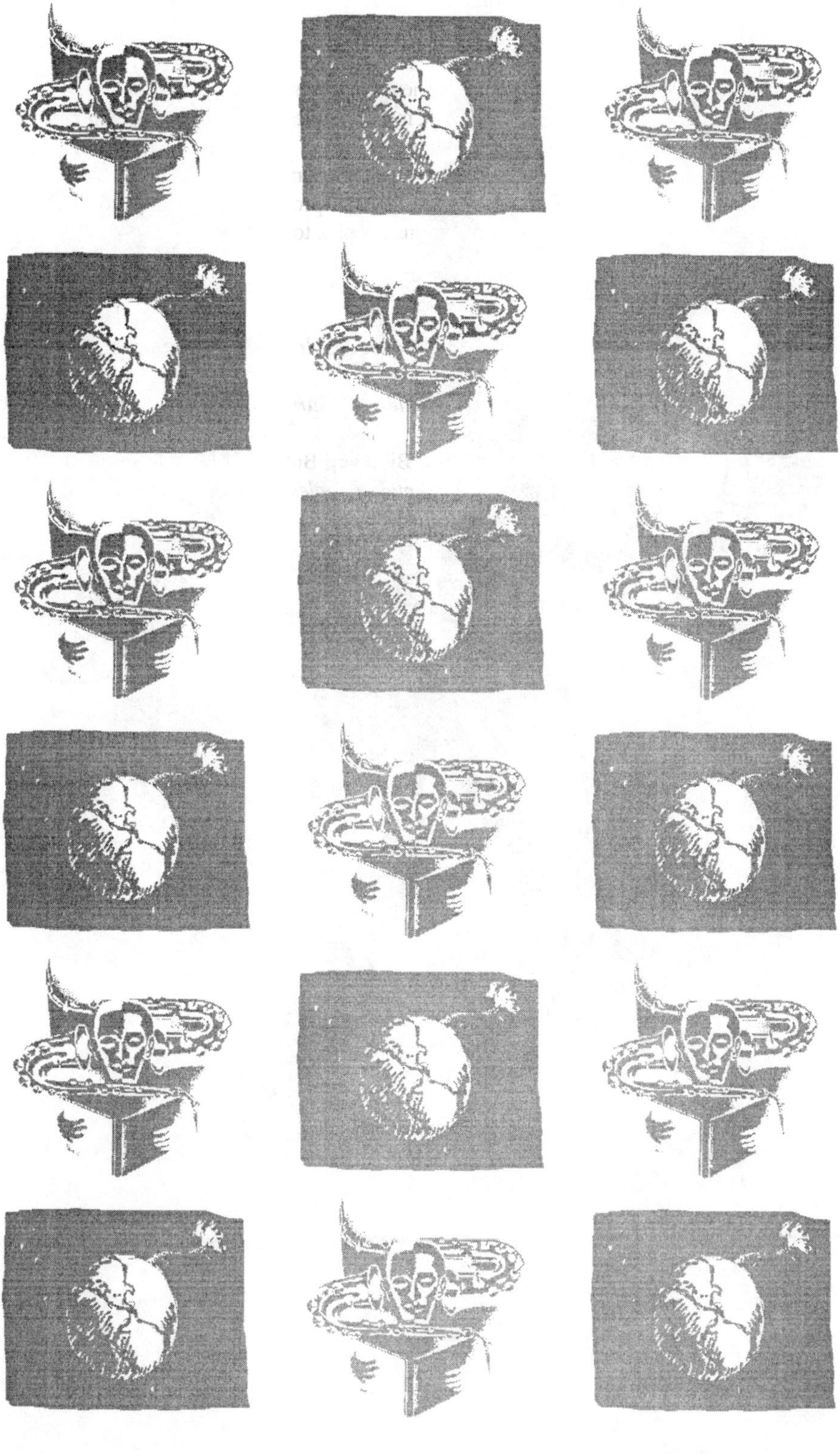

Isiah Dodd

The Contributors

Miekal And & Elizabeth Was along with their son, Liaizon Wakest, divide their life between growing gourds and ethnobotanical rarities, building a time machine, designing a functional low cost bioshelter and preparing for the return of the millennium. They also spend day after day directing Dreamtime Village, a permaculture, hypermedia eco-village in southwest Wisconsin and *Xeroxial Endarchy*, an umbrella arts organization cultivating real-life adventures on the edges of media. For books, cassettes, computer disks and visiting Dreamtime contact them at Rt.1, Box 131, LaFarge, WI 54639.

Robin Balliger has a B.A. in music from the University of California at Berkeley and is currently a graduate student in anthropology at Stanford, focusing on the politics of music in the Caribbean. Prior to graduate school she was a professional musician, composer and recording engineer. As an electric bass player, she has been involved in oppositional music from punk to Afro-beat. Ms. Balliger is also a co-founder of Komotion International, an artists' collective and performance space in San Francisco.

Hakim Bey has returned to India to work as an unpaid negotiator for the Naga Liberation Front in Bhogavati. He left behind a CD of recordings with ambient music by Bill Laswell (Axiom), and a book on Immediatism (AK Press, Edinburgh/San Francisco, 1994). He can be reached (maybe) through Autonomedia.

Jean Binta Breeze is a reggae dub poet. Born in Jamaica, she attended the Jamaica School of Drama with such dub poetry luminaries as the late Mikey Smith and Oku Onuora, and went on to record with Mutabaruka. Currently, she lives in London where she works with dub poet/activist Linton Kwesi Johnson, and has begun a new phase of her career by performing as a jazz vocalist.

Herbert Brün was born in 1918 in Berlin. He left Germany for Palestine and then left Israel in 1955 for France. He roamed Europe from 1956 to 1962. He has lived since 1963 in the USA teaching and composing Music, Prose, Poetry, Plays and Projects. His Projects generate Groups of People. The Groups of People compose Music, Prose, Poetry, Plays, and Projects.

Darryl Cherney is a singin'/songwritin' EarthFirster! who knows that guitarist rhymes with forest. He has been known to record with Judi Bari (on *They Sure Don't Make Hippies Like They Used To!* and *Timber!*). While organizing together against the lumber barons during Redwood Summer in 1990, their car was bombed by the forces of law and order who, then, in a cowardly FBI attempt to disrupt, destroy and discredit EarthFirst!, framed them for bombing themselves.

Chris Cutler is the author of the book *File Under Popular* and numerous articles. He is also a composer, librettist, improviser, lecturer, editor of the *ReR Quarterly* and founder of the inde-

The Contributors

pendent distribution network Recommended Records and the experimental music label ReR. As a musician, he plays drums and electronics on musical projects including: Henry Cow, Art Bears, News From Babel, Cassiber, Pere Ubu, Oh Moscow, and collaborations with such artists as The Residents, Kalahari Surfers, Aqsak Maboul, Jon Rose, Fred Frith, Lutz Glandien, Peter Blegvad, Hail, and the (EC) Nudes.

Mark Enslin studied composition, acting, cybernetics, bassoon, group interaction, protest, and teaching, while completing degrees in music composition at the University of Illinois. He is a member of the Performers' Workshop Ensemble.

Tom Frank edits *The Baffler* magazine, a journal of abrasive cultural critique and lucid, flowing prose. He has also written a long study of American advertising in the 1960s.

Carol Genetti is an interdisiplinary Chicago artist working with the experimental potential of the human voice. She has appeared with various performance art troupes and musical combos in Minneapolis and Chicago. Presently, she is working with Red Moon Puppet Theater in Chicago, composing a new performance work for shadow puppets and original musics, and will soon publish her first book of cartoons entitled *Zen Boobism*. She also leaves her cookies laying around wherever she wants.

Andrew Goodwin is a teacher, writer and musician. He is the author of *Dancing in the Distraction Factory: Music Television and Popular Culture* (University of Minnesota Press, 1992) and co-editor of *On Record: Rock, Pop and the Written Word* (Pantheon, 1990) and *Sound and Vision: The Music Video Reader* (Routledge, 1993). He has written for *Screen, Cultural Studies, Critical Quarterly* and *Socialist Review*, in addition to writing popular criticism for the *New Statesman, Society Sight and Sound,* and the *East Bay Express, the Chicago Reader* and *San Francisco Weekly*. He is associate professor of communications at the University of San Francisco and occasional host of KUSF's "USF Today."

Joe Gore is a recording artist, and the Senior Editor of *Guitar Player* magazine, an international periodical devoted to all things guitaristic. He maintains a workaholic's performance and session schedule. He holds an M.A. in Music Composition from the University of California at Berkeley.

Amendant Hardiker: Dreamtime traveler & effigy mound dweller in mysterious Wisconsin.

Fred Wei-han Ho (formerly Houn) is a revolutionary socialist Chinese American baritone saxophonist, composer/arranger, leader of the Afro Asian Music Ensemble and the Monkey Orchestra (formerly Journey Beyond the West Orchestra), and a long-time activist in the Asian American Movement. He has five recordings to date as a leader: including *Tomorrow is Now!* (Soul Note Records 1985, featuring the Afro Asian Music Ensemble); *We Refuse to be Used and Abused* (Soul Note, 1989, featuring the AAME); *Bamboo that Snaps Back* (Finnadar/Atlantic, 1986, featuring the Asian American Art Ensemble); *A Song for Manong* (AsianImprov Records, 1988, featuring the Asian American Art Ensemble and San Francisco Kulintang Arts); and *The Underground Railroad to My Heart* (Soul Note, 1994, featuring the AAME).

The Contributors

James Koehnline is a renowned (starving) artist, 'zinester, Moorish Orthodox activist, and long-time Autonomedia collective member. He lives in Seattle with wife Andrea.

Tuli Kupferberg is a singing cartoonist, founding member of the sempiternal Fugs, and all around nice guy. His current project is a book of collages called: *Great Moments in the History of Journalism.*

Peter Manuel is an ethnomusicologist specializing in musics of India and the Caribbean who teaches at John Jay College (CUNY). His recent books include *Cassette Culture: Popular Music and Technology in North India* and *Popular Musics of the Non-Western World: An Introductory Survey.*

Scott Marshall is a practicing visual artist, writer, graphic designer, audio collagist, performer, cassette-networker, and former radio broadcaster. If he didn't have creative outlets he'd probably be either an ascetic or an assassin. He searches for new citizenship in a more ecologically-correct and intellectually stimulating community or *bolo*. Loves a good dry red, and dreams often of UFOs.

Tripp Mikich has been a cultural activist and political activist for at least the last 28 years, starting with his expulsion from high school for organizing activities during "Stop the Draft" week in 1967. From rank-and-file labor organizing in the canneries and electronics factories of Oregon, to tour and concert production for the San Francisco Mime Troupe, Quilapayun, Carlos Mejia Godoy, Wallflower Order and many other political performance groups from Europe, Latin America, Asia and the U.S.; his efforts have continually tried to weave the fabric by which the social, political, and cultural become one. He has been a national board member of the Alliance for Cultural Democracy for the past seven years, and is currently devoting his efforts to developing computer and Internet multimedia on alternative and community-based cultural work in the U.S. and around the world.

Ivor Miller is a Ph.D. candidate in the Department of Performance Studies at Northwestern University. His articles on graffiti and African American shamanistic dance have appeared in *Race and Class* and *Caligraphy Review*, and his photos have appeared in the book, *Face of the Gods: Art and Altars of Africa and the African Americas* by Robert Farris Thompson, who he studied with at Yale. He has lived abroad in Cuba on and off in recent years, researching Afro-Cuban religion.

Negativland is a music/noise group who has been sued twice for copyright infringement over collage and parody works and has recently devoted itself to advocating reform of U.S. copyright laws. Their recently published book/CD *FAIR USE: The Story of the Letter U and the Numeral 2,* tells the story of those two lawsuits. For more information on this and other Negativland CD releases write to: Negativland, 109 Minna #391, San Francisco, CA 94105 or point your web browser to http://sunsite.unc.edu/negativland.

Sheila Nopper has been involved in community radio in Toronto, Canada for eight years as a music programmer and a producer of audio documentaries. Throughout the last decade she has published articles on various topics promoting equal rights and justice, focusing this theme more recently on musicians.

The Contributors

John Oswald is Director of Research at Mystery Laboratory in Canada, and Musical Director of the North American Experience. He is the third recipient of the Freddie Stone Award ('93) for "musical integrity, innovation, and a long-term contribution to the Canadian music world," and *Eye Weekly*'s 1994 year-end report appointed him a "God-like being." In 1990, Oswald's most notorious recording, *plunderphonics,* was destroyed by prudes in the recording industry representing Michael Jackson.

Susan Parenti received her doctorate in music composition from the University of Illinois in 1988. She works with Herbert Brün and the Performers' Workshop Ensemble, a group of teaching performers and performing teachers whose projects connect art and society. Currently, the Ensemble teaches in the Campus Honors Program at the University of Illinois at Urbana-Champaign.

Stephen Perkins is a graduate student in the University of Iowa's School of Art and Art History, a long-time art-networker, and a founding member of the Iowa Chapter of the Aggressive School of Cultural Workers. He lives with his wife Arda Ishkanian and their daughter Nina in Iowa City.

Hal Rammel has been an active participant in the world surrealist movement since 1976. As a visual artist, experimental multi-instrumentalist, and historian, his drawings, cartoons, collages, reviews, and articles have appeared in *Cultural Correspondence, Arsenal, the improvisor, Experimental Musical Instruments, Mannen På Gatan* (Sweden), and *Analogon* (Czecholsovakia). His book, *Nowhere in America*, a history of comic utopias in American folklore and popular culture, was published by University of Illinois Press in 1990. A CD of his electroacoustic music *Elsewheres* was released by Penumbra Music in 1994. He makes his home in southeastern Wisconsin with surrealist painter Gina Litherland.

Tricia Rose is currently an Assistant Professor of History and Africana Studies at New York University. She is the author of *Black Noise: Rap, Music, and Black Culture in Contremporary America* (Wesleyan Press, 1994), and co-author, with Andrew Ross, of *Micro-Phone Fiends: Youth Music and Youth Culture* (Routledge, 1994).

Kalamu ya Salaam is a New Orleans, African American writer and arts producer. He is the author of *What Is Life?—The Reclamation of the Black Blues Self* (poetry and essays/Third World Press, Chicago), and the producer/scriptwriter for Crescent City Sounds, a nationally syndicated, weekly radio program of authentic New Orleans music. He and Chinese American musician/composer Fred Ho form the Afro Asian Arts Dialogue, a poetry and music performing ensemble.

Ron Sakolsky does occasional radio shows (on both pirate and community radio) and is the dancehall selector for the Fool's Paradise Sound System. He has conducted interviews, written about radio, and done music reviews, essays and criticism for such national periodicals as *Sound Choice, Cadence, Social Anarchism, Cultural Democracy, Upfront, Griot,* and *In These Times,* and in such books as *A Passion for Radio* and *Cassette Mythos.* Currently he is a national board member of the Alliance for Cultural Democracy and a regular contributor to *The Beat.* He teaches a colloquium on "World Music" at the University of Illinois at Springfield (formerly Sangamon State University). With James Koehnline, he is co-editor of the inspirational anthology, *Gone to Croatan: Origins of Drop-Out Culture in North America* (Autonomedia).

The Contributors

Anthony Seeger is an anthropologist, ethnomusicologist, archivist and musician. He holds a B.A. from Harvard University and an M.A. and Ph.D. in Anthropology from the University of Chicago. A specialist in the Amerindian communities of lowland South America, he has published four books and over sixty articles on a variety of subjects. He has taught at the Museu Nacional in Rio de Janeiro (1975–1982) and Indiana University (1982–1988). Currently, he is Curator of the sound archives of the Smithsonian Institution's Center for Folklife Programs and Cultural Studies, and Director of Smithsonian/Folkways Recordings.

Jean Smith is the lyricist and singer in the band Mecca Normal, and is the author of a chunk of fiction entitled *I Can Hear Me Fine* published by Get To The Point. She and David Lester (also of Mecca Normal) are co-founders of the Black Wedge—a group of anti-authoritarians who have toured in North America and Europe spreading the damned difficult word of how to combine music and poetry with activist resistance culture and have a fun time doing it!

Miyoshi Smith is a multimedia worker based in Philadelphia. Her works include: *Even The Sounds Are Blue (Parts I and II)*, *Common Spaces*, and *First And Last Words*.

Jilli Streit-Warburton is a post-graduate student in the Department of Anthropology and Sociology at the University of Queensland, in Brisbane. She holds an undergraduate degree with a major in anthropology from Deakin University and a Diploma of Fine Art from the South Australian School of Art. She is currently writing a research thesis on Aboriginal women's contemporary music in Australia and has a particular interest in the nexus between music and the construction of identity. She has three teenage children and lives on the escarpment of the Great Dividing Range near Toowoomba in Queensland.

Scott M.X. Turner is a songwriter/guitarist who has been in punk bands since Commun-ism was scaring the beejesus out of the Carter Administration. In 1993 he released his first solo album, *Ya Got A Kalashnikov... Ya Got A Job*, on Brooklyn-based Triage Records. The same year he joined with the Devil's Advocates to release "Fire In The Hole," a bene-fit single for the Community/Labor Campaign to Save Taystee Jobs. The summer of '94 saw M.X. annoy Lincoln Center patrons with a live Devil's Advocates performance of music he wrote for a dance piece there by Kun-Yang Lin, and that fall he co-wrote with Peter Gingerich the score to *The Story of Dou-e/Snow In June* at New York's La Mama Theater. M.X. is also a highly irregular contributor to *Forward Motion* magazine.

Batya Weinbaum lives in Vermont with her dog and daughter. For several years she was active in the women's music festival community, in which she gave workshops on making music with matriarchal consciousness. She belongs to the Vermont Composers Consortium for which she occasionally writes and has her compositions performed, many of which involve chant-like audience participation and experimental improvisation. During the time that she studied ethnomusicology in the American Studies program at SUNY buffalo, she went to Hawaii to research the hula as a women's community art forum. Lately, she has been doing doctoral work on chant and orality in American literature at UMass-Amherst in the American Studies Program.

Benjamin Zephaniah was born in Birmingham, England in 1958, and grew up in Jamaica and in Handsworth, where he was sent to an appwoved school for being uncontrollable, rebellious and a 'born failure,' ending up in jail for burglary. After prison he turned from crime to music

The Contributors

and poetry. Zephaniah has since become a master of oral and perfomance art, with many appearances in films, on TV and radio. He has been Writer-in-Residence for the City of Liverpool with the Africa Arts Collective, and now lives in London's East End, where he is Chairperson of Hackney Empire Theatre. His books include *The Dread Affair* (Arena) and *City Psalms* (Blood Axe).

Index to the Artists

Scott Marshall front cover collage
Carol Genetti front cover design
Maurice Caldwell 1
Marcelo Lima 3

Part I. *Theorizing Music and Social Change*
James Koehnline 10
Freddie Baer 12
James Koehnline 28
Monica Sjoo 40
Davey Williams 52
Dreamtime Collective 60
James Koehnline 65
Scott Marshall 66
John Oswald 86
Negativland 90
Esau Underhill 96
Tom Frank 108
Ron Sakolsky 120
Darrell Johnson 132

Part II. *In the Belly of The Beast*
Carol Genetti 144
Andrew Rawson 146

Paul Miller 154
L. F. Productions 170
Wm. Crook, Jr. 172
Tuli Kupferberg 178
Panic Productions 210
The Tape-beatles 216
Mark Enslin 226

Part III. *Shattering The Silence of the New World Order*
Marcelo Lima 234
Ricardo Levins-Morales 240
Bonnie Rubenstein 246
Carol Genetti 260
Chicago Dzviti 270
Amy Cordova 276
Ivor Miller 286
Ernesto Javier 293, 294
Wendy Allen 306
Tripp Mikich 320
Robert Lancefield 330
Michael Schwartz 338
Isiah Dodd 346
Tim Blunk back cover collage
Scott Marshall page design

A companion **Sounding Off** musical CD,
with 77+ minutes of soundtracks by book contributors

HAKIM BEY	SUE ANN HARKEY	NEGATIVLAND	KALAMU YA SALAAM
JEAN BINTA BREEZE	FRED HO	JOHN OSWALD	SCOTT M.X. TURNER
BROTHER RESISTANCE	THOMAS MAPFUMO	PERFORMER'S WORKSHOP	LIZ WAS / MIEKAL AND
CAROL GENETTI	SCOTT MARSHALL	HAL RAMMEL	BATYA WEINBAUM

among others, is available for $10 postpaid from
Autonomedia, POB 568, Brooklyn, New York 11211 USA